D0760840

DINO
The little Ferrari

Motor racing as it used to be: the main road through Stavelot village rings to the Dino V6 as a works Ferrari mechanic drives Olivier Gendebien's car up to the Spa-Francorchamps circuit for the start of Belgian Grand Prix practice, 1958. The Standard in the foreground was owned by English stock-exchange man John Maitland, seen focusing his camera to record the happy scene. This shot was taken by David Thirlby, the great Frazer-Nash authority

DINO
The little Ferrari

V6 and V8 racing and road cars — 1957 to 1979

DOUG NYE

John W. Barnes, Jr. Publishing, Inc.
Box 323 Scarsdale, New York 10583

Published in the USA only by
John W. Barnes Jr. Publishing Inc.
Box 323 Scarsdale, New York 10583

First published in 1979 by Osprey Publishing Limited,
12–14 Long Acre, London WC2E 9LP
Member company of the George Philip Group

© Copyright Doug Nye 1979

This book is copyrighted under the
Berne Convention. All rights reserved.
Apart from any fair dealing for the
purpose of private study, research,
criticism or review, as permitted under
the Copyright Act, 1956, no part of
this publication may be reproduced,
stored in a retrieval system, or
transmitted in any form or by any
means, electronic, electrical,
chemical, mechanical, optical,
photocopying, recording, or
otherwise, without prior written
permission. All enquiries should be
addressed to the Publishers

British Library
Cataloguing in Publication Data

Nye, Doug
  Dino
  1. Dino automobile
  I. Title
  629.22'22   TL215.D/

ISBN 0-914822-24-1

Editor Tim Parker
Design Gwyn Lewis
Filmset and printed by BAS Printers Limited,
Over Wallop, Hampshire, UK

*Superstition abounds in the world of motor racing—hence
no Chapter 13. Ferrari would never use the number. Or
would they? *Above is Ginther testing a 246SP at Modena in
June 1961. The car never raced with that number. Why was it
tested with it?*

Contents

When I was first asked to produce a history of the Ferrari Dino cars my instinctive reaction was to refuse. While I have followed Ferrari fortunes very closely for almost twenty-five years and saw many of the Dino variants in their element, racing, I have never counted myself a rabid Ferrari enthusiast. The motoring and motor racing world would be a far poorer place without the man the Italians call *Il Drake*—the Dragon of Maranello—and the cars his men have built to carry his name, but for many years Ferrari was incredibly reactionary in the technical sense. They seemed incapable of sustaining a competitive team effort for more than short periods of time and while generally dominant in long-distance sports-car racing with some mouth-watering examples of most exciting machinery I was often left wondering, well, who are they beating?

This is to in no way denigrate the astonishing fecundity of the Ferrari competition and production teams, for no other manufacturer in history can match Ferrari's bewildering range of engines, gearboxes, chassis, bodies and so on, their incredible reaction speed in producing new components or new variations of old at the drop of a hat, and their often very effective competitive development of the same.

When this Dino project was broached, my mind instinctively pictured the pretty little 206S sports-racers of the mid-nineteen-sixties, and the little Ferrari production cars which have now begun to outsell their exotic up-market brethren. A moment's clearer thought recalls the very first Dino competition cars, and the V6 Formula 1 models which carried Mike Hawthorn to his sensational World Championship title, the first ever for a British driver, in 1958. Hawthorn came from my home town of Farnham, in Surrey, and was a boyhood hero to me. Having recalled those cars I then remember the V6 Dino F1 and F2 models which succeeded them in 1959, driven by men like Tony Brooks, Phil Hill, Dan Gurney and Jean Behra, Cliff Allison and 'Taffy' von Trips. Then there were the 1960 Formula 1 Dinos, the ultimate expression of the front-engined racing car theme, fighting a fierce and desperate rearguard action against the British-inspired mid-engined revolution.

When Carlo Chiti designed his 120-degree V6 Grand Prix engine for the 1961 1.5-litre Formula it appeared with 'Ferrari' lettering cast into its cam-covers, in place of the now hallowed 'Dino' script. The works continued to run the bewildering array of sports car V6 and V8 engines under the 'Dino' name of Mr Ferrari's long-lost son and heir, while the Formula 1 cars continued popularly to be called the Dino 156s. . . . Right or wrong, in my opinion they formed an integral part of the Dino family, and they brought Ferrari and Phil Hill the World Championship titles in 1961, and as late as 1964 helped John Surtees and Ferrari to yet more

World Championship success as Lorenzo Bandini won the Austrian Grand Prix with a V6, and deprived *Il Grande John's* main rivals of a chance to stretch their points advantage over him, and over *La Ferrari*.

The more I examined the Ferrari Dino saga the more fascinating it became, for it is ground rarely covered in a marque history which has been picked over, reheated, and served up again as many times as have so many Ferrari engine, gearbox and chassis combinations.

I talked to Dino drivers like Phil Hill, Dan Gurney, Tony Brooks, Cliff Allison, David Piper, Dick Attwood, Derek Bell and Chris Amon. I recalled and unearthed notes of conversations with drivers like Scarfiotti, Bandini, even Hawthorn and Collins, whom senior colleagues had known well while I was still a schoolboy, looking-on admiringly, from afar. Eventually I had to back down and admit it—I had caught this wretched Ferrari bug! One might not altogether admire Ferrari cars for the way they were built and operated, but they all, with few exceptions, carried fine power units and had a flair and aura which few other marques have ever come even close to achieving. Just to look at one of the cars is to imagine its searing exhaust note and to sense how it must have felt for its driver, in the later years at one with his car—a svelte thoroughbred racing machine—earlier on a wild thing not so much to be tamed as to be persuaded to channel its fine engine and usually indifferent handling into competitive pace around a circuit. So the cynical sceptic became hooked on Ferrari lore in general—and on the job in hand, the Dinos in particular.

Perhaps it would help to explain the arrangement of this history. I have presented it in chronological form, expecting the critics to chop my head off for producing another 'and then they did this' book, but having tried it other ways this is the clearest and most intelligible way of recording not only what was built, but who did what with which and where, and how the bewildering series of Dino cars interrelated. Most of the chapters essentially cover one calendar year, in the busier seasons dealing with the sports cars first, the Formula cars second. The years from 1968 are presented in one section, together with the story of the latter-day Lancia–Ferraris—the exciting Ferrari Dino V6-engined Stratos rally cars. In the text I have attempted to paint a clear and detailed picture not only of the cars' specifications, but also of the incidents, successes, trials and tribulations they experienced in International competition.

Finally, don't blame me for the absence of a Chapter 13 in this book— it was my publisher Tim Parker's idea; of course he caused all the trouble in the first place, and it was he who won Ferrari a convert. Now read the Dino story of cars thus far sadly underrated and overshadowed by their Ferrari brethren. For Dino is a noble name.

DOUG NYE
Lower Bourne, Farnham, England
July 1979

Ferrari—man and boy

The autostrada was packed as we beat south away from the industrial sprawl of Milan. Amongst this roaring, grumbling throng of trucks and coaches and cars our transporter hummed along, pitching monotonously over the rippled surface. On either side the flat plain of the Po Valley stretched away, patterned into geometric fields by lonely rows of straight trees merging into the grey-blue haze.

For those fated to use this autostrada every day this must have been a bore. For the tourists heading south to Rome and the sun-soaked beaches beyond this was the time to snatch some sleep, or perhaps to read. But for the lover of fine motor cars, for the motor-racing enthusiast, this autostrada is the road to Mecca; the way to Modena, adopted homeland of Maserati, and to Maranello—Enzo Ferrari's kingdom.

No matter how many times you return, images of that first pilgrimage always remain vivid in the mind. There's something special and indelible about that first time. You pass the service areas on the modern autostrada and visualize Ferrari's great drivers stopping off, pondering the forthcoming interview on their way to meet the great man, or on their way back, agonizing over what had been said. As the signs flick by, 'Modena', 'Modena', 'Modena', anticipation mounts....

Down into the bustling city streets with their hopelessly congested traffic you can picture Ascari and Fangio, Hawthorn and Collins, Phil Hill and Richie Ginther, later Surtees, Ickx and Amon carving through the throng on their way to work, being recognized and besieged by in-comers, while the experienced locals would just nod and smile as the familiar *condottieri* passed on their way.

On one side here is a long and high square-buttressed wall, with peeling posters clinging to its red brickwork. Behind it lies the Modena Aero-Autodrome, where Formula 1 and 2 races were once held and where Ferrari and Maserati and the other Modenese racing teams tested their wares. Here Castellotti and *Ingegnere* Fraschetti died while testing single-seat Ferraris, and the luckless Giulio Cabianca crashed his Cooper through an open gateway into a taxi on the street. Here Mike Hawthorn up-ended his 1952 Cooper-Bristol on the day of his first Ferrari test—and here the Formula 1 Ferrari Dinos had an early race success....

The whole place oozes motor racing history, for just outside the city Enzo Ferrari was born; in its centre he based his pre-war Scuderia

Viale Trento Trieste 31, Modena, today—the Ferrari Assistenza with the top floor flat in which the Ferraris lived, built on what had in 1929 been open ground next door to the original Scuderia building. That can be seen to the right, the Sinclair service station with the pillared balcony. Through the gateway on the left is a courtyard; turn right inside and the facing garage block houses the shrouded shape of Dino's last road car, parked more or less where he left it for the last time

8

Ferrari, and today in the Viale Trento Trieste there stands the Ferrari *Assistenza*, from which customers buy their cars and have them serviced. Just a few minutes' drive outside, in the ochre-coloured village of Maranello, lies the Ferrari factory, long, low buildings nestling fortressed within a walled compound. Here is the famous guarded gateway with its electrically opened gate and the office block archway with its large Ferrari lettering. Here is the dowdy reception area '... where millionaires and future champions await the pleasure of Enzo Ferrari'.

Here this truly remarkable man, this larger-than-life industrial and sporting entrepreneur, has long reigned supreme—and alone.

He was born on 18 February, 1898, second son of Alfredo Ferrari, a structural engineer whose small workshop attached to the family home produced sheds and gangways for the railway. The Po Valley is traditionally rich in artisan talent, and highly skilled metal-workers and pattern-makers were and remain ten a penny throughout the region, Modena being just one of several centres of employment. Enzo had a brother, Alfredo, who was two years his senior. Alfredo was good academically, while Enzo was useless (he claims), detesting school and dreaming of the day when he could earn his own living.

His early ambitions were to be an opera singer, until he regretfully concluded that he 'had neither voice nor ear', and secondly a sports-writer, which in some small measure he later fulfilled. His third aim was to become a racing driver. He had listened to his father and brother discussing cars with ever-growing interest. In 1908 they took him to see a motor race on the Via Emilia at Bologna. He recalls he saw Vincenzo Lancia set fastest lap, and Felice Nazzaro win at nearly 74 mph. A year later the eleven-year-old took himself to see a straight-line sprint on the Navicello Straight, a section of the Modena–Ferrara highway. A driver named Da Zara won at around 87 mph. Ferrari was thrilled: 'I found these events immensely exciting,' he wrote later in his memoirs.*

Then came the Great War and in 1916 his father contracted pneumonia and died. Within months Alfredo was dangerously ill in an army hospital, and he too passed away. Enzo Ferrari does not tell us what happened to his mother, née Adalgisa Bisdini, merely writing that he found himself 'alone and afraid in the world'. He was conscripted into the army in 1917 and assigned to the Val Seriana detachment of the 3rd Mountain Artillery. In typical military style his engineering background won him a job shoeing mules. But then his health was broken. He fell seriously ill, spent time in the military hospital at Brescia and eventually found himself in the Barracano in Bologna—a hutted camp 'reputedly intended for incurables'.

After the Armistice, Ferrari emerged from the Barracano, recovered though still weak, and began hunting for work with a million others. His colonel gave him a letter of introduction to Fiat in Turin, but they had no job available. He landed on his feet with a Bolognese named Giovanni,

*'Le Mie Gioie Terribili'; Casa Editrice Licinio Cappelli, Bologna, 1962. In English 'The Enzo Ferrari Memoirs; My Terrible Joys', Hamish Hamilton Ltd, London, 1963. Five subsequent editions. New title 'Le Briglie del Successo', works-published, March 1970, second edition November 1970, private edition 1974.

who was stripping second-hand light trucks, which he sold as running chassis to a specialist coach-builder. Ferrari was employed to test and deliver the chassis to the Carozzeria Italo-Argentina in Milan. He was a driver at last, and in both Turin and Milan he began frequenting bars where 'automobile people' could be found.

The Bar del Nord at Porta Nuova was a favourite, 'where I made many good friends'. The closest seems to have been Romolo Bonacini, who had been racing driver Pietro Bordino's mechanic before the war and then flight engineer with the legendary Italian pilot Francesco Brack-Papa during it. He also met and came to know established racing drivers like Felice Nazzaro, hero of that Bologna race more than ten years before, and his nephew Biaggio, Moriondo, Evasio Lampiano, Cagno and Salamano.... He was clearly regarded as 'a good lad', a young man from Modena with his heart in the right place. But times were still hard, he was running through the small legacy his father had willed him, and Giovanni could not pay well.

His trips to Milan had taken him to the Bar Vittorio Emanuele, a meeting place for the sporting fraternity, and there he befriended Ugo Sivocci, who had just retired from a successful bicycle-racing career. He had become chief tester for Costruzioni Meccaniche Nazionali, or CMN, which was based in the Via Vallazze. They made cars powered by surplus 3-litre four-cylinder Isotta-Fraschini engines and had room for another driver, and Ferrari was taken on.

CMN had modest racing ambitions to publicize their cars, and the pushy young man from Modena found an ally in Sivocci and got his wish. He made his racing debut for them in the 1919 Targa Florio in Sicily, the first major postwar motor race, and was placed ninth. The following year he drove a CMN again in the Parma to Poggio di Berceto hillclimb and was placed third.

At this time Alfa Romeo of Milan were getting themselves back into gear as a manufacturer of civilian transport and could offer a brighter future than tiny CMN. Somehow Ferrari found a job there, and as Alfa Romeo used their test-drivers to race, and they too were developing formidable competition ambitions, he was on the verge of his brilliant career ... not that it was to be as a great racing driver....

He had a works Alfa Romeo drive in the 1920 Targa Florio and put his previous knowledge of the course to good effect, finishing second, but in 1921 he could do no better than fifth, while placing second in the less important race at Mugello. In 1923, driving one of the Merosi-designed 3-litre RL Alfas, Ferrari won the Savio race at Ravenna, and that brought him his Prancing Horse insignia. According to Ferrari this famous symbol was given to him by the parents of Italy's wartime air ace Francesco Baracca, 'for luck'. Baracca flew Nieuport and SPAD fighters and downed thirty-four enemy aircraft before being killed by ground fire at Montello on 18 June, 1918. Enzo's elder brother, Alfredo, had been on the ground crew of Baracca's *Squadriglia* when he contracted his fatal illness, while Baracca himself had been a military graduate of the Modena academy. Count Enrico and Countess Paolina Baracca got to know Ferrari after his Ravenna success, and these multiple links led them to

Enzo Ferrari—racing driver—in his Alfa Romeo before the start of the 1923 Targa Florio. On the right is Giorgio Rimini, Alfa executive from whom he learned so much about the ways of business. Between them in the background wearing the gent's natty headgear is Vincenzo Florio's distinguished guest, King Constantine of Greece

suggest that he should adopt the squadron insignia made famous by their late son and his fellow airmen.

However, in comparison to his team-mates, like Sivocci, who had followed him from CMN to Alfa Romeo, and especially Antonio Ascari and Giuseppe Campari, Enzo Ferrari was at best a driver of modest talent. He was proving more valuable to Alfa Romeo in other ways, for his days spent hanging around the cafés and bars had made him known to almost everybody who was anybody in motor racing. He was an insistent and persuasive man, not shy of making himself known and acting as Alfa Romeo's agent in all manner of business deals. He has been described as an important 'industrial spy and pirate' for Alfa Romeo, and he certainly developed rapidly into their motor racing 'Mr Fixit'.

He learned much from a young Catanian engineer named Giorgio Rimini, who was in charge of Alfa Romeo's sales and racing promotion. Ferrari described him as 'swarthy... with staring eyes and a cigarette permanently hanging from his lips. Keen, intelligent and full of drive, it was he who spurred me on to the formation of that band of men — a virtual automobile "general staff" — that was to help build the fortunes of Alfa Romeo for many years to come....'

Rimini even conned Ferrari over the sale of an Alfa Romeo, and the dynamic and aggressive Modenese doubtless logged away his method for future reference.

It was during 1923 that Ferrari was used by Alfa Romeo to open negotiations with top Fiat design personnel, whose Grand Prix cars at that time dominated racing. Ferrari had already lured his friend Luigi Bazzi from Fiat in Turin to the Alfa works at Portello, Milan. With the Bazzi capture to his credit, Ferrari was then sent after Vittorio Jano, another young and brilliant Fiat engineer, and after his initial approaches Alfa were successful in securing Jano's services. Bazzi had described Jano as a man of 'formidable will' and Ferrari was to consider that '...no description could do credit to this extraordinary man and his fertile brain'. Other Fiat technicians followed Bazzi and Jano to Portello, and the Torinese company eventually abandoned racing in disgust at being used as a training academy for their rivals.

Ferrari's racing ambitions reached their height in 1924, when he drove his Savio-winning Alfa Romeo RL in the Coppa Acerbo at Pescara, and after the retirement of Campari's new P2 Grand Prix model he and his riding mechanic, Eugenio Siena (who later became a good driver in his own right), won the race.

The Acerbo Cup was donated by Fascist cabinet minister Giacomo Acerbo in honour of his brother Tito, who had been decorated for gallantry in the Great War. In addition to the Cup, he arranged for an honour — that of *Cavaliere* — to be bestowed upon the winner, and so *Cavaliere* Enzo Ferrari returned to Portello. For further services in the motor racing field he was later elevated to *Cavaliere Ufficiale*, and finally (before his thirtieth birthday he claims, which would have been in 1928) to *Commendatore*. In postwar years, as the Ferrari legend has grown, so he has been known as *Commendatore* Ferrari, yet all Fascist honours were abrogated after the war as he emphasizes in his memoirs. Although holders could apply for confirmation of their titles if they wished, Mr Ferrari made no such application and thus was no longer *Commendatore*. He sometimes made this clear at his annual press conferences, rounding on nervous journalists who addressed him as *Commendatore* —or even as 'Mister'—Ferrari and snapping 'Just call me Ferrari!'

He was given his big chance after the Coppa Acerbo when he was entered to drive one of the potent P2s in the French Grand Prix at Lyons. He was a non-starter, and at his press conference in 1976 he revealed that he had suffered a nervous breakdown, and had backed out after testing the car on the French course. He did not race again for some time, and then resumed only in minor touring events, usually in aged Merosi-designed Alfa Romeos, as a means of publicizing the marque he was by this time selling. According to the Italian Automobile Club listing of his race performances, his last event was the Bobbio-Passo del Penice hillclimb of 1931, in which he took a first-place award.

Meanwhile Alfa Romeo themselves had been absent from big-league racing for a while. They had struggled financially since the Armistice, and although racing had proved a very successful promotion, productivity was low and 1925 saw the company absorbed by the Government *Istituto di Ricostruzione Industriale* (IRI), which had been created to save otherwise bankrupt concerns vital to the national economy. (IRI still exists and owns Alfa Romeo today.) After Antonio Ascari's fatal accident while leading the 1925 French Grand Prix at Montlhéry, Alfa withdrew from racing and concentrated upon selling their race-bred products to wealthy sporting gentlemen.

Enzo Ferrari became a link in their sales chain. He knew everybody who was anybody and described his work with Alfa as '...driver, organizer, racing manager and other things besides, without any clear-cut boundaries to my fields of responsibility. At the same time I was in charge of Alfa Romeo sales in Emilia–Romagna and the Marche, living alternately in Milan and Bologna and managing to avoid complete severance of my ties with Modena.'

Jano was building up a line of aggressive new high-performance Alfa Romeo sporting cars that were to capitalize in private hands on the Grand Prix reputation established by the factory, and on 1 December 1929, Enzo Ferrari formally established the Scuderia Ferrari in Modena, with a number of share-holding partners; initially the Caniato brothers, Ferrara hemp processors, and Mario Tadini, an amateur driver. Alfa Romeo had officially re-entered racing—with IRI's blessing—in 1928, but the Depression and the Wall Street collapse had intervened and they were forced to cut back once more. Scuderia Ferrari came into being apparently as a quasi-works operation, intended to sell customers their sporting cars, then to service, prepare and maintain them and in some cases even to enter and transport them, so the proud owner need merely present himself and find his car ready to go. According to former Alfa draughtsman Luigi Fusi, Ferrari was officially their Sales and Racing Consultant at this time, and with its independent funding Scuderia Ferrari emerged in 1930 as a pure Alfa Romeo racing headquarters, complete with a permanent staff of leading technicians, regular visits from Jano and even comprehensive machine-tool and engine test-house facilities. Ferrari had applied the yellow of Modena as background to his variation of the Baracca prancing horse, and under this symbol his new Scuderia went to war.

Their history is a busy and confused one, highlighted by immense motor racing success for Alfa Romeo in all departments of the sport from Grand Prix and big-league sports-car events such as the Mille Miglia and Le Mans 24-Hours to bush-league affairs like local club hillclimbs. In addition to their circle of gentleman customers, the Scuderia operated cars for a quasi-factory team at top level, and from 1932 to 1934 they also ran a motorcycle team of British Rudge and Italian Bianchi machines for riders like Giordano Aldrighetti, Carlo Baschieri, Giuseppe Fagnani, Aldo Pigorini, Francesco Lama, Guglielmo Sandri and a young man named Piero Taruffi.

But it was the Alfa Romeo cars that formed the Scuderia's main programme, with drivers like Tazio Nuvolari, Achille Varzi, Louis Chiron, Dreyfus, Fagioli, Sommer, Borzacchini, Brivio, Moll, Cortese, Pintacuda and many, many more.

Jano introduced his legendary Tipo B or 'P3' *Monoposto* Grand Prix design in the factory team in 1932 with instant success, but when the works withdrew from racing in 1933 they placed the single-seaters under dust sheets and Scuderia Ferrari had to struggle on in Grand Prix racing with the old wide-bodied, offset-seat *Monza* models. They did their best by fitting uprated engines, but the old cars' transmissions then wilted under the strain. Nuvolari was one who stamped out in disgust and went to Maserati, and began winning in their 8CM *Monoposto*, much to Alfa's distress. Consequently the Tipo Bs were released to the team, and they carried the Scuderia Ferrari badge to a string of magnificent Grand Prix successes, even in the face of early forays by the state-backed German teams of Mercedes-Benz and Auto Union until they quickly out-gunned their less well-financed Italian rival.

In 1933 the Scuderia briefly campaigned an Indianapolis special built by Augie Duesenberg, driven for them by their President, Count Trossi, but it was unsuccessful and they were not long diverted from their Alfa loyalties. Then in 1935 they built their own fearsome *Formule Libre* specials, the two now-famous *Bimotore* cars designed principally by Luigi Bazzi. By 1936 the German teams had established a stranglehold on the major *Grandes Epreuves* which the Italians could not dislodge. Consequently they began to look towards 1500 cc *Voiturette* racing as a class in which to show their mettle, Maserati leading the way with designs which wrested a brief initiative from the British ERA concern. In 1937 Nuvolari, in a Scuderia Ferrari Alfa Romeo 12C-36, managed to beat Hasse's lone Auto Union in the Milan Grand Prix in Sempione Park, and in the Rio de Janeiro Grand Prix, on the tortuous Gavéa circuit, Carlo Pintacuda's old 8C-35 proved more nimble than Stuck's Auto Union — and won again.

According to Ferrari, he had the idea of building a racing car of his own in Modena that year, designed by Gioacchino Colombo, who had just been 'ceded' to the team by Alfa Romeo's general manager, Ugo

Gobbato. With engineers Nasi, Giberti and Massimino the designs were completed and (again according to Ferrari) he sold the completed prototype to Alfa Romeo in 1938 together with parts for four cars under construction. The cars were certainly assembled at Modena, but many parts were made in Milan and they were certainly prompted by Maserati's success in a class of racing where thus far the Germans had not ventured. Ferrari claims these little 1500 cc *vetturette* as his own, but they were undeniably Alfa Romeos by lineage, and became famous as the Alfa Romeo 158/159 *Alfetta*. Ferrari's own successful racing cars were still to come....

Lack of success against the German teams prompted Alfa Romeo to re-enter the fray in their own right in 1938, and the 158 purchase was only part of a bigger deal under which the Scuderia Ferrari hardware in Modena was absorbed and future Alfa Romeo racing operations were centralized at the Portello factory, under the new name Alfa Corse. Enzo Ferrari accompanied the move, as Directive Consultant.

By this time Ferrari had grown beyond Alfa's parental restraint, and with his well-practised skills and experience of running a massive racing operation virtually on his own he reacted poorly to life at Portello. He was used to running things his way, and squaring snap decisions with the parent company after the event. At Alfa Corse it did not work that way, for Gobbato was strictly a big industry man, who believed in stern adherence to long-range planning. While Ferrari knew that a racing car should be built by a specialist staff, quick to react to its designers' findings and insulated from normal industrial practice and delay, Gobbato considered Alfa Corse should combine the best work of every department of his whole massive factory. When Spanish engineer Wilfredo Ricart was introduced into this situation, as Alfa Corse's chief engineer, Ferrari took an instant and lasting dislike to him. He unburdened himself to Gobbato, but the Alfa manager sided with Ricart. The rift became unbridgeable, and led eventually to Ferrari's dismissal in 1939.

He retained ownership of the Modena premises and emerged from the break with considerable capital, though he had to refrain from racing—other than with Alfa Romeo—for four years.

He returned to his native Modena, where he established a small machine shop in the old Scuderia buildings under the name Societa Auto Avio Costruzioni, sub-contracting machining for a minor aero-engine manufacturer.

But during the winter of 1939 he was back into the racing car business, with Alberto Massimino designing and Enrico Nardi helping to develop a pair of 1500 cc sports-racing cars based largely on Fiat components. The cars were simply dubbed '815' because of Ferrari's severence contract clause with Alfa, which precluded use of his name, and in April 1940 they were entrusted to young Alberto Ascari (son of the late Antonio) and to the Marquis Lotario Rangoni Machiavelli for the Brescia–Mantua–Verona Mille Miglia race. Neither car survived to the finish.

Nardi brought Ferrari together with a Torinese machine-tool dealer named Corrado Gatti. Ferrari's AAC company was hungry for work and Gatti pointed out the great demand for oleodynamic grinding machines, used to make ball bearings. One German machine was very good, but in short supply, and Ferrari applied to the manufacturer for a licence to reproduce it. They refused, on the grounds that they could not provide adequate technical assistance, but since nothing in Italian law prevented him copying the machines without a licence, Ferrari responded by doing just that. The result was a great success. By 1943 he had a staff of 150 or more in his Modena machine-tool plant, but late that year a Government plan for industrial decentralization forced him to move.

He already owned a tract of land at nearby Maranello, and he moved his company into a new building there, only to have it damaged by Allied bombing on 4 November 1944 and again the following February. The works was entirely rebuilt in 1946 and subsequently enlarged on several occasions, as Ferrari SpA began its rapid growth. . . .

Once the war had ended and Italy's internal politics were resolved, Ferrari began phasing out the production of machine tools and set his sights firmly on a return to motor racing.

During the war years he had kept in touch with Colombo, the *Alfetta* designer, and he had work for him in 1946—when the engineer had his problems, since he had been prominent in Fascist party politics during Mussolini's final years. As historian Griffith Borgeson has pointed out, Enzo Ferrari was not exactly a man given to blaming anyone for loyalty to iron dictatorship.

Colombo was to design the new V12 Ferrari racing car, based on their joint experience of Jano's Alfa Romeo V12s, and Colombo's detailing of the Wilfredo Ricart-conceived mid-engined 1.5-litre Alfa 512, which had been tested in 1940–41. They decided on a short-stroke V12 engine offering greater piston area and crankshaft speed than Alfa Corse's revived 158 straight-8s. So the Ferrari mould was cast, and after the slow development to success of those early Colombo V12s and their descendants, (devised by the brilliant engineer Aurelio Lampredi), Ferrari went on through world championship-winning 4-cylinder models until 1955, when Vittorio Jano returned to the fold. Jano had been with Lancia and was responsible for their 1954–55 D50 V8 Grand Prix cars. By 1955 Ferrari were on their knees before Mercedes. Lancia finances crumbled and Gianni Lancia presented his entire racing department assets to Ferrari. During this period the World Sports Car Championship became indisputably a Ferrari preserve, mainly with a bewildering variety of V12 engines, but also with 'fours' and 'sixes', each apparently designed, built, developed and tested and put into racing trim with breathless speed.

But Ferrari was not always successful, and indeed killing-off the Alfa Romeo 159s in 1951 was not achieved lightly, nor were Maserati and Mercedes-Benz ever dominated in the mid-fifties, rather the opposite, in fact. Ferrari had his bad times to set against the good and the story of these cars is adequately told elsewhere, as can be seen from the bibliography at the close of this book. For here we are concerned with the evolution and career of the Ferrari cars called Dino, and having set the scene we should examine the sombre story of Enzo Ferrari's heir.

Ferrari is a proud man, dynamic, successful and arrogant, as befits the master of such creation. He has been attractive and attracted to women, and his memoirs reveal explicitly his attitude to the opposite sex. He wrote: 'When I was a racing driver myself, I had a girl in the pits. This was my wife, who accompanied me everywhere. I think, however, that I should have done better not to have married. Marriage brought me the terrible joy of having a son whom I was later to lose; but I should never have married, for a man who is dominated by an overriding passion such as mine is rarely able to divide himself in two and find time also to be a good husband. What is more, marriage takes away from a man at least half his freedom. Had I listened to my wife, I should have gone and got myself a job with the local tramway company.'

He explains that he married somewhere around 1920; he forgets exactly when because he has mislaid the marriage certificate. He met Laura, pretty and smartly dressed, one evening under the arcades of Turin's Porta Nuova. She came from a wealthy family, from the village of Racconigi, some twenty miles outside the city, and she became his wife soon after despite parental opposition. Many years later Ferrari declared that he felt sure men were inferior to women if not in intelligence then in vitality and hardness. 'This feminine superiority is apparent above all in marriage: it is the woman who chooses her mate, not vice versa ... we think we have wooed and won, whereas in reality we are merely the slaves of our desire, on which the woman has played with consummate skill,' he wrote; '... I am convinced that when a man tells a woman he loves her, he only means that he desires her; and that the only total love in this world is that of a father for his son.'

Laura Ferrari gave her husband the son he craved on 19 January 1932, much later in marriage than most. He was christened after his late uncle Alfredo, which became inevitably 'Alfredino' or 'Dino' for short. With his birth, Ferrari tells us he surrendered his ambitions to be a racing driver.

Dino Ferrari studied for his diploma at the Corni Technical Institute in Modena, and progressed later to take an engineering degree in Switzerland, using for his thesis a project for a 1.5-litre 4-cylinder engine with two inlet valves and one exhaust valve, Bugatti-fashion, in each combustion chamber. He was also enrolled as a first-year student in the faculty of economy and commerce at Bologna University, just a few miles down the road from home in Modena.

Enzo Ferrari consciously groomed his son to carry on the business, as any ambitious father would in that position, and Dino was by instinct a motor racing enthusiast. Mr Ferrari gave him a little Fiat 500 *Topolino*, in which he learned to drive, then came a Fiat 1100 TV and finally a 2-litre Ferrari of his own, which father let him thrash around Modena Autodrome. But just as Enzo and his brother Alfredo had suffered ill-health in their youth, Dino was never strong and Ferrari worried about his apparent deep intent to become a successful student, to drive his cars, to enjoy their racing and perhaps to make himself a worthy heir. Ferrari was concerned '... not so much for any risks he might run, but because his health was precarious and I was afraid he might overtax himself'. It is almost an embarrassment to read Ferrari's tortured laments for his lost son as set down in his memoirs; one feels almost an intruder spying on intensely private emotion. But Dino was to win unusual immortality.

Dino Ferrari, after whom the Ferrari Dino cars were named, pictured with his mother, Signora Laura, at Imola in 1954. After his death at the age of 24 in 1956 the Imola circuit was named in his honour, together with the training school at the growing Ferrari plant at Maranello

The *Commission Sportive International* of the FIA—motor racing's international governing body—had announced that a new unsupercharged 1.5-litre Formula 2 class would take effect in 1957 to provide an adequate single-seater stepping stone towards the contemporary 2.5-litre Formula 1.

Ferrari briefed his ailing son and his senior engineers under Jano to investigate suitable engine layouts for the new Formula. He has published a letter from his son written as late as August 1955, in which Dino suggests a smaller version of the contemporary Lancia-derived V8, but in his memoirs Mr Ferrari goes on to record that he and Jano spent long hours at Dino's bedside during the long and cold winter of 1955–56, discussing the pros and cons of using a straight-4 or six-cylinder, a V6 or V8. The grieving father in Ferrari recalls: '. . . for reasons of mechanical efficiency, he (Dino) came to the conclusion that the engine should be a V6, and we accepted this decision.' In view of Vittorio Jano's impeccable engineering credentials and vast experience, this is a little hard to believe.

But Dino Ferrari had been fighting a lingering and losing battle against muscular dystrophy, and that winter what in health would have been only a minor secondary infection brought on nephritis—a kidney disease—and Dino Ferrari fell into chronic renal failure.

At that time, Italy led the world in treatment for such disorders and the administration of low-protein, high-carbohydrate diets was considered vital to maintain life . . . for a limited period. Ferrari wrote: '. . . I had deluded myself—a father always deludes himself—that we should be able to restore him to health.' He spent time every day drawing up tables detailing the diet which could sustain his son, and tracing graphs of Dino's latest sample analyses. He filled a notebook with columns of figures recording his son's condition, but abruptly on 30 June 1956 Dino's struggle ended. His desolated father wrote 'the match is lost', and closed the notebook for the last time. Muscular dystrophy was considered to be congenital; passed on via the mother.

For many years following Dino's death Mr Ferrari seldom missed a daily visit to his grave to commune and seek inspiration for the business. Dino's portrait hangs in a place of honour on his office wall at Maranello, and his small chapel there is another part of the Ferrari legend, as is the shrouded little Fiat saloon, still parked in the Modena *Assistenza*, where Dino switched it off, shut the door and walked away for the last time.

But let Dino Ferrari's objective epitaph be the regard and affection which the Ferrari staff clearly held for him. Like Phil Hill: 'He obviously wasn't well, but he was pleasant enough and always spoke to us, even when we were new boys, strangers in the camp. . . .' Mr Ferrari—of course—best put it into words: '. . . it was only after he had passed away that I realized to the full the goodness of this young man, who knew that he was going to die yet never inflicted the burden of his infinite suffering on me, his father, or on the friends who went to see him. He was a noble lad and a generous one. . . . I never thought a son could leave his father a legacy. But my son did. . . .'

In one small part, that legacy became his own memorial, the long race-bred series of Ferrari Dino cars.

The baby grows

After those initial discussions with Mr Ferrari and his son, Vittorio Jano pondered deeply the problems of crystallizing his knowledge and experience into a 1500 cc Formula 2 engine which would have a competitive life of several seasons, and which might also stretch for other applications.

For purposes of adequate dynamic balance various included angles between the cylinder banks of vee engines had become accepted. A vee-8 balanced well, fired properly and was compact enough to install easily with a 90-degree included angle. A V12 or V6 suited 60 degrees and preliminary schemes for the new 1.5-litre as agreed with Enzo and his son adopted this included angle. But Jano intended to produce a full-blooded racing engine, and the state of the art at that time indicated that space demanded by double overhead camshafts and their covers would severely restrict intake duct shaping within the vee necessary for adequate breathing. Jano toyed with the problem, and finally added 5 degrees to the included angle within the vee, widening it to 65 degrees—not much wider but sufficient—and he still maintained normal 120-degree phasing between firing impulses.

He achieved this by considering the engine as three V-twins coupled together in series rather than as two conjoined banks of three cylinders in line, and he drew up its crankshaft with some crankpins disposed at 55 degrees and others at 185 degrees. He reasoned that 55 degrees advance, plus the 65 degrees built into the engine vee, gave 120 degrees phasing. Then 185 degrees minus 65 degrees again provided 120 degrees phasing.

As the first 'vee-twin' fired it would be followed in turn by the second vee-twin (we cannot call it a V2) and then the third. The cylinders of each pair should fire 120 degrees apart. When number 1 fired, the opposing number 2 would be 120 degrees of rotation away from firing. As the opposing cylinder bank had 65 degrees advance built into it by the engine layout, its crankpin required only 55 degrees spacing. Then to phase the centre vee-twin correctly, its number 3 cylinder should fire 120 degrees after number 2 in the first 'vee-twin'. Because of the 65-degree vee this crankpin spacing then had to be 185 degrees. In this way the new V6 fired six times at equal intervals during two crankshaft rotations.

The cylinder blocks were staggered relative to one another, since fork-and-blade connecting rods sharing a common big-end had long gone out of favour. The new V6 was staggered with its left bank advanced forward of the right, opposite to Ferrari's well-established V12s, which had their right bank forward of the left, but matching Jano's Lancia V8. Take-offs from the short four-main-bearing crankshaft's nose powered the twin-overhead camshafts via chains, plus the oil, water and fuel pumps. Unlike the V12's cam-drive, the V6's chains were controlled by two tensioners. Two valves per cylinder were actuated via typical Jano mushroom-type tappets screwed onto the valve stems. There were two 14 mm spark plugs set in each combustion chamber, fired from twin magnetos, one on the nose of each inlet camshaft. Induction was handled by three Weber twin-choke 38DCN carburetters sitting within the vee. Three exhaust primaries on each side fed into single tail-pipes. All castings were in Siluminum light alloy, and dry-sump lubrication was used.

A one-piece casting formed the crankcase integrally with both three-cylinder blocks. The con-rods were split at a 45-degree angle, having a tongue-and-groove cap-joint location to enable them to pass through the bores. Whereas previous Ferrari racing engines had employed cylinder liners screwed into the head to avoid the use of a gasket, the new V6 followed the D50 Lancia-Ferrari V8 practice of nipping the liner between block and head. There was a seating flange some $1\frac{1}{2}$ inches beneath the top of the liner, while a copper-nickel gasket formed a fire joint with the head.

Bore and stroke dimensions were 70 mm $\times$ 64.5 mm, giving a swept volume of 1489.35 cc. Nominal compression ratio was 10.0:1, as Formula 2 regulations demanded the use of premium-grade pump fuel as opposed to the alcohol mixes still allowed at that time in Formula 1.

Work proceeded rapidly during the summer of 1956, and five months after Dino Ferrari's death the new Formula 2 Ferrari V6 was motored over in a Maranello test-cell. Oil and water flows were checked and verified, the fuel system was tested and eventually the new unit's ignition was switched on. It howled into life, ran quite satisfactorily, and work began in earnest to design and build a chassis for its racing debut.

The Ferrari engineers tackled the problem as simply as they knew how. They were aware that the funny little British firm of Cooper Cars had built an uprated version of their successful 500 cc Formula 3 mid-engined design for Formula 2, and that the Lotus sports-car company were forging ahead with an ultra-lightweight front-engined model—actually their first-ever single-seater. Both were to use the proprietary Coventry Climax FPF twin-cam light-alloy 4-cylinder engine, and that was expected to produce about 140 bhp at 7000 rpm. On the test-bed, the new Ferrari V6 was already showing around 180 bhp at 9000 rpm.

Ferrari at this time was firmly convinced that engine power was all, the chassis was purely secondary. He has set down his philosophy like this, talking of his prototype V12 design: 'All we wanted to do was to build a conventional engine, but one that would be outstanding. Perhaps in designing this car, as in the years that followed, I underestimated the importance of the chassis. In fact I have always given great importance to the engine and much less to the chassis, endeavouring to squeeze out as much power as possible in the conviction that it is engine power which is—not fifty per cent but eighty per cent—responsible for success on the track.... When one has this extra power, chassis deficiencies are not a handicap....'

So the new V6 Formula 2 car was designed as a scaled-down version of the Formula 1 Lancia-Ferrari 801 models being developed for the 1957 World Championship season. The whole thing was quite simply scaled down from that basis, using a tubular chassis frame with two large-diameter bottom longerons welded to a lighter superstructure for additional rigidity. It was by no means a true spaceframe, with all members in tension or compression, it was closer to a simple twin-tube ladder frame in effect.

It carried the new V6 engine at an angle to pass its propeller-shaft low to the left under the driver's seat, into a four-speed and reverse gearbox in unit with the final-drive assembly. The propshaft drove the gearbox through bevel-gears and projected beyond them to terminate in a starter-dog exactly as on the Lancia–Ferraris. Both types of car could be started in the same manner, using Ferrari's standard trolley-starter shaft inserted in a tail tube.

This final-drive assembly filled the entire width of the frame, its cast magnesium alloy casing containing input-bevels, clutch, four-speed gearbox and final-drive gears combined with a ZF limited-slip differential. Input was by a pair of straight-tooth bevels of almost equal diameter on the left side. Inboard of these was a tiny multi-plate clutch with fabric-lined driving plates. The clutch shaft passed across the car's centreline to the right, forming the first motion shaft of the two-shaft gearbox. It carried free-running gear-wheels engaged by stub dogs similar to those in a synchromesh 'box, but minus the synchronizing cones. Vertically above this shaft lay the second motion shaft carrying constant-mesh fixed gears. On its inboard end—actually on the car's centreline—was a pinion meshing with the straight-tooth final drive, which in turn enclosed the ZF differential. The encased clutch was cooled via tangential slots in its housing and there was a right-hand gearchange without a gate, an interlocking mechanism being provided in the gearbox itself.

Front suspension was by unequal-length double wishbones with interposed coil springs and an anti-roll bar, and used Houdaille dampers mounted on the main chassis longeron beneath the lower wishbones. The wishbone outboard ends carried short vertical king-pins and a forged stub-axle carrier. At the rear a de Dion beam ran behind the gearbox/final-drive assembly in Formula 1 style, but instead of having the centre location ball fitted to the chassis and a guide channel below the tube as on the F1s, the new F2 had the guide-channel on the frame and the ball on the de Dion beam. Forward-facing twin radius rods located each end of the beam, and a transverse-leaf provided the springing medium, high-mounted above the final drive. Dampers were again by Houdaille.

Front brakes were an amalgam of existing components, using thin cast-iron back-plates and shoes from the Lancia–Ferraris. Rear brakes were special to the new F2, but followed established Lancia–Ferrari practice, with wide drums bearing thin peripheral cooling fins.

The car's hand-made aluminium body shell was scaled directly from the latest Lancia–Ferrari 801 design, with thirty-seven gallons of fuel housed in a large tail tank wrapped over the gearbox/final-drive and in a subsidiary tank low to the left side of the cockpit alongside the driver's leg. His seating position was accordingly offset slightly to the right. An oil tank occupied the extreme tail of the car, with a neatly fared flap covering its filler neck. The steering wheel was set on an almost horizontal stub column passing through the dash and scuttle, where a universally jointed shaft snaked over the engine's left-side exhaust cam-cover into a steering-box mounted high by the left-front top wishbone pick-ups.

A long, beautifully flared megaphone exhaust emerged from each side of the engine bay to terminate just ahead of the rear wheel. The cockpit sides were cut low to give the driver a little extra room, and in prototype form carried an abbreviated wrap-round Perspex screen. An induction air box humped on the engine cover, matching a similar section on the scuttle-top, which incorporated a cold-air cockpit ventilator closed-off by an adjustable flap. Borrani 15-inch wheels were fitted in preference to the Formula 1 cars' 16-inch, accentuating the new F2's scaled-down appearance.

Its wheelbase of 2160 mm (85.1 in) compared with the latest Lancia–Ferrari 801's 2280 mm (89.8 in); track was 1270 mm (50 in) front and 1240 mm (48.8 in) rear, compared to 1320 mm (51.9 in) for the Grand Prix car; and weight was around 512 kg (1129 lb), compared to the 801's 650 kg (1433 lb).

While the project was still under development, Mr Ferrari decreed it should be named 'Dino' in honour of his lost son, who had been so interested in its early evolution.

This decision coincided with another intended to simplify Ferrari's type number system. Formerly this identified models by the nominal displacement in centilitres of one engine cylinder. Thus the figures '125' when applied to a V12 engine indicated 1.5 litres, because 125 cc × 12 cyls = 1500 cc. Similarly '250' applied to one of the V12s indicated 3 litres, for 250 cc × 12 = 3000 cc, and '750' as applied to the big *Monza* 4-cylinder sports-racer also indicated 3 litres, since 750 cc × 4 = 3000 cc. Now the new F2 Dino '156' classification indicated simply a 1.5-litre 6-cylinder car. This more simple system for single-seater Ferrari identification survives to this day, with detail suffixes such as the 1979 312T4 Grand Prix car, indicating a 3-litre 12-cylinder *trasversale* (transverse-disposed gearbox) of the fourth series. This simple system is also applied to all the Dino family, while other Ferrari sports and road cars adhere in the main to the original single-cylinder displacement system with suitable suffix letters, of which more anon....

During 1956 the side-panniered Lancia–Ferrari V8s had taken first and third places in the Driver's World Championship for Juan Fangio and Peter Collins. Their other drivers had included Luigi Musso, Eugenio Castellotti, Olivier Gendebien, 'Fon' de Portago and Wolfgang von Trips. Mike Hawthorn had attempted to find success with British

Above Factory test driver Martino Severi photographed by Walter Breveglieri on the Maranello–Serramazzone road during initial testing of the unpainted F2 Dino 156 prototype '0011' in April 1957. Breveglieri raced a 1.5-litre Formula 1 Cooper in 1961 under the pseudonym 'Wal Ever'

Left On the Naples grid, '0011' is dwarfed by its basically 1956-style Lancia–Ferrari sisters driven by Collins (centre) and Hawthorn (right). The portly figure of Ferrari crew chief Parenti leans forward expectantly on the left

This page These photographs of '0011' on its race debut at Naples in 1957 were taken by Denis Jenkinson of *Motor Sport* magazine with his Rolleiflex. 'Jenks' was often the only English-speaking journalist at these Italian meetings. The new Dino's cockpit has a cut-down Perspex windscreen, a tachometer red-lined at 8000 rpm and (from left) fuel pressure, oil pressure and water temperature gauges. The cockpit fuel tank resides on the left-hand side; Naples' Posillipo circuit was unusual in being lapped anticlockwise, which placed this tank on the inside of most turns. The 156 engine shows off its angled chassis mounting, twin-plug ignition sparked by two six-cylinder magnetos driven off the inlet camshaft noses, and 'Ferrari' lettering on the cam-boxes—not yet the 'Dino' script

Right On the 1983 cc V6 engines adapted for the Modena GP in September 1957 a single double-bodied magneto appeared. The cam-covers are still 'Ferrari' lettered, but have gained their distinctive strengthening web at the rear

23

cars in 1955–56 after two quite good seasons with Ferrari in 1953–54, and as Fangio returned to Maserati for 1957 so Hawthorn cabled Ferrari saying, 'I am interested if you are.' Mr Ferrari replied enthusiastically, and just before Christmas Hawthorn flew to Milan, took the train to Modena, and after 'the usual wait before Ferrari was able to see me' found himself being offered very favourable terms, which he accepted. At Modena Autodrome they watched Castellotti testing the latest 3.5-litre V12 sports-racing car and then Ferrari took Hawthorn to Maranello and showed him the new Dino being built.

Hawthorn wrote: 'Ferrari claimed that the engine was producing nearly 190 bhp, or over 125 bhp per litre, which was really phenomenal, and said that Vittorio Stanguellini, one of his neighbours in Modena, who knows a great deal about extracting power from small engines, had maintained that it could not possibly produce more than 160 horsepower. He had furthermore bet Ferrari that for every horsepower he could produce over 160, Stanguellini would buy him a dinner for five people. When I saw him, Ferrari was looking forward to eating well and cheaply for some time. . . .'*

Work proceeded on the Dino while the Formula 1 team began its World Championship defence, unsuccessfully, in Argentina, and Castellotti crashed at Modena while testing an 801 and lost his life. Soon after, in the Mille Miglia, the Spaniard De Portago had a tyre burst at very high speed in his works Ferrari 335S and plunged into the roadside crowd, killing himself and his navigator, 'Ed' Nelson, and eleven bystanders.

Ferrari found himself attacked on all sides. The Italian press, the inevitable band-wagon politicians, even the Vatican launched into him as a murderer, no less. He could not be held responsible for a tyre failure, but the death of De Portago following upon that of Castellotti and now of so many members of the public all rebounded directly upon Maranello. Mr Ferrari (still chilled, remember, by his Dino's death) threatened to quit racing (not for the last time) and was rewarded by assurances of sympathy and support from all over the world. He pressed on.

In April the spring sun sparkled on the prototype Dino 156 — numbered '0011' in the Lancia–Ferrari series — as works tester Martino Severi gave it its first shake-down laps at Modena Autodrome. Towards the end of the month Hawthorn and Collins arrived to try it between testing their Lancia-Ferraris on 23 April. Musso was unwell.

On 28 April the non-Championship 14th *Gran Premio di Napoli* was held on the serpentine Posillipo street circuit high in the city, and Ferrari arrived with a brand-new double-deck transporter carrying two Formula 1 Lancia–Ferraris and the brand-new Formula 2 Dino V6, now painted. The new car was entered for the faithful Luigi Musso, while Collins and Hawthorn had a pair of pannier-bodied 1956 Lancia–Ferrari specials, the former's with low-pivot swing-axle independent rear suspension on coil springs, and the latter's a long-cockpit model tailored to the tall English driver with 1955 Ferrari Super Squalo front suspension grafted on.

*'Champion Year' by Mike Hawthorn, William Kimber, London, 1959.

This magnificent shot of the prototype Dino 156 V6 engine was released by the factory in 1957. It demonstrates the monobloc construction with detachable twin-cam heads, shallow sump pan and the original magneto arrangement. Ferrari camshafts had provision for power take-off at either end. The engine weighed 126 kg (277 lb) dry, compared to the Climax F2 engine at 260 lb on magneto ignition or 280 lb with coil, dynamo, etc.

Practice held its problems for Ferrari, but the trio ended up on the front row of the grid, Hawthorn on pole alongside Collins with 2 min 0.08 sec and Musso in the Dino with 2:09.2. English privateer Horace Gould was on row two with his Maserati and he warned his compatriots that with his lower bottom gear he intended to dodge between them at the start. Hawthorn and Collins knew the burly Bristolian motor trader would do just that, and they moved apart as the flag fell and sure enough Gould blasted through to lead them all.

Halfway round the first lap he moved over and let Collins and Hawthorn through, but Musso was another matter and he was held off for two laps before slashing by and wailing the V6 after its big-engined team-mates in third place. On lap 13 Hawthorn stopped because the fuel pressure gauge feed-pipe had split and was spraying onto him, and Musso's Dino inherited second place behind Collins. Hawthorn lost six places, but tigered furiously after rejoining and he barged past Musso on the very last lap to demote the Dino to third place—as of right.

The new car had been flogged mercilessly by Musso for two days of arduous practice and throughout the Naples race itself and had emerged with flying colours, trouble free. Hawthorn's fantastic race lap record for the circuit of 2:05.6, 117.515 km/h (73.02 mph) was only 1.7 seconds faster than the little Dino's, which in those days was a remarkably small margin, and Ferrari now knew they had a tremendous Formula 2 prospect if only the class would take hold in Europe.

Despite the Mille Miglia catastrophe a full Ferrari team went to Monaco for the year's first European World Championship round, on 19 May, and fielded no less than six cars, including the little Dino—four V8s being intended for the race. Collins, Hawthorn, Wolfgang von Trips and Maurice Trintignant were the drivers and in between the serious business of running their Lancia–Ferraris they all took turns to hurl the little Dino around the Principality's street circuit, to obtain comparative figures for the future. Once again it withstood a considerable hammering, but the race was a shambles for Ferrari, only Trintignant surviving to finish fifth....

Collins had severely damaged his Lancia–Ferrari in a practice accident and in the race crashed a second car and was hit by Hawthorn. All three wrecks were virtual write-offs and with the works sports cars impounded after the Mille Miglia disaster and Ferrari refusing to run in another Italian event until the authorities had cleared his cars of responsibility, it really did look as though he would stop racing altogether. But at Maranello, the work of rebuilding the Formula 1 cars got under way, and the promising little Dino was temporarily set aside.

In the French Grand Prix at Rouen, Musso (recovered from a recurrent tummy bug which had kept him out of the team at Monaco) was second, Collins third and Hawthorn fourth in their Lancia–Ferraris behind Fangio, whose majestic driving skills in the good-handling lightweight Maserati 250F had left them all for dead.

One week later, on 13/14 July, the Reims weekend saw a non-Championship Formula 1 race supported by the first major continental Formula 2 event and the International 12-Hours for sports cars. Musso beat Jean Behra's Maserati and Stuart Lewis-Evans's Vanwall in the sixty-one-lap Reims Grand Prix and Olivier Gendebien and Paul Frère won the 12-Hours in their Ferrari 250GT. Then the thirty-seven-lap Formula 2 race was also Ferrari's, being won by Maurice Trintignant—in the Dino....

Twenty cars had started, with the Dino '0011' out-paced and lonely against a dozen Coopers, five Lotuses and lone sports cars from OSCA and Porsche. Trintignant was involved in a slip-streaming battle for the

The two works Formula 1 interim cars in the Ain Diab circuit pits at Casablanca prior to the non-Championship Moroccan GP in October 1957. Number 2 with the four-spoke steering wheel is Hawthorn's 2195 cc '0011'; number 4 is Collins's 2417 cc '0012'. Both carry the new high-cockpit side bodywork and the high-level exhaust systems introduced with 1983 cc engines at Modena the preceding month. The factory's 1974 list provides evidence that these engines were 77 × 71 mm, 1983.72 cc, though reported at the time—and since—as 1860 or 1877 cc

lead with the spidery little mid-engined works Coopers of Jack Brabham and Roy Salvadori from the start, all three swopping places round the very fast Champagne circuit. Brabham and Trintignant shared a 2 min 38.2 sec (188.914 km/h, 117.391 mph) lap record, but faces fell in the Ferrari pit as it seemed Trintignant stood little chance while the two Coopers were working together. But on lap 24 Brabham coasted to rest just short of the finish line with a broken valve in his Coventry Climax engine. Two laps later the beautiful front-engined Dino and its crude-looking adversary lapped the American Herbert Mackay Fraser's stripped sports Lotus and he latched onto their slipstream and stayed with them and was towed past the third and fourth place men.

Tragically Fraser lost control next time round on the flat-out curve before Gueux village and crashed fatally: only the week before he had starred for BRM in the French Grand Prix

Still Trintignant and Salvadori were racing hammer and tongs, but on lap 31 the Ferrari appeared in the pit straight alone and Salvadori eventually went by with his engine far off song. Trintignant was howling round happily on his own at 9200 rpm much of the time, easing off comfortably at the finish to score the Ferrari Dino's maiden victory at an average of 114.39 mph (184.087 km/h). Still the writing was on the wall, for the little backyard special Cooper-Climax cars had given the Prancing Horse's tail a pretty firm tweak before the Dino's power had stretched them to destruction.

There were no major Formula 2 dates remaining in the season's calendar, and while the team continued their (unsuccessful) defence of the World Championship title with the Lancia–Ferrari V8s, engineer Massimino's men at Maranello were completing a second Dino 156—chassis '0012'. This car differed from the Reims-winning prototype in having its twin magnetos mounted on the rear of the inlet camshafts, and the steering box was mounted behind the top-right suspension pick-up

Ferrari's release picture of the 1957–58 winter Formula 1 Dino 246, taken at the 'Aerautodromo di Modena' on a typically misty day. The Englebert tyres were Belgian made and were often troublesome

instead of the left, with its multi-jointed column re-routed accordingly.

This second car began an extensive test series at Modena, where it was driven by the very promising young Ferrari engineer Andrea Fraschetti. He had largely been responsible for the 6-cylinder in-line Ferrari sports car engines, and had collaborated closely with Vittorio Bellentani on the 1956 860 *Monza* 4-cylinder sports of 3.4 litres and 310 bhp, which placed 1–2 in the Sebring 12-Hours, and the 3.5- and 3.8-litre V12 sports car units known as the 290MM and 312LM. Many years later, Ferrari likened Fraschetti to Rudolf Uhlenhaut of Mercedes-Benz, who combined brilliant engineering ability with first-rate driving skill. Fraschetti owned a sports Stanguellini which he raced in national events, but the second Dino got away from him on 29 August at Modena; it crashed and he was killed.

Fangio in the Maserati gave Hawthorn and Collins an unforgettable driving demonstration in beating them into second and third places in the German Grand Prix at Nürburgring. The Pescara Grand Prix was the next Championship round, Ferrari entering just one car for Musso as a 'privateer', and at Monza the Italian Grand Prix was run as normal—the post-Mille Miglia hysteria having more or less evaporated—and Vanwall and Maserati ruled the day, Fangio clinching his fifth and final World Drivers' Championship crown while Maserati lifted Ferrari's Constructors' Championship.

The Lancia V8-based cars were clearly at the end of their development when compared to the nimble handling and smooth power promised by enlarged versions of Jano's successful little Dino V6, and both F2 cars were now fitted with revised engines reported as 1877 cc; bored from the original 70 mm to 78.6 mm while retaining the 1.5-litre crankshaft assembly with its 64.5 mm stroke. Power output was quoted as 215 bhp at 8500 rpm. Ferrari records reveal 77 × 71 mm, actually 1983.72 cc and c.220 bhp at 8500 rpm.

The first of these models was tested back-to-back with the Lancia–Ferrari 801 at Modena and Monza and proved itself both slightly quicker and much easier to handle.

At this time 2.5-litre Formula 1 was approaching the end of its initial three-year term, and it had been announced that it would be extended for three further seasons, to the end of 1960. However, in response to pressure from publicity-conscious fuel companies, alcohol fuels were to be banned in the new year, and 130-octane AvGas aviation fuel was to be substituted. Mr Ferrari had a very close relationship with Shell, and here he was with the V6 engines already well developed to run on straight petrol—against the British alcohol-fuelled establishment of Vanwall and BRM, who would clearly have a lot of work to do during the coming winter. What Mr Ferrari had not, possibly, bargained for was the reduction in minimum race distances from the classic 500 km (312 miles), or around three hours, to only 300 km, or two hours. This change gave the British 'special builders' their head, with lightweight cars on bolt-on wheels running non-stop throughout a Grand Prix. . . .

The Modena Grand Prix for Formula 1 cars was to be held on 22 September, two weeks after the Italian Grand Prix, and the two '1877 cc'

Dinos formed the Ferrari works entry, Musso in '0011' and Collins in '0012'. The scuttle hump ahead of the cockpit had gone on the later car and both engine covers were now cut away to expose the Weber carburetters' induction trumpets, protected within a clear plastic 'screen' open at the top and rear. Both cars had been finalized with high-sided cockpit/long-nosed bodywork.

Practice proved these beautiful miniaturized Grand Prix cars to be very fast despite their lack of cubic inches and use of AvGas petrol against full 2.5-litre alcohol-fuelled opposition. The race was arranged in two heats, with final result on aggregate time, and Musso lined up for heat one on the outside of the front row beside the Maseratis of Jean Behra and Harry Schell, with Collins on row three. Behra made a poor start and Schell led away only for Musso to force ahead on lap two and give the Dino the lead in only its second Formula 1 race. By lap 11 Behra had caught Schell and then Musso and drew away, finally winning by 20.5 seconds from the older Ferrari Dino, with Collins fourth behind Schell in the latest Dino. Musso shared fastest lap with Behra, a new circuit record.

In heat two Behra led from start to finish, while Schell found himself involved in a torrid battle with Musso and Collins, who outnumbered him in his Maserati. Eventually the result was as in heat one.

This result was extremely promising, and at Maranello the whole stock of Lancia–Ferrari cars and parts was tidied away into store preparatory to scrapping. The Dinos became the sole object of attention for Formula 1.

The season was to close with the first Moroccan Grand Prix on 27 October at Casablanca's Ain-Diab circuit and Ferrari entered his two Dino chassis with their V6 engines further enlarged. The stroke was increased by just 1 mm to 71 mm and allied to a bore of 81 mm in Hawthorn's engine for a swept volume of 2195 cc and to an 85 mm bore in Collins's for 2417 cc. Weber 42DCN carburetters replaced the 38DCNs used with the smaller displacements, and power output for these two interim engines was quoted as 240 bhp at 8500 rpm and 270 bhp at 8300 rpm. Weight was up to about 560 kg (1235 lb). Rear suspension geometry was altered to lower the roll-centre. This was achieved by fitting a fabricated fork extension below the de Dion tube which rode on a pivot fixed to the frame beneath the final-drive. Originally a ball on the tube-centre had ridden in a slide on the back of the final drive casing.

In practice the Dinos again showed competitive pace after some early problems, but their drivers in common with several others picked up some nasty Asian 'flu virus and were suffering on race day. Collins resolved to have a go in Dino '0012' and leapt into an immediate lead, using his car's low startline weight to full advantage, but on lap 8 he spun. While trying to make up time he spun again on lap 16, clobbered some straw bales and damaged his car too badly to continue. Hawthorn was unhappy, knew he was in no condition to go motor racing, and when Schell went by signalling furiously he pulled '0011' into the pits. Team engineer Amorotti's men found the gearbox leaking oil, so Hawthorn gratefully retired, having completed ten laps. Some reports attribute his withdrawal to a burned piston, but this was not substantiated.

However, Ferrari's V6 revolution was under way. . . .

1958 Title won — Championship lost

Immediately after the '1877 cc' Dinos' successful showing at Modena in September 1957, Alberto Massimino's chassis design team began development of an all-new Formula 1 frame to carry Dino V6 engines in the 1958 World Championship series.

It was closer to a true spaceframe with near same-size tubes used throughout the bottom ladder-frame and top superstructure. This 'same-size tube' frame saved a claimed 25 lb weight over the shallower side-truss 'big bottom tube' frame of the two prototype 1957 cars. It was announced at the time as Ferrari's standard Formula 1 chassis for the coming season, but for the Argentine races in January a third 'big-tube' frame was provided for Hawthorn carrying new short-nose 1958 body panelling. The prototype small-tube frame was subsequently taken out for Trips, but it does not seem to have been a success. Its torsional rigidity was almost certainly a disappointment, and of the seven cars which Ferrari records suggest they raced that year only two—possibly three—used the new frame. A typical Ferrari mystery enshrouds this question, for their records give the same chassis number to vehicles which are known to have appeared with the small-tube frame at one meeting, and in big-tube form at another. As a rough guide the 1958 frames '0011' (a new one, replacing the 1957 first prototype), and '0004' were small-tube quasi-spaceframes, '0001'–'3' and '5'–'6' and almost certainly '7' were big-tube, shallow truss, chassis. Collins's car '0002' had both types! Denis Jenkinson's *Motor Sport* race report notes for the period record a chassis 'No. 6' being driven by Trips at Monza, but this appears in fact to have been a new big-frame '0005'. Equally his notes list Hawthorn's disc-brake Monza car as 'No. 5'. This machine was certainly Mike's personal car '0003', which may perhaps have been physically renumbered on its disc-brake conversion. In what follows and in the appendices I have considered the cars in this light, with the aid of some access to the factory records.

Jano and Bellentani's engine development men standardized the 1958 Formula 1 V6 around Collins's Casablanca unit, with the 85 mm bore and 71 mm stroke giving 2417.3 cc. The model was given the official type classification 'Dino 246'....

The racing season began with the traditional Argentine *Temporada* races in January, including the World Championship Grand Prix, the

Hawthorn's Casablanca 1957 'big-tube' chassis frame '0011' stripped out at Maranello after the Moroccan GP. The main structural members are the two cranked bottom longerons in *c.* 60 mm tube tapering rearwards, with a same-size vertical carrying the rear suspension radius rod mounts; the whole being stiffened by a smaller-tube superstructure. The cockpit fuel tank is still in place, while the Lancia–Ferrari suspension wishbones and gilled front drum brake are clearly visible. The massive water radiator partially blanked by the oil cooler was standard practice

In comparison the 1958 'small-tube' quasi-space-frame Ferrari Dino chassis was hailed upon its introduction in the Argentine Temporada as the new year's 'Formula 1' chassis in place of the big-tube 'Formula 2' type. It saved a claimed 25 lb weight, using *c.* 40 mm bottom tubes, with *c.* 30 mm top tubes. The seven cross-members in the bottom bay increased in diameter from rear to front, where there were two closely spaced 30 mm tubes between the bottom members at fabricated box section front-suspension pick-ups

non-Championship Buenos Aires City Grand Prix for *Formule Libre* cars and the Buenos Aires 1000 km Sports Car World Championship event.

Ferrari shipped three Dinos south of the Equator, the original cars '0011' and '0012' for Collins and Musso and the prototype 1958 spaceframe 246 (looking suspiciously like '0003') for Hawthorn. This car was fitted with an abbreviated aero screen which he always preferred to the modern wrap-round transparencies of the ex-F2 cars, and, of course, had his favourite style four-spoke steering wheel. It also carried experimental angle-vaned drum brakes, and dispensed with cockpit fuel tankage.

The field comprised just ten cars, for the *Temporada* had been an on-again, off-again series which was finally confirmed as being 'on' with only four weeks to go. Some of the British teams (still struggling to convert their engines to run on AvGas) felt aggrieved at such short notice, and

since the Royal Automobile Club had not received copies of the regulations from the Argentinian organizers within the minimum notice specified by the CSI, a British protest was registered, demanding that the race should not be allowed to count towards the 1958 World Championship. The CSI responded by saying they would consider the matter at their next meeting, in Monte Carlo after the Rally had finished, and after the Argentine Grand Prix had been run. Ferrari of course was eminently well prepared, and sent his full team as usual, while Stirling Moss (in Vanwall's absence) was entered by Rob Walker in a 1960 cc F2-based Cooper–Climax . . . taking a leaf out of Ferrari's book.

Practice began at the Buenos Aires Autodrome on 15 January and the V6 Ferraris were fast but troubled by understeer, which slowed them badly. In Saturday qualifying, Collins and Hawthorn managed to place their Dinos alongside Fangio's pole position Maserati, equalling each other's time of 1 min 42.6 sec, 0.6 slower than the reigning champion. Musso was on the middle of row two on 1:42.9, splitting the Maseratis of Behra and Argentinian polo-player Carlos Menditeguy.

Race day was pleasantly cool for a change, but at the start Collins's Ferrari bounced forward and stopped immediately as one of its F2-sized half-shafts failed. Fangio led away from Hawthorn, Behra and the rest with Moss's quaint little baby car running strongly in touch with the leaders.

Hawthorn found his car understeering and was in early trouble with his experimental brakes locking the offside front wheel. As he lost time, Fangio established a comfortable lead with Moss second ahead of his compatriot's new Dino, but around the thirty-lap mark Hawthorn saw his oil pressure drop and he stopped. He asked Adelmo Marchetti, the chief mechanic, to check the tank level. It was full and he was sent back into the race. Naturally he did not want to risk his brand-new engine, but they promised him all was well and he re-entered with a will.

Fangio lost the lead when his Maserati stripped a tyre tread, and while he was in the pits Moss scuttled by in first place. Hawthorn caught and passed the ailing Maseratis of Fangio and Behra, but meanwhile Luigi Musso was running consistently second and waiting for what the team thought would be Moss's inevitable tyre change. Phil Hill was present as spare driver, and he vividly recalls the anticipation in the Ferrari pit changing to doubt as Moss droned round and round and showed no sign of stopping, then to disbelief and finally despair as it became evident Musso was not close enough to put pressure on the Englishman and his funny little car. Should Moss be forced to stop, the Cooper's bolt-on wheels would cost him dearly in time, but he eased off to conserve his tyres, and although they were down to the breaker at the finish, Musso had started his charge from too far back, and was still over 2 seconds behind as the chequered flag swept down. Hawthorn was third, and the atmosphere in the Ferrari pit was one of disbelief at having been beaten by the baby Cooper. Phil recalls glum-faced Amorotti walking around with his fingers interlaced, palms upward, waggling his finger-tips. Compared to his beautiful tool room-built Ferraris the Cooper was like a bug on its back. . . .

In the wet Buenos Aires City GP for Formule Libre 'Taffy' von Trips's new space-frame car—probably '002'—briefly leads Luigi Musso's 1957 '0011' in the rain, during the first heat. Trips crashed later, while Musso finished second overall on aggregate behind Fangio's Maserati 250F

Musso was furious, claiming the pit had given him no signals, but Collins had done so several times and both English drivers felt the Italian should really have tried harder, though they kept their opinion to themselves. Both surviving Ferraris had suffered understeer, though it diminished as the fuel loads dropped, and Hawthorn's finished with its right front tyre through to the canvas, where the brake had locked. On the whole he thought the new brakes worked adequately well, 'but they were to get much worse as the season wore on....'

Back in Europe the Royal Automobile Club were now in the position of having a protest pending which could rob their leading driver of eight World Championship points! BRM sportingly withdrew their companion protest about the Grand Prix's status, and the CSI rejected the British club's, so in a perverse way all was well.

After the 1000 km sports car race the following weekend, the V6 single-seaters were prepared for the two-heat City Grand Prix on 2 February. It used another of the BA Autodrome's circuit combinations, and Ferrari fielded four Dinos; Collins, Hawthorn and Musso retaining their former mounts, while a brand-new 246 fresh from the factory was to be handled by von Trips in heat one and by Phil Hill—getting his single-seater chance at last—in heat two. This car had the cockpit fuel tank

replaced by an oversize tail tank similar to Hawthorn's. All four V6 engines used the single 12-cylinder magneto driven from the rear of the left-side inlet camshaft. Hawthorn's had the standard brakes refitted.

Heat one began in pouring rain, which should have given Moss a distinct advantage in the nimble and well-balanced little Walker Cooper, but he was thundered out of the race at the first corner by Iglesias's Chevvy Special. Collins again broke a half-shaft on the line to put one Dino out, while Hawthorn splashed away into a handsome lead and won, well clear of Fangio, with Musso third. Trips was going well in the brand-new chassis when he hit a puddle on the straight, got badly out of shape and spun off into a stout concrete post. This left Phil Hill without a drive in the second heat, and he was heart-broken. Still that Formula 1 car drive eluded him.

Hawthorn had a 31.8-second time cushion on Fangio for heat two, but Amorotti and team-manager Romolo Tavoni were fearful of another half-shaft failure like Collins's and implored him to be gentle at the start. Accordingly he restricted himself to around 4000 rpm and fed in the clutch gently as the starter's flag swept down. The car rolled forward, there was a clunk and Mike stopped with a half-shaft broken. They were still the F2 shafts, designed for 150 bhp and not 250.... 'Tavoni was very good about it and said that it was tough luck but they'd got plenty of time to get it right....'

Musso did his best to come to grips with Fangio, but was not in that class, and after a spin, Menditeguy passed him and he brought the sole surviving Dino 246 home third in the heat but second overall on aggregate.

The European season began with two important Internationals close together; Goodwood on Easter Monday (7 April) and the Syracuse Grand Prix on the 13th. Ferrari made two works entries at Goodwood, one a new Dino 246 for Hawthorn in the forty-two lap Formula 1 Glover Trophy race, and the other a brand-new sports-racing car for Peter Collins in the accompanying twenty-one lap Sussex Trophy.

The new 'Dino 246S' sports car used a 2-litre version of the V6 engine, mated to a live rear axle on coil-springs, with a new four-speed competition gearbox (intended also for the 250GT *Berlinetta*) in unit with the engine. Front suspension and brakes came straight from the contemporary Formula 1 car. Bore centres for the 2.0 and 2.4 Dino V6s were identical, the 206S unit being under-bored 8 mm to provide a 77 mm bore, which combined with the standard 'big Dino' stroke of 71 mm for a swept volume of 1983.72 cc. The unit was rated at 220–225 bhp at 8500 rpm, though its tachometer was red-lined at only 8600. It carried three twin-choke Weber 42DCN carburetters and had a compression ratio of 9.8:1. Coil ignition replaced the Formula V6's magnetos. The new car's chassis number was '0740'. It was rumoured that this 'Dino 206S' heralded development of a full 3-litre V6 sports-racer matched to the new capacity limit recently imposed for the year's World Sports Car Championship.

Collins handled the left-hand-drive car (which had Scaglietti bodywork very similar to that of the second-series 250TR V12s) in the

Ferrari team manager Romolo Tavoni shows off the brand-new Dino 206S 2-litre four-cam sports-racer to John Morgan, Secretary of the organizing BARC club, at Goodwood's Easter Monday 1958 meeting. Note the 'Dino' script cam-boxes on its V6 engine. The coil-ignition twin-plug system with two six-cylinder distributors driven from the inlet camshaft noses is clearly visible. Collins shows off the Scaglietti body's lines on the

entry to the Goodwood chicane, while the cockpit shot shows the spartan interior finish, 8600 rpm red-lined tachometer, tall centre gear-change and Baroclem battery mounted in the passenger footwell. The fuel tank dipstick lies across the seat. The 206S engine appears to have been effectively the 196F1 of Modena 1957 fame, with coil instead of magneto ignition . . .

Sussex Trophy. Moss's 3.8-litre Aston Martin DBR2 led Archie Scott-Brown's Lister–Jaguar from the Le Mans-type start, with Collins third in the Ferrari, which was understeering (naturally). Scott-Brown slammed past Moss, but retired when his car's steering tightened, leaving the Aston Martin to win by 47.6 seconds from Collins and his new sports Dino.

Hawthorn took the stage with his F1 Dino 246, chassis '0003' fitted with a Perspex cover extending right over the carburetters and with an aero-screen mounted within the model's standard Perspex wrap-round. He was opposed by two BRM P25s for Behra and Schell—these drivers having been abandoned by Maserati, whose racing programme had been drastically curtailed, and by Moss, Brabham and Salvadori in Coopers plus a few makeweights.

Moss stalled at the start and Behra led away with Hawthorn hard on his heels, but on lap four the BRM's brakes failed and the Frenchman had an almighty collision with the brick-built chicane, Hawthorn dodging his Dino through the gap with showering bricks to his left and the careering BRM wreck to his right. Moss was charging through the

35

Both left Luigi Musso's big-tube '0001' at Syracuse in April 1958. These shots by Denis Jenkinson demonstrate the new car's compact design, the far-forward angled engine mounting within the 2160 mm wheelbase, rear-opening Perspex induction shroud, stone/spray deflectors behind the front wheels and transverse leaf spring De Dion rear suspension with rear-mounted Houdaille dampers. At the flag Musso has the rear Engleberts smoking as the leaf-spring tips bow upwards under squat. The empty grandstand in rear was incomplete—not a reflection upon Sicilian enthusiasm

field after his delayed start, but Hawthorn found he could maintain the gap quite easily before the Cooper broke. Eventually he gave the Dino 246 its maiden Formula 1 race victory by a 36-second margin from Brabham and Salvadori in the works Cooper–Climaxes. His only complaint was that the car still understeered excessively....

The following Sunday saw Ferrari's Dino racing in far-off Sicily in the Syracuse Grand Prix, where Luigi Musso ran a lone '58-specification Dino 246—the new '0001'—with 46DCN carburetters against ten Maseratis, all privately owned but some works supported, and a 1500 sports OSCA. In practice Musso was the only man below the 2-minute lap time barrier, and in the race he ran away at a rate of some 5 seconds a lap and lapped everybody else, easing up later to score an easy victory. Two in a row for Dino's memory....

Third race for '0740', the Goodwood 206S, came at Naples in May 1958 in the aggressive hands of Luigi Musso. There was a lot to hit around Posillipo and in his efforts to better the sports car lap record Musso hit his share

Collins's Goodwood Dino 206S reappeared in its native land on 13 April when Gino Munaron was loaned it for the national *Trofeo Shell* at Monza. He led the 2-litre race until a UJ failed. On 27 April, when the Naples Grand Prix was run as a two-day four-race sports car meeting instead of the scheduled Formula 1 event, which had been banned in the wake of the Italian Government's post-Mille Miglia moratorium on road racing, Luigi Musso drove the car in the forty-lap 2-litre event, and was faced by four 1957 4-cylinder Ferraris and seven Maserati 200S models, though none should have been a match for the new car. Unfortunately, the shortened Posillipo circuit's surface had broken up in the heat, and in his determination to improve on Giulio Cabianca's sports car lap record with the winning 1500 cc OSCA in an earlier race Musso got carried away. He spun twice, the second time buckling both left-side wheels and crumpling the car's bodywork and exhaust on that side. He dropped back to fourth, and while trying to regain lost ground the Dino's clutch failed and Musso was out after twenty laps, with fastest lap of 1 min 29.7 sec, 100.132 km/h, only 62.22 mph, to his credit, still 1.2 seconds outside Cabianca's time with that wretched OSCA....

Silverstone's non-Championship BRDC International Trophy race was held on 4 May and Ferrari again made a lone Formula 1 entry, this time for Peter Collins, who had an Argentine-specification Dino 246 with tubular top front wishbones instead of the latest forged components seen on Musso's Syracuse car, but using the new angular-finned broad-drum brakes tried by Hawthorn in the Argentine Grand Prix and now standard wear. It was '0002' using (temporarily) a small-tube frame.

Practice shocked many of the front-engined Grand Prix car faithful, as the 1960 cc Cooper-Climaxes of Salvadori and Brabham annexed the first two grid places, with Moss's Walker car next up and Collins just scraping onto the outside of the front row with his Ferrari.

At the flag Moss stalled yet again and Collins blared away from the BRMs of Behra and Flockhart, and Masten Gregory's private Maserati

was fourth ahead of the Coopers. Collins and Behra soon shared a new lap record of 1 min 40 sec on the second lap, and three laps later the Frenchman's British car was ahead and drawing away. On lap 11 Behra was lapping a back-marker when the usual BRM luck struck him, along with a flying stone, which smashed his goggles and cut his eye. Collins inherited a comfortable lead until lap 18, when he hit some oil at Copse Corner and careered along the verge in a full-lock slide, bouncing off the grass bank and charging away without damage and minimal loss of time. His healthy sounding Ferrari V6 completed the fifty-lap distance after 1 hr 26 min running to win handsomely from Salvadori, Gregory and Behra. Three in a row for Dino's memory. . . .

It was Hawthorn's turn to contest the supporting twenty-five-lap 'over-1500 cc' sports car race for Ferrari, and once again they sprang a surprise by delivering their threatened 3-litre Dino V6-engined sports car to the airfield circuit. Designated the 'Dino 296S', this left-hand-drive model had a transverse leaf-spring de Dion rear suspension, unlike the Goodwood/Naples 206S on live axle and coils. Still, in practice Hawthorn found it very similar; '. . . it had formidable understeer . . . [it] was tremendously fast down the straight, but going round corners was absolutely terrifying. . . . With a dry weight of some $13\frac{1}{2}$ cwt and a power output of over 300 bhp at 7800 rpm it was fantastically quick . . . on Woodcote the understeer would lift the inside front wheel two or three inches off the ground, which was a little alarming to say the least. . . .'

Mike ran sixth from the Le Mans-type start, moved up as others retired and finished a breathless third behind a titanic 3.8-litre Lister-Jaguar battle in which Gregory beat little Scott-Brown's works car for the first time. Hawthorn later recalled the new Dino would '. . . catch up everyone on the straight, only to lose it again on the corners. It would get a sort of roll on it and start oscillating; I believe the designer was having kittens just watching his pride and joy doing such horrible things in full view of everyone. . . .'

Above and right The original print of this Testa Rossa-like chassis frame photograph, taken at Maranello early in 1958, states that this was to become the new 3-litre Dino 296S sports-racer. The car emerged as '0746' and gave Hawthorn a frightening ride at Silverstone in the May meeting. The V6 was subsequently removed and replaced by a TR V12 for the Nürburgring 1000 km, but the car reacted badly to the 70 lb extra weight up front and was retired thereafter. In 1960 it was rebuilt and rebodied, the works papers describing it at that time as a type 529C *Bastarda*! That's just what Hawthorn called it first time out

This largest Dino V6 engine yet employed the same 85 mm bore as the Formula 1 type 246 engine, allied this time to a long-stroke crank; stroke increasing from only 71 mm in the well-oversquare 2.5-litre unit to 87 mm in this new four-cam 3-litre—making it one of the very rare 'undersquare' Ferrari engines; apparently only the second after the 102 mm × 105 mm *Tipo* 860 *Monza* 4-cylinder sports of 1956.

The new engine displaced 2962.08 cc, had a compression ratio of 9.0 : 1 and with three Weber 46DCN carburetters was rated at 300 bhp at 8000 rpm—according to the factory. Obviously this is not what they told Hawthorn. . . .

After its race debut the car was taken home to Maranello, where its unique V6 engine was allegedly craned-out and adapted to fit the Dino 296MI track-racing special for the Two Worlds Trophy Monza 500 Miles on 29 June. The engineless sports car chassis—'0746'—was run experimentally with V12 engine in the ADAC 1000 Km and then stored before being totally rebuilt during 1960, its wheelbase lengthened from 2280 mm to 2320 mm (89.76 in to 91.33 in) and a V12 engine and five-speed transmission were installed in place of the V6/4-speed assembly. With Dunlop disc brakes, right-hand steering and a new

39

Fantuzzi bodyshell this new *Testa Rossa* was sold to Luigi Chinetti's North American Racing Team (NART), of whom we will be hearing much more. It was driven by the youthful Mexican Rodriguez brothers, Ricardo and Pedro, at Sebring in 1961, where they finished third in the annual 12-Hours classic.

The first European outing for the full team followed at Monte Carlo, where the World Championship Monaco Grand Prix was held on 18 May. Four Dino 246s were fielded by Ferrari for Collins, Hawthorn, Musso and Trips, including the two ex-F2 1957 chassis and a third to similar specification with the larger-diameter bottom longerons and cross-members. Of these three only Musso's had the latest forged top wishbones, while all had the 'turbo-finned' broad brake drums. The

James Allington produced this superb cutaway of Peter Collins's Silverstone Dino 246 in the team's garage at Brackley, Buckinghamshire. According to factory records this was '0002', which as James depicts used a small-tube spaceframe chassis. Two weeks later, '0002' ran at

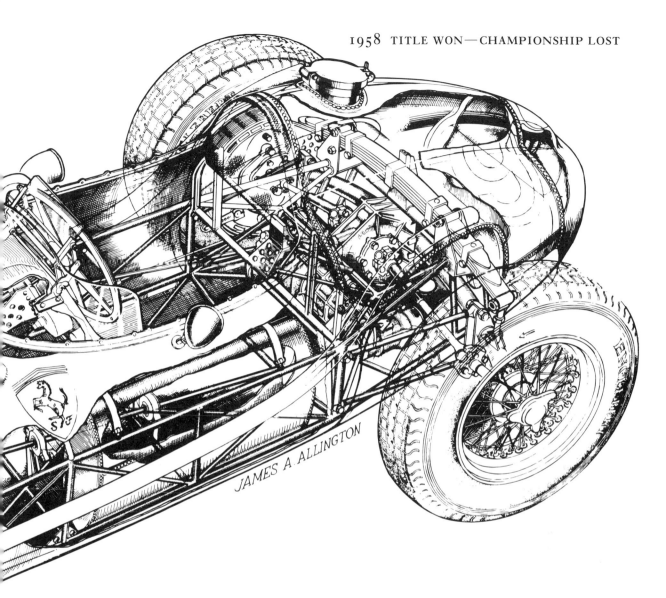

JAMES A. ALLINGTON

Monaco looking very similar externally but built around a big-tube frame. Such minor conundrums are typical of Ferrari. The concentration of mass around either end of the wheelbase is very apparent. This 'dumb-bell' principle was considered to resist break-away of either end. It made the car unhappy to react to sudden changes of direction and did not impress drivers. Massive brake drums were 13 by 2 inches at the front and 12 by $1\frac{7}{8}$ inches at the rear. The 246 engine weighed 286 lb dry

fourth car was a true lightweight 1958 F2 version with a small-tube frame and forged top wishbones, but since full 246 engines were still in short supply, one was held back as spare and this latest car was fitted with a 206 2-litre for practice, and was entrusted to Trips. Since visibility and cockpit cooling can be vital at Monaco, all the cars had cut-down plastic screens for practice and all except Musso's also mounted aero-screens. In first practice they used early-type open-top carburetter cowls and these were changed to rear-open bubble covers on the second day. None of the Ferraris carried fashionable bumper protection on their long nose cones.

Since none blew up, Trips's car was fitted with the spare 2.4-litre V6 engine for final practice, and the bigger engine with its fifty-plus extra horsepower made a 'night-and-day' difference to the handling of his car. Grid positions were resolved with Brooks's Vanwall on pole at 1 min 39.8 sec, flanked by Behra's BRM and Brabham's Cooper. The Coopers of Salvadori and Trintignant comprised row two and Hawthorn was a

41

lone blob of red on the inside of row three, with a best of 1:41.5, with the Vanwalls of Lewis-Evans and Moss alongside him. Collins and Musso occupied row four, with 1:42.4 and 1:42.6 respectively, while Trips sat on the centre of the fifth rank on 1:44.3.

Hawthorn was seventh on lap one and then cut out Lewis-Evans and Trintignant for fifth. When Salvadori went into the pits he inherited fourth place, and soon after caught Moss, who waved him past. After some trouble with Brooks, who could not see the Ferrari in his mirrors, the Vanwall hit trouble and Hawthorn was second trying really hard in pursuit of Behra's leading BRM. But on lap 27 the green car headed into the pits, and Hawthorn was leading, to which Moss responded by pressing harder in the Vanwall. Trintignant's little 2206cc Walker Cooper was third, ahead of Musso, Collins and Trips in the other Ferrari Dinos, and on lap 31 Moss was nibbling at Hawthorn's tail and Mike waved him through, since it was easier to be led than to lead and there were many miles to go.

First Moss broke the lap record, then Hawthorn (finally) at 1:40.6, when smoke puffed from the Vanwall and its race was run. Mike was left well ahead of Trintignant in second place and the three sister Ferraris, but on lap 46 his Dino engine missed down by the station and towards the tunnel it went woolly and cut out. Hawthorn stopped and summoned assistance from *Motor Sport* man Michael Tee, who happened to be standing there taking photographs. Hawthorn took the bonnet off and it was Michael who spotted the fuel pump dangling from the front of the

Right Mike Hawthorn winning the Glover Trophy at Goodwood on Easter Monday 1958 with his personal car '0003', distinctive for its low-cut cockpit sides, which he preferred. The tall Hawthorn found this the first Ferrari in which he was comfortable

Below right Peter Collins winning the BRDC International Trophy at Silverstone to give the Dino 246 a hat-trick of Formula 1 non-Championship race victories. His car is '0002', running with a cut-down Perspex screen outside the toughened-glass aero-screen, and high cockpit sides in comparison to Hawthorn's. It was built around a small-tube space-frame at this time, and flexed badly, as this fine Geoff Goddard study apparently captures

---

Mike Hawthorn was born in Mexborough, Yorkshire, but father Leslie raced motorcycles at Brooklands and moved his family south to Farnham, Surrey, to be closer to it. He established Tourist Trophy Garage there and postwar both Leslie and young Mike began racing Rileys.

In 1951 Mike drove both the family's 1500 Riley Sprite and 1100 Ulster Imp after Leslie had hurt his back, and he won two events in Ireland and was consistently successful at Goodwood. Family friend Bob Chase bought him a brand-new Formula 2 Cooper-Bristol for 1952, and on Easter Monday at Goodwood, 'Mick' Hawthorn burst to prominence on his debut with the car, winning two events and placing second in another behind Froilan Gonzalez's *ThinWall Special* Ferrari 375. He was fourth in the Belgian GP—at Spa in the rain—on his first continental foray and third in the British GP. He led a Formule Libre field at Boreham in the rain, including Villoresi's works Indy Ferrari. Mr Ferrari invited him to join the Maranello team for 1952 and Hawthorn accepted.

He beat Fangio at Reims to win a classic French GP and won long-distance events for Ferrari, like the Spa 24-Hours. Early in 1954 he was burned at Syracuse, and father Leslie died in a road accident. Mike won the Spanish GP ending the season, but for 1955 had to spend more time in Britain running TT Garage and opted to drive for Jaguar and Vanwall. He won Le Mans but was involved in the catastrophic Mercedes accident there, and his Formula 1 season was poor. For 1956 he moved to BRM but found nothing but frights and more frustration, and in 1957 he returned to Ferrari. He was hounded by British press factions for alleged conscription dodging and for driving 'foreign', but a kidney problem made him ineligible for the Army and when he drove 'British' he won in sports cars, and suffered in Formula 1. Ferrari made the most of the tall, extrovert Englishman with the green helmet and ever-present bow-tie. . . .

John Michael Hawthorn
b. 10 April, 1929
d. 22 January, 1959

engine. Its retaining nuts had not been wired on, and had vibrated free. As he marched back to the pits Hawthorn caught the eye of a lovely blonde girl watching from a hotel room, and he asked for a glass of water. She could hardly refuse and he climbed in through the window and was caught in the process by a photographer. After several glasses of water he felt better, and returned to the pits and took up station at the Gasworks Hairpin to urge his team-mates on.

Trips lost ground when he had to refuel his small-tanked car, and Trintignant had a long lead over Musso and Collins, who were finding a terrible flat-spot in their engine response, where all the power seemed to die away. Musso could do nothing to close the gap on the Cooper and Collins was unable to close upon his team-mate, and so Trintignant won the Monaco Grand Prix for Cooper and Rob Walker in a car costing perhaps a quarter as much as the Ferraris in second and third, over 20 seconds adrift. Trips's engine seized on lap 91, and Musso found himself leading the World Championship after another helpless second place, while Hawthorn picked up just one point for his fastest lap.

Monaco had been a great disappointment for Ferrari, humbled for the second *Grande Epreuve* in succession by a Cooper-Climax 'special' after winning three consecutive non-Championship races in between.

One week later the Dutch Grand Prix took place at Zandvoort and there the straight-line speed and power of the Dinos seemed a better prospect. The three older chassis were used as at Monaco, with Hawthorn, Collins and Musso driving, and only the Italian's used the forged top wishbones, and they were all in trouble from the moment practice started....

Their understeer on the hairpins was 'incredible' in Hawthorn's words; inducing lurid oversteer was the only cure and that cost too much time. And instead of only two cars suffering a bad engine flat-spot cum vibration period, this time all three had it. It came in around 7200–7400 rpm 'and it took ages to get through it and build up ... at 8000 it was all right, but the snag was getting there....'

Practice was a Vanwall demonstration, with all three team cars packing the front row, Lewis-Evans on pole at 1 min 37.1 sec from Moss and Brooks. Hawthorn had the best Ferrari Dino time, on the inside of row three at 1:39.1, with Collins a row behind at 1:39.3 and Musso in the middle of row five at 1:39.5. It was a sorry race for Ferrari, with Hawthorn and Collins embroiled in an early scrap for fifth place with Brabham's Cooper and Allison's similarly small-engined Lotus, while the Vanwalls and BRMs battled it out up front. Musso fluffed his start and had to clamber through the field from thirteenth place and did so nobly, he was so angry. He passed Collins before the Englishman's gearbox seized on lap 35 and spun him off, but was beaten by Allison's Lotus and finished seventh behind Hawthorn, who was fifth and furious.

His Dino had steered, handled and accelerated badly and when Moss lapped him around two-thirds distance on his way to win for Vanwall he could swallow that. But when the second- and third-placed BRMs of Schell and Behra came up to lap him he really fought, but still could not hold them off. He had walked out of BRM in disgust at their poor management and preparation in 1956, and when the Dutch race ended he gave his car back to Tavoni and told him it was useless and if Mr Ferrari really wanted to win the Constructors' Championship then he would have to do something really drastic before the next race. The handling and the engine had got progressively worse since the Argentine and Ferrari's chances, which had looked so bright, were being simply thrown away....

All this time Ferrari was successfully defending its World Sports Car Championship title with the 3-litre V12 cars, but on 15 June the Belgian Grand Prix was held at Spa-Francorchamps, fourth round of the Formula 1 Championship. Mr Ferrari had assured his drivers that the Dinos would improve, and four were entered for Hawthorn, Collins, Musso and—if none were broken—for the Belgian Champion Olivier Gendebien; his being painted in yellow national racing colours before Friday practice. Two of the new lightweight small-tube frames were used, the others being the earlier type, and the Perspex carburetter bubbles were dropped in favour of aluminium 'power bulges' formed into the bonnet panels. Musso ('0004') and Gendebien ('0011') had the lightweights.

The drivers quickly felt at home on Spa's super-fast curves and long straights, and Hawthorn was fastest overall after the first Thursday sessions and started the Grand Prix from pole position with a 3 min

Dino 246/58 front-end as in mid-season with co-axial coil-damper front suspension, far-forward angled engine mounting and turbo-finned cast-iron drum brakes with magnesium back-plates. The tubular top wishbones appear in this shot, though some cars ran forged members

57.1 sec lap. Musso was next quickest on 3:57.5 and Moss's Vanwall completed the front row on 3:57.6. Collins was alongside Brooks's Vanwall on the second row, fourth fastest at 3:57.7, and Gendebien was quickest on row three—last man below 4 minutes at 3:59.3. This was an excellent team performance, but the Belgian officials bungled the start procedure and the cars were kept waiting too long on the grid with their engines running and radiators coming rapidly to the boil. Collins's gauges were off the dial as his Dino began spouting steam and water, and the starter hesitated as the Ferrari's bonnet paint began to blister. Still with 10 seconds to go according to the timekeeper the starter hastily waggled his flag and drivers with nerves a-jangle muffed their getaways. The Dinos had no special low starting gear as did the Vanwalls and Maseratis and both Hawthorn and Musso hung fire, allowing Moss and Brooks to boom away.

Leaving Stavelot Corner on the far side of the circuit during that opening lap Moss missed a gear and the Vanwall's engine blew apart, and it was Brooks who led across the line from Collins, whose oil and water-temperature gauges were still reading way up in the red. Gendebien was third to the Belgian crowd's delight and Hawthorn fourth, with Musso seventh behind Behra's BRM and Lewis-Evans's Vanwall. On the second lap Collins scorched into the lead and Hawthorn displaced Gendebien for third. Collins and Brooks swopped the lead, while on lap 4 Gendebien was shunted in the tail while braking for La Source hairpin and spun into the outside retaining wall. The engine stalled and he manhandled the car until it pointed downhill towards the pits and pulled

Hawthorn on the limit at Spa in '0003' climbing the Eau Rouge turn beyond the pits. The nose cowl has been reprofiled and a front-opening aluminium air-scoop replaces the various top- and rear-opening Perspex cowls used previously. Note the extreme wheel cambers

Luigi Musso
b. 29 July, 1924
d. 7 July, 1958

'Luigino' was the youngest of three sons of an Italian diplomat, who spent many years in China. The Musso clan had produced generations of Champions in the 'manly' sports; Luigi was a fine horseman, an outstanding fencer and crack shot. Brother Giuseppe led the way into motor racing and bought an old 750 cc Giannini. He raced it in the 1950 *Giro di Sicilia* and crashed. He crashed again in the Mille Miglia, won his class in the *Giro di Calabira* and won again at Naples.

From these early days a rivalry developed between the aristocratic Roman and Castellotti, the commoner from the north. For 1952 Giuseppe lent his brother a 750 Stanguellini with which he won the Orsis's attention, and their Maserati company sold him a 2-litre sports car which they would prepare. He won the Coppa Perugina and the class national championship and by 1954 was in the full works sports and Formula 1 teams, winning at Naples, Pescara and Senigallia, placing second in the Spanish Grand Prix and Targa Florio and third in Calabria and the Mille Miglia.

He had a good 1955 season with Maserati, emerging as Italian Champion and for 1956 he moved to Ferrari, starting his career there with victory in the Argentine Grand Prix—sharing his Lancia–Ferrari V8 with Fangio. In the Nürburgring 1000 km he broke an arm and was out for the rest of the season, but in 1957 he won the non-championship Marne GP at Reims-Gueux for Ferrari and added victory in the Buenos Aires 1000 km. He underlined his smooth skills with consistent second places in the French, British, Syracuse and Venezuelan Grands Prix, but after Castellotti's death he was the last front-line Italian racing driver . . . and surrounded by foreigners in Italy's premier team this fast and competent Italian gentleman tried too hard.

in to have the damaged nose intake opened up. Brooks appeared alone in a comfortable lead from Hawthorn, and when Collins emerged from the forests before La Source his Dino was coasting. He had wisely switched off as water and oil temperatures showed no sign of decreasing and then the oil pressure had zeroed.

Musso had even worse luck, and a thick line of oil spread diagonally across the road at Stavelot showed where Italy's sole Formula 1 works driver had suffered a tyre burst at over 160 mph and had bounced from one side of the course to the other, escaping with nothing worse than a strained back and a shaking, while the car was not too badly damaged.

The wreck itself was lying below road level in a field, and Hawthorn, seeing the marks, convinced himself it was his friend Pete, whose boiling engine had probably seized and thrown him off course, and he could see no way that such an accident was survivable. 'I honestly thought he had had it and I was in no mood to go on motor racing,' he wrote, 'but I felt that I had to go on. . . .' Some laps later he caught sight of Collins standing at the pits, and soon after spotted Musso watching the race from the roadside at Stavelot. Thus encouraged he set about Brooks's 41-second lead, with ten laps to go. He doubted he could catch the Vanwall, but wanted the extra Championship point for fastest lap, taking it next time round at 3:59.3. David Yorke, Vanwall team manager, responded by speeding up Brooks, and although he did not better Mike's time the Ferrari pit thought he had and signalled Hawthorn as much. Consequently on the last lap he strung together his best-ever time round Spa. . . . The Dino's average speed for the 8.7 miles was 132.36 mph.

Brooks swung round La Source to head downhill across the finishline and won with his gearbox tightening up. Less than 30 seconds later Hawthorn hurtled into the Clubhouse turn before La Source, felt his Dino broadside and thought, 'Hell... I've ruined it now, I've lost the fastest lap!' He rounded the hairpin and was accelerating flat-out for the flag when a piston collapsed and the Dino plumed white smoke, Hawthorn crossing the line in neutral. He stopped beside Brooks's stranded Vanwall at the bottom of the pits when Lewis-Evans's third-place Vanwall drew up with the right-front wheel hanging at a drunken angle as a wishbone had just failed. Then Hawthorn was told he had set a new lap record of 3 min 58.3 sec on that spectacular last lap, despite the slide and covering the last 150 yards with a wrecked engine. He had six points for second place, plus one for fastest lap . . . and that one was to prove vital. . . .

Before the next Grand Prix, which would be the French race at Reims, Europe's second fastest road circuit, Ferrari was involved with the Monza 500-Miles track race, against an imported flock of Indianapolis cars and drivers from America. Every year the Italian club offered a bag of gold for the most successful Italian car, but in 1958 they amended the rules to state that any manufacturer who wished to compete for the annual prize must enter cars not only in the Italian Grand Prix but also in the Monza 500-Miles, which Ferrari had passed up the previous year. So Ferrari entered, though under protest, and since he had to do the job Mr Ferrari decided to do it properly and set his engineers ferreting once more through the parts bin. Maserati had built a big and brutish 4.2-litre V8 monster for BP oil and Mr Zanetti, owner of the Eldorado ice-cream company, and Stirling Moss was engaged to drive it. Ferrari responded with two specials, one a crude 4.1-litre V12 single-seater based on the old 1951–52 Tipo 375 chassis design and the other a modern Formula 1 Dino-type spaceframe with a 60 mm wheelbase carrying the 3-litre Dino stretched 296S V6 engine, which had impressed Hawthorn—despite its chassis behaviour—in the Silverstone sports car race in May.

This track-racing Dino, named the '296MI' (Monza-Indianapolis) carried the Formula 1 Dino series chassis number '0007', although I have seen it suggested that the car actually used the prototype 1957 Formula 2 Dino frame—presumably meaning '0011'—suitably cut about. It featured uprated springs, wishbones, steering arms and track-rods, and double dampers (friction and hydraulic) appeared at each corner. Experimental coil springs were used in the rear suspension, where the de Dion layout was retained. These springs were initially bonded into a solid rubber block, while the front coils were rubber covered to provide different characteristics. Later all these were replaced by conventional coil springs, and those at the front enclosed additional telescopic damper barrels. In general the bodyshell followed Dino 246 style, though the midships section was wider and the tail shortened and taller. Special treadless Englebert track tyres were tested, but Firestone Indy specials subsequently replaced them.

The race was run on 29 June in three sixty-three lap heats around the Monza *Pista de Alta Velocita* speedbowl, and the brave Luigi Musso qualified the V12 Ferrari special on pole despite his Belgian fright. Phil Hill was entrusted with the 296MI and qualified fourteenth of nineteen starters at 259.468 km/h (over 161 mph).

Heat one saw Musso rocket into the lead, hammering around the very top of the bankings, while the American drivers in their specialized Indy cars wondered which way he had gone. Phil Hill was storming around amongst his oval-racing compatriots, sixth with the big Dino, but was soon sidelined when its 'magneto failed' after eleven laps. There was a lot of oil about. . . . He subsequently shared the big V12 with Musso and Hawthorn and played a major part with the Italian in placing it third overall behind two of the American bolides.

One week later came the French Grand Prix at Reims, and Ferrari arrived feeling well prepared and confident. Collins, Hawthorn and Trips had the heavier-framed cars, while Musso's had the lighter, later style. All had new front coil springs enclosing co-axial telescopic dampers and the metal carburetter intake cowls were retained as at Spa. The team's Fiat–Bartoletti transporter also disgorged a new Formula 2 Dino 156 for Collins to drive in the supporting *Coupe de Vitesse* event.

Hawthorn won 100 bottles of Champagne as the first driver to top the 200 km/h lap during first practice. He was timed at 2 min 23.9 sec, which bettered Fangio's 1956 Lancia–Ferrari D50 lap record of 2:25.8. The Dino touched 8600 rpm along the Soissons straight, just on 180 mph. Hawthorn asked Ing Carlo Chiti (who had joined the team from Alfa Romeo after Fraschetti's death) whether it was all right to hold the V6 there and he replied it was, though 8400 or 8500 rpm 'would make him happier'. Hawthorn then asked for a higher back axle ratio, but they were already running the highest available.

Thursday evening practice found Hawthorn winning more Champagne as the first driver to lap Reims at 210 km/h and his 2:21.7 time was followed by Musso at 2:22.4. There was trouble in the camp, as Tavoni wanted Collins to drive only in the F2 race, and he responded angrily that he would drive in the Grand Prix or not at all. When Hawthorn backed his viewpoint, Tavoni relented and Collins drove in both races, yet they assigned his regular F1 car to von Trips. Considering Collins had won this race the previous year he was furious, and although his recent Formula 1 performances had lacked some fire, his inspired sports car driving had played a major part in putting the World Sports Car Championship once more in Ferrari's pocket. Collins set fourth fastest time at 2:23.3 and the grid was decided with Hawthorn on pole flanked by Musso and Harry Schell's fleet BRM, with Collins alongside Brooks's Vanwall on the second row.

After the 12-Hour sports car race, won for Ferrari again by Gendebien and Frère, the Formula 2 *Coupe de Vitesse* took place over thirty laps of the 5.2-mile course. Jean Behra's sports-bodied central-seat special Porsche took pole at 2:34.1 ahead of Collins with 2:35.3 and Moss's Cooper, 0.5 seconds slower, and the Frenchman led away, and once Moss retired Jeannot won as he pleased, for Collins and the Dino 156 could do nothing about the modified mid-engined sports car. Behra's victory was greeted with huge delight, while Ferrari looked acutely embarrassed by the whole thing and the British Climax-engined brigade could not believe their failure, having formerly had this class sewn up.

Collins snatched a very brief rest before the Grand Prix cars were wheeled out for the fifty-lap main event, and Schell stole an immediate lead before Hawthorn hurtled by on the curves towards Muizon. Trips muffed his start completely and was last away. Musso was hanging onto Hawthorn's tail and Collins onto his, with the Vanwalls, BRMs and Fangio's special lightweight Maserati wheel-to-wheel behind the Ferrari Dino trio. On lap 5 Collins had a metal scoop above his car's magneto drop down and wedge behind the brake pedal at Muizon hairpin and he flurried up the escape road, losing time to sort it out.

Musso was driving very hard to stay in touch with Hawthorn. He was very conscious of being the last hope of Italy, and had been in over his head for most of the season to justify that fact. Reims was no place to take such chances, and ending lap 10 he was close to Hawthorn's tail as they hammered under the Dunlop bridge, entering the curve before Gueux village at 155–160 mph. On the way out Hawthorn glanced in his mirrors to see if he had gained anything on his team-mate, and to his horror he glimpsed the other Dino sideways across the road then shooting backwards out of his view. Next time round he saw the flattened corn where Musso had disappeared, and the medical helicopter clattering away overhead, but the car was hidden. He hoped Luigi had walked away as he had at Spa, but actually the thirty-three-year-old Italian had suffered grave head injuries and died soon after in hospital.

Hawthorn hammered on and won as he liked, putting in a sprint on light tanks near the end to make sure of fastest lap and that extra Championship point, achieving it at 2:24.9, 206.254 km/h (128.17 mph), forty-fifth time round. He came up behind Fangio after the World Champion's pit stop and felt he really ought not lap 'The Old Man'. Mike followed him, admiring his immaculate placing of the car, despite having

Peter Collins drove this Formula 2 Dino 156 in the Coupe de Vitesse race supporting the 1958 French GP at Reims. He then climbed into a Formula 1 car for the Grand Prix itself. The 156 used the small-tube chassis frame quite happily, in this case using the 1957 big-tube number '0011' to simplify internal paperwork. The 156 ran 15-inch wheels in place of the F1's 16-inch and was identifiable by its longer air-intake scoop. Musso ran car number '2' in the GP, and crashed it fatally

Mike Hawthorn, French
Grand Prix 1958, in Dino 246
'0003'—totally dominant

not raced since the *Temporada* in the winter. Fangio fully appreciated the gesture, and Hawthorn was glad he held back, as this subsequently proved to be the Argentinian maestro's last motor race. Moss was second behind Hawthorn, Trips an excellent third after his early delay, and Collins pushed his car across the line out of fuel for fifth, Fangio overtaking him on the run in.

Enzo Ferrari had the last word on this Grand Prix: 'I have won at Reims, but the price is too high. I have lost the only Italian driver who mattered in Formula 1 racing....'

The British Grand Prix followed at Silverstone on 19 July, where Vanwall hoped to repeat their home-ground victory of the previous season. In theory their fine-handling chassis were better suited to the medium-fast curves of the airfield course than the Dino 246s, which had excelled on the power circuit at Reims.

Three Dinos were fielded for Hawthorn, Collins and Trips, all using the big bottom-tube frames. The Collins and Trips cars both carried additional fuel tanks on the left of the driving seat, while Hawthorn's had only the normal tail tank. He discarded the wrap-round Perspex screen and ran with the aero-screen alone. The Dinos were all at sea, their drivers finding understeer converting into vicious oversteer in the turns. Hawthorn: 'Going round Woodcote was a very shaky do. One would go into it with a good deal of understeer. In fact, the inside wheel kept coming off the ground, as a number of my friends told me....'

The team was also troubled by an Argentine problem in which the engine breather tossed back oil onto the windscreens. Pipes were rigged to connect the breather direct into the tail oil tank. At Reims all three surviving cars had worn out their drum brakes, and at Silverstone they were bedded-in carefully during practice.

One interesting experiment was to run a car on Dunlop RS5 tyres in place of Ferrari's contracted Belgian Engleberts. Hawthorn used Trips's

51

personal Dino for the tests after having some trouble squeezing into it, and the Dunlops killed the understeer but gave lurid oversteer instead. Later, some pressure juggling indicated that the Dunlops were a great improvement, but the team raced—of course—on Engleberts.

Hawthorn was set fair in the World Championship chase against Moss, and before the Grand Prix Collins offered to do everything he could to improve Mike's chances. He planned to take the lead if he could and attempt to break up the Vanwall opposition.

Hawthorn qualified best amongst the Ferraris, on the outside of the front row, fourth fastest at 1 min 40.4 sec compared to Moss's pole time with the Vanwall of 1:39.4. Schell's BRM and Salvadori's incredible 2.2-litre Cooper-Climax split them. Allison's spidery 2.2-litre front-engined Lotus-Climax was next up at 1:40.4 alongside Collins at 1:40.6, last man below the 1:41 mark. Trips was eleventh quickest, on the outside of row three at 1:42.0.

Hawthorn again started hesitantly as Moss catapulted away and Collins blared through from the second row and sliced ahead of the Vanwall through the left-hand sweep at Maggotts. On the Hangar Straight Collins's Dino powered away from the Vanwall with Hawthorn sitting third awaiting developments. Trips was embroiled in a midfield dispute with Salvadori, Graham Hill's Lotus, Brabham and Behra, while Collins streaked on in the lead with Moss unable to do anything about it and Hawthorn comfortable but lonely in third place. On lap 26 the Vanwall failed and Moss drove straight into the paddock, leaving the Dinos first and second. Hawthorn was worried by spasmodic puffs of smoke from the left side of the engine bay, and his oil pressure was falling from its normal 7 kg/cm² to 2 kg.... Remembering the Argentine race he opted to press on, but Collins showed no sign of weakening, and on lap 43 Hawthorn pointed to the oil tank as he passed the pits and slapped his helmet, the usual signal that he was coming in. Tavoni had both oil and tyres ready as he bustled in, shouting 'Olio'. He rejoined just ahead of Salvadori's third-place Cooper and set fastest lap on lap 50 in 1:40.8, 164.96 km/h (104.54 mph), in ensuring the car stayed in third place. Trips lost his battle with Brabham when his oil pressure fell and he coasted into the pits with his Dino's bearings run. Collins won by twenty-four seconds from Hawthorn, having averaged 163.41 km/h (102.05 mph) for the seventy-five lap distance. During the closing stages of this hot race Hawthorn saw marshals he knew at Becketts Corner sipping beer from pint mugs. On the cooling-off lap he stopped the Ferrari, picked up a pint of shandy and toured back round to the pits with his crash helmet off, sipping his pint—'... it foxed a lot of people'.

With two *Grandes Epreuves* victories in a row, Scuderia Ferrari journeyed happily to Nürburgring for the German Grand Prix on 3 August. They took five cars; two normal Formula 1 246s, one lightweight 246, the Formula 2 Dino 156 with its lightweight chassis and the experimental 296MI frame—chassis '0007'—from the Monza 500-Miles, now re-engined with a 246 Formula 1 V6, but retaining its coil-spring, telescopic-damped de Dion rear suspension.

Hawthorn, Collins and Trips were to drive the F1 cars while Phil Hill

'0007' heads the Ferrari line-up at Nürburgring, ahead of Collins's '0002' and Trips's sister car. In this form the MI has a 246 Formula 1 engine and a reprofiled road-racing nose cowl to admit more cooling air at lower speeds. Peter Collins is in discussion in the foreground, while Trips is to the right of his car, American Scarab car constructor Lance Reventlow (with camera case) to the left

was at last entrusted with a single-seater, the F2 car for the sub-class run concurrent with the main race. The '246MI' was tried by all the regular drivers, and Hawthorn in particular was enthusiastic, finding its road-holding better than the normal cars, though the steering was dead and it wandered along the bumpy straights. The Dino 156 began practice with ribbed brake drums 1957-style, later replaced by the normal 'turbo-finned' type, and overnight before the race Collins's car was fitted with the engine from the MI experimental chassis, which was not to be raced.

The circuit record stood at 9 min 17.4 sec, set by Fangio during his legendary drive against the Lancia–Ferraris of Hawthorn and Collins the previous year, but some resurfacing helped Mike take pole position in his big-tube framed low cockpit side '0003' at 9:14.0, while the Brooks and Moss Vanwalls lined up between him and Collins's '0002', completing the rank on 9:21.9: four British drivers, two in green cars, two in red. Trips was fifth quickest with a second low cockpit car, probably car '0001' on the inside of row two at 9:24.7, while Phil Hill's Dino 156 was best placed in the Formula 2 class—tenth overall with 9:48.9 and starting on the third row. He was six seconds faster than Ian Burgess's F2 Cooper, which was next up, but had actually been slower than Brabham's works F2 Cooper, which managed a 9:43.4 lap, but covered too few training laps and so was banished to the back of the pack.

Under overcast skies Brooks and Moss made the best starts, Schell diving into third place for BRM from the third row ahead of Hawthorn

Mystery car: the Monza 500 Dino '296MI' was reported at the time to use the V6 engine from '0746'. According to Ferrari's engine registry a '326MI' engine was built in 1958 and factory sources state this was used at Monza, not the 2.9 litre. The 296S block survives today numbered '0006'. Normally new Ferraris carry matching chassis and engine numbers. The MI was noted at Monza as chassis '0007'. The car used a big-tube frame, possibly '0012's' from 1957, lengthened to 2220 mm wheelbase, with modified short-tail bodywork, the oil tank being removed to the cockpit. It had experimental coil-spring De Dion rear suspension, and is seen here in practice on experimental Englebert tyres. Firestones were used for the race. The

Peter John Collins
b. 8 November, 1931
d. 3 August, 1958

Pat Collins, a Kidderminster motor trader encouraged his son Peter's racing. In 1949 17-year-old P. J. Collins was hurtling around in a 500 cc Formula 3 Cooper-Norton and in 1950 an 1100 cc hillclimb Cooper-JAP was added to the Collins's stable. Early in 1951 John Heath and George Abecassis were testing a new HWM F2 car and Pat Collins appeared asking if his son could have a drive. Peter impressed, and was taken into the team alongside Stirling Moss and Lance Macklin.

For 1952 he won a works Aston Martin sports car drive, and Tony Vandervell signed him to handle his fearsome *ThinWall Specials*. Through 1954 Collins showed enormous potential, ending the year seventh in the Italian GP with the 2.2-litre Vanwall interim F1 car.

BRM took him on in 1955, handling initially their Maserati 250F special and later the potent prototype P25 4-cylinder BRM. He shared Moss's Mercedes-Benz 300SLR to win the Targa Florio and edge Ferrari out of the sports car title. Then Collins had an offer from Ferrari, which he accepted, and 1956 saw him winning the Belgian and French Grands Prix and challenging team-leader Fangio for the World title. The Italian GP was the decider and Collins voluntarily handed over his car to the ageing *maestro* when the Argentinian's own had failed. This sporting gesture gave Fangio his fourth World Championship title, and endeared Collins to racegoers worldwide, and to Mr Ferrari. His relationship with Collins was particularly close, until Peter married and his driving seemed to lose some of its fire.

When Hawthorn rejoined the team alongside Collins, his great friend, for 1957 this extrovert duo enjoyed pranks and practical jokes verging on sheer hooliganism—but for both, it was a good time. . . .

Monza speedbowl was lapped anticlockwise. Phil Hill was instructed to stop on the ninth lap, tell anybody who asked that he had magneto trouble and return to the pits as quickly as possible to take over the big 4.1 V12. In fact the car suffered piston failure after eleven race laps

and Collins. Mike had again fudged his start, this time slipping his clutch too much and burning most of it out. There was hardly any free movement in the clutch pedal at the first corner, and he was furious with himself.

Both Ferraris picked off Brooks, but could do nothing about Moss, who was driving brilliantly in the Vanwall, until lap 4, when its magneto failed and he was stranded at the *Schwalbenschwanz*. Hawthorn was left in the lead despite his clutch problem with Collins close behind. Phil Hill was seventh overall and leading the Formula 2 section by miles, but Trips had visited the pits early to complain he had no brakes, and had rejoined to drive on carefully, slowing the car on its gearbox.

With Moss out, the Vanwall pit urged Brooks forward, and his car proved itself faster than the Dinos around the Nürburgring. Collins drew alongside Hawthorn and indicated by hand signals he wanted him to win, but Brooks was in sight and Hawthorn waved his team-mate on. By lap 8 Brooks was with the Dinos, catching them on the twisty sections and only losing ground along the main straight. On lap 10 he nipped off Hawthorn on the inside of the North Curve, but was repassed on the straight. On lap 11 he retook second on the South Curve, caught Collins along the return straight behind the pits and forced his Vanwall into the lead round the North Curve. Collins fought back on the frighteningly fast winding section downhill towards Adenau, mindful of the battle lost against Fangio here the previous year. Brooks held him off and Hawthorn was sitting close behind watching his two compatriots jockeying for position.

55

They raced up through the *Karussel* and over the hill at *Hohe Acht*, then up and down, winding through the forests towards the *Pflanzgarten*. On a tight left-hander just before this corner Collins may have missed a gear, for Hawthorn drew alongside, front wheels level with his team-mate's cockpit, then tucked behind again as Collins made no sign to wave him through. They plunged into the *Pflanzgarten* dip in hot pursuit of Brooks, fast in third, then a dab at the brakes and second. Out of the dip they came into a right-hand curve which was taken accelerating hard. Hawthorn was suddenly aware Collins was going too fast, and was off line: '...only a yard, maybe two yards, but it was enough. He went round the corner perfectly normally but running wide, and the car slid, drifting out. His back wheel hit the bank and the car lifted, running with the rear wheels on the bank, which is about twelve inches high. God, I thought, the silly fool, we're both going to be involved in this...I was just thinking up some choice words to say to him when...without the slightest warning, fantastically quickly, his car just whipped straight over.... There was a blur of blue as Pete was thrown out and I put the brakes on hard and almost stopped as I looked round. I saw the car bounce upside down in a great cloud of dust, before it came to rest....'

Hawthorn drove on like an automaton, but behind the pits his transmission failed and after trying to limp round to the accident site he stopped near Adenau. After being assured initially that his friend was all right, he later discovered Collins had been thrown against a tree and had suffered severe head injuries from which he later died in hospital at Bonn.

Phil Hill meanwhile found his Dino 156 quicker than its brakes

Above Phil Hill drove a brave race in the Formula 2 section of his first Grand Prix for the Ferrari team, at, Nürburgring. Here is '0011' hurtling towards Adenau showing body damage sustained in a wild slide brought on by failing brakes and non-existent damping. Phil was a brave and exciting driver to watch in action in these cars. He had driven a Maserati 250F on his GP debut at Reims a month previously

provided for, and on lap 6 he hit some oil near Adenau and had a lurid spin, bouncing off the verges and banks but pressing on, eighth and still F2 class leader. But his excursion had torn away the oil breather pipe beneath the car and it was now pumping oil mist onto the rear tyres. With dampers losing their efficiency over the Nürburgring's bumps the little Dino 156 was virtually uncontrollable, but the determined American persevered and carried on until the finish, ninth overall and fifth F2 behind three Coopers and Edgar Barth's sports-derived Porsche. Wolfgang von Trips managed a remarkable fourth place, driving virtually brakeless throughout.

For Ferrari, Collins's death following so close upon Musso's was another body blow. Mr Ferrari seemed to have a special soft-spot for the fair-haired Englishman, which diminished only when he had married and seemed to lose some of his will to win during the 1957 season. Three men had now died in Ferrari Dinos, and from a range of twenty years Phil Hill recalled that day at Nürburgring and considered the cars' braking and damping shortcomings were possibly responsible for Collins's death. With the Houdaille dampers you had some spring control when the race started, but after a few hard laps around the Nürburgring they were virtually shot. The drum brakes were always hit and miss, and Phil feels that where a brush on the brakes was necessary just to steady the cars before that fatal curve, Collins may have hit the pedal and found the retardation he required was not there. Committed deep in his pursuit of

Right Peter Collins at Nürburgring. His car was '0002', now using a big-tube frame as it had since Monaco. The pipe leading into the oil tank had been rigged from the engine breathers before Collins's victorious drive in the preceding British GP at Silverstone. It prevented breather mist coating the windscreen and the driver's goggles. The ineffectual Houdaille rear dampers and monster front brake drums mounted well into the airstream are clearly visible in this shot

Brooks there would have been no margin left to compensate....

Hawthorn was heart-broken and embittered by his friend's death. From this point forward he still drove for that World Championship, but after every race he would declare 'that's another one I won't have to do again....' Whatever happened in the Championship chase he had decided to retire at the season's close.

The remorseless Grand Prix calendar continued with the Portuguese Grand Prix at Oporto on 24 August. Ferrari entered only two cars, Hawthorn's normal low-side Dino 246 and the coil-spring rear suspension 246MI for von Trips, though the Englishman tried it in practice. Hawthorn set second fastest practice time at 2 min 34.26 sec, splitting the Vanwalls of Moss (on pole at 2:34.21) and Brooks on 2:34.60; it was going to be a very competitive race. Trips was sixth with 2:37.04 on the inside of row three.

They started gently on a damp track and on lap 2 Hawthorn punched his Dino into the lead from Moss with Schell third and Trips going well, fourth, and soon third. On lap 8 Hawthorn was displaced by Moss, and Trips by Behra. Moss was making the most of his Vanwall's disc brakes while Hawthorn realized his drums were being over-stressed. On lap 33 he signalled he was coming into the pits, where the brakes were adjusted, but Behra stole second place. Hawthorn chased the BRM desperately, realizing Championship points were at risk, and when he set a new lap record at 2:32.37 the Vanwall pit signalled 'HAWT REC' to Moss, telling him the Ferrari team leader had his hands on that extra Championship point. Moss did not respond, mystifying the Vanwall crew, and afterwards he explained he had misread the sign as 'HAWT REG'—'Hawthorn regular', meaning the gap was stable. Hawthorn's sprint brought him up on Behra on lap 42 and he scrabbled by into second place. Moss had lapped his fourth-placed team-mate Lewis-Evans and was towing him round in his slipstream. As Behra struck trouble Lewis-Evans inherited third place and Hawthorn—his brakes deteriorating—was signalled '+4 Evans'. Looking in his mirror he saw a Vanwall, assumed it was Evans, though in fact it was Moss set to lap him with Evans right behind, and began to hurl the Ferrari around, slowing it savagely on the gearbox. He broadsided into some bales, but bounced straight again, and the Vanwall drew alongside, whereupon Hawthorn saw it was Moss not Lewis-Evans and looked so appalled at the indignity of being lapped that Moss waved him ahead and slotted back onto the Dino's tail! Moss took the chequered flag to win with Lewis-Evans being flagged off a lapped third in his wake just as Hawthorn commenced his fiftieth and final lap. But he forgot that Lewis-Evans would already have finished and still driving hard he found his brakes had vanished altogether, shot up an escape road and stalled his engine. After a long delay, fighting off outside assistance in fear he would be disqualified, a miserable and exhausted Hawthorn toured back to the pits, convinced he was last. When Tavoni smiled and said 'You're second and you've made fastest lap' he just could not believe it. A subsequent protest that he had pushed his car against the direction of the race was rejected, on Moss's evidence that the Ferrari had been on the footpath and not on the road, and his seven points stood. Trips meanwhile had soldiered steadily home into fifth place with the MI special.

For the Italian Grand Prix at Monza on 7 September, Hawthorn was adamant his car must carry disc brakes to replace those untrustworthy drums. On the Thursday after the Oporto race, he telephoned Mr Ferrari from his Farnham home to press his case. Collins's road Ferrari 250GT was at Maranello, and on its last trip to England he had had it fitted with a set of Dunlop disc brakes similar to those used on the Jaguar XK150. Before the German Grand Prix he had driven the car to Maranello for the Ferrari engineers' inspection. Ferrari agreed to have these brakes transferred to Hawthorn's Dino 246, and Mike called Dunlop for their approval and they responded by sending engineer Harold Hodkinson and fitter Maurice Roe to Italy to supervise the job. They found Ferrari wanting to fit discs on the front only, but Hodkinson insisted Hawthorn required them front and rear. Many detail fittings had to be made, along with brand-new hubs, and Roe was deeply impressed by his first sight of Italian fitters at work ... 'they walked through one entrance of the shop with a hunk of metal in one hand and a drawing of the hub in the other. They disappeared through the door at the other end and in the evening out they came—with the finished hubs!' The strength of *La Ferrari*....

Hawthorn arrived on the Wednesday before the race to find his disc-braked car—chassis '03/05'—was almost ready. Among the detail work required was Industria Meccanica Rho's almost overnight construction of new-type Borrani wire wheels for the car, with the spokes re-laced towards the outer ledge to clear the new brake calipers. Neither had Ferrari's engine men been marking time, and the usual Monza crop of innovations was on hand....

An enlarged Dino 256 V6 engine was now available with the standard 72 mm stroke combined to a 1 mm larger 86 mm bore, increasing swept volume to 2474 cc, closer to the 2.5-litre capacity limit, and this new unit, rated at 290 bhp at 8800 rpm, was fitted in the 'Hawthorn Special' for the start of practice, a second appearing later.

The three other cars included a standard F1 chassis, a lightweight small-tube chassis and the coil-spring rear suspension 'MI', now modified with taller coil springs and Koni telescopic dampers in place of

Trips racing the 246MI at Oporto in the Portuguese GP. Hawthorn had been given race number '22' as the meeting began, but swopped with Trips for '24'. Both Musso and Collins had carried race number '2' when they died, Collins in the second race after Musso's death; no way would Hawthorn race under double-two

the Houdailles fitted to the other cars. Each of these three was Dino 246-engined and drum-braked, although the drums were new bi-metal components, cast in alloy with a steel liner. Early in practice the alloy carburetter cowls were discarded and replaced by large front-opening Perspex scoops.

Hawthorn and Trips were joined in the team by Phil Hill—set for his long-overdue Formula 1 debut—and Olivier Gendebien. Both Hawthorn and Trips ran new 256 engines in first practice, but Brooks and Moss were fastest for Vanwall with Hill displaying his long-caged promise third ahead of Lewis-Evans, Hawthorn and Trips. Using the

This magnificent Jesse Alexander study of Hawthorn's car before the 1958 Italian GP at Monza shows off its four-spoke steering wheel, tank and body construction, de Dion rear suspension and offset engine mounting. The number '0005' was observed on this car at Monza, but it was probably '0003' disc-braked

Michael Tee, son of the proprietor of *Motor Sport* magazine, took this classic Ferrari pit-stop picture of Hawthorn's car at Monza during the 1958 Italian GP. The rear disc brakes are clearly visible as Hawthorn waits impatiently. Adelmo Marchetti stands with the 'go' flag by the car's nose while team strongman Carlo Amadessi heaves a fresh Englebert towards the hub and Ener Vecchi dodges by behind him. On the right stands a worried Boasso, the Englebert technician

246 engine Hawthorn improved later to place his special Ferrari in third spot on the front row, with Vanwalls all around, Moss on pole at 1 min 40.5 sec, then Brooks 1:41.4, the Dino's 1:41.8 and Lewis-Evans's 1:42.4. Row two was solid Ferrari, one-tenth of a second apart, with Gendebien quickest in the '246' at 1:42.5, Trips's apparently new '0006' with 256 engine on 1:42.6 and Hill's rebuilt '0004' on 1:42.7. A tremendous race was in prospect.

Of course Hawthorn's start was hesitant and the Vanwalls boomed into a brief 1–2–3 lead. The starter held the grid too long, Hawthorn knew his clutch was suffering, popped it in with a bang and managed to save most of the lining, but knew he was heading for trouble. Hill shot through from row two to lead all the Vanwalls ahead of Schell's BRM, then Trips and Hawthorn. Into the *Curva Grande* Trips rammed the tail of Schell's car and his Dino somersaulted into some trees, throwing the German out. He escaped with a leg injury, but the car was virtually crushed in two. While Hill tore round in the lead, Gendebien had been rammed by Brabham on the grid and was forced out with the MI's de Dion tube bent.

Hill led, looking very relaxed and comfortable, until Hawthorn moved ahead of the Vanwalls and took over on lap 5, but then Moss cut out both Ferraris and the real battle began. Hill had a puncture on lap 7 in the *Parabolica* and stopped for a wheel change and rejoined tenth. Hawthorn was on his own, with Moss, Evans, Brooks and Behra all in touch. The race developed with Hawthorn finding his car quicker than the Vanwalls and BRM everywhere save round the *Parabolica* corner before the pits and he drew out a seven-second lead, knowing he needed much more cushion as he would have to stop for fresh tyres at half-distance. Moss's gearbox broke on lap 18 and Hawthorn knew that if he could hold his lead and win, he would become Britain's first-ever World Champion Driver, and Ferrari would probably have another Constructors' Championship to their name. Hill had slammed into the fray and when Behra made a pit stop and Lewis-Evans hit trouble he forced his way back into second place; Hawthorn now had some support.

Half-distance was thirty-five laps and with thirty-eight seconds lead Hawthorn made his stop, Hill taking the lead and Masten Gregory's private Maserati displacing Hawthorn briefly from second place while he warmed his new tyres. Two laps later Hill made his stop and Hawthorn displaced the Maserati, not realizing it was actually on the same lap, and challenging for the lead. Hawthorn was irritated at being slipstreamed so closely, for it slows the leading car, and only when he spotted Gregory's number '32' on Monza's illuminated scoreboard did he appreciate the situation. 'It gave me quite a shock, so I turned it on a bit, and next lap past the pits I swerved and knocked him out of my slipstream....'

Brooks was closing fast, and Hawthorn now found his clutch beginning to slip. Hill was third, twenty-two seconds behind the Vanwall, and as the leading Ferrari's clutch-slip worsened so Brooks closed and went ahead on lap 60 right in front of the main grandstand. On the last lap the Hawthorn car was creeping along and its driver signalled frantically to Phil Hill to stay behind, the Dinos finishing second and third some twenty-five seconds behind the winning Vanwall. Hill had driven a superb race, and he set fastest lap on lap 26 at 1:42.9, 201.166 km/h (125.004 mph), a new record, robbing Moss of a possible Championship point, for which Hawthorn was to be very grateful.

With only the Moroccan Grand Prix left, five weeks hence at Casablanca and this year a World Championship round, Hawthorn had 40 points (only a driver's best six performances counting) and only Moss with 32 points could challenge him for the title. Stirling Moss was acknowledged as the outstanding driver of his day since Fangio had retired, and while Fangio was around he had been the eternal second in the Championship. To take the title from Hawthorn he had to win at Casablanca and set fastest lap with Mike lower than second place.

This exercise of mental agility nagged at both men during the five weeks between Monza and Casablanca, on 19 October. The Dunlop disc brake Hawthorn Special '03/05' was on hand for Ferrari's Champion elect, fitted with a 256 engine, while Hill had the F2-framed lightweight '0004' with bonded bi-metal drum brakes and Gendebien was to try his luck again in the '246MI' '0007', which had now been fitted for comparative purposes with British Girling disc brakes.

Hawthorn was very upset when he discovered he had been allotted race number '2', while Hill had '4' and Gendebien '6'. Both Musso and Collins had been carrying '2' when they were killed and Hawthorn

I don't care—you can't leave it here. The Monza park authorities were less than happy with Wolfgang von Trips's excursion into the brambles with his apparently new Dino 256 on the opening lap of the 1958 Italian GP. Trips escaped with a knee injury, which is more than can be said for the car. If the tank inscription is correct, this was '0005'. The frame number '0006' was noted at Monza. The photograph was taken by Henry Manney, who enjoys pastoral scenes

implored Tavoni to change the number. Gendebien said he would swop, he was not at all superstitious. At Oporto Hawthorn and Trips had swopped.

In a hot first practice Hawthorn tried both disc-braked cars and found the Girling-equipped MI poorly balanced and prone to lock-up at the rear. Later a sea-mist drifted in from the Atlantic and drivers found salt being deposited on their visors and goggles. To counteract the sun's glare the Perspex carburetter scoops were painted matt-black along with the scuttle surface inside the wrap-round screen. Hawthorn had a dark plastic visor made and found it worked very well. He had been accompanied to Morocco by his friend and mentor F. R. W. 'Lofty' England, the Jaguar team manager, and Tavoni made use of him as a welcome extra timekeeper. Hawthorn wanted to know just how he was placed in the coming race, the time intervals to cars ahead and behind, and reliable information on anyone closing up through the field. He intended driving for second place; that was all he required to win the Championship. Moss had to go flat out in the Vanwall and had to win and make fastest lap. . . .

After practice Hawthorn had the edge, with pole position his at 2 min 23.1 sec, Moss alongside on 2:23.2 and Lewis-Evans's Vanwall completing the front row on 2:23.7. Behra's BRM was on row two at 2:23.8 with Phil Hill alongside him at 2:24.1. Gendebien, Brooks's Vanwall and the Swede Joakim Bonnier's BRM occupied row three, with 2:24.3, 2:24.4 and 2:24.9 respectively. The first five cars were covered by 0.9 second, the first eight by only 1.8 seconds.

The race erupted as a furious free-for-all from the starting flag, with Hawthorn starting desperately gently to conserve his clutch and Moss charging away with Phil Hill hot on his heels ahead of Lewis-Evans. Hawthorn quickly established himself behind his American team-mate, who was harrying Moss mercilessly wheel-to-wheel. On lap 3 Hill tried to outbrake the Vanwall, found his drums could not match the British car's Goodyear discs and hustled up an escape road. Moss put his head back and set about establishing a lead, while Hill tore back through the field, caught Hawthorn, was waved ahead into second place again on lap 8 and set about Moss. But the Vanwall was lapping back-marker F2 cars by this time and Hill could make no impression through the traffic. Gendebien found his car's adjusted Girling disc brakes quite good, and was arguing sixth place with Behra and Lewis-Evans.

Brooks had got into his stride with the second Vanwall and on lap 14 was alongside Hawthorn to dispute third place. His task was clearly to keep the Ferrari away from second. At twenty-five laps, nearly half-distance in this fifty-three lap race, Moss led Hill by twenty seconds, Brooks was forty-two seconds behind in third with Hawthorn in close touch. Bonnier was a distant fifth, and Gendebien sixth.

Hawthorn occasionally swopped places with Brooks around the back of the circuit, but had noticed that the Vanwall was trailing smoke. He could see Brooks having to wipe his goggles and windscreen clean and felt assured the tall green car could not last long. By lap 30 he was ahead of the Vanwall when its engine blew apart, dumping oil on the rear tyres and producing an enormous slide which the phlegmatic Brooks did well to catch. François Picard's Cooper crashed heavily on the oil and Gendebien also lost control, smashing into a rock which completely sliced off his car's tail, behind the seat. Picard was badly hurt, but the Belgian escaped, only bruised and shaken.

Moss now looked secure in the lead, he had set fastest lap on lap 21 at 2:22.5, 173.23 km/h (117.86 mph), and with the oil down there was little prospect of bettering it. Tavoni signalled Hill to ease off and let Hawthorn by into second place. The only threat to them now came from Bonnier's fourth place BRM, which was going very well, but the two Dinos had his measure. With ten laps to run Lewis-Evans's Vanwall broke its engine and crashed heavily, exploding into flame. The slightly built, delicate Englishman suffered burns which tragically were to prove fatal.

Mike Hawthorn: 'Three laps to go and Phil toured gently round behind me, a loyal and brilliant driver, who at both Monza and Casablanca had done his best to help me. Two laps to go...one lap...and then there it was; the chequered flag...I had just become the Champion Driver of the World, the first Englishman to achieve the title.'

He had taken the title literally on a 'points decision' rather than by a 'knock out', and Moss's Vanwall victories that season, added to those of his team-mate Tony Brooks, won the British team the coveted Constructors' Championship title ahead of Ferrari. Still Tavoni and the crew were overjoyed for Hawthorn and simply disbelieved him when he explained he had driven his last motor race and was hanging up his famous green jacket, crash helmet and visor. The Ferrari team had lost four drivers and one engineer killed in two seasons, and Hawthorn's defection hurt Mr Ferrari deeply, which is never difficult....

Their contract had always been on a yearly basis and when Hawthorn wrote to him after Casablanca thanking him for all he had done but telling him formally of his retirement he heard nothing for several weeks. Eventually he received a letter from Tavoni saying that Mr Ferrari was fearfully upset. Hawthorn had asked as a special favour if Ferrari would sell him his World Championship-winning Dino 'special', purely for sentimental reasons. He wrote in his account of that season, 'I have not heard since about the car, although I feared that probably it had been scrapped....' And within weeks Mike Hawthorn, Ferrari World Champion, was dead, killed in a road accident near his Farnham home.

At Maranello, Ferrari set about picking up the pieces....

1959 Creeping obsolescence

Even before Mike Hawthorn had clinched his World Championship title at the wheel of the Formula 1 Ferrari Dinos, Maranello was busily preparing for the new season's competition. After the tentative Dino quad-cam sports car forays of 1958 a more comprehensive programme was contemplated for 1959, while of course the Formula 1 cars' natural development progressed.

It seemed obvious to Ferrari by this time that the Jano-originated four-cam Dino V6 was far too complex and expensive an engine to offer to customers, and a scheme rapidly developed to produce a more simple and economical second-generation Dino V6 with single overhead camshafts on each bank, like the established 250GT and TR V12s, which would become a serviceable sports car power unit. It is thought that this may have been seen as the foundation of a new line of small-capacity GT cars, production 'Dinos' in fact, for as our picture shows, the engine was tested in touring trim.

The new engine was in fact launched more as a simple bisection of the existing Colombo-originated 250 *Testa Rossa* V12 than as a simplified variant of the Jano four-cam V6, and it had the V12's simple 60-degree vee angle. The prototype in fact used the same cylinder dimensions (73.0 mm × 58.8 mm) to form a '156S' 1.5-litre, but this was never raced.

It was instead overtaken by a 2-litre '196S' version with bore and stroke dimensions of what had been the 206S in 1958, 77 mm × 71 mm to provide a swept volume of 1983.72 cc. The single overhead camshaft on each cylinder bank was chain driven, and actuated roller followers and rocker arms controlling two inclined valves per cylinder, returned by coil springs. A belt-drive from a pulley on the crankshaft nose powered a six-blade cast-alloy fan, water pump and generator. The engine used single-plug ignition with a distributor mounted vertically on the tail of the left-side camshaft. Unlike its pure-bred racing sister, the Jano 65-degree V6, this unit employed wet-sump lubrication. It carried three Weber 42DCN twin-choke carburetters, and was rated at 195–200 bhp at 7800 rpm, running on straight petrol with its 9.8:1 compression ratio.

A typical Ferrari welded-steel sports-racing frame was built to accept this power unit, derived from the successful *Testa Rossa* 1958 frame design, but smaller. It had a 2250 mm (88.6 in) wheelbase compared to

The prototype Dino 196S two-cam 60-degree V6 engine set up on an assembly stand in the winter of 1958–59, showing its road-going prototype GT form with air-cleaner, fan, dynamo and wet sump. The distributor is mounted vertically at the rear of the left-side camshaft, not on top of the oil filler/breather pipe as it looks here. The engine was never used in production, being raced shorn of its road-going accessories

the V12 TR-58's 2350 mm (92.5 in), while front track was 1250 mm (49.2 in) and rear track 1225 mm (48 in) compared to the V12 cars' 1308 mm (51.5 in) and 1300 mm (51.1 in) dimensions. The new V6 drove through a single dry-plate clutch directly to a four-speed gearbox bolted to the engine. The rear suspension used a live axle located by parallel trailing arms and suspended on coil springs with telescopic dampers. Front suspension was by unequal-length double wishbones, coil springs and tele-dampers. Dunlop disc brakes replaced the Ferrari drums, fitted outboard all round within Borrani centre-lock wire wheels.

The prototype car was completed in March 1959 and was tested at Modena with Scaglietti bodywork almost identical to that seen on the 1958 four-cam prototype '206S' and '296S' sports Dinos raced at Goodwood, Naples and Silverstone. It had greater affinity to the 206S/58 than to the 296S as the head fairing of the large-engined car cut down almost vertically at the rear, while that on both quad-cam and two-cam 2.0 bodies curved more gently into the tail. One change was that the rear-opening carburetter blister, which was formed into the aluminium engine cover of the earlier cars, was now replaced by a GP-like front-opening clear Perspex cowl.

Ferrari sports car bodies changed at this time, however, with the deep-chested Scaglietti form being dropped in favour of a new design, still by Pininfarina, but now built by Fantuzzi; formerly Maserati's body-builder. Scaglietti's works were full to bursting at this time with Ferrari Californias and 250GT *Berlinettas*. The Fantuzzi-built sports car bodies were easily identifiable by their rather fussy-looking aluminium trimmed and grilled air outlets behind the wheel arches, and round instead of tall, oval brake cooling intakes on either side of the radiator orifice.

Ingegnere Carlo Chiti (burly and bespectacled on the left) supervises Tony Brooks's first test run in the prototype F1 Dino 246/256 at Modena early in 1959, the photograph being dated by the Englebert tyres on the sports-racer in the background. Marchetti makes a final check on the right. The 1959 Dinos had a big-tube chassis, with the longer 2220 mm wheelbase of the 1958 MI, forged wishbones as standard, coil springs all round and bulbous but beautifully formed Fantuzzi bodywork. Modena gossip of the time described the bodywork as being just like Medardo Fantuzzi himself . . . of ample girth. Brooks signed with Ferrari on the understanding he would not be required to drive at Le Mans. He had crashed heavily there in 1957, and was not anxious to return

Meanwhile Formula 1 development continued for the new season, the big bottom-tube F1 Dino chassis being adapted to carry all-new bodywork again by Fantuzzi, with Dunlop disc brakes and also Dunlop tyres now standard wear. The new body style was voluptuous and rather bulky, with a 'torpedo' tail replacing the down-tucked affair of the 1958 cars, higher straight-edged cockpit sides and a more elegantly curvaceous nose treatment. The fuel and oil tanks were hidden by the body-panelling around the tail, and the 1958-style upswept exhaust pipes exiting above the rear suspension were dropped in favour of a low-level system passing beneath the rear suspension. Experiments were made to improve gas extraction by fitting 'Snap' turbo-vaned exhaust extractors, these devices being claimed by their manufacturer to improve performance and fuel consumption. Ferrari toyed with them for some time, and every self-respecting 'boy racer' in Europe soon had them fitted to his Renault Dauphine and Ford Popular. . . .

These 1959 Formula 1 Dinos used forged upper and lower front wishbones with interposed coil springs enclosing co-axial Koni telescopic dampers, while the de Dion rear ends adopted similar coil/damper assemblies as standard in place of the original transverse leaf spring, and fore-and-aft location of the axle beam and hubs was by parallel radius

rods on either side. A revised gearbox was produced, now with five forward ratios, and the chassis' wheelbase was increased to 2220 mm (87.4 in) from the 1958 models' 2160 mm (85.1 in). This 2.3-inch increase was based upon experience with the long-wheelbase 'MI' Monza-Indianapolis special.

Ferrari had their cars ready, but drivers were now a problem. Having lost Musso, Collins and Hawthorn, and with Trips having fallen from favour, Mr Ferrari found himself left with the promising but in single-seater terms inexperienced Phil Hill, and the steady Olivier Gendebien, who was obviously not about to set the Grand Prix world alight. But Vanwall had retired after their World Championship success due to the loss of Lewis-Evans and Mr G. A. Vandervell's failing health, and so Tony Brooks was available and was signed up. Another Englishman, Cliff Allison, was added since he had shown great promise with the embryo Lotus team the preceding season, and finally Jean Behra joined Ferrari...having lost patience with BRM. Of these five only Brooks had proved himself a truly first-rate driver, capable of winning Grand Prix races. So the driver team looked adequate, but was it the weakest Ferrari had ever fielded?

After the controversy of 1958 there was no Argentine *Temporada* in 1959. In the season's sports car races Ferrari lost their World Championship narrowly to Aston Martin—who largely had Stirling Moss to thank for their surprising success—but the new Dino sports-racers played little part in the title defence.

On 3 May Giulio Cabianca and his Scuderia Eugenio Castellotti gave the new Fantuzzi-bodied Dino 196S its debut in the Coppa Sant' Ambroeus race at Monza. The car was described in the Italian press as a perfect replica of the latest V12 *Testa Rossa*, only the six carburetter stacks beneath that Perspex scoop giving it away. It is thought that this car used the same chassis, number '0740', as the Scaglietti-bodied prototype shown at Modena that March, but its debut yielded little.

The same car was shared by Cabianca and Giorgio Scarlatti in the Targa Florio Championship race on 24 May, where it was again entered under the Scuderia Eugenio Castellotti banner though tended by Maranello racing shop mechanics. Cabianca had the car catch fire under him early in the race, and once that problem had been quelled the gearbox failed and its race was run.

On 7 June the same driver pairing ran the Dino in the ADAC 1000 km at Nürburgring, but its engine failed in a big way after ten of the forty-four laps. At Goodwood for the RAC Tourist Trophy on 5 September, Scarlatti and Ludovico Scarfiotti faced the works 2-litre Porsches (which had won the Targa) in the Fantuzzi Dino, but retired yet again as its rear suspension collapsed.

At Le Mans on 20 June much was expected of Scarlatti and Cabianca in the car, but they were out after five hours with another engine failure.

It was left to Luigi Chinetti to salvage something for the new Dino 196S. He bought a brand-new car, '0776', on November 18, 1959, and had it air-freighted to New York. 'Papa' Rodriguez had agreed with Chinetti to finance the car's running at Nassau, in Cuba, and the 1960

Sebring 12-Hours and Targa Florio, where it would be driven by his sons Pedro and Ricardo. At Nassau its gearbox broke under a ham-fisted mechanic, and Ricardo drove his Porsche in Cuba.... At least Ferrari had found a customer, and things would improve in the coming year.

Meanwhile Scuderia Ferrari had achieved much more on the Formula 1 front with their 65-degree four-cam V6 Grand Prix Dinos.

They passed up Easter Goodwood in favour of the Aintree '200' on 18 April on Mrs Mirabel Topham's circuit around the perimeter of her world-famous Grand National horse-race course at Liverpool. Two of the revised Fantuzzi-bodied cars were entered, one with a 256 engine for Behra and the other with 246 power for Brooks. They arrived on hired lorries, 'each with four mechanics . . . [plus] some spare wheels, a couple of tool-boxes and one electric starter'. The British Grand Prix was to be held on this circuit in July, and this meeting provided an ideal opportunity to test the new cars in preparation.

With only one starter for two cars the Ferrari mechanics had to work very rapidly on the grid, and on a damp and cloudy day Behra and Brooks got away slowly, running seventh and ninth against Cooper–Climax (now with full 2.5-litre engines) and BRM opposition, while Moss had Walker's new Cooper–BRM.

The Ferraris were visibly faster than anything else on Aintree's Railway Straight, running 'with a delightful high-pitched scream', but seemed outclassed through the twists. Retirements allowed Behra into fourth, then third place behind Schell's BRM and Moss's leading Walker Cooper. Behra was inspired by the sight of Schell, his former team-mate, in the BRM ahead and moved into second place after twenty-eight of the sixty-seven laps. Schell fought back, but broke his car in an effort to

Sports-racer—the rebodied and re-engined chassis '0740' from 1958 now carrying Fantuzzi bodywork with its distinctive air exit vents behind the front and rear wheel-arches being fisted through Goodwood's St Mary's ess-bend in the 1959 Tourist Trophy, where it was shared by Giorgio Scarlatti and newcomer Ludovico Scarfiotti. The car is still left-hand drive

repass the Ferrari. Then on lap 30 Moss's Colotti gearbox failed, so Behra was left leading, and Brooks had moved into second place, and they held these positions to the finish; a Ferrari 1–2, but hardly a convincing one.

The following weekend found the team in Sicily for the Formula 2 Syracuse Grand Prix, with a Fantuzzi-bodied Dino 156 for Behra. His opposition included Moss in a Cooper–Borgward and Brabham and Gregory in works 1500 cc Cooper–Climaxes, and Moss took pole position at 2 min 2.7 sec from Behra on 2:03.0 and Gregory at 2:05.0. Behra managed to lead narrowly at the end of the opening lap and then commenced a torrid dice with Moss in which the lead changed several times. On lap 12 Moss gave Behra the slip while lapping back-markers, but the Frenchman pulled back, setting fastest lap at 2:01.2 and on lap 20 the Dino was two lengths in the lead. On lap 30 Moss took the lead from Behra, gained yards through traffic but in trying to fight back, Behra spun and dented his car's nose on a wall. He managed to restart, but Moss had set a new fastest lap. Behra responded once he had got the Dino restarted and pointing in the right direction by hammering it to 10,000 rpm through the gears, and on lap 45 he clocked 2:00.0 for another new fastest lap. By lap 49 Behra was down to 1:59.0, 166.3 km/h (103.4 mph), but with only six laps to run he could not close more on Moss, who ran out the winner by twenty-two seconds from the beautiful little F2 Dino.

On 2 May the BRDC International Trophy race at Silverstone saw Phil Hill joining Brooks in a pair of Dino 246s. Brooks was third quickest on the front row, with Hill on the inside of row three on the unfamiliar

Tony Brooks, from Dukinfield, Cheshire, was son of a dental surgeon. he qualified in dentistry himself and while still studying, his father's interest in sports cars set him racing in British club events. He began with a secondhand Healey Silverstone in 1952, moved on to a Frazer-Nash and rapidly developed the smooth and elegant style for which he became famous.

John Riseley-Prichard gave him his first single-seater drive in an F2 Connaught at Crystal Palace in August, 1954; he finished fourth behind F1 cars driven by Hawthorn, Schell and Salvadori. After a driver test he was signed on by Aston Martin for 1955, and late that year Connaught gave him both his first Formula 1 ride and his first race overseas, at Syracuse in Sicily. He beat off a horde of Maseratis led by Musso and gave Britain her first continental Grand Prix victory for both car and driver since Segrave and Sunbeam had triumphed at San Sebastian in 1924.

Brooks joined BRM for 1956 but the year was punctuated by a fiery accident at Silverstone which broke his jaw. Then he joined Moss in the 1957 Vanwall team and fulfilled his promise. He crashed an Aston Martin, uncharacteristically, at Le Mans, and was still battered and bruised when he drove in the British Grand Prix at Aintree, held his car in contention and when Moss took it over he was able to score Britain's maiden World Championship race victory. Into 1958 Tony Brooks was clearly one of the World's best-six drivers, and he won the Belgian, German and Italian Grands Prix for Vanwall.

He married an Italian girl, Pina, and joined Ferrari in 1959 after Vanwall's withdrawal. In 1960 he drove private Coopers and in 1961 spent the first 1.5-litre year with BRM, but found himself left cold by the new cars' lack of power. He retired to concentrate on his Weybridge garage business—still an outstandingly skilful driver, well respected.

Charles Anthony Standish Brooks
BDS (Manc), LDS (Manc)

b. 25 February, 1932

circuit. The Englishman ran third before retiring with misfiring, while Hill looked very uncomfortable in his car, had a spin and finally finished fourth, one lap behind Brabham's winning mid-engined 2.5-litre Cooper–Climax and the Aston Martin of Salvadori (on its debut) and Flockhart's BRM.

The following Sunday, 10 May, saw the World Championship open at Monte Carlo. Would the mid-engined Cooper–Climaxes now that they had full-sized 2.5-litre engines prove superior to the less manoeuvrable front-engined cars?

Ferrari entered Behra, Hill and Brooks in three of the latest Dinos, all reportedly with 246 rather than 256 engines. In preparation for close racing their long nose cowls were abbreviated, leaving specially enlarged radiators designed to cope with Monaco's potentially high temperatures well exposed. A normal-nose fourth car was available as spare, and in addition Behra's Syracuse Dino 156 F2 car was on hand to give Allison his Ferrari single-seat debut in the concurrent 1500 cc class.

Early in practice Brooks spun entering the tunnel while passing Bruce Halford's F2 Lotus 16, but continued unabashed. Behra began a struggle with Moss in which they swopped fastest time back and forth, but Brooks unobtrusively pipped his team-mate to run second quickest behind Moss's Walker-entered Cooper–Climax. On the second day Phil Hill was trying both his own car and the spare and fighting hard to learn the way round Monte Carlo. Allison inadvertently changed down from fifth to second and brought his F2 car in with 10,600 rpm on the clock, but it seemed perfectly happy. He only just qualified right at the close of practice, while Moss took pole at 1 min 39.6 sec, alongside Behra on 1:40.0 and Brabham's Cooper at 1:40.1. Brooks and Hill were on row two with their Ferrari Dinos, at 1:41.0 and 1:41.3 respectively—an excellent effort by the American on his first appearance at Monaco. Allison was on the back of the grid with 1:44.4, only Halford qualifying slower.

Behra led the initial charge, and on lap 2 at Ste Devote corner the F2 entry eliminated themselves as von Trips's Porsche broadsided on spilled oil and was rammed by Halford and Allison in the Dino 156. All three cars were badly damaged, and out of the race, but it was significant that the mid-engined Porsche had out-qualified both front-engined machines.

The race developed with Behra leading narrowly from Moss, Brabham sitting comfortably third awaiting developments and Phil Hill falling away fourth. Brooks was involved in a mid-field battle farther back, as was his habit early in a Grand Prix, but he found himself hemmed in by BRMs and lost contact with the leading bunch, where he should rightfully have been. By lap 20 Behra was still narrowly ahead, while Hill and Brooks were fourth and fifth, but two laps later the leader slowed abruptly, Moss and Brabham went by and as Behra set out on his twenty-fifth lap his engine burst at the Gasworks Hairpin, and strewing oil and hot pieces all over the road he stopped behind the pits.

Moss had a comfortable lead from Brabham, who was in turn well clear of Hill, but on lap 36 Hill spun in the Casino Square and dented the

Dino's tail and allowed Schell and Brooks—who had been displaced by the BRM—to catch him. Two laps later they both passed the hot and bothered American, and on lap 44 he spun again in the Square. Soon afterwards Schell crashed at the same place and Brooks was left alone third behind the Coopers of Moss and Brabham. On lap 68 Phil Hill had his third spin by the Casino, and this time he hit something hard which buckled both left-side wheels, and a stop to change them dropped him to sixth and second to last. He was being gassed by cockpit fumes.

In the final stages Brooks made a big effort to close on Brabham for second place, but the Australian responded by setting a comfortable fastest lap, whereupon Moss abruptly fell back with transmission trouble. Brooks was suffering from heat and fumes in the tightly enwrapped Ferrari cockpit and settled for second place, which he took some twenty seconds behind the works Cooper–Climax. Trintignant's Cooper was third and Phil Hill, three laps down but driving as though his life depended on it, finished fourth, having frequent broadsides around the Gasworks Hairpin and putting the Casino Square crowd on their toes

'Jeannot' leads the way at Monaco—Jean Behra in his short-nosed '0004' enters the Station Hairpin ahead of the Coopers of Moss and Brabham—the mid-engined revolution gaining ground. The special short nose is very apparent here, cut back to prevent accidental closure during Monaco's crowded early laps

every time he appeared. It had been very hard work for Scuderia Ferrari—these mid-engined cars were quick, and they gave their drivers an easier time....

The Dinos would have excelled at Spa, where they could be wound-up in top gear, but the Belgian GP was cancelled. Every time Brooks had been to Spa he had won. It was a bitter blow to his Championship hopes.

The Dutch Grand Prix was held at Zandvoort on 31 May and Ferrari appeared with their three Monaco Formula 1 chassis refitted with long-nose body panels and the repaired F2 chassis carrying an experimental 256 engine. This had Weber 50DCN carburetters instead of the normal 42DCNs, and in consequence had a larger Perspex cowl covering them. While the true F1 frames rode on 16-inch wheels, the 156-derived F2 car ran on 15-inch, all four cars using Dunlop disc brakes and tyres. There was also a true Formula 1 spare car available.

Behra tried both the experimental model and the spare in first practice, deciding he preferred the F2-derived machine. Allison took over the spare with no real chance of starting in the race, more of gaining experience. Brooks and Hill meanwhile were in trouble with their regular cars, which as in 1958 were understeering and/or oversteering madly on this seaside circuit. The circuit's fast back section demanded a nimble car, quick to change direction. This the big Dinos could not do.

On the second day Behra's F2 experimental had the big-carburetter engine replaced by a standard 246, while the big-Weber V6 went into Allison's F1 chassis. Behra was quickly down to the 1:36 mark with his 'special', but Brooks and Hill were having trouble cracking 1:40 and both were unhappy at not being allowed to try the F2 chassised car. The team was in a shambles, juggling springs, dampers and tyre pressures, and Brooks and Hill were not too impressed when Behra drove the spare F1 car and said it felt fine to him. Tavoni got the rival team managers to agree to a proposition which he put to the Dutch organizers, asking them to allow Allison to start in the spare F1 chassis with the big-carburetter engine, and this was agreed to, although he had set no time in it.

The grid formed with Bonnier on pole for BRM at 1 min 36.0 sec alongside Brabham and Moss, while Behra's F2 'special' was next up on row two at 1:36.6. Brooks was on the outside of row three at 1:37.9, Hill was very unhappy on row five at 1:39.2 and Allison was behind him.

Brooks made an excellent start to run third ahead of Behra as Gregory and Bonnier made the running. Behra got ahead of his team-mate to lead the bunch squabbling over third place and Brooks was soon in trouble as an oil-pipe union had split and was pumping oil mist onto his rear tyres. After a vicious slide he fell to eleventh place, behind a group comprising Phil Hill, Innes Ireland's Lotus 16 and Trintignant's Cooper. Brabham had moved into third place and drew away from Behra, who was manfully blocking off Moss and Graham Hill who were both climbing all over him in an effort to get by. On lap 24 Moss ran round the outside of the Dino on Tarzan Hairpin and by the end of that lap Graham Hill was past as well, though soon his Lotus made a stop.

Brooks survived until lap 43, when he retired with the Ferrari quite undriveable and its tail smothered in oil, while Allison was lapped. Behra suffered a similar fate, lost his temper because he had earlier been dicing with Moss, who was now lapping him, and slithered broadside onto the verge, but recovered. The race ran out with Moss's Cooper again breaking its transmission and Bonnier winning BRM's first-ever *Grande Epreuve*. Behra was fifth, one lap down, with Phil Hill sixth and another lap behind. Allison, lapped four times, was ninth. It was not a happy Ferrari crew who returned to Maranello, but the next race was to be the French Grand Prix at Reims, and on that power circuit the Dinos should excel . . . and Brooks loved such fast courses.

The French race was on 5 July, accompanied by the usual *Coupe de Vitesse* F2 event, and Ferrari's Fiat–Bartoletti transporters disgorged six cars, three the regular '59 F1s, one with a 256 engine, and the fourth the F2-framed 'special' from Zandvoort. The fifth car was the normal F1-frame spare, and the sixth a second Dino 156 for the Formula 2 race, these F2 chassis frames all retaining the short wheelbase of the 1958 Dino 246, though the difference was minimal to the naked eye. The F1 cars were geared to 180 mph at 8800 rpm, while the Dino 156 ran to 10,200 rpm, developing its peak at 9800, around 160 mph.

Some rear suspension modifications had been made. Formerly the single-seat Dino's de Dion tube had been located laterally by a steel ball mounted on the rear of the gearbox/final-drive case engaging in a forked guide projecting below the de Dion tube's centre. Now the Reims F1 cars all had the arrangement reversed, with a ball mounted on a plate bolted to the de Dion fork now running in a hardened guide bolted to the final-drive case. The de Dion tube ends were machined to provide a small degree of negative camber and toe-in and these modifications vastly improved handling on high-speed corners. The F2 car was left unchanged as its lower power and terminal speed did not produce the problems found in the Formula 1 cars.

Brooks was fast almost from the moment practice began and everyone was staggered by his speed, particularly Behra, whose short-chassis F2 'special' was nothing like as quick. Hawthorn's race lap record of 2 min 24.9 sec toppled as Brooks clocked 2:19.6 and then 2:19.4, an over 133 mph average Behra managed 2:23.0 early on, but eventually despaired of going much faster in his special.

On the second day all five F1 Ferraris were out, driven by Brooks, Hill, Behra, Gendebien and the newly signed American sports car driver Dan Gurney. Behra took Gendebien's standard car in an effort to improve, and Hill drove his heart out to get down to 2:19.8. Final practice was run in slower conditions, and the grid was resolved with Brooks on pole with his 2:19.4 alongside Brabham at 2:19.7 and Phil Hill. Moss's non-works BRM was next up on row two with 2:19.9 to his neighbour Behra's 2:20.2 in the ex-Gendebien F1-framed Dino. Gendebien and Gurney were on the fifth row with 2:21.5 and 2:21.9 respectively.

Reims on race day was as hot as an oven with sections of the track surface melting and breaking up. Brooks took an instant lead, unusual for him, and simply drove the opposition into the ground, leading all the way, relaxed and happy to win as he pleased for Ferrari Dino. Behra stalled on the line and was push-started to hare away after the field. He

1959: Reims organizer 'Toto' Roche decreed that no circuit testing should take place on the Saturday preceding the big race. Ferrari wanted to test something on Gendebien's F2-based car '0011', but could not find the Belgian driver. Phil Hill was available, but didn't have his helmet with him. Gurney's helmet was found and Phil took off amongst the public. The team based themselves on the grass traffic island at Thillois and Phil reappeared hurtling through the traffic at around 140 mph. He stopped to say Roche was at the pits 'going bananas'. He was told to do another lap, and this time Roche tried to swat him with a flag as he went by. Next time round Roche was airborne and fit to explode. When he tackled the team he said he would disqualify Gendebien, he had got the car's number. When Olivier explained he had not been present, Roche threatened Gurney; it was his black helmet. Dan protested truthfully he had not driven a Ferrari all day. Baffled, Roche let the matter drop. Pete Coltrin took the picture of Hill amongst the traffic

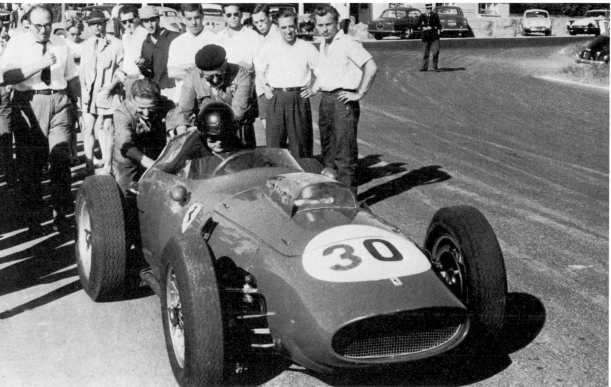

and is seen extreme left in Geoff Goddard's shot of Phil being push-started. Also visible is Chiti and, in the beret, the venerable Luigi Bazzi. Behra took over this car, with its over-sized induction cowl, for the race

Above right Brooks loved fast circuits and in the Dino 246/59 he had a fast-circuit car. Unfortunately for him, his and Ferrari's World Championship hopes, the year's Belgian GP was cancelled. Tony had won at Spa on all his previous visits.

Reims matched both his relaxed high-speed style and his car admirably, and on a roasting day he won the French GP untroubled — leading all the way in his regular car '0002', seen here at Thillois. He started from pole and determined to lead

from the flag to run in clean air. In this way he stayed relatively cool, while many other drivers collapsed with heat prostration. He had a drinking bottle rigged in the cockpit, but recalls his first sip; 'orange juice at around 90-centigrade is horrible!'

caught and tore through them as the race progressed and was sixth by lap 10, behind Phil Hill but ahead of Gurney and Gendebien. On lap 18 Gurney blared past the pits signalling something was amiss, and next time round he retired with overheating, his radiator having been holed by a flying stone. Brooks was leading from Brabham, while behind him Behra had caught Phil Hill and Moss and all three were closing on the Australian's Cooper. Behra was driving furiously; he picked off Moss and on lap 24 took third place from Phil Hill. Ending the next lap he braked too late at Thillois Hairpin and skated round the far side of the grass triangle junction there, dropping back to fourth. Next time round Phil Hill had overtaken Brabham to run second behind Brooks. Behra equalled the fastest lap of 2:23.5 on his twenty-eighth lap, but next time round his Dino was trailing pale smoke from its left-side exhaust. He slowed, trying to complete thirty-five laps of the scheduled fifty to be classified as a finisher, but a piston collapsed and that was that.

All the drivers were suffering from the heat, Brooks less than most since he was well clear of traffic, Hill suffering badly. He was driving in a wild daze, overshooting the hairpins and spinning on almost every lap. Moss was closing on him until his BRM spun on melted tar at Thillois and he could not restart it. Brabham was utterly exhausted and had settled for third, so Hill was able to relax and toured in second behind his team-mate. Olivier Gendebien had driven steadily apart from one spin and was fourth on the same lap as the leaders at the finish.

Soon afterwards the F2 race began with Allison on the centre of the front row with his Dino 156, flanked by Moss on pole and Hans Herrmann's Porsche. Cliff's start was hesitant and he was instantly engulfed by private Coopers, and after establishing himself a distant third behind Moss's winning Cooper–Borgward and Herrmann's second place Porsche his V6 engine blew up at Muizon with two of the twenty-five laps to run.

After his retirement in the Grand Prix Behra had a set-to with Tavoni in the pits and punched the team manager, the Frenchman being summarily released from his contract once Mr Ferrari got to hear about the incident.

The British Grand Prix followed at Aintree, but there were no Ferraris present owing to labour disputes in Italy. Brooks attempted to enhance his World Championship points standings with a lightweight Vanwall entered half-heartedly by the Vandervell Products company, but it proved a forlorn hope, and Brabham won handsomely for Cooper–Climax from Moss in the British Racing Partnership-entered BRM.

Ferrari's problems were effectively resolved by 2 August, when the German Grand Prix was held for the second and last time at Berlin's artificial AVUS speedway. This very high-speed course consisted of two autobahn lanes connected by a flat wide-radius 180-degree curve at one end and by a superfast banked wall-of-death at the other; an ideal venue for Ferrari power. The Grand Prix was to be run in two thirty-lap heats, with the overall result decided by addition of times.

Ferrari fielded four Dino 246s for Brooks, Hill, Gurney and Allison, and practice soon saw both Allison and Gurney taking to ultra-high-

Right Cliff Allison rounds Thillois in the Formula 2 156/59 '0012', showing off its Fantuzzi body lines and undersized wheels

Below and below right Brooks up the wall at AVUS driving with supreme confidence and subtle skill to win the controversial 1959 German Grand Prix. Here '0002' shows off its shapely lines, the still left-side angled engine mounting and its very roomy cockpit. The car is in a stable understeering drift on the brick-built banking at some 165 mph. It was on this banking the previous day that Jean Behra crashed fatally in his private Porsche. It was an event which set all his former Ferrari team-mates on edge, yet still they finished 1–2–3, as shown here with Brooks leading across the line from Hill and Gurney at the end of the second heat. The high banking is visible in the background

speed motoring very well and slipstreaming their team-mates to great effect. The Ferraris took a hammering on the bumpy brick-built banking, but were better capable of resisting it than the flimsy Lotus and Cooper British opposition. Brooks later took pole at 2 min 5.9 sec, next to Moss's Cooper-Climax on 2:06.8, Gurney at 2:07.2 and Brabham on 2:07.4. Phil Hill was in the centre of the second row, having been narrowly eclipsed by Gurney, at 2:07.6, while Allison wound-up on row four with his reserve entry, despite a staggering quickest-of-all lap at 2:05.8, 191.34 km/h (147 mph)!

Gurney crept at the start, hesitated and was engulfed as the field took off, Brooks taking an immediate lead. Gurney recovered to run second ahead of Brabham and Phil Hill, while Allison's clutch packed up on lap 3. Gregory stole a brief lead in the Cooper before Brooks pinched it back, and as the five leading cars arrived at the South Turn, Gurney rammed one of Gregory's rear wheels, closing the Dino's nose cowling, though not enough to cause his engine to overheat. Brooks, Gurney and Gregory fought a tremendous wheel-to-wheel battle with Hill sitting back in fourth place worrying that he was hitting 9000 rpm on the straights and convinced his team-mates had been carried away in the heat of battle and were wildly over-revving. Unbeknown to him his tachometer was at fault, and they were pulling 8500–8600 rpm on the same gearing as his car. All three up front chopped and changed position constantly until lap 24, when Gregory's Climax engine broke a big-end bolt and the unit literally exploded in a shower of bouncing fragments. The three majestic Ferraris were able to run out as they pleased, with Brooks winning from Gurney and Hill, the intervals being 1.3 and 3.2 seconds.

Before Heat Two Allison's clutch was repaired and Gurney's car had its nose cowl beaten straight. Allison took position on the back of the grid, but just before the start the organizers ushered him off, having decided he should not take part. Bruce McLaren's works Cooper took an initial lead, but the three Ferraris stormed by on the straight along with Bonnier's

Dan Gurney shone in his new car '0007' in the Portuguese GP at Lisbon's Monsanto Park circuit and is seen here ahead of Moss's Rob Walker team Cooper-Climax. The nose of '0007' was badly made with its air intake raised into the air and a shelving under-surface presenting itself to the airstream. 'It was great for lifting the front wheels off the ground,' Dan explains, 'but whenever I complained about it they looked at me like I had a hole in my head.' He was immensely proud of his third place that day in Portugal

BRM, and Phil Hill led the way back across the timing line, from Bonnier, Brooks and Gurney. On lap 3 the Ferraris took total command and after swopping places amongst themselves they ran out 1–2–3 again, with Brooks winning by 0.3 second from Hill, who was in turn 0.3 second clear of Gurney. The overall result showed Brooks first, Gurney second and Hill third, while Brooks set fastest lap at 2:04.5.

Lisbon's Monsanto Park circuit was used for the Portuguese Grand Prix on 23 August. Four Ferrari Dinos were present, their regular cars for Brooks, Hill and Gurney—Dan's having begun life as the last-built Fantuzzi-bodied car, the spare at Monaco. The Lisbon spare was the F2-frame big-carburetter engined ex-Behra special, and each driver tried it. Its low-down punch away from Monsanto's hairpins was pathetic, and it was quickly put away. No record survives outside Ferrari of which engines were used, as for reasons of team psychology the magic '256' big-engine covers had been replaced, and all units were now '246s' to everyone except the team engineers. Gurney's car differed visibly from the others in having a large cylindrical gear-knob and a three-spoke steering wheel with unequal spoke spacings.

Practice quickly showed the Ferraris to be like fish out of water on this circuit, giving their drivers a very hard ride, and Gurney's best of 2 min 8.02 sec was only sixth fastest behind Moss's Cooper pole of 2:07.99. Hill was alongside his team-mate on row three with 2:08.02 and Brooks was on the row behind with 2:10.96, having come to grips neither with the circuit nor his car. David Yorke, former Vanwall team manager, was present and Tavoni had asked him earnestly during practice: 'This man Brooks, how do you make him try?' Tony was unable to adjust his car to neutral steer, and was always too intelligent to drive a car beyond its limits.

From the start Gurney and Hill ran fifth and sixth with Brooks way back having been baulked on the grid. On the next lap Hill shot up an escape road and dropped behind, and while trying to regain lost time he

1959 Dino cockpits; Gurney's with the thick-rim unequal-spaced solid-spoke steering wheel, massive gear-change grip and tall screen, which he favoured; firstly because his hands had always been prone to blistering and he wanted to spread the load over a larger area, secondly because he was well over six feet tall, very strong and had a reputation for dragging steering wheels and gear-shifts out by the roots. In comparison the cockpit of Brooks's car shows the Lancia–Ferrari derived drilled-spoke standard steering wheel and the ball gear-change. Tony recalls the car as having 'a truly fabulous gear-change unlike the Vanwall's I had driven in 1957–58, which you could describe at best as agricultural'

met Graham Hill's Lotus 16 broadside-on in the dual-carriageway section of the course and clobbered it very hard indeed. The American was annoyed, and out of the race.

Behind four leading Coopers Gurney was the only Ferrari hope, embroiled in a scrap with Trintignant. Brooks was buried and when the Ferrari pit signalled him a lap time of 2 : 18.0 he could not respond. After more signals in similar vein he came into the pits to explain his engine would not rev. He rejoined, last.

Brabham crashed, and Gurney was firm in fourth place by half-distance before inheriting third, in which position he finished, one lap down on Moss's winning Cooper–Climax, despite riding up over Trintignant's rear wheel and damaging his car's nose cone (again) six laps from the end. Brooks finished ninth.

Monza and the Italian Grand Prix followed, on 19 September, and Ferrari pinned their hopes on Brooks for this fast circuit, where he had won for Vanwall the previous year. Pre-race tyre tests indicated that the quiet Englishman's smooth driving would run through the race non-stop supposing a 1 : 40 lap time. Five Dinos were presented for Brooks, Hill, Gurney, Gendebien and Allison, the Belgian's being the F2 framed Formula 1 'special'.

Left A proper Grand Prix team—the gorgeous Ferrari Dino fleet in the Monza paddock prior to the 1959 Italian GP. The cars are respectively number 30 Brooks's '0002', 32 Hill's '0003', 34 Allison's '0004', 36 Gurney's '0007', with its upturned nose form, and 38 Gendebien's F2-framed '0011'. The porphyry setts surfacing the Monza paddock formerly covered the *Porfidano* corners before the pits until the speedbowl was built in 1955. They could tell a tale. . .

Practice saw Moss stealing pole in his Walker Cooper at 1 : 39.7 from Brooks, who clocked 1 : 39.8, driving now with all his naturally elegant artistry. Brabham was on the outside of the front row with 1 : 40.2, while Gurney and Hill occupied row two with their Dinos, on 1 : 40.8 and 1 : 41.2 respectively. Gendebien went well with 1 : 41.4 on the inside of row three, and Allison was on the outside with 1 : 41.8, the Dinos being split precisely by Schell's BRM.

As the flag fell and the field set off, smoke belched from the tail of Brooks's Ferrari and it moved away with cars passing on both sides. Its new clutch, replaced after practice, had burned out and Brooks's race was already over. For Ferrari this was a body blow.

Phil Hill nipped out Moss to lead on lap 2 with Gurney on the Cooper's tail, and Gendebien and Allison were involved with Schell and Ireland's Lotus in the second bunch. From laps 10 to 20 the two

Above and above right In preparation for the 1959 US GP at Sebring, Ferrari modified three of their cars with coil-and-wishbone independent rear suspension and built up one, a short-wheelbase de Dion model, with a two-cam 246 engine providing little more than 255 bhp outright but with much improved mid-range torque. The cars are shown here in the factory while work was under way. Note the two-cam engine retained the left-side offset at this time. Forged wishbone front suspension is visible, together with the rear-calipered mildly drilled Dunlop brake disc

Right Richie Ginther impressed Ferrari with his first test laps at Modena Autodrome and is seen here with the two-cam de Dion car '0006', which Phil Hill drove in American blue and white national colours at Sebring. The enormous induction cowl and sagbacked tail show clearly

American Ferrari drivers and Moss ran unchanged, having sized each other up, and the Englishman was relaxed, for he knew the Dinos were wearing out their tyres faster than his Cooper. This game of cat-and-mouse continued until lap 33, when Hill was called in for new rear tyres, and despite a very quick stop he fell back to fourth. Next time round Gurney changed all four wheels so Moss was alone, with Allison a distant second. When he stopped to change tyres on lap 36 the Ferrari bolt was shot, since Gendebien was out of contact and he too had to change tyres on lap 38. Ferrari were waiting for Moss to change, but he was running comfortably non-stop and paced himself home to an easy victory. Hill was second ahead of Brabham, while Gurney was fourth, and Allison and Gendebien were fifth and sixth—and lapped. Hill set fastest lap, on the lap before his tyre stop, at 1:40.4, 206.175 km/h (128.11 mph). If only Brooks's clutch had survived. . . .

81

The World Championship-deciding Grand Prix was the first United States event, held at Sebring on 12 December. The three leading teams, Cooper Cars, Walker Racing and Scuderia Ferrari all made the long trip; the Italian team taking four cars for Brooks, Hill, Allison and the back-in-favour Wolfgang von Trips. In the Drivers' Championship Brabham led with 31 points from Moss's 25½ and Brooks's 23.

The Dinos presented a rare combination in Florida. Three carried 246/256 four-cam engines, but were fitted with prototype independent rear suspensions, taking a leaf out of the British constructors' book with a double-wishbone system in which the A-arms were rigidly cross-braced, sprung by co-axial coil/damper units picking up behind the axle line, whose top mounts were outrigged on either side of the frame. An enlarged version of the 196S-type two-cam V6 engine was mounted in a de Dion-axled F2 chassis for Phil Hill, this car being painted in American national colours of blue and white for the occasion. If one is to believe contemporary reports two of the four-cam Dinos used 'regular' F1 frames while the third had a 10 cm longer 'F1' frame. In any case Brooks and Trips took the two shorter F1 cars and Allison the mysterious 'long car' alongside Hill's two-cam special, which was hoped to have more mid-range torque for this stop-go circuit.

Ferrari continued to be troubled by transitional under- and oversteer during practice, emerging with Brooks quickest on the inside of the second row at 3 min 5.9 sec, comparing poorly with Moss's Cooper pole of 3 minutes dead. Row three carried the other three cars, Trips, Allison and Hill, with 3:06.2, 3:06.8 and 3:07.2 respectively. Brooks's place was hotly disputed, Tavoni sure he should have been third on the front row,

Ferraris leave the line at Sebring, Brooks alongside Maurice Trintignant's Walker Cooper on the second row of the grid, with Hill's two-cam US-liveried special, Allison and Trips on row three. Halfway round this first lap Brooks found 'a kerfuffle at a tight right-hand corner and I had to take the escape road and got thumped from behind by Trips....' Always a thoughtful racing driver—indeed many felt Brooks was too intelligent to be racing at all—Tony stopped at his pit to check damage and lost his World Championship chance. At Silverstone in 1956 he had suffered painful injuries when pressing on in a damaged BRM. He did not forget that lesson

but the organizers placed Harry Schell's Cooper there in his stead.

On the opening lap Brooks's chances evaporated when he was rammed by Trips, and pulled into his pit to check for damage. Hill was running fourth and Allison seventh in pursuit of Moss, Brabham and McLaren, all in Coopers, but Phil lasted only nine laps before his special lost its clutch and he was forced to retire. Allison was running comfortably third behind McLaren and Brabham after Moss's transmission failed yet again, but after twenty-three laps the Yorkshireman was out with his Ferrari defunct after sounding sick for some time. Trips was running well despite his car's crushed nose cone, but as the leading works Coopers barked into their last lap the German's V6 engine broke and he coasted to a halt before the finish line, ready to push over when the flag came out, while a pool of oil spread beneath his car. Brabham ran out of fuel on that lap, allowing his team-mate Bruce McLaren to go by and score his maiden Grand Prix victory by half a second from Trintignant's Walker car. Brabham was pushing his silent Cooper towards the line when Brooks appeared and blared by to snatch third place, but Brabham's points for fourth gave him the World Driver's Championship to add to Charles and John Cooper's Constructors' crown. Trips pushed over, but the organizers refused to allow his last lap, which demoted him to sixth in the final result.

The Cooper–Climax World Championship success set the seal on what has become known as Grand Prix racing's 'rear-engined revolution'. In 1960 the Ferrari Dinos were to become the ultimate front-engined Grand Prix cars, but Maranello's own revolution was slowly on the way....

1960   Rearguard action

Before 1959 had ended Ferrari announced their 1960 version of the Dino 196S 2-litre sports-racing car, which differed principally from the 1959 prototype in having right-hand instead of left-hand drive. The car was also fitted with a new full-height windscreen in response to new CSI regulations, which were to prove very unpopular with the drivers, causing problems of parallax and cockpit fumes. The V6 engine was slightly *désaxe*, angled across the frame from right-front to left-rear, effectively to balance driver-weight as in the TRs. It was still rated nominally at 195 bhp at 7800 rpm.

One car was prepared for the Dino sports-racers' first appearance in 1960. It was the *Tipo* 544 Sport chassis '0778', which appeared in Buenos Aires for the 1000 Km race on 31 January. It carried an 85 mm × 71 mm, 2417.33 cc two-cam 246S engine derived directly from that used by Hill at Sebring the previous month. The works specification sheet for the car reveals test-bed figures for the engine peaking at 248.8 bhp at 7500 rpm with as much as 232 bhp at 6500. Even at 5500 rpm it still produced 199.8 bhp. Test figures stop at 244.9 bhp at 7900 rpm. This was engine '169 No. 4'. The car's wheelbase was listed as 2160 mm (85.0 in), front track 1245 mm (49.0 in) and rear track 1205 mm (47.45 in); it was shorter but had wider track than its 1959 '196S' predecessor. In the Argentine it was entrusted to Ludovico Scarfiotti and the Argentinian veteran Jose Froilan Gonzalez. He was very enthusiastic about it, praising its 'fine handling and remarkable power' and emphasizing that it rode far more comfortably than its larger sisters. It ran fourth behind Dan Gurney's leading Maserati and the works Ferrari V12s of Phil Hill and Richie Ginther before retiring with ignition problems after thirty-nine laps.

At Sebring at the end of March, the Dino 196S of Ricardo and Pedro Rodriguez ran very strongly in the 12-Hours race, lapping very rapidly and lying fourth before a series of stops with drive-line problems ended in retirement due to clutch failure.

On 8 May the incredible Targa Florio race around the Madonie Mountains in Sicily saw three Dinos fielded by the factory, including the Rodriguez brothers' car. The leading works entry was a 246S modified with coil-and-wishbone independent rear suspension as developed for the Formula 1 *monoposti*, and entrusted to Phil Hill and 'Taffy' von Trips. The works' second car was a new rigid-axle 246S for Willy

The Mexican madmen, Pedro and Ricardo Rodriguez, hammered their Chinetti-operated Dino 196S '0776' home seventh in the 1960 Targa Florio, despite a body-crushing double roll-over en route! Here Ricardo, the younger of these two youthful brothers, pushes the long-

Mairesse/Scarfiotti/Cabianca, while the Mexican boys' car was '0776', the 196S, also with a live axle. One of the boys bent its tail in practice, and in the race, although Bonnier/Herrmann proved uncatchable in their nimble 1630 cc Porsche RS60, the Trips/Hill Dino '0784' was placed second and its same-size sister '0778' was fourth. The Mexicans' 2-litre car meanwhile had a torrid time, Ricardo bending both ends early in the race, his brother Pedro spending minutes finding his way out of an olive grove into which he had fallen, and then having a remarkable accident, rolling it over twice to land on its wheels and find it still driveable. After some panel-bashing in the mountains he brought it back to the pits, handed over to Ricardo and the battered wreck was driven home in seventh place....

The sports cars next turned out for the Nürburgring 1000 km on 22 May, where the independent rear suspension '0784' was shared by new works tester Paul Richie Ginther and Scarfiotti and the live-axle '0778' by Scarlatti and Cabianca. The Rodriguez brothers ran their works-prepared North American Racing Team-backed 2-litre 196S. During the first refuelling stops the Ferrari crew contrived to set fire to Scarlatti and his car in a sensational incident which briefly threatened the whole pit row. Scarlatti escaped with mild burns on his left hand, but the car was a carbonized wreck. The second 246S lost its water, while the Rodriguez brothers challenged strongly against the Porsches in the 2-litre class until their engine failed.

All this time the works 250TR V12s had been running very strongly and the overtaxed racing shop at Maranello was really hard pressed to lavish the Dinos with the careful preparation required for arduous

suffering little car through the Cerda pit area
The 196S had a 60° two-cam engine of Ferrari's second generation, like the 246S sister cars in 1960. A 276S V6 of 90 × 71 mm, 2710.09 cc was also available, giving 255 bhp at 7500 rpm

Both left The ex-Rodriguez '0776' in Rob Walker's far more sympathetic hands; showing the functional cockpit and the two-cam 2-litre engine with its massive cam-covers lettered in the Dino script. The 'bed-knob' cam-cover grips were typically Ferrari. The engine was offset slightly across the frame to balance driver weight. This practice was common to the Testa Rossas and mid-engined SPs

Below left, below and right Jesse Alexander's picture of the Scarlatti fire exploding in the Nürburgring pits in 1960 has often been published, but the second shot showing Stirling Moss racing with others to the Italian driver's aid is seldom reproduced. The Rodriguez brothers' '0776' is hastily wheeled to safety, while *Tipo* 544 '0778' burns. On the pit roof a refuelling system attendant looks on, chin on hand, apparently unmoved. With new wheels and tyres fitted to allow movement, '0778' looked a sorry sight. It was actually rebuilt

long-distance racing, and no Dinos were entered for Le Mans—effective end of the Sports Car Championship season—in which other Ferraris placed 1–2–4–5–6–7.

The Formula 1 Argentine Grand Prix was revived on 7 February 1960, as the opening round of the new year's World Championship, and Ferrari were ready with four cars. Dan Gurney had read the rear-engined writing on the wall, and having seen BRM's prototype mid-engined car on test at Monza before the Italian Grand Prix he had talked to them about the coming year. When they offered better money terms than the parsimonious Mr Ferrari, Dan made the move. The loyal Phil Hill stayed behind, and he was joined for the Argentine race by von Trips and Cliff Allison, while a guest drive was given to Froilan Gonzalez, who had won Grands Prix for Ferrari in 1951 and 1954.

Phil's Buenos Aires car carried a two-cam 246 engine for the second time, apparently mounted in his Sebring short-wheelbase (2220 mm, 87.4 in) chassis '0006', but this time set back some 25 cm (9.8 in) from its '59 position closer to the centre of the wheelbase. In a further move to improve weight distribution, kill some of the front-engined cars' understeer and make them more amenable to sudden changes of direction, much of the fuel load was concentrated in deep but slim pannier tanks on either side of the cockpit. An additional tank remained in the tail, along with the oil tank. Phil's two-cam Argentine special had these pannier tanks exposed.

Meanwhile the Trips and Allison cars both ran four-cam 246 engines, similarly moved back in the chassis and now angled the other way across the frame from left-front to right-rear, passing the propshaft through intermediate bearings low to the right of the cockpit. The very compact and relatively lightweight 1959 final-drive/gearbox assembly was turned about-face and its internals revised to provide a right-side instead of left-side power input. The gearchange moved to the left side of the cockpit, and adopted a real brain-teaser pattern just to test the drivers. The 1959 de Dion slide survived on the final-drive casing, but now faced forward—and empty—right behind the driver's seat. Both these cars shrouded their pannier tanks in Fantuzzi body panelling very reminiscent of the 1954 *Squalo* model 2.5-litre Ferraris. Chiti had realized the error of promoting top-end performance at the expense of mid-range torque, and these 1960 four-cams were rated at 275 bhp at 8500 rpm with 'better punch at low revs'. Hill's two-cam was rated at around 255 bhp and would presumably have resembled the 246S sports-racer's power curve. Finally Gonzalez drove the 1959 model which Brooks had used at Sebring, '0004', with minor tankage modification and a four-cam motor, and not surprisingly set the early pace in practice on this his home circuit. Final grid positions saw three Ferraris on the second row, Trips, Hill and Allison, with Gonzalez on row three. It was the first-ever Argentine Grand Prix without a Ferrari on the front row, which was occupied by Moss's Cooper, Ireland's sensationally fast new mid-engined Lotus 18 and the front-engined BRMs of Graham Hill and Jo Bonnier. Phil Hill drove hard in fifth place behind the British cars early on, but fell back

Top Cliff Allison drove consistently quickly in the Argentine GP opening the 1960 season at Buenos Aires to finish second in this bulbous enclosed side-tank car '0001'. In these cars the engine offset was altered to the right- instead of the left-hand side and the V6 was moved back bodily in the frame while fuel tankage was concentrated on either side of the cockpit within the wheelbase

Below, left and right The prototype 1960 side-tanked right-side offset engine F2 car won at Syracuse in March and is shown here subsequently at Monza, on 27 April, still bearing its Syracuse numbers though fitted with a 246 F1 engine, where it was tested against the Argentine 'semi-Squalo' enclosed side-tank right-side offset car shown head-on. The F2 layout was an improvement.

behind Allison, who seemed impervious to the heat that day. Profiting by retirements McLaren won in his works Cooper, while Allison came home second, Trips was fifth, and Phil Hill a troubled eighth. Gonzalez had a long delay with tyre problems and finished tenth and last.

The European season commenced on 19 March with the Formula 2 Syracuse Grand Prix and Ferrari entered a lone prototype Dino 156/60 for 'Taffy' von Trips. This little car—inheriting the Formula 2 chassis number '0011'—was based on a 2160 mm (85 in) wheelbase, big-tube frame, carried its four-cam 1476.60 cc engine raked left-front to right-rear providing a right-side prop-shaft feeding an about-face gearbox-cum-final drive and housed its fuel in exposed strap-on pannier tanks either side of the cockpit.

The team juggled with alternative exhaust tail-pipes in practice, both low-level systems, but one terminating under the tail and giving better top-end power while the other terminated just ahead of the rear axle and provided extra mid-range torque, which was expected to be helpful out of Syracuse's slower corners. Trips preferred the longer pipes with their top-end edge, and qualified fifth on row two of the grid with a time of 1 min 59.0 sec, compared to Moss's pole time of 1:57.6 with his Walker-entered Porsche 718 flat-four.

In the race Moss led handsomely from a battle between Trips, Brabham's Cooper and Ireland's new Lotus 18. The Dino 156 was easily fastest on the straights, but both English cars caught it under braking despite the new ventilated discs it was using, and Ireland could pass both the Cooper and the Ferrari through the corners, but lost time with a tricky gear-change. Brabham hit trouble, and Trips was second ahead of Ireland when rain began to fall and Moss found the Porsche a real handful. With a delirious Sicilian crowd cheering him on Trips closed up and on lap 26 of the fifty-six laps distance the Porsche dropped a valve and the pretty red Ferrari led. Once Ireland made a pit stop Trips was left

untroubled and he won as he pleased by 19 seconds from Trintignant's Cooper.

After this success the Syracuse 156 was returned to the works and fitted with a 246 engine for comparative tests at Monza with one of the 1959-based Argentine cars. On the results of these tests Carlo Chiti advised that the season's new Formula 1 cars be based on the 156/60 layout.

Ferrari abstained from further Formula racing until 14 May, when two new Dino 246/60s were entered for Phil Hill and Cliff Allison in the BRDC International Trophy race at Silverstone. Practice was wet and marred by the death of Harry Schell in a Yeoman Credit team Cooper. Moss, inevitably, was on pole with a Cooper on 1:50.4 with the mid-engined BRMs of Bonnier and Gurney beside him, flanked on the outside by Phil Hill's Dino with 1:55.6. Allison was seventh qualifier on the outside of row two on 1:56.2. In the race neither Dino driver could do anything about the new mid-engined cars and while Ireland scored a magnificent victory in his Lotus 18, hastily rebuilt after a practice accident, Hill could only manage a lapped fifth place and Allison was

Left Phil Hill on the outside of the front grid row at Spa in '0007'—the Dino looking handsome but antiquated alongside the mid-engined Cooper-Climaxes of Brooks (Yeoman Credit) and Brabham (works' lowline) on pole. Note the X-braced rear wishbones on the Dino and its angled engine mounting. This car survives today, owned by Neil Corner in England

Above Monaco 1960 first lap with Trips's short-chassis '0011' scuttling round the Gasworks Hairpin ahead of team mate Richie Ginther in the important prototype mid-engined Ferrari '0008'. Graham Hill's BRM (number 6) and Surtees's Lotus 18 (26) add scale and perspective to the new Ferrari, which owed more to Cooper practice, like the car outside it. It is particularly noticeable how Ginther is seated very little lower — considering his own diminutive stature — than the tall von Trips ahead of him, and how Surtees and Hill's cars are lower-slung still

eighth, another lap down. Cliff had made a stop to repair a crumpled nose cone, which was causing overheating, and Hill's tail was dented....

Two weeks later, on 29 May, the Monaco Grand Prix saw Moss scoring Lotus's first-ever *Grande Epreuve* victory in the brand-new car bought for him by Rob Walker after Ireland's International Trophy demonstration. Ferrari brought three of the new side-tanked Dinos for Hill, Trips and Allison and more significantly an experimental mid-engined car which had only turned its wheels for the first time the previous Sunday. It was entrusted to Richie Ginther and consisted of a new multi-tubular Cooper-style frame picking up double-wishbone independent suspension like that of the front-engined cars. The front anti-roll bar passed through a chassis cross-member, and the rear wishbones carried cast-alloy instead of fabricated steel uprights. The standard four-cam Dino 246 engine had twin-coil and distributor ignition and was in unit with a brand-new five-speed and reverse gearbox in unit with the final drive and carrying an overhung clutch on its rear end. The preceding gearbox/final-drive aggregate of the front-engined cars could not be used in a practical mid-engined layout, and the new

Ferrari overhung in-line transmission used three-shaft design. From the 246 engine, mounted centrally and square in the frame, a primary shaft passed beneath the final-drive to a set of quick-change spur gears at the rear. They spaced the second motion shaft to the right-hand side (viewed from the rear of course) and the exposed clutch was carried on the rear of this shaft, offset from the engine centreline. Drive from this second motion shaft transmitted to the third, set more centrally and higher, the front end of which carried the final-drive bevel pinion. Dunlop disc brakes with radial drillings were mounted outboard at the front and inboard on the final-drive cheeks at the rear. Wheels were 15-inch Borrani centre-lock wires with Dunlop 5.25-15 front and 6.50-15 rear tyres. Wheelbase was 2300 mm (90.6 in)—some 3 inches longer than that of the front-engined 246/60s—and track 1200 mm (47.2 in) front and rear. Weight was quoted at 550 kg (1213 lb), less fuel and driver.

Chiti was experimenting with the effect of wheelbase on weight distribution in the front-engined cars, Trips running the 216 cm F2 chassis '0011', Hill a 222 cm wheelbase Formula 1 frame, '0003'* and Cliff a full 232 cm frame, '0004'.

During Friday practice Trips's Syracuse Dino broke the rear of its chassis and poor Allison crashed very heavily at the chicane, somersaulting his car after clipping the straw bales and being flung out. He was picked up unconscious and was taken to hospital quite badly hurt. Practice ended with Moss's brand-new Lotus 18 on pole, alone in the 1 min 36 sec bracket, while the Ferraris were grouped in mid-grid; Trips best placed on the outside of the third row, eighth-quickest qualifier with 1:38.3, and Ginther and Hill behind him, having both lapped in 1:38.6, the diminutive crew-cut Ginther having looked particularly happy in his mid-engined experimental car during his first GP practice sessions.

On the second race lap Trips had to stop to beat out an oil fire in his car's undertray, sparked by its short 'high-torque' exhaust pipes, while Bonnier's BRM led with Moss, Brabham, Brooks (Cooper) and Phil Hill behind him. Ginther was driving sensibly at the tail of the field, but by one-third distance rain was falling and Hill spun at the Gasworks Hairpin, but managed to keep his engine running. He rejoined sixth, with Trips a long way back seventh and Ginther still eleventh and last . . . and lapped. Interest centred on Phil Hill and he moved into third place, but he could not fight off McLaren's Cooper, which he eventually had to allow past. When Bonnier stopped, this Ferrari/Cooper duel was for second place, but just at the end Phil was baulked by a back-marker and settled for third. Ginther made a stop to enquire about 'grumbling noises' from his car's transmission, and pushed across the finish line for sixth place, thirty laps behind Moss. Trips's clutch failed after sixty-two laps.

The Dutch Grand Prix on 6 June at Zandvoort saw Ferrari having their usual problems. While the mid-engined prototype was run briefly in practice, the team fielded their three conventional Dino 246s for Hill, Trips and Ginther. They were the only front-engined cars to make the race, the Aston Martins and Scarabs scratching, and qualified twelfth, thirteenth and fifteenth, Ginther quickest on the centre of row five with

*See notes an these chassis, Appendix page 304.

Right Phil Hill hurtling round Monaco in his *Tipo 546* 2220 mm 1959-wheelbase car '0003', showing off its handsome Fantuzzi fish-mouth despite the onset of practicality rather than styling in the strap-on side tanks. Compare the proportions of this car with those of Trips's 2160 mm '0011' and the extra wheelbase length becomes apparent. The car which Allison crashed in practice at Monte Carlo was longer yet, by 100 mm, and this 2320 mm wheelbase was to become standard

Below 'Taffy' von Trips looks for the source of trouble at Monaco 1960 and is about to abandon his 2160 mm short-wheelbase chassis '0011', though he has covered sufficient race distance to be classified eighth. The tiny build of the Formula 2-chassised Syracuse car is very apparent in this beautiful Yves Debraine picture. It shows the new engine offset, and the 'Z'-form rear wishbones and single-filler (oil tank only) tail of this Formula 2 chassis. The F1 frames carried 'X'-braced top rear wishbones most of the season and had a supplementary tail fuel tank ahead of the oil reservoir.

Richie Ginther was youngest of three children, born in Hollywood, California. Just after his birth his family moved to Dayton, Ohio, then back to Santa Monica in 1935. Eleven years later diminutive little Richie was driving around in a 1932 Chevvy when he met a fraternity friend of his older brother; his name was Phil Hill.

In 1948 Richie joined Douglas Aircraft, where his father worked, and 18 months later he became a mechanic at International Motors, then moved on for better pay as Bill Cramer's mechanic and occasional driver. In 1951 he made his race debut in Cramer's MG TC-Ford, but on his 21st birthday he was taken into the US Army and spent two years as a helicopter mechanic—some of the time in Korea.

On his discharge in 1953 Ginther became manager of a foreign car shop, renewed his friendship with Phil Hill and became his co-pilot in the *Carrera Panamericana*. In 1955 he travelled with Hill to Le Mans, then returned to manage John von Neumann's Ferrari agency in California, racing Ferraris and Porsches on occasion. Chinetti fostered his career as he had Hill's, and Ginther made his Le Mans debut in 1957—his Ferrari *Testa Rossa* running second in class when it failed.

By 1959 he was the most successful Ferrari driver in the USA and in 1960 won a Ferrari factory contract, and became their official chief test driver. . . .

After leaving Ferrari he drove for BRM in 1962–64 but never showed the fire necessary to win major races, and in 1965 he led the Honda team and won the last 1.5-litre Formula 1 race, at Mexico City. In 1966 he handled Cooper-Maseratis and in 1967 Eagles as Dan Gurney's number two, but when he could not qualify for Monaco, nor for Indianapolis he realized it was time to stop—and he retired.

Paul Richard Ginther
b. 5 August, 1930

1 min 36.3 sec, Hill alongside him with 1:36.4, and Trips behind on 1:36.7. Moss's Lotus 18 pole time was 1:33.2. Hill ran a new 2320 mm-framed car '0005', Trips took over Phil's Monaco 2220 mm '0004' and Ginther had a second 2320 mm car, '0006' . . . according to Ferrari.

Hill made a tremendous start and was fifth at the end of the first lap, and became involved in a dice with Gurney's BRM and young Chris Bristow's Yeoman Credit Cooper. After various alarums and excursions, Brabham held the lead with the three Ferraris running 6–7–8 in the order Hill, Ginther and von Trips. Phil slowed due to erratic throttle control and Ginther conceded sixth place to Trips, but was pacing along behind him quite comfortably. On lap 41 Hill stopped for attention to his car's carburetters, and Moss (recovering ground after an early delay) caught and passed Ginther and Trips. When Hill rejoined, his engine was cutting violently in and out and eventually after fifty-five laps he gave up. Brabham ran out the seventy-five laps the winner in his works lowline Cooper-Climax, while Trips and Ginther finished lapped but fifth and sixth overall.

The scene shifted to Spa–Francorchamps for the super-fast Belgian Grand Prix on 19 June, and Ferrari were present with three Dino 246s for Hill, Trips and the Belgian Willy Mairesse. Hill was in his element on the high-speed open curves of the Ardennes and although the Dino's chassis deficiencies prevented him being a true match for the 2.5-litre Coopers, Phil set third quickest time at 3 min 53.3 sec and started on the outside of the front row beside Brooks's Cooper and Brabham's works car

Edward Eves shot V6 engine '0005' *in situ* during 1960. It is evident how far back in these chassis frames the 246 engine was eventually sited in an attempt to approach mid-engined car weight distribution. When chassis '0007' was fitted with a Testa Rossa V12 engine for Tasman racing at the end of the year, only the front crosstube had to be excised, extra braces from the front end of the V12 taking its place. The chassis was not lengthened to accommodate the small-bore 3-litre V12, which of course was not twice as long as the big-bore 2.5-litre V6 which preceded it

on pole at 3:50.0. Unfortunately practice accidents had beset the Lotus 18s, and Moss was in hospital quite badly hurt. Trips was back on row four with 3:57.8, having tried both available Dinos in practice, while Mairesse was on the centre of the next row at 3:58.9. The 2320 mm wheelbase was now standard.

Hill drove tremendously hard in the opening stages to make a race of it with Brabham and several others, and the Australian drew out a slight lead, but Hill was making the pace and forcing him on. After fifteen laps Brabham held a 12-second lead from the Ferrari, while farther back Trips lost a wheel-to-wheel battle with young Chris Bristow's Cooper when he lost the use of his clutch; though he kept going Mairesse moved past him. At half-distance, eighteen laps, Hill was closing on Brabham, with Gendebien, Graham Hill (BRM) and McLaren battling for third place on his heels. Some way behind Mairesse was fighting a desperate duel with Bristow for sixth place and Trips was slowing since a gearbox vibration had begun. On lap 19 Bristow got off line on the daunting Burnenville curve, hit a fence and died in a horrifying accident — ending his duel with Mairesse, who just missed the gyrating wreck. Later in the race Alan Stacey was struck in the face by a bird, his Lotus crashed and he too lost his life.

On lap 24 Mairesse retired abruptly at the pits with transmission failure, and on lap 29 Hill disappeared and had stopped to investigate a cold spray of petrol onto his leg, finding that the capillary tube to the fuel pressure gauge had cracked. The spray ignited, but he managed to douse it, and drove back to the pits, where the crack was sealed as Brabham passed by to lap him. He rejoined and finished fourth, while Trips had retired with a broken drive shaft, which had put him into a big broadside near Stavelot.

Once again Ferrari's hopes were pinned on Reims and the French Grand Prix, fielding three cars for Hill, Trips and Mairesse, although Ginther was around and Tavoni was under pressure to give him the drive. When it was not to be, Ginther rather shocked the Ferrari establishment by doing some laps in Lance Reventlow's Scarabs. Brooks's Ferrari practice record of 2:19.4 was the immediate target, and Phil Hill drove forcefully to clock 2:18.2 for centre place on the three-car front row. Brabham, however, was on pole at 2:16.8, and Phil's namesake Graham in the latest BRM was on the outside, only 0.2 second slower than the front-engined Ferrari. Mairesse was fifth quickest on row two, having been credited with 2:19.3, although his factual best time had been 2.3 seconds slower — and he should have been back on the fifth row. Trips's genuine 2:19.4 put him on the inside of row three.

At the completion of the first lap Hill and Trips were second and third, hard on Brabham's heels amongst a wheel-to-wheel slipstreaming bunch, with Mairesse sixth across the timing line. On the second lap the timekeepers singled out Trips for a new lap record in 2:19.6, and by lap three the bunch had split apart, Brabham with a modest lead and Trips and Hill together and almost touching, clear of the rest. On lap 4 Hill had snatched the lead, and Brabham was being harried by Trips, and so it went on between these three, the Ferrari pair asking and giving no quarter with Brabham and all the time running at speeds approaching 190 mph along the main straights. At one time Brabham felt a jar, glanced in his mirrors and saw Hill's Dino rearing into the air, its air intake buckled out of shape by contact with a Cooper rear wheel, but Phil brought it down to earth safely and pressed on. Trips was holding a watching brief until Hill's braking went awry at Thillois, and he skated round the island, rejoining third behind his team-mate.

Mairesse dropped out of the pursuing bunch on lap 15, when his drive failed at Thillois and he pointlessly attempted to push the car in to the pits. On lap 19 Hill and Brabham slammed past the pits side by side, with

Trips on their tails, and at half-distance the two Italian V6s yowling away at 8400 rpm were still drowning the Climax's 4-cylinder 6800 rpm exhaust note, but the British car had led six consecutive laps past the pits.

On lap 29 Hill's car's input bevel broke just before the pits and he coasted to a stop at the end of the pit-row, ending a terrific piece of full-blooded motor racing. Two laps later Brabham barked out of Thillois alone, for Trips's transmission had failed just like his two team-mates, and for Ferrari the French Grand Prix was over.

16 July saw the British Grand Prix at Silverstone, and Ferrari—disheartened—entered only two Dino 246s, for Hill and Trips, both fitted with Snap exhaust extractors. Neither was at home on the airfield circuit's medium-fast corners, yawing wildly from lock to lock to match the mid-engined Coopers, Lotuses and BRMs.

Brabham was again dominant, taking pole at 1:34.6, while Trips was rewarded for a desperate practice effort by seventh spot on the outside of the second row at 1:37.0, and Hill was tenth quickest on row three with 1:37.8. This was understandably depressing, and as the race took shape the two Ferraris ran eighth and ninth in the second bunch of cars chasing the leading group, and they fought their cars home, profiting by retirements ahead to finish sixth and seventh, Trips ahead of Hill, and both lapped twice by Brabham, scoring his third consecutive *Grande Epreuve* victory of the season.

The following weekend Ferrari entered their mid-engined experimental car in extensively revised Dino 156 Formula 2 form for the annual *Solituderennen* on the superb public road circuit just outside Stuttgart, with a conventional front-engined Dino 156 in support. Phil Hill had the conventional car, von Trips the experimental.

Chiti had been working on the Jano V6 in its 70 mm × 64.5 mm Formula 2 Tipo 156 trim, and he evolved a second-series version with bore and stroke dimensions of 73 mm × 58.8 mm (1476.60 cc) while the shorter stroke reduced corrected piston speed at 9000 rpm to 3860 ft/min from the original unit's 3970 ft/min. In this form the V6 (with 'Dino 156' lettered cast cam-boxes) used 38 mm Weber carburetters and produced around 180 bhp and this was more than adequate in Formula 2 racing against the 145–160 horsepower of the Climax and Porsche brigade.

Modifications to this mid-engined car had reworked the suspension, repositioning new-pattern wishbones on the chassis frame, although the actual system-type was unaltered. The 1500 cc four-cam 156 engine was mated to the five-speed transaxle with inboard brake discs used at Monaco and in Zandvoort practice, but instead of the clutch-operating mechanism being mounted on the rear chassis cross-member it was now on an alloy casing bolted to the rear of the gearbox case and hooking round the left side of the clutch body, which was still exposed. The chassis tube extensions beyond the gearbox had consequently been cut short. There was no water header tank above the engine so the high head fairing was removed and replaced by a flat engine cowl with a front-opening Perspex bubble over the carburetters. The car's tail ended in an aperture fitted with a neat six-bar grille, and two slender megaphone exhausts protruded far back from beneath the rear suspension. The car's

Adelmo Marchetti motoring the revised and partially rebodied experimental mid-engined car '0008' through the Solitude paddock during the Formula 2 meeting in July 1960, which von Trips dominated in this car. Compare with the Monaco GP start picture on page 91. The transaxle gearbox/final-drive of this car had provision for electric starting, as would be required by 1500 cc Formula 1 regulations in the coming year. At this time the British teams were still arguing the toss, trying to side-step the Formula change, while Ferrari was quietly getting on with the job. The horrible welding of the 'Cooper-tube' chassis is typical of Ferraris of this period. On the extreme right the chassis plate is visible, welded on to the chassis cross-tube. It is legible on the original print as '0008'. Note also the thin but ventilated inboard Dunlop disc brakes on either side of the final-drive housing, and the exposed clutch drum on the end of the gearbox with its cooling holes. Clutch actuation reacts against the rearmost chassis cross-tube in this Monaco photo, the chassis frame being abbreviated and a cast clutch slave cylinder brace being adapted at Solitude

snub nose was much as before and the cockpit was enclosed by a deep-fronted wrap-around windscreen. This was very much a prototype for the 1.5-litre Formula 1 due to take effect in six month's time.

Von Trips tested the car at Modena with the new engine installed two days before the start of practice at Solitude and it was an immediate success. At Solitude in the first very wet practice session Trips found the car felt very safe, and he threw it around in lurid slides with total unconcern. At one time he was an incredible 30 seconds *a lap* faster than anybody else, and he flurried past the works Porsches on this their home circuit and left them standing. In later (drier) practice the car was still very fast, but fast-developing Jimmy Clark took pole in his works Lotus 18 at 4:23.6 and Trips was content with the centre of the front row, 0.5 second slower. Hill was in the middle of row five on 4:48.7, wondering which way his team-mate had gone.

Race distance was twenty laps and it began as a furious sprint with any one of nine cars leading at some point round the course and Trips in amongst them. Clark eventually established himself and drew away until lap 9, when his water temperature rose alarmingly and Herrmann's Porsche was closing in second place with Trips's experimental Ferrari on its tail. Ending lap 10 Clark boiled into the pits and Herrmann led from Trips, while eight cars in a wheel-to-wheel bunch flashed by 'third', including Hill's conventional Dino 156.

Herrmann and Trips proceeded to set progressive fastest laps until, on lap 17, the German Count clocked 4:04.7, which was best of the day and his new Dino fled into the lead. He held it to the finish, beating Herrmann by 3.6 seconds, while Hill was seventh, by half a second, behind Ireland's works Lotus.

Extensive experiments continued, with special mounts being made up to accept Lola/Lotus-type long parallel radius rods. Rear roll stiffness was reduced and the new geometry induced more rear-wheel toe-in. It was replaced on the finalized 1.5-litre chassis design for 1961, though the rear hub carriers were in fact redesigned to provide a degree of permanent toe-in. The same test series saw the car's wishbone front suspension modified, with the same geometry adopted late in the season by the front-engined cars, in which the upper wishbones were angled steeply downwards towards their chassis pivots, so ensuring when in a corner that the outside wheel maintained negative camber throughout its arc; formerly the wheels had adopted positive camber at points in their travel. The rear suspension pivots were also modified to preserve negative camber and to maintain a high rear roll centre, for the front suspension arrangement was said to place the front roll-centre some 5 inches above ground level.

The following week found the teams at Nürburgring for the German Grand Prix, but to give the home Porsche team some chance the organizing AvD club opted for Formula 2, and Ferrari withdrew, opting to send Phil Hill and Ginther instead to Brands Hatch for the fifty-lap Silver City Trophy Formula 1 race on the newly extended 2.65-mile circuit, on the August Bank Holiday Monday.

Ginther qualified thirteenth (on row four) and Hill eighteenth (row five) with times of 1:46.6 and 1:47.4, compared to Clark's Lotus pole time of 1:39.4. It really had become no contest between mid-engined and front-engined Grand Prix cars.

Hill became embroiled in a fourth-place battle with the McLaren and Salvadori Coopers, and driving desperately hard he got the better of them and by lap 30 had lapped Ginther and finished fourth while Richie was ninth, was behind. . . .

In Portugal on 14 August Moss made his comeback in Walker's Lotus, having recovered from his Belgian Grand Prix injuries. Ferrari fielded two of their usual Dino 246s, this time for Hill and Trips. The Oporto circuit record still stood to Hawthorn's Dino 246 in 1958 at 2:32.37, and for a change both Ferraris were running quite well and all things considered were showing better form. Surtees's Lotus 18 took pole at 2:25.56, while fourth row of the grid was Ferrari's with Trips on 2:28.40 and Hill on 2:28.42.

Trips clobbered some straw bales on the opening lap, twisting his car's always vulnerable nose and Phil Hill again showed the fire he had displayed at Brands Hatch, running fourth behind Gurney's leading BRM, Moss and Surtees. On lap 11 Gurney backed off as he thought his car was sliding on its own oil, and Surtees, Moss and Hill slammed by. Slowly the Lotuses outpaced the Ferrari and Brabham's delayed Cooper appeared in Hill's mirror, climbing though the field. Brabham pushed and Hill shoved as the Cooper and Ferrari came alongside each other on lap 24 of the fifty-five, and although the Australian got ahead and showed Hill a great deal of the Cooper's side panels, the American was unimpressed and hacked ahead of him again. On lap 29 the Ferrari's hydraulic clutch actuation failed, and Hill missed a gear, ran wide on a turn and bounced into some straw bales. He limped into the pits with the nose cowling crushed and steering bent, and after an inspection took position ready to push across the finish line when the flag came out. The organizers ordered him to move on, and trying to push-start his car without clutch disengagement exhausted him and so he had to retire. Trips meanwhile had driven as hard as he could, and kept pace with the leaders and finished fourth, Brabham winning his fifth consecutive Grand Prix of the season and clinching his and Cooper's World Championship titles.

The Italian Grand Prix was run under a cloud as the organizers used the combined road and banked speedbowl track, which the British establishment decided they objected to and consequently boycotted. In the absence of works Cooper, Lotus and BRM opposition, the Grand Prix provided some consolation to Ferrari supporters, who loved to see the Prancing Horse in front and winning, regardless of whom they had to beat.

It had been intended to run the mid-engined car at Monza with a full 246 engine installed, but with the British works teams' defection the opportunity was taken to run it again in 1.5-litre trim. The 65-degree short-stroke Chiti engine was reinstalled together with a smaller radiator, which allowed a more slender nose to be adopted for the high-speed track, and air scoops were added to cool both driver and magneto. An

Snapping noses scenting victory at Monza before the 1960 Italian Grand Prix, which the leading British teams all boycotted because the controversial banked speedbowl track section was being used. These are chassis '0007' (number 20 for Phil Hill the winner), '0003' for Richie Ginther, number 18, who finished second, and '0006' for Willy Mairesse, number 16, who finished third

Mairesse dutifully doing his job of 'towing' von Trips's Dino 156-engined '0008' Formula 2 car along in fourth place during the 1960 Italian GP at Monza

Having blotted his copybook by stopping to check tyre wear, a slipstream-begrimed von Trips and '0008' are waved out of the Ferrari pit by Dunlop tyre engineer Vic Barlow, while Marchetti, Vecchi, Chiti, Amadessi and the team look on. This photograph was taken by a brave Ami Guichard, Swiss publisher of the annual *Automobile Year*

Above The Drama of a Ferrari pit-stop, again at Monza, 1960, this time with Phil Hill's winning Ferrari being serviced. Pasquale Cassani drops the badly worn left rear to the ground while Ener Vecchi spins on the right-rear hub-nut—Phil Hill looks well wound up in the cockpit and Marchetti and Barlow consult up front. The right-side tail-starter socket is visible just inboard of the Snap exhaust extractor

Below left Fish on the banking; Trips at speed during the 1960 Italian GP in which he finished fifth and won the F2 class by miles. The 'Prova Mo 53' number on the car's tail was a road-test registration used for public-road work around the factory and between Maranello and the Modena Autodrome

auxiliary fuel tank was fitted to enable the car to run non-stop.

SEFAC Ferrari entered three front-engined Dino 246s for Hill, Mairesse and Ginther, all with stiffened chassis, while the Solitude-winning mid-engined 156 was entered in the make-weight Formula 2 class for von Trips.

High-spot of practice was when Enzo Ferrari himself, on his annual visit to Italian Grand Prix practice, was ejected from the pit area by one of the notorious Monza police, because he did not have the correct pass. Uproar ensued, and the Ferraris only resumed practice after fulsome personal apologies from the track authorities. Reputedly the policeman was last seen locked in his own jail.

Phil Hill took pole at 2:41.4 from Ginther on 2:43.3 and Mairesse with 2:43.9. Trips was fastest F2 runner, on the inside of the third row with 2:51.9. At least Trips was opposed by works F2 Porsches for Hans Herrmann and Edgar Barth, and as Ginther led as planned from Hill, so Mairesse fell back to give Trips a 'tow'. Ferrari planned to run 1–2–3–4 in this way, but Giulio Cabianca spoiled their plan with his Scuderia Castellotti Cooper-Ferrari (using an old 4-cylinder engine) and he stormed round, splitting the team in third place. His team-mate Gino Munaron caused further embarrassment by splitting Trips from Mairesse's slipstream, and on lap 16, when Ginther stopped for a rapid rear-tyre change, the two Cooper chassis were showing the Italian crowd what they could do. Next time round Hill stopped and changed both rear wheels and the right front. Mairesse made an identical change, leaving

Trips all on his own though far ahead of the Porsches, and when Cabianca and Munaron made stops, half-distance (twenty-five laps) found Ginther leading Hill and—by one lap—von Trips, while Brian Naylor's JBW-Maserati special was fourth ahead of the rapidly closing Mairesse. On lap 26 Hill retook the lead, Ginther was towing Trips though the German was a whole lap behind, and Mairesse was fourth. Ginther expected the Belgian to take over the job of giving Trips a slipstream to ride in, but Mairesse had had enough of pussy-footing around to team orders and he blasted straight by. Richie responded and stormed back, so poor Trips was left all on his own, wondering if it was something he'd said. . . . Ginther assumed Mairesse had been a whole lap behind him, but he wasn't taking any chances.

The 246 Ferraris made their second tyre stops very slickly, and Trips halted to allow the Dunlop tyre technicians to check his rear tyre wear. He was hurried back into the race without a change, but his stop had allowed Cabianca to retake fourth place, spoiling the Ferrari display. As the mid-engined Ferrari covered the whole fifty laps without refuelling, this stop was an unfortunate decision by the German.

With eight laps left Mairesse hustled in to inform Tavoni and Chiti that his transmission was making awful noises, and then Phil Hill had finished, winning his first Grand Prix and the first for an American driver since Jimmy Murphy and Duesenberg in the 1921 French race. More important, he set a new record race average of 132.07 mph in the process.

End of an era; the last front-engined Ferrari single-seater made its swansong appearance in the Formula 2 Modena GP on 20 October, 1960. Here it is (number 26, chassis '0011') parked behind its replacement, the mid-engined 156 '0008'. Richie Ginther, who drove '0011' home into a fighting second place behind the winning Porsche, sits on the pit counter, back to Pete Coltrin's camera

Ginther drove excellently into second place, while Mairesse was third one lap down and Trips easily won the F2 section, fifth overall.

It was the Dino 246's last Championship Grand Prix, since Ferrari did not enter the United States Grand Prix, ending the season and the 2.5-litre Formula, at Riverside. The cars went out on a high note, but if there had been worthwhile opposition would it have been so?

The future was foretold in the season's one remaining F2 race....

This swansong for the front-engined Dino came in the sixth Modena Grand Prix run for Formula 2 cars on 2 October. Ferrari entered their experimental mid-engined car once again for von Trips with the now unconventional front-engined Dino 156 in support for Ginther. Three works Porsches and Moss in a private Lotus-Climax provided major opposition. This was Ferrari's home ground and they were determined to recoup some of their waning prestige, but the single Saturday practice session ended with Bonnier's Porsche on pole in 59.2 seconds, flanked by Moss on 59.3 with Trips's mid-engined Dino outside him at 59.4. Ginther was sixth quickest with 60.5.

The Porsches of Edgar Barth and Bonnier led Moss and Trips from the flag with Ginther sixth, but Trips quickly took second place as Barth and Moss fell back, and almost immediately Ginther blared past them all to chase Bonnier's Porsche, catching and passing it to tremendous acclaim from the Modenese crowd. The Ferraris were running first and second on home ground when Moss began to close, only for the Lotus's

Modena, 28 September, 1960: Luigi Bazzi watches Ginther on test in the mid-engined prototype '0008'

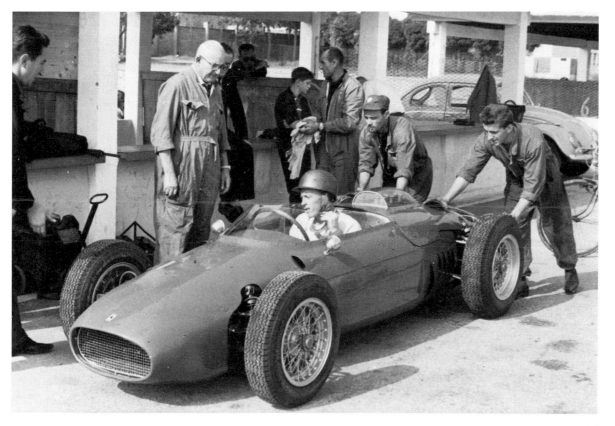

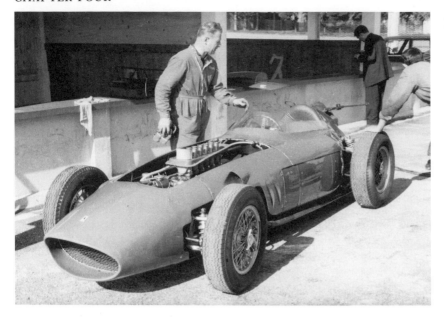

Modena, 26 October, 1960: Adelmo Marchetti tends Hill's Italian GP-winning car '0007' in re-engined Tasman form using the Testa Rossa 3-litre V12 engine '0788' on test at Modena—the car being bound for Pat Hoare in New Zealand. Pat Hoare was said to have a good relationship with Ferrari since his wartime experiences in this part of Italy with the Allied Armies. Contemporary Kiwi rumour had it that he had either saved Mr Ferrari from the Germans or had ordered a hold-fire just as artillery was ranging-in on the Maranello works

Anthony Bamford's JCB Excavators Ltd company raced this exhibition-prepared 222 cm wheelbase car—probably '0003'—in British historic events in 1978. Here the car is under preparation at David Clarke's Graypaul Motors, Loughborough

engine to fail. On lap 22 Ginther braked early at the end of the main straight and waved Trips by, and for the next twenty-four laps the Dinos continued their 1–2 demonstration, until Bonnier found second wind, displaced Ginther and hared after Trips. On lap 60 the silver car took the lead, only for Trips to repass, and they began swopping the lead between them—the crowd almost fighting each other in their excitement. With eight of the 100 laps remaining Trips hit trouble with failing brakes and slowed, allowing Bonnier to get away into a secure lead and win easily, gaining Porsche's revenge for Monza. Ginther caught and passed the mid-engined car on lap 97 and so the front-engined Dinos' career ended, with second place on the circuit where they had first been brought to life, four seasons before. Trips was third in the Dino of the future. . . .

The stripped chassis frame of '0788' née '0007' (the *Tipo* 546 design) in 1979 during its rebuild in V12 Tasman trim for new owner Neil Corner. The top chassis tubes had been cut to allow the fitting of a two-seat GT 'O' for 'Orrible body in New Zealand, but Pat Hoare and interim owner Logan Fow had saved every excised tube and all the original Italian GP body panels. The right-side drive-line and about-faced gearbox/final-drive is clearly visible.

Above right Ferrari driver tester—the five-speed gearshift gate for the about-turned transmission of '0007'. The reverse gear lock-out is hinged open here. It would appear that the gearbox assembly was reversed in the frame to move the axle centres slightly forward alter weight distribution. The modest bulk of the gearbox was then slightly overhung to the rear. This about-turn demanded a switch in engine alignment from left-side towards right-side

At the end of the season, with the new mid-engined 1.5-litre cars on the stocks, the hard-raced Dino 246 chassis were surplus to requirements. Ferrari had found a New Zealand customer named Pat Hoare who had commissioned a special car for the Tasman series and national Championship races there. This first car consisted of a retired Tipo 500 chassis frame carrying a 625 4-cylinder Le Mans sports car engine enlarged to 2.8 litres. A *SuperSqualo* transmission was adopted to give a low seating position and the machine was clothed in a neat Dino-like bodyshell incorporating a Lancia–Ferrari tail tank. This car was moderately successful, but Hoare set his heart on a 'proper' Ferrari V12.

Consequently he ordered a new Tasman special for the 1960–61 summer season, and Maranello sold him one of the newly retired

Dino 246 chassis fitted with a 250 *Testa Rossa* sports-racing V 12. The chassis was actually that of Phil Hill's Italian Grand Prix winner, though numbered 'F 0788'—a customer number as opposed to the original works team serial, '0007'.

Hoare's first race in the new car was the 1961 New Zealand Grand Prix at Ardmore airfield, in which he finished sixth, and he won fourth time out at Waimate—against only national opposition. He was second in the season's New Zealand Gold Star Championship, behind Denis Hulme. In the 1961–62 series he won the coveted Gold Star after a string of good placings with his front-engined Ferrari special.

For the 1963 season a 2.5-litre limit was applied and Hoare found himself left with a 3-litre GP-derived Ferrari he couldn't even give away. Eventually in 1965 he had the single-seat bodywork removed and replaced by a rather ghastly mock 250GTO bodyshell apparently drawn by an architect friend and hand-beaten from 16-gauge aluminium sheet by McWhinnie's, a local coachbuilder. Ernie Ransley and inveterate special builder Hec Green modified the chassis to suit, though retaining the original riveted-up Tasman fuel and oil tanks in the tail. Thus the one-time Dino 246 became a V 12 road-going Grand Prix car, reported to accelerate from rest to 150 mph and stop again within a mile and to reach 185 mph flat out. It ran 0–100 mph in 10.8 seconds, 0–100–0 mph in under 15 seconds and covered the standing-start quarter-mile in 11.98 seconds. In 1967 Hoare sold the car to a fellow enthusiast named Logan Fow, from Hamilton in New Zealand's North Island. He christened her *Charlotte* and ran her happily for several years. In 1969 the car made an attempt on the New Zealand Land Speed Record with Don McDonald driving, but the attempt was cut short due to timing apparatus problems, and the best one-way speed achieved was a disappointing 169 mph.

In 1978 the car was acquired by British historic car driver Neil Corner, and as these words are written it is being returned to its Tasman single-seater V 12 trim for another season's racing. By coincidence a second surviving 1960 Dino 246 appeared in Britain at the same time, this being a 2220 mm frame with engine '0003' prepared as a show car in 1962 for the Henry Ford Museum. The car had lived in Luigi Chinetti's New York premises for many years. It was acquired, for a small fortune, by Ferrari collector Anthony Bamford and was rebuilt for racing in 1979 by David Clarke's Graypaul Motors company for Willie Green to drive. On his initial test-drive at Silverstone before the car had been stripped, Green found he could lap the Grand Prix circuit in under 1 min 45 sec with little effort, since the old chassis put its smooth power down onto the road so well. In 1960, remember, von Trips's best practice lap for the British Grand Prix at Silverstone had been 1:37.0—and eighteen years later the circuit included a new chicane, slowing cars drastically at Woodcote Corner. During 1979 this pretty little Dino carried Bamford's JCB Excavator's colours to total domination in British historic car racing. The ultimate in front-engined GP car design lives on.

Phil Hill and Ingegnere Carlo Chiti got on together quite well in the 1960 Ferrari team. Here at Monaco Phil tells what it's like out there. In September 1979 the author arranged for Phil to test drive the JCB Excavators team's 222 cm wheelbase Dino—probably '0003' seen here—at Silverstone, and within a very few laps he was down to within 0.3 seconds of the car's standing Historic class lap record

The third surviving 1960 Dino 246 F1 car is '0005', on permanent display in the magnificent Biscaretti Museum in Turin. It is shown with pannier tanks and all mechanical parts in place but minus body panels. The Biscaretti Museum must be seen by any historic racing car enthusiast—it is simply too good and too well stocked to miss

1961 Year of the Champions

The Ferrari press conference at Maranello in February 1961 created a sensation, and proved although the competition department had been in trouble in 1960 they had not been idle. In addition to the new mid-engined Dino 156 1500 cc Formula 1 cars, Ferrari unveiled their latest Dino 246SP sports-racing cars—and they were also mid-engined. The 'P' suffix was added for 'prototype'.

These products of engineer Chiti used a first-series Dino four-cam 65-degree V6 engine derived from those of the retired 2.5-litre Formula 1 cars, with the 85 mm bore and 71 mm stroke providing 2417.3 cc. It had dual ignition with twin distributors mounted on the front of the inlet camshafts up against the rear cockpit bulkhead. The rear, top chassis cross-member prevented their being mounted at that end. Three Weber 42DCN *Speciali* carburetters were fitted, and with a 9.8:1 compression these dry-sump engines were rated at 270 bhp at 8000 rpm, as opposed to their former 285 at 8500 with Formula 1 cams and tuning, For mid-mounting, these V6s were assembled upon re-cast blocks having provision for transaxle cushion-drive.

The V6 mounted amidships in a simple multi-tubular chassis frame owing much to single-seater developments, using unequal-length wishbone and coil/damper suspension front and rear. A unitary final-drive and gearbox was bolted direct to the rear of the engine, drive passing beneath the crown-wheel and pinion housing to a clutch overhung on the rear of the gearbox, then back through the five-speed gear cluster to the final-drive itself. This transmission was based on that used in the prototype mid-engined Formula 1/2 car during 1960.

It was the body styling which caused so much sensation, for at chief engineer Chiti's instigation Ferrari had installed a wind-tunnel, and from model tests Chiti and his team had developed a high-tailed body form with a headrest fairing rearwards into a sharp-edged aerodynamic fin. Fuel tanks were amidships in either sill. The bulkhead behind the cockpit reared to head height, the high rear deck then curving smoothly down to a cut-off Kamm-theory tail, the upper lip of which was just about on a level with the smoothly humped front wing peaks. The cockpit was enclosed by a high, curved Perspex windscreen (conforming with new minimum screen height rules), which merged into the tumble-home of the high bulkhead and rear deck, providing a kind of 'Targa-top' impression, like

Original factory press release photograph of the prototype Dino 246SP mid-engined sports-racing car showing off its wind-tunnel and CSI high-screen regulation dictated body shape with the original headrest and tail fin.

a coupé with the roof panel removed. As shown at Maranello there were two grilled vents set into either half of the tail's transom panel, ramped vents to release wheel-arch air behind each wheel, and inlet ducts on either hip in line with the rear cockpit bulkhead. There was a carburetter blister on the rear deck. The twin-inlet 'nostril' nose was to become a Chiti–Ferrari trademark, as it appeared also on his monoposto designs.

Hans Tanner—late Ferrari historian—explained its origin as having been brought to Ferrari by Fantuzzi, the former Maserati body-builder after he had bodied three *Piccolo* Maserati 250Fs for sale to private customers. These cars carried twin-nostril nose cones to make them look a little exotic and more attractive to race organizers, the shape having been sketched by Tanner himself, who in turn copied it from the still-born Sacha-Gordine mid engined Grand Prix car of 1953.... On Fantuzzi's suggestion it was adopted by Chiti's design team.

In addition to this startling new Dino 246SP, Ferrari also showed the open-mouthed pressmen their prototype TRI/61 front-engined V12, whose high-tailed nostril-nosed bodywork mirrored Chiti's latest thinking on aerodynamics.

Two days after that press announcement, von Trips was testing the

As shown the car lacked its front-wing fuel fillers. This side shot demonstrates admirably the short-nose nostril configuration, extended in much prettier form in 1962

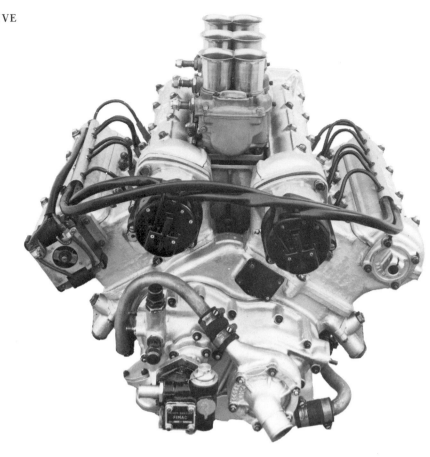

prototype high-fin 246SP ('0790') at Modena when, charging fast into the sharp left-hander before the pit straight, a brake disc apparently failed, knocking back the pads as Trips braked. With only the rears effective he was unable to slow the car sufficiently, and it clipped the inside kerb and rolled over, bounced and landed upside down. Trips crawled out unhurt from beneath the car and luckily its damage was confined to the bodywork and front suspension. On 14 March at Monza Richie Ginther tested all the works sports-racers intended for the Sebring 12-Hours. During these tests it was found that the curved elevation body form created inherent instability which the optimistic headrest fin could not control. Chiti's crew worked on the spot with Medardo Fantuzzi to correct the car's aerodynamics, adding a second fin at one point and even trying converging fins. Richie sat on the pit counter, examining the problem in his mind. He recalled the aerodynamic effect of trim tabs on aircraft and after some argument with the engineers, Fantuzzi's panel beaters fashioned an aluminium vertical fence which they tacked across the lip of the car's tail. Instantly the car was transformed. After further modifications to the 'spoiler' and to the tail's top edge to break up this effect, Ginther immediately found that although top speed dropped and he was not achieving such high revs on the Monza straights, the car's handling through corners was so much improved that lap times dropped. He declared the 246SP the best-handling sports car he had ever driven.

The tail lip had broken up airflow over the high tail, thus killing lift which reduced the rear-tyre loading at high speed. Properly made triangular section double-skin 'spoilers' were fitted to the sports-racers for Sebring.

The Floridan 12-Hours was run at Sebring's Hendrick airfield on 25 March, and the Ginther/Trips prototype Dino 246SP appeared with an ugly aluminium carburetter air-scoop fitted on its rear deck, the headrest-cum-tail-fin removed—despite having been repaired after Trips's Modenese inversion—and with a three-louvre panel on the left-front tail deck area. The car proved itself very fast and handled very well, leading the race until Trips slid and bounced it too hard over a kerb and had to retire with the steering broken.

Texan oil man Jim Hall and George Constantine shared a high tail-bodied two-cam front-engined Dino 246S entered by Luigi Chinetti's North American Racing Team and finished seventh behind the winning Hill/Gendebien V12 TRI/61, four more Ferrari V12s and a Porsche RS61. The Dino 196S two-cam of Helburn/Fulp/Hudson was eighteenth overall and won its class despite interminable troubles, while Ed Hugus/Alan Connell ran their Fantuzzi-bodied two-cam Dino 246 as high as fifth before the gearbox failed. But heroes of the piece were the youthful Rodriguez brothers, who were the fastest thing on the track much of the time with a 1960-style front-engined V12 *Testa Rossa*.

The Le Mans test weekend early in April saw Ginther charging his 246SP around the Sarthe within 2 seconds of Phil Hill's 3-litre V12 lap record, and on 30 April a second works 246SP was available in time for the Targa Florio.

Factory press release photographs showing the Chiti-designed 120-degree Formula 1 V6 engine of 1961 compared to its 65-degree (top) Jano-designed/Chiti developed predecessor. The two engines ran parallel into 1961 and 1.5-litre Formula 1 racing. Note the twin distributors driven from the inlet camshaft noses on the older unit, off the ancillary-drive gears on the later one. The wider vee allowed greater freedom in induction manifold length and shape. While both units were mechanically viable to sustained speeds of 9500 rpm and more the 65-degree's top-end power levelled off due to poorer breathing. The slightly lower C of G height of the 120-degree promised to improve handling. Claimed dry weight for the 120-degree was 225 lb, some 30 lb lighter than the Coventry-Climax FPF 1.5-litre four-cylinder in comparable trim

The big Dinos joined a TRI/61 in the three-car Maranello entry, Trips and Ginther being named to drive the Sebring Dino 246SP while Hill and Gendebien had the new one. This was so new in fact that someone had forgotten to fit the normal conical fuel filler baffle, and on its first run the car spun repeatedly on fuel slopped out of its side tanks. The 12-cylinder car was being driven by Ricardo Rodriguez and Willy Mairesse and 'those two madmen' kept the Ferrari mechanics busy throughout practice beating out dented body panelling. Strangely the once-crashed '0790' was nicer-handling than its virgin sister '0796'. Everybody wanted to drive it.

At the start—cars leaving the pit area at 30-second intervals as was traditional in the Targa—Ferrari had something of a flap since they had agreed that if anything happened to the Hill/Gendebien Dino early in the race, they should take over the Trips/Ginther car. The Belgian Gendebien was scheduled to take the start in the number one car, but he apparently realized that if it should fail early on somewhere around the 45-mile lap he would be out of the race and Phil Hill would be left in the pits ready to take over the sister car. So Gendebien announced he would not take the start and Hill was forced to jump into the car in a terrible flap and he charged away thoroughly ruffled and twitchy. He literally battered his way past slower runners, brushing them aside, and about two-thirds of the way around this opening lap he lost the car in a big way, bounced off walls and ditches and wrote off its front end.

Trips was more cautious, while the nimble Porsches of Moss and Bonnier broke the lap record, and then the German Ferrari driver responded nobly. His Dino 246SP bore the marks of Hill's car barging past on that torrid opening lap, and Ginther stepped down to allow Gendebien to take it over at the scheduled refuelling stop. But the race was Trips's after Moss's Porsche broke down, and the German drove superbly to give the Dino its first sports-car victory and to set a new record lap for the Madonie circuit at 40 min 3.4 sec, 107.847 km/h (67.013 mph), which might not sound very fast if you haven't seen the circuit.

Left Richie Ginther on test in the finned 246SP '0790' at Modena, where Trips rolled the inherently unstable car. It was rebuilt sans fin, and during Monza tests Richie Ginther invented the tail air-dam, or 'spoiler', which transformed the SP's handling—though it remained a demanding and sometimes daunting proposition

Above right Major sports car victory came to the Ferrari Dino at last on 30 April, 1961, when Trips, Ginther and Gendebien drove this prototype car, '0790', home first in the Targa Florio. Here is Trips at speed, showing off the regulation-height windshield greenhouse with its high side-screens faring back into the tail section. The tail spoiler was large, and very effective

Right Luigi Bazzi, wearing his familiar beret, ponders the rear end of 246SP '0796' on the pit apron at Nürburgring prior to the 1961 ADAC 1000 km, which the car led, setting a new lap record, before crashing heavily in mist and rain. This Jerry Sloniger photo shows how the hip intakes ducted cool air on to the inboard rear brakes, while an induction air-box was formed into the open engine cover

Far right Trips racing '0796' at Nürburgring, showing the clear-vision slot which a relaxation in the regulations permitted at the last moment. The 246SP were ungainly looking devices from most angles

The ADAC 1000 Kilometres race at Nürburgring on 28 May found the two Dino 246SPs shared by Hill/Trips and Ginther/Gendebien, and during practice the FIA issued from Paris an amendment to the windscreen regulations which had caused drivers to complain of poor visibility for over a year. The amendment permitted the cutting of a slot in the windscreen, no more than 35 cm wide. Consequently teams with Perspex windscreens cut out the entire section ahead of their drivers, leaving just a small deflector at the bottom.

Once again Moss's skill shone as he led in a Porsche with Hill and Ginther leading the pursuit. But Phil Hill went ahead completing lap 2 of the forty-four scheduled, and he put on a display of prodigious sports-car driving, breaking the lap record every time round to leave Moss for dead. His eighth lap was an all-time record in 9:15.8, 147.0 km/h (91.34 mph), clipping over 16 seconds off the old figure. Ginther displaced Moss for second behind his team-leader, and ending lap 10 the first-placed Dino

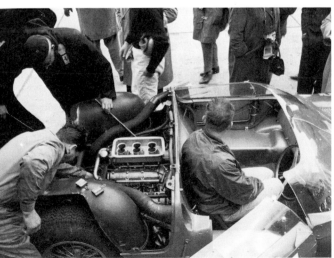

stopped to refuel, change all four wheels and allow Trips to take over on his home ground. He did so before the Ginther car appeared in second place. Richie stopped next time round and Gendebien rejoined sixth. Trips was way out in front with Gendebien back in second place when rain began to fall and temperatures fell dramatically.

Ending lap 20 Trips went by with Moss second, and Gendebien arriving late to enter the pits. He had spun and had the greatest difficulty restarting. Rain had been fed into the carburetters by the intake ducting, and the low temperatures had then created carburetter icing. The ducts were hammered flat, and when Trips stopped for fuel and tyres the ducts on his car were also closed up and Hill rejoined still in the lead. Ginther's car was running very badly and clearly was still drowning. He stopped to have the intake ducts taped off, but this still proved ineffective. Now Hill was suffering similarly in the drizzle and freezing mist, and early into lap 25 he spun at very high speed and had a comprehensive accident from which he fortunately escaped unscathed, though bitterly disappointed....

The Ginther car was struggling around in seventh place until conditions improved, then Trips took it over and right at the end it was running clean and fast, salvaging third place behind the Rodriguez brothers' TRI/61—which had survived a wheel collapse—and the winning Gregory/Casner Maserati.

The *Grand Prix d'Endurance* followed at Le Mans on 10–11 June and there Ferrari relied upon their proven V12 *Testa Rossa* but fielded one

Phil Hill was born in Miami, Florida, but raised in Santa Monica, California. In the late 1940s he acquired an MG TC and taught himself to drive it quickly. He won his first race with it at Carrell Speedway, Los Angeles, and other races followed before he went to England in 1949 as a Jaguar trainee.

He returned to the USA with an XK120 which he raced and he became a drive-anything skilled mechanic, enjoying increasing success. In 1952 he drove a Ferrari home sixth in the mighty *Carrera Panamericana* road race through Mexico, and in 1953 he shared a 4.1 Ferrari in the *Carrera* with his friend Richie Ginther, and both escaped when it crashed over a cliff. And he drove an OSCA at Le Mans.

Luigi Chinetti gave Hill drives at Sebring, Le Mans and Reims and in 1954 he and Ginther brought Allen Guiberson's Ferrari home second in the *Carrera* behind Maglioli's winning Lancia. At Sebring in 1955 Hill and Carroll Shelby were a disputed second behind the Hawthorn/Walters D Type Jaguar and with Chinetti's recommendation Enzo Ferrari invited Hill to drive a works car at Le Mans. He had one of his best-ever seasons in 1955 and in 1956 was racing again, sharing the second-place Ferrari with Gendebien in the Buenos Aires 1000 km. Ferrari took him to Europe and he found himself alongside Fangio, Musso, Castellotti, Collins and others in the Maranello team. . . . He won the Swedish GP.

Phil grew in stature during 1956–57, but always with sports cars, and his delayed Formula 1 debut came in 1958 after a false start in the Argentine, and then a drive in Bonnier's Maserati in the French Grand Prix at Reims. He finished seventh and found his way into Ferrari's F1 team via the Monza 500-Miles and German GP F2 class. . . .

After leaving Ferrari at the end of 1962 the World Champion's career slumped with ATS in 1963 and Cooper in 1964, but the three-time Le Mans winner shone in Ford's GT40s and GT Mark 2s in 1964–65 and then with Chaparral in 1966–67. After winning the Brands Hatch 1000 km with Mike Spence in 1967, Phil Hill retired—typically without frenetic publicity.

Philip Toll Hill Jr

b. 20 April, 1927

Richie Ginther hurling his 246SP '0790' through the Le Mans esses during the 1961 24-Hours race. Le Mans additions of the cross-beam driving lamps set within the nose intakes and the bonnet-top bug deflector are noteworthy. The steady-stay for the mirror is clearly visible, along with the engine-cover safety strap. The high tail proved a great advantage in night racing, preventing the headlights of following cars flaring on the bug-spattered windscreen

Dino 246SP for von Trips and Ginther. The car was troubled by water loss in the race, but led in the second hour, ran third and fourth for a long time and finally went out early on Sunday morning when lying second. Trips was driving and through a terrible miscalculation by the team the car ran out of fuel at Mulsanne. There was nothing the German could do, as it was too far for him to push all the way to the pits. He drove it as far as he could on the starter motor, but the battery died and the Dino was out. Gendebien/Hill won again, in a TRI/61, and Ferrari had taken their seventh World Championship sports car title.

On 15 August the Pescara 4-Hours had a lone factory 246SP entry for Ginther and Giancarlo Baghetti, who had made a meteoric entry into Formula 1 during the season. Ginther broke the lap record in practice on the tricky Adriatic coast public road course, and led Casner's Maserati from the Le Mans-type start. After his ten-lap stint Ginther handed over the leading Dino to Baghetti, but he pushed too hard, careered off the road and broke the car's steering. With the works Ferrari Dino out, Casner took the lead only to crash quite seriously, and Lorenzo Bandini/Giorgio Scarlatti won in a Scuderia Centro-Sud Ferrari TRI/60-61.

Since the InterContental Formula had died (predictably) on its feet, the Canadian Grand Prix scheduled for Mosport Park near Toronto was run instead for sports cars on 1 October. The Rodriguez brothers appeared with two Ferraris to face a bevy of stars, including Moss and Gendebien in mid-engined Lotus 19s. Ricardo had a front-engined Dino 246S with the current high-tailed body style, Chinetti's '0784', while elder brother Pedro drove the Le Mans-winning 250 TRI/61, rebodied in anticipation of the forthcoming low-screen/low-tail 1962 style.

The Lotus 19s were dominant with their 2.7-litre Climax 4-cylinder engines' fat mid-range torque on this winding circuit, and the Dino 246 retired with its oil pressure gone away, after running third.

At Ferrari's February press conference, Chiti's brand-new Dino 156 Formula 1 cars were unveiled, to become famous as the 'Shark-nose' Ferraris. With the mid-engine position decided there was plenty of room available to use a wider, lower engine, which would help the car's

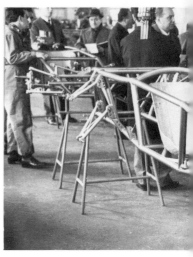

handling by reason of a reduction in centre-of-gravity height. The wide-angle engine offered potential for weight-saving since its crankshaft could adopt a simpler form than that of the 65-degree unit, and since it was designed from scratch as a 1500 cc racing engine some flesh could be saved from the castings which with the 65-degree had accommodated capacities from 1500 cc to 2500 cc. The broad vee angle would provide ample space to accommodate experimental carburetter or fuel-injection sets, and also allowed the heads' inlet tracts to be straightened in search of better efficiency and higher power. Such a broad engine would not have been practical mounted in the front of a single-seat chassis since incredibly wide-track front suspension would be required to allow for steering lock.

Chiti saved more weight in his new 120-degree V6 by shortening con-rod length and reducing big-end diameters. He based it on the 73 × 58.8 mm 65-degree engine which had won at Solitude and the Monza F2 class. This produced a swept volume of only 1476.6 cc. The simple deep-sided crankcase construction was retained, with a very wide finned oil pan enclosing the dry sump underneath. Pressure and scavenge pumps were driven from the front end of the short four-main-bearing crankshaft, and a disposable oil filter mounted vertically in front of the unit. Oil galleries passed down the centre of the vee as in earlier Dino V6s, with transfer passages to the heads at the rear of the block.

Each head was retained by only eight studs instead of the earlier unit's twelve, and the camshaft chain-drive was retained, although on this wide-angle V6 the chain was free as on the V8 Lancia engine, instead of being run around an additional idler wheel. Cam-drive originated from two half-speed gears on the crankshaft nose, and the right-hand chain passed over an additional sprocket on the tension side between the drive and inlet-cam wheels which was intended to power a fuel injection pump at a later date.

The cylinder head assemblies followed Jano Dino V6 configuration, with broad cam lobes reacting on the Jano mushroom tappets, which screwed direct to the valve stems for adjustment. Valve return was

Left Enter the sharknose Formula 1 Ferrari—Ginther on test at Modena with the unpainted prototype 120-degree-engined car '0001' early in 1961. Marchetti, to die regrettably soon after from natural causes, peers paternally at his charge, while in the background Bazzi's familiar figure rubs hands in anticipation. Richie and his wife lived in a small apartment at the 'Cavallino Bianco' inn across the road from the factory, where Collins and Hill had both stayed and where the works' *Mensa* or canteen was established. Phil recalls he could not sleep there, due to the noise of engines running all the time

Above Not a thing of beauty—the 1961 Ferrari Formula 1 chassis frame on display at the factory press conference before the season commenced. This is a 120-degree engine frame with the bulged engine bay top rails. In the right background is a TRI/61 Testa Rossa sports car chassis with V12 engine installed

provided by coil springs, as before. However, Chiti did not have both cam housings machined in the same plane, returning instead to cutting at right-angles to the valve stems.

There were two valves per cylinder, the inlet inclined at 28 degrees from the vertical and the exhaust at 32 degrees to provide a 60-degree included angle, unchanged from the Jano engines. Chiti settled on 34 mm diameter exhaust valves, but provided for alternative 38.5 mm and 42 mm inlets. The small valves were intended to promote more mid-range torque, while the large valves were intended for top-end power.

One major difference between this engine and those Jano-originated designs that preceded it was that the cylinder bank offset was transposed, Jano having followed his own Lancia V8 lead in setting the left-side bank ahead of the right. Chiti set his own signature on the 120-degree engine and brought it more into line with previous Ferrari engine practice by moving the right-hand bank ahead of the left.

The upper and lower main frame longerons were $1\frac{1}{2}$ in (c. 40 mm) tube spaced apart vertically 15 in at the cockpit. The cockpit space was 25 in wide between top-tube centres narrowing to 20 in at the bottom. From the dash panel the top frame tubes tapered slightly inwards and swept down to meet the front suspension mount structure. The top tubes ran parallel to the lower longerons in the engine bay terminating in two bridge tubes over the rear suspension pick-ups. A triangulated rear frame supported a final bottom cross-member beneath the gearbox. The 120-degree engine demanded curved top chassis tubes to allow clearance upon removal, while the 65-degree frame tubes were parallel in planform.

The unit was fitted with two specially designed triple-bodied Weber 40 IF3C carburetters. Initially 190 bhp was claimed at 9500 rpm and there was talk of 200 bhp or more, while initial tests yielded 177.

In parallel with this rapidly constructed engine, some development work had also been undertaken on the 65-degree Jano/Chiti V6. These were to continue as second-string power plants.

Both V6 engines were mated to developed versions of the five-speed and reverse transaxle seen in the 1960 mid-engined prototype, still with the clutch body exposed in cool air on the unit's endplate. It used a rigid input drive-shaft, torsional cushioning being provided by a large coupling with eight rubber elements, which were described as being 'under compression when the engine is pulling', this coupling being inserted where a conventional clutch would have been between engine and final-drive, the gearbox being overhung outboard behind the final drive. Compared to the engine the transaxle was very long, measuring 16.25 in from drive-shafts to main casing rear face. In fact the transaxle casing provided a spacer between final-drive and engine, moving the V6 well amidships to optimize weight distribution, and also to allow for the fitting of the larger 87 mm × 82 mm, 2925 cc Dino 296 V6 engine, which Ferrari announced as being available for InterContinental Formula racing should the class succeed. This unit was rated at 310 bhp* at 7500 rpm and would have produced a fearsome single-seater, for Ferrari's drivers were to discover that the Maranello credo was still all about horsepower and not about chassis sophistication in the season

*Claimed by the factory at the time—now listed by them as 295 bhp.

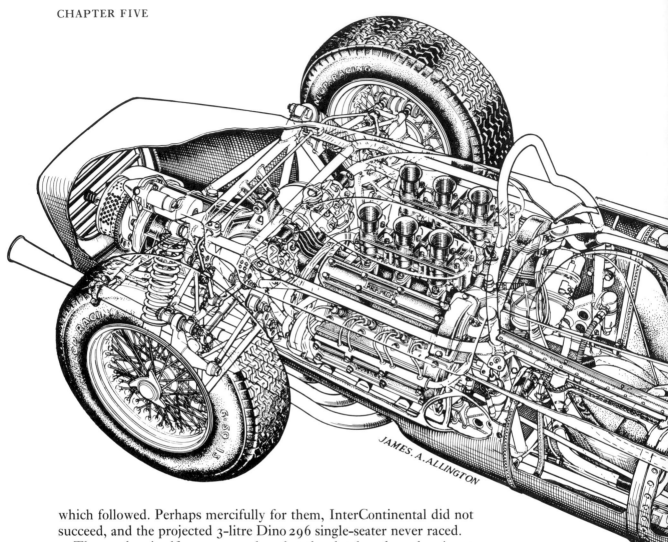

JAMES.A.ALLINGTON

which followed. Perhaps mercifully for them, InterContinental did not succeed, and the projected 3-litre Dino 296 single-seater never raced.

The gearbox itself was arranged so that the clutch and gearbox input shaft ran at less than engine speed, was an all-indirect type with five, and provision for six, forward speeds all without synchromesh and was equipped with an integral pressure lubrication system. Clutch actuation was by an hydraulic plunger exposed on the rear of the assembly, the toothed flywheel engaging with the regulation onboard starter motor which sat above the gearbox. The 12-volt battery made necessary by such provision was carried behind the oil tank in the car's nose, mounting just behind the water radiator and above the steering rack.

The multi-tubular chassis was derived directly from that proven in the 1960 prototype, heavy and crude-looking with Cooper-style members in comparison to the small-diameter latticework developed by Lotus and BRM in Britain. The Formula 1 and projected InterContinental cars were intended to be identical except for the engine and wheelbase. While the F1 car retained the 2300 mm (90.6 in) wheelbase of the 1960 prototype, the InterContinental would have run 2 in longer. The F1 61/120-degree car was claimed to scale 420 kg (925 lb); the F1 61/65

This drawing depicts the conventional and more widely raced 1962 Formula 1 Ferrari 156 rear end, with traditional camboxes and overhung gearbox. Turn to pages 142–43 for comparison with the 24 valve centre gearbox prototype

440 kg (970 lb) and the 296IC 500 kg (1100 lb). The $1\frac{1}{2}$ ran 5.00-15 front and 6.00-15 rear tyres, the 296IC demanding 5.50-15 front and 7.00-15 rear Dunlops.

Front suspension was by welded-up tubular unequal-length double wishbones with the new 'negative-camber' attitude built into them, carrying forged uprights on ball-joints at their outboard ends. An interposed coil-spring/Koni damper unit provided the suspension medium. Rear suspension was similar in system, with adjustment provided for lever arm length and alternative chassis pick-ups. Anti-roll bars were adopted on the rear as well as the front, but the rear was very thin throughout the season and its effect minimal.

The bodywork was very much cleaned up from that of the 1960 car, with a very low and flat snout up front and a long graceful tail ending in a miniature Kamm transom with a grille-covered aperture to allow cooling air flow. The twin-nostril nose of the sports cars reappeared.

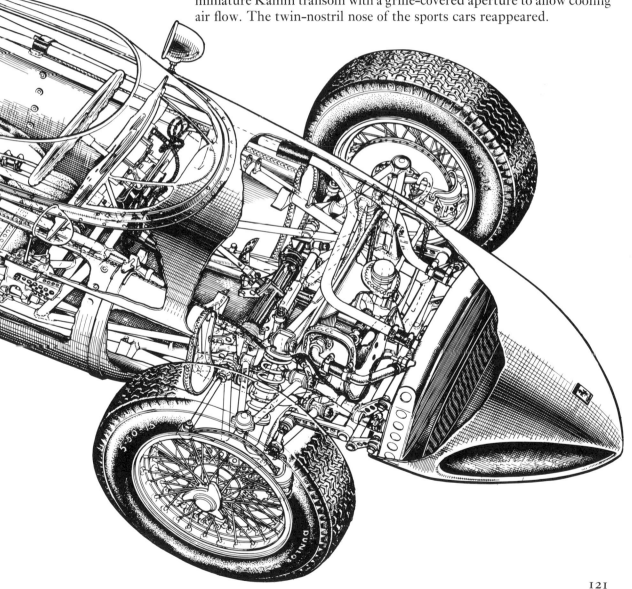

Solid Dunlop disc brakes were mounted outboard on the front hubs and inboard on the transaxle cheeks at the rear, while pannier-style fuel tanks hung on either side of the cockpit, being of riveted construction and adding a little extra rigidity to the frame structure. Borrani 15-inch centre-lock wire-wheels were retained—Ferrari remaining the last bastion in Formula 1 of these wheels, as he had been formerly with drum brakes. Dunlop racing tyres were standard wear. Wheelbase remained at 2300 mm (90.6 in) as in the 1960 prototype.

The four-valve-per-cylinder development had been initiated by Chiti following valve-spring breakages in 1961. These were possibly related to the Jano valve-gear design with the cams operating direct on a collar threaded onto the valve stem, which thus absorbed some side-thrust from the cam, so subjecting the springs to slight bending as well as torsional loads. Honda had achieved 180 bhp per litre with four-valve motor-cycle engines. Ferrari were trying hard. They failed—like BRM's V8 the four-valver never showed any advantage over the two-valve—probably because the high-peaked piston crown hampered good combustion.

During the winter various Italian racing teams had banded together to form the *Federazione Italiana Scuderie Automobilistiche*, or 'FISA', and they arranged with Mr Ferrari to enter one of the new Dino 156s in certain Formula 1 races with the intention of bringing forward a new generation of Italian Formula 1 drivers. They chose Renato Pirocchi, Lorenzo Bandini and 25-year-old Milanese Giancarlo Baghetti as their prime candidates, the latter being number one choice, and he actually gave the new Formula 1 Ferrari its debut, at Syracuse on 25 April.

Ferrari had made a works entry for Ginther in the very latest 120-degree car, but it was withdrawn at the last moment owing to oil

Typically quietly, in shadow at the back of the Syracuse pit, Giancarlo Baghetti cleans his goggles preparatory to winning the Sicilian non-Championship Formula 1 race on his and the shark-nose Ferrari's GP-class debut. Romolo Tavoni, managing the FISA team at this meeting, in the dark glasses and trilby hat, talks with his staff. The car is '0008' rebodied and fitted with a 65-degree Dino 156 engine beneath that massive Perspex bubble. The 1.5-litre engines were very critical on exhaust pipe length. The total pipe run from exhaust port to Snap extractor tip on this car measures around five feet

The determined and likeable German Count 'Taffy' von Trips was raised on the family estates near Cologne and taught himself to drive just postwar in an old Opel he patched up himself. A 250 cc JAP motorcycle followed which he entered in trials before dropping it and breaking an arm. At agricultural college he acquired a BMW motorcycle and returned to competition.

An early Porsche followed quickly, and he did well in local rallies. On a visit to the factory in search of assistance, competitions manager, Baron Huschke von Hanstein offered instead a works drive in the Mille Miglia. Sharing a car with Hampel, Trips won his class. Works drives for Porsche followed at Le Mans, and then for Mercedes-Benz in the RAC TT at Dundrod.

In 1956 Trips drove Porsche, won the 1500 class at Le Mans and then appeared with Collins in a Ferrari, placing second in the Swedish Grand Prix. In an expansive moment Mr Ferrari offered him a Formula 1 drive at Monza, but in practice there the car's steering failed and pitched Trips into the trees, breaking an arm again. His explanation of the crash was disbelieved, until the wreck was stripped. Ferrari gave him another chance in 1957, he made his Grand Prix debut at Buenos Aires and was second behind Piero Taruffi in the Mille Miglia, holding back since he knew how much victory meant to the veteran Italian. He drove for Porsche when events did not clash, and won the European Mountain Championship.

When Porsche tackled Formula 2 seriously in 1959 Trips drove for them, but in 1960 returned to Ferrari. The 'yellow' press dubbed him 'Von Crash' because he did have his fair share of accidents, until 1961 when he seemed to have things well under control. . . .

Wolfgang, Graf Berghe von Trips

b. 4 May, 1928
d. 10 September, 1961

scavenge problems while on test at Modena. Baghetti was left on his own with the FISA-entered 65-degree car, presumably the 1960 Monza tests prototype, since its chassis number was '0008'—apparently carrying on the 1960 Dino 156/246 serials. There was no reason for the usual carnet-juggling at this event as the cars did not have to cross any national frontiers on their way down to Syracuse, so the number visible should have been genuine. It was the 1960 frame revised and rebodied.

This car had a Perspex centre bubble over its carburetters, with small openings cut towards the front on either side to allow air entry. On either side behind this tear-drop were Perspex scoops directing cooling air down onto the inboard rear brakes. The car started practice, under Romolo Tavoni's experienced eye, with Snap exhaust extractors, but they were quickly replaced by normal Ferrari shallow megaphones.

Baghetti was faced by Gurney and Bonnier in the latest ex-F2 works Porsche 718s, until the British brigade of works Coopers, Lotuses and BRMs arrived, all using 1500 cc Coventry-Climax 4-cylinder engines. Baghetti was comfortably quicker than the Porsches for much of practice, despite his total inexperience of this type of racing, and only by driving right on the ragged edge did Gurney manage to steal pole position by one-tenth of a second from the young Italian's 1 min 57.0 sec best time, while Surtees's special-bodied Cooper–Climax was on the outside of the front row with 1 : 57.8.

In the race, Surtees took the initial lead with Baghetti starting carefully, eighth amongst the Britons. But lap by lap he moved forward to run third on lap 5, and next time round he had displaced Gurney and Surtees and to the Sicilian crowd's joy was leading. Gurney drove his heart out to press Baghetti, but the chubby youngster reacted with

Richie Ginther stood the *tifosi* on their ears at Monte Carlo in 1961 when he took up the chase of Stirling Moss's nimble Walker Lotus 18 after leading, as seen here, in the opening stages with his 120-degree-engined (note the small humps) 156 '0001'. Even as recently as 1961 Grand Prix racing was 'different', for this Pete Coltrin shot immediately after Richie's heroic chase prompts the questions 'But where were the media?' and 'Where were the hangers-on?' In fact little Ginther in his perspiration-soaked overalls is being greeted only by Tavoni, an enthusiastic Franco Gozzi and the even smaller Jenks of *Motor Sport*

phlegmatic calm until lap 25 (of fifty-six), when Gurney's experience in traffic won him the lead while they were lapping back-markers. Gurney drew some lengths ahead, but in one lap Baghetti not only caught and passed the Prosche but established a 100-yard lead. He maintained it with the apparent assurance of a master and won as he pleased to FISA's and Ferrari's utter delight, although after the finish he looked bewildered by this schoolboy dream come true: victory in his Formula 1 debut. His average for the race distance was faster than Moss's 1960 Formula 2 lap record, and although the British attributed their crushing defeat to their use of 'last year's engines' Porsche and Ferrari had both run old 1960 units. The only other explanation was that the new Ferrari was a wonder car, for Baghetti's driving could not possibly match Gurney, Brabham, Moss, Clark and the rest. As Dan Gurney recalls, 'It was obvious that Ferrari was some tool.'

The serious business of the World Championship began at Monaco on 14 May, with the still-experimental 120-degree V6 entrusted to Ginther, and Hill and Trips having 65-degree-engined cars. Gauze covers appeared over the carburetters, a large central orifice in the rear deck identifying the 65-degree cars, while two smaller vents set apart were provided for the wider 120-degree unit's intakes.

The story of this great motor race has often been told, for Stirling Moss in his obsolete Lotus 18 with Climax 4-cylinder engine took on the more powerful Ferraris and beat them all. However, it should be remembered that Monte Carlo puts a premium on nimble handling and the Ferraris, though greyhounds by Maranello standards, were still carthorses by a Lotus yardstick. Phil Hill has described the race as 'similar to seeing which is quickest round a living room, a race horse or a dog'.

The grid saw Moss on pole with 1 min 39.1 sec alongside Ginther's 1:39.3 in chassis '0001' and Clark's new Lotus 21 at 1:39.6. Phil Hill was alongside Graham Hill's BRM-Climax on row two with 1:39.8 in chassis '0003', while Trips was on row three with 1:39.38 in '0002'. Ginther led the initial charge from Moss and Clark, while Hill and Trips were buried in the pack. Moss and Bonnier moved into first and second with Ginther, Phil Hill and Trips chasing them. On lap 24 Hill displaced Ginther and was climbing all over Bonnier's Porsche, and two laps later Hill and Bonnier were lapping wheel-to-wheel with Trips and Ginther breathing their exhaust fumes. Moss was holding a level 10-seconds lead, and on lap 32 diminutive little Richie Ginther repassed Trips to see if he could sort out Bonnier, as Hill was now established in second place.

Ginther left Trips breathless and on lap 41 he nipped off Bonnier at the Gasworks Hairpin and tore after his team-mate, Hill. Bonnier was needled into hanging on to the Ferrari tail and they both caught Hill and pushed him along so that the gap to Moss began to close. By lap 55 it was only 4.5 seconds, and when Bonnier's Porsche broke, the two Ferraris were being kept behind the Lotus only by Moss's greater speed through traffic. By lap 72 Moss was drawing away again and three laps later Ginther elbowed past a hot-and-bothered Hill and tore into the Lotus advantage. On lap 84 Ginther set a new fastest lap of 1:36.3, only a tenth off the 1960 2.5-litre lap record, but Moss immediately equalled his time. Four laps later they doubled von Trips, and Moss drove his hardest to stave off Ginther who—in the race of his life—finally finished second, 3.6 seconds behind. Hill finished third and on his slowing-down lap found Trips stopped by the roadside, his car's ignition having packed up. He was classified fourth. All the Ferraris had in fact been handicapped by carburetter flooding, which hampered initial pick-up out of the hairpins, but Moss's victory and his battle with Hill and Ginther was a golden moment in motor racing.

On the same day as Monaco, the Naples Grand Prix was run over sixty

laps, ninety-two miles, of the Posillipo circuit, and Baghetti headed the entry with his FISA 65-degree Ferrari '0008'. He was confronted by nine British Climax 4-cylinder cars, a couple of De Tomaso-OSCAs and a Cooper–Maserati driven by Lorenzo Bandini. He was beaten into third place on the front row of the grid by Gerry Ashmore and Roy Salvadori, whose Lotus and Cooper both clocked 1 min 21.3 sec, 0.6 seconds quicker than Baghetti. Salvadori led for two laps from the start, before Bandini hurtled by, then Baghetti, who took the lead on lap 4 and held it easily to the finish, setting fastest lap on the way at 1:20.2, 111.96 km/h (69.57 mph). Two wins in two races for Ferrari—Baghetti looked quite promising....

Whit-Monday, eight days after Monaco and Naples, saw the Dutch Grand Prix with the teams all scrambling to prepare their cars in time. Ferrari provided three 120-degree V6 cars for Hill, Trips and Ginther; Hill's being a brand-new chassis carrying his Monaco serial number '0003', Trips's a new chassis '0004' and Ginther's the original 120-degree frame '0001'. As usual the Ferraris handled 'horribly', to quote von Trips, on the Zandvoort circuit, but as practice progressed so suspension settings were juggled with great success and the grid was decided with the Ferrari trio occupying the front row; Hill and Trips sharing a time of 1 min 35.7 sec with the American on pole as he had achieved it first, while Ginther was 0.2 second slower. On the warm-up lap Hill found his

Experience counting as Luigi Bazzi personally tests one of the team cars at Modena on the eve of their departure for Spa and the Belgian GP. His adjustments counted for something, as that weekend Ferrari became one of the rare Formula 1 teams to achieve a 1–2–3–4 finish in a Grande Epreuve

clutch pedal was not operating and in the pits his mechanics found a pivot pin had fallen out. A substitute was found and hurriedly fitted so that the pedal dipped, though in a wobbly fashion. Trips and Hill squeezed out Moss, who tried to split them off the second row, while Ginther had too much wheelspin and was swallowed by the British cars. In three laps Trips established a 3-second lead, while Hill prepared to hold off the opposition, with Clark and Graham Hill on his tail and Moss wheel-to-wheel with Ginther.

Ahead of them Jim Clark began to make his name by harrying Hill mercilessly, forcing his 4-cylinder Lotus 21 into second place and setting

Olivier Gendebien's yellow-painted 156 '0002' hustles into Spa's Beau Rivage corner ahead of Hill's winning '0003', Trips's second-place '0004' and Ginther's third-place '0001', which set fastest race lap. This was a noble demonstration of superiority by the Italian team, though it is interesting to see the different lines being taken by each driver on this very high-speed course, which left little margin for error

off after Trips, employing the car's fine handling to the full through Zandvoort's curving back section. Hill barged back ahead and the pair battled for many laps, though Hill always dictated the pace once he was ahead, while Ginther's engine improved and he made progress only for a seat support to break, which left him flopping about in the cockpit round the corners. Trips was well established in the lead when Hill decided he had had enough of dicing with Clark and he put in some flat-out laps which took him up onto Trips's tail. They circulated like this for the last fifteen laps, while Clark fell away. Moss was running just behind Ginther, looking for fourth place, when the Californian's main throttle return spring broke and he had to hook back the pedal with his toe. During one lurid moment into the *Hunzerug* hairpin behind the pits, Moss nipped by and Ferrari's Dutch Grand Prix ended with Trips first by 0.9 second from Hill, and Ginther fifth after his eventful afternoon.

This event proved that Ferrari could fulfil the Championship potential their cars clearly had, but as Phil Hill has subsequently explained: '... that very possibility of success brought into focus another source of tension peculiar to driving for Ferrari. Instead of being a team we were a collection of individuals who happened to operate out of the same pit ... we were racing each other for the designation as Numero Uno from Ferrari, a promised decision which he nonetheless withheld race after race and, indeed, never did make. The tension was excruciating and

127

1961 French GP, Reims: Phil Hill's spin on melting tar at Thillois—the Ferrari '0003' was clipped by Moss's Lotus and stalled. Phil ran himself over before successfully restarting it

could not be relieved by a frank expression of competitiveness, not acceptably anyhow, between friends and team-mates....'

The Belgian Grand Prix followed at Spa–Francorchamps on 18 June, where Ferrari fielded the Zandvoort cars for Hill, Trips and Ginther plus a 65-degree V6 for Gendebien on his home soil, this car being painted yellow and on loan to Equipe Nationale Belge, although Maranello mechanics were caring for it. The chassis was possibly '0002' ex-Trips. Practice had Vic Barlow of Dunlop very worried, for the Ferraris' excessive negative camber was burning out the inner edge of their tyre tread. Chiti was persuaded reluctantly to wind off some of the camber, but to his suprise and the drivers' joy the cars' handling improved while

---

THE 1.5-LITRE FORMULA 1 (1961–1965)

On 29 October, 1958, the British motor racing fraternity gathered at the Royal Automobile Club in London's Pall Mall to witness presentations to World Champions Mike Hawthorn and Tony Vandervell. Monsieur Auguste Perouse was present on behalf of the governing CSI and he used the occasion to announce new Formula 1 regulations which would replace the then-current 2.5-litre Formula from 1 January, 1961. Pat Gregory—RAC Press Officer—read out the English translation and his audience listened in stunned silence as he detailed a new capacity limit for unsupercharged engines of only 1500 cc, plus a minimum weight limit of 500 kg (1100 lb).

When he finished the uproar began. Count Lurani shouted that this did not have Italian support, and constructors like Colin Chapman, Charles and John Cooper and Peter Berthon of BRM were outraged. Each nation represented on the CSI committee had one vote. Britain and Italy were the only two actively involved in Grand Prix racing, and both had voted for continuance of the 2.5-litre limit. The USA favoured 3 litres and abstained from the vote. France, a nation without F1 or major sports car involvement at that time, had proposed the 1.5-litre limit, and had been supported by Germany (Porsche were happy . . .), Holland, Belgium and Monaco. Sweden, Switzerland and Mexico did not have representatives present at the deciding meeting, and therefore the 1.5-litre Formula came into being by five votes to two.

The furore lasted for several weeks, fuel companies announcing initially they would not support the Formula. British and American interests cooked-up a 3-litre limit for a so-called InterContinental Formula to replace Formula 1, but after first denouncing the 1500 class Mr Ferrari sat back, thought, and went very quiet. . . . The weight limit was cut subsequently to 450 kg for them. Into 1960 British constructors came to realize the change was inevitable, and they set about building suitable multi-cylinder 1.5-litre engines. They were one season too late—and Ferrari capitalized on a French Formula without French cars.

---

tyre temperatures were more even and manageable across the tread. Predictably Ferrari dominated again with three cars on the front row; Hill's 3 min 59.3 sec putting him on pole, alongside Trips with 4:00.1 and Gendebien with 4:03.0. Surtees's Cooper was on the inside of row two with 4:06.0 and Ginther alongside him, a tenth slower.

In the race Gendebien drove his 65-degree-engined car very hard to head his regular team-mates on occasion, but Hill soon established himself in the lead he held until the finish, beating Trips by 0.7 second. Gendebien had been passed by Ginther as he acclimatized so well to the strange and very daunting circuit that he set fastest lap of the race in 3:59.8, 221.676 km/h (137.743 mph), and Ferrari had achieved the rare distinction of a 1–2–3–4 *Grande Epreuve* finish for the second time, the first having been at Nürburgring in 1952.

Reims on 2 July; the forty-seventh *Grand Prix de l'ACF*: the three regular works Ferraris were entered for Hill, Ginther and von Trips (nominated in that order) with a FISA entry for Baghetti. He had the 65-degree-engined '0008' while the others were full 120-degree-engined cars, and all four were run under Tavoni's eye from the SEFAC Ferrari pits. Early in practice Moss latched his Lotus onto Trips's tail, and while the German tried to shake him off he unwittingly towed the English ace round to a very quick lap time. Thereafter the Ferraris were very careful about who was following them. Hill managed a 2 min 24.9 sec lap to take pole position, but Trips was unable to improve on 2:26.4 for the centre of the front row and became very agitated. At the start of the season the drivers had agreed amongst themselves not to ask to drive a team-mate's car, as they had done happily before for comparative purposes. Now Hill saw Trips asking Tavoni to suspend the rule and to put Hill in his car. The American did not want to swop to help prove his team-mate's car was slower than his, for Phil was leading the World Championship at this stage by 19 points to the German's 18. At that point they heard somebody had dropped oil at Thillois, so with this as a cover Hill agreed to take out Trips's car quite prepared to show a slow time. When he found there was no oil to worry about at Thillois he tried his hardest for three laps, was almost a second quicker than Trips had been and returned to the pits to say that the car didn't feel too bad, but that the track was so oily he hadn't had a chance to push it. . . . Trips was thoroughly unsettled, and they kept their regular cars for the race. . . .

Ginther tried a tall, humped engine air-box in practice, with a gauze-covered air entry just behind his head, but found little improvement. In 1971 Lotus reinvented the engine air-box and set a fashion which was effective, and which grew until regulations were changed to restrict such fittings. He completed the front row with a 2:26.8 lap while Baghetti was back on the middle of row five with 2:30.5.

Hill, Ginther and Trips led initially from Moss, Surtees, Clark and Ireland, but at Muizon hairpin on lap 4 Ginther spun. Baghetti was embroiled in a massive battle for fifth place and seemed at home, giving and asking no quarter on this very fast, slipstreaming circuit. On lap 6 Ginther repassed Moss for third place, and on lap 13 Hill let Trips by into the lead. But seven laps later Trips peeled off into the pit lane with water dribbling from the car's right-side exhaust pipe. A stone had holed his radiator and the engine was ruined.

Hill was leading Ginther by around ten seconds, but on lap 25 Richie slithered up an escape road and lost some time. Behind them Baghetti was having a really rough race against the Lotuses and works Porsches, but by lap 34 he headed the bunch and was third behind his senior team-mates in his first *Grande Epreuve*.

On lap 38 Hill, possibly having relaxed his concentration although it was another very hot day, spun on melted tar at Thillois and Moss slid in sympathy and clouted the Ferrari, and its engine stalled. The starter wouldn't work, and Phil tried to push it, but it slipped his grip and ran over him. Finally he got it going but had lost two laps, and Ginther was left in the lead while Baghetti was second with Gurney's Porsche alongside him to his left and Bonnier's to his right. Ginther stopped abruptly at his pit to complain his oil pressure was falling, but regulations now forbade adding oil during the race and he was despatched, still in the lead. On lap 41 his oil pressure gauge zeroed and mindful of his engine's survival he switched off and retired out at Muizon.

Ferrari's last hope now rested on Baghetti's young shoulders, but he looked to have little chance with the old hands Gurney and Bonnier climbing all over him in their silver Porsches. Bonnier's engine cried enough, however, and it was suddenly a straight battle between Gurney's Porsche and Baghetti's Ferrari, the young Italian again displaying the

Battle royal at Reims between Dan Gurney's Porsche 718 and Baghetti's FISA-entered fourth-string Ferrari 156 '0008' was resolved in Italy's favour. The stone-scarred Ferrari nose bears witness to the no-holds barred racing seen that hot July day, while Gurney has a gag gripped in his teeth to help him breathe without being smothered as he towers out of the Porsche

extraordinary calm seen against Gurney at Syracuse. After sitting second in Gurney's slipstream on the final run-in to the line, Baghetti timed his move to perfection, ducked out and surged alongside like a slingshot, winning by 0.1 second in a truly sensational finish.

Ferrari were beside themselves with excitement, Hill and Trips were still virtually level for the Championship and Giancarlo Baghetti had gone into the history books . . . though he was never to do so well again.

The British Grand Prix was at Aintree on 15 July, the Reims driver-car pairings appearing once again. Still Ferrari horsepower combined with adequate if not outstanding road-holding ruled the day, and practice saw the team happy wet and dry, although Hill and Ginther's identical time of 1 min 58.8 sec was shared by Bonnier to place the Porsche alongside the Ferraris on the front row. Trips was the fourth driver to clock the time, the British timekeepers operating only to one-fifth-second divisions, and he started the race alongside Moss's Lotus on the second row. Baghetti was nineteenth on row eight with 2:02.0 after a lurid spin in practice.

Rain was falling heavily at the start and in showers of spray the three works Ferraris led away in the order Hill, Trips, Ginther. On lap 6 Ginther had a big slide which allowed Moss through to third, and when Hill began to lap back-markers he was outfumbled and Trips took the lead. On lap 10 Hill found himself in a terrifying aquaplaning slide headed straight for a huge gate post at the Melling Crossing ess-bend, and he shaved it by millimetres, as by luck the front tyres cut through and found some steerage. Hill, the thinking man's racing driver, recalls the incident to this day. 'A few years earlier it would have been forgotten, like a letter dropped in a mailbox, the instant that the wheel caught hold, but by 1961 it stayed with me.' His concentration was ruined and Moss splashed by and was trying very hard to displace von Trips, before settling down to stay in contact and rely on something happening to the Ferrari.

When Moss had a huge spin at Melling Crossing on 'Hill's puddle' Trips established a clear 10-second lead, and while lapping Baghetti, who had run tenth, the youngster lost control and pirouetted '0008' into the rails at Waterways Corner, which bent both car and rails badly.

Moss stopped with brake trouble, Ginther displaced Hill until the circuit began to dry, when Phil retook second place, and the Ferraris ran out 1–2–3, with Trips some 45 seconds clear of Hill, who finished inches ahead of Ginther.

Still Hill knew the Nürburgring at least as well as Trips and always excelled there, and the German Grand Prix was next, on 5 August. The regular 120-degree trio were joined by the 65-degree car '0002' replacing Baghetti's Aintree wreck, for Willy Mairesse to drive. Moss's 1958 lap record with the Vanwall was 9 min 9.2 sec, while Hill had managed 9:15.8 with his sports Dino 246SP in the 1000 km earlier in the season. Though the cars were leaping and bounding around from bump to bump, Hill was soon lapping in 9:03.0 and on soft Dunlop rain tyres which the Ferrari would burn out in a couple of hard laps in the dry he suddenly strung together a lap in which he got almost every corner right at near ten-tenths effort, and clocked the stunning time of 8:55.2, coming in staring-eyed and trembling from the effort. Brabham had the prototype Coventry Climax V8 engine installed in his Cooper and was second fastest on 9:01.4, while Trips was fifth on the inside of the second row with 9:05.5, Ginther was on row three with 9:16.6 and Mairesse was alongside him on 9:15.9.

Moss ran the rain-mix Dunlops in the race, against the makers' advice that they could not last, and starting from the front row (with a 9:01.7 practice time) he led away. Hill shook himself free of the pack, Brabham spun off on the opening lap, and second time round Moss was drawing away on his soft and sticky tyres while Hill had Trips closing behind him. The German began setting new fastest laps and closed rapidly on Hill,

Graf Berghe Wolfgang 'Taffy' von Trips, victorious in the 1961 British Grand Prix at Aintree in Ferrari 156 '0004'. This was the car he died in at Monza, killed when the unbraced roll-over bar collapsed as the car landed upside down

and on lap 8, although Moss had just clocked 9:02.8, Trips trimmed 1.2 seconds off that time and passed Hill for second place. 'Taffy' became the first driver to break the nine-minute Nürburgring barrier in a race, on lap 10, with a time of 8:59.9, but Hill was responding, returned 8:57.8 and the Lotus's lead was down to a precarious 9 seconds—Trips and Hill could see the blue car's tail on the long switchback straight.

Then on lap 13 rain began to fall and Moss's rain tyres would now survive and came into their own. Surrendering hopes of winning Hill and Trips raced each other for second place and Championship points. As Moss took the chequered flag the Ferraris stormed off the straight to find the Tiergarten Curves awash and both broadsided dramatically and nearly crashed. Trips gathered his car up first, and blared over the line for second place, 1.1 seconds clear of Hill. Mairesse lost a certain sixth place when he was caught out by the slippery road on the last lap and crashed heavily, and Ginther was eighth—a long way behind.

With only the Italian and United States Grands Prix remaining on the calendar either Hill or Trips was going to be World Champion, and if either failed to score at Monza and the other won, it would be decided there, on Ferrari territory, on Sunday 10 September.

The importance of the race was demonstrated by Ferrari giving the preceding Modena Grand Prix a miss, and arriving at Monza with five cars; Hill, Trips and Ginther all in their regular 120-degree-engined chassis plus a 65-degree model for young Ricardo Rodriguez, while Baghetti was to drive a 120-degree model not for FISA but for his local Milanese team the Scuderia Sant'Ambroeus. The prototype 65-degree-engined car was on hand as a training hack.

Once again the combined road and high-speed track circuit was being used, and Ferrari had tested extensively on it in August and again early in

the week before practice began. Both Brabham and Moss had Climax V8 engines available and Graham Hill was out in the brand-new V8 BRM, which he put amongst the Ferraris' lap times. Tavoni was keeping Baghetti and Rodriguez at work, even when rain fell and the young Mexican drove his car in lurid slides through the high-speed corners while looking quite unconcerned by the whole business. At the end of practice Trips emerged on pole at 2 min 46.3 sec with the remarkable Rodriguez a tenth slower on the front row for his Grand Prix debut. Ginther and Hill were on row two on 2:46.8 and 2:47.2 respectively, while the third row was occupied by Graham Hill's BRM-Climax 4-cylinder at 2:48.7 and Baghetti on 2:49.0.

For the race all five Ferraris ran with their engine side panels removed and had high back-axle ratios with consequently high first gears. They made painfully slow starts, but the 2-by-2 grid spacing ensured they got away, though Clark stormed his new Lotus 21 through from row four to lie second on the opening lap behind Ginther, with Phil Hill, Rodriguez, Trips, Brabham and Baghetti all in close contact. Completing the first lap Hill led Ginther, Rodriguez, Clark, Brabham, Trips and Baghetti spread across the broad roadway in a bunch. Going into the *Parabolica* for the second time at the end of the 165–170 mph back straight Trips was aiming to take fourth place from Clark. It appeared he did not see Clark still alongside him and moved across, and the cars clipped wheels. The Ferrari spun into the left-side bank, flipped up it and bounced along the packed spectator fence before somersaulting back onto the roadway as so much scrap metal. Clark's Lotus spun to a halt further along the left-side verge without hitting anything or anyone and he sprang from the cockpit to see poor Trips lying in the grass and chaos in the spectator area, where fourteen people were dead or dying. 'Taffy' von Trips was beyond help.

The race continued with the drivers unaware of the accident's severity, and the surviving Ferraris running 1–2–3–4, Hill leading from Ginther, Rodriguez and Baghetti. Brabham did his best to upset their formation, while Ginther and Hill swopped the lead between them. Rodriguez and Baghetti both suffered engine failures (the Italian after setting fastest lap at 2:48.4, 213.776 km/h (132.84 mph)) and limped in to retire, and Hill and Ginther eased their pace and began to feel a little vulnerable. On lap 22 Ginther began to fall away, obviously in trouble, and two laps later he entered the pit lane, his engine having failed him.

Hill was racing with a new engine installed after practice, and he drove impeccably to win his second consecutive Italian Grand Prix by 31.2 seconds from Gurney's Porsche, and become the first American ever to win the World Drivers' Championship. 'It was a warming relief, a soaring feeling', he later wrote; 'But it was to be a short flight. When the race ended I asked Chiti about Trips. He muttered something, but I could tell from his face that it was not the truth. I suspected the worst, but it was not until after the Champagne and congratulations on the victory stand that I was told....'

As after the Mille Miglia catastrophe of 1958 Mr Ferrari found himself attacked on all sides, and again he issued a statement that he was giving up all forms of racing. The works cars did not race again that season, and

Above Ferrari's shoal of sharks at Monza during practice for the 1961 Italian Grand Prix, which clinched their World Championship for Phil Hill but cost von Trips his life. The cars include '0008' standing spare in the foreground; Hill's number 2, '0002', then Trips's ill-fated '0004', Rodriguez's '0006', Ginther's '0001' and Baghetti's number 32, '0003'. Extra header-tank cooling scoops were cut in four of the cars' noses. Before the start the cars' racing numbers were placed on the other side of the nose

Above right Phil's lap: at Nürburgring in practice for the 1961 German GP Phil Hill strung together a staggering practice lap which left him nervously exhausted—the first man around the 14.2-mile mountain circuit in under nine minutes. Here his '0003' hammers round the Karussel turn

Ricardo Rodriguez looks round with justifiable apprehension as his failing 156 coasts towards the Monza pits and retirement in the 1961 Italian GP. After setting fastest race lap Giancarlo Baghetti's sister car heads the same way, the Milanese driver's hand aloft to warn those behind him he is slowing and in trouble

Phil Hill did not have the opportunity to celebrate his title before his own crowd at Watkins Glen. But when Phil went to see Ferrari in his Modena home some days after events at Monza, he was asked if he would stay with the team for 1962. The American responded emotionally that he would; he would remain loyal. It was a gesture, a decision, he was to regret and only after he had signed his contract was he informed of a great political upheaval at Maranello which was to leave Ferrari not the team he had known for so many years....

1962 Troubled year

What Mr Ferrari had neglected to inform Phil Hill before the new World Champion signed his 1962 contract was that a major dispute within the corridors of power at Maranello had led to the resignations of Romolo Tavoni, Carlo Chiti, Giotto Bizzarini, Ermano Della Casa (their financial wizard), commercial manager Girolamo Gardini, Maranello works manager Federico Giberti (a veteran of the pre-war Scuderia Ferrari), personnel chief Enzo Selmi and foundry controller Giorgio Galarssi.

In the design sense only Chiti and Bizzarini counted, but still Ferrari should have been lamed by such a mass defection, though Della Casa and Giberti were to return. Chiti and Tavoni found outside backing to set up *Automobili Turismo e Sport* to out-Ferrari Ferrari and produce the disastrous ATS Formula 1 cars of 1963. Phil Hill had got along particularly well with Tavoni and with Chiti, and he and the new team manager Eugenio Dragoni shared a healthy mutual dislike....

Ferrari grieved and railed at his loss, blaming the defectors for disloyalty and treachery, but much of this despair was typically theatrical, for the wily old fox of Maranello had always developed strength in depth — to Ferrari no man was indispensable.

With Chiti gone, his engine development colleagues Franco Rocchi and Walter Salvarani assumed extra responsibility, while the veteran consultants Jano and Bazzi were always available and two young design office engineers were briefed on Formula 1. Their names were Angelo Bellei and Mauro Forghieri....

On 24 February 1962, the press arrived at the fortress-factory to see the new year's Ferrari crop. The driver team was announced as Phil Hill, Giancarlo Baghetti and Lorenzo Bandini, with Willy Mairesse taking Ginther's place as chief tester since the American had moved to BRM. Olivier Gendebien had changed his mind about retiring, and was to be under contract along with Ricardo Rodriguez. In addition, for sports car events Ferrari could call on British engineer-driver Mike Parkes and on Ricardo's elder brother, Pedro Rodriguez.

Before his departure, Chiti had been developing an extensive series of alternative head designs for the '156' V6 racing engines. The first was a two-valve per cylinder with twin-plug ignition; the second two valves with three spark plugs; the third three valves with two plugs, and the fourth four valves per cylinder with a single, central spark plug. All the

24 February, 1962, the Ferrari press-conference line-up in the factory courtyard at Maranello, with the new allegedly four-valve headed and certainly six-speed centre-gearbox car '0007' in the foreground, with the two 248SP, the 268SP and 196SP sandwiched between it and the mouth-watering 250FTO prototype. The Formula 1 car's lengthened wheelbase caused by the provision of the gearbox between engine and final-drive created the short-tail impression seen here. This car also had a distinctive snub-nose upturn

time he was chasing better filling and combustion within the cylinder to improve power output, but progress had been unusually slow.

It was apparent that Ferrari's newly promoted men would be taking time to find their feet, and in the interim period development of the existing Formula 1 cars was effectively stalled. The Grand Prix car on display in the courtyard at Maranello for the press conference was fitted with prototype 4-valve heads and its short-tailed bodywork betrayed the removal of its now six-speed gearbox from the former overhung position behind the final drive to a new mounting between engine and diff, though the clutch was still exposed on the tail of the whole assembly. The only visible differences in the car's outward appearance concerned a more sleekly raked windscreen, the shortened tail and bulged fairings behind the cool air intakes on each side of the engine bay. The rear suspension wishbones were cross-braced and an extra transverse link was introduced, picking up halfway down the forged uprights to provide better toe-steer control.

Power output of the new-head 24-valve 120-degree engine was claimed as 200 bhp at 10,000 rpm, while the modified chassis offered a wheelbase of 2350 mm (92.5 in), compared to the 1961 cars' nominal 2300 mm (90.6 in), and accounting for the short-tail appearance. Weight was around 490 kg (1080 lb). Bore centres were 3.635 in apart and the crankcase measured only 16 in overall from front to rear facing. Front-end ancillaries occupied a further 6 in. These comprised angularly spaced six-cylinder distributors and a gear-driven low-mounted water pump with individual inlets and outlets to each bank, plus the oil pressure and scavenge pumps. A Fimac fuel pump drove from the forward end of the left-side exhaust camshaft.

But while Formula 1 hopes appeared to have stagnated, there were three new mid-engined sports-racing cars on display, plus the Giotto Bizzarini-originated 250GTO grand tourer, which was to become such a legend within the greater Ferrari saga.

The three sports-racing models were virtually indistinguishable externally, and each had its type number painted neatly onto the upper edge of the windscreen. They were all Dinos—two-cam 60-degree 196SP and 286SP and an all-new 248SP fitted with a two-cam V8 engine, which was completely new to Ferrari and the Dino family. The new bodyshells were tailored to the FIA's backdown on windscreen height after the 1961 season, Ferrari having lowered the rear body sections to match this new windshield height. Otherwise the nostril-nose and tail treatment was similar to the 246SP of 1961, but without the hunched tail the whole set and balance of the cars was improved. They looked really sleek and beautiful, a schoolboy's dream of front-engined good looks despite the mid-mounted engine.

The two-cam Dino 196S engine of 1958 origin was virtually unchanged apart from normal development extracting a wee bit more power, rating 210 bhp at 7500 rpm. The new 286SP also was based on the Chiti-originated second-series 60-degree 'half-V12' block with a bore and stroke of 90 mm × 75 mm producing the swept volume of 2862 cc. Compression was quoted as 9.5:1 and output was 260 bhp at 6800 rpm, but this was a very marginal power unit, the two-cam 196S block being taken right out to its extreme limit. It must have used liners like cigarette paper. It was never to be raced.

But there were two examples of the new Chiti-developed Dino 248SP V8 on display, which quite overshadowed the simple V6s. This engine was developed from a study which Carlo Chiti had produced for a stillborn '248GT' project which was abandoned upon his departure. It was a 90-degree V8 with bore and stroke dimensions of 77 mm × 66 mm for a displacement of 2458.70 cc. Like the V6s it had single overhead camshafts on each cylinder bank, the tail of the left-side shaft driving a

Buck Fulp and Peter Ryan shared the unloved new Dino 248SP at Sebring after it had been rejected by its scheduled drivers Stirling Moss and Innes Ireland. The new 2.4-litre two-cam V8 power unit seemed under-powered and overweight, the car showed no particular inclination to go, stop nor corner well and its American–Canadian driver team did quite well to bring it home thirteenth. The large prancing horse badge on the side is Luigi Chinetti's North American Racing Team emblem

THE RODRIGUEZ BROTHERS:
Ricardo Valentine Rodriguez de la
Vega

b. 14 February, 1942
d. 1 November, 1962

Pedro Rodriguez de la Vega

b. 18 January, 1940
d. 11 July, 1971

Don Pedro Rodriguez, father of these famous sons, was a former motorcycle champion who became head of Mexico's state motorcycle patrols, and — reputedly — secret service chief for successive Mexican presidents. His position of power and authority accumulated wealth with property holdings and diverse business interests.

The brothers had an older sister, Conchita, and a younger brother Alejandro; born in 1955.

Both boys began motorcycle racing as children, Pedro and Ricardo winning the national championship at the ages of 14 and 13 respectively. Pedro raced Jaguar XKs and Chevrolet Corvettes before opting out during a spell at an American military academy. Ricardo raced an OSCA 1500 bought by Papa in 1957, and that December saw both brothers at Nassau; Pedro in a Ferrari, Ricardo a Porsche. In 1958 Ricardo was Mexican motor racing champion, and in 1959 he shared an OSCA at Sebring with Bruce Kessler. NART entered the boys in European races in 1960, and in 1961 they made their single-seater debuts in Formula Junior at Mexico City; Ricardo won, Pedro was fourth. Mr Ferrari offered both Formula 1 rent-a-drives late that year but Pedro's business commitments forced him to say no — Ricardo accepted, and showed instant promise though his naturally wild style took months to mature. He had married and his wife wanted him to retire. Ferrari did not attend the first Mexican Grand Prix in November 1962, Ricardo drove one of Rob Walker's Lotus 24s instead, and was killed in practice.

Pedro developed through sports car racing to some one-off Lotus and Ferrari Grand Prix drives in the mid-1960s, then in a trial drive for Cooper-Maserati he won the 1967 South African Grand Prix. With BRM in 1968 he proved himself a driver of natural talent but zero mechanical knowledge, and in 1969 a chequered season of freelancing saw him in Parnell BRMs and replacing Brambilla in the lone Ferrari 312 for the Italian Grand Prix. In 1970 Pedro blossomed as the king of sports car racing in the Gulf-JW team Porsches and as a leading Grand Prix driver for the revived BRM team, winning the Belgian Grand Prix for them. In 1971 the impeccably well-mannered Mexican gentleman with the dark brown spaniel eyes stayed on with both teams. Someone described his driving as being like an ammeter, maximum charge all the time....

One weekend that July neither Gulf-JW nor BRM were racing and Pedro Rodriguez de la Vega accepted a ride in Herbert Muller's Ferrari 512M at the Norisring. It crashed and burned, and Pedro was killed. We all mourned him.

single distributor. Induction was by four twin-choke Weber 40 IF2C *Speciali* carburetters which matcd with straight inlet ports in the heads and mounted at a 45-degree angle within the vee. This unit was very quickly enlarged by use of a new crankshaft with the now familiar 71 mm stroke in place of 66, providing the new displacement of 2644.9 cc. With a 9.8:1 compression ratio, the original 248SP V8 was rated at 250 bhp at 7400 rpm, while in enlarged Dino 268SP form it was claimed to produce 'over 260 bhp' at 7500 rpm.

In this enlarged form the new V8 was tantamount to two-thirds of the 400 *Superamerica* production V12, with the vee angle broadened from 60 to 90 degrees. This allowed some standardization of parts and numerous production V12 components became adaptable to the customer V8 sports-racing model. Like its V6 sisters, the 248-cum-268SP engine was mated to a standard five-speed and reverse transaxle. All three engines ran single-plug ignition. These simplified sports-racing cars for 1962 were a far more saleable proposition for a team, in any case overstocked with chassis, than had been the four-cam 246SPs of the previous year.

The 1962 sports car racing season got under way at Daytona Speedway on 11 February, where the 3-Hours race was won by Dan Gurney in his much-modified Lotus 19, staggering past the chequered flag on its starter motor after throwing a rod in the closing laps. Phil Hill led initially in a Dino 246SP '0796' now rebodied, but lost ground in changing over to Ricardo Rodriguez whose Papa was paying the bill. Phil set fastest lap on the Daytona 'road' course at 108.9 mph. Buck Fulp finished eighth in the Chinetti 246S '0784' in which Rodriguez started the race.

The Sebring 12-Hours on 24 March began the series of classic endurance races for the season, but the Sports Car World Championship had died at the CSI's whim to be replaced by a nebulous organizers' competition. Consequently Maranello did not run works cars in Florida, but relied upon NART to make the entries. The Rodriguez brothers led in their low-tailed 246SP/62 into the fifth hour, when their hard-charging ways blew its clutch; or the engine....

Stirling Moss and Innes Ireland had been entered to run the new 248SP in its debut, but after trying it in practice they opted instead for the well-tried (and faster) TRI/61, which had won both Sebring and Le Mans the previous year. Buck Fulp and Canadian Peter Ryan were entrusted with the new V8 '0806' and finished a poor thirteenth, thirty laps behind the victorious Jo Bonnier/Lucien Bianchi Serenissima-entered V12 250TRI/62.

In Europe the Targa Florio was held on 6 May, and Ferrari entered three Dinos; the Daytona 246SP for Mairesse/Ricardo Rodriguez, a new 196SP '0804' for Baghetti/Bandini and one of the two 268SPs '0802' for Hill/Gendebien. Early in practice Hill was out in the new V8 when its throttle stuck open and he went hurtling into a corner, leaving long black marks from locked wheels before the car launched itself over a cliff to land on its wheels badly wrecked. At the time Hill was starting his season-long battle with the new team manager, Dragoni, who insisted that the American had been 'Impressioned' by Trips's death and considered this 'evident psychosis' had triggered the accident through pure driver error. Hill was often characterized as being excitable, and that summation was one of the main things which got him really excited! Dragoni's smug belief that he knew what was really going on inside the American's head simply made Hill climb the walls, and on this occasion in Sicily he finished up without a drive, and extremely disgruntled.

Meanwhile Mairesse took the start in the 246SP and covered his first forty-five mile lap in 40min 43.02sec, which was close to Trips's lap record. Baghetti inherited second place when Gurney's Porsche crashed, but on the third lap the Milanese driver spun his Dino 196SP and crumpled its tail, limping to Ferrari's remote depot in the mountains, where the damaged section was wired in place, and he slammed away fourth. Bandini took over at the pits and began a furious drive.

Mairesse set a new lap record on his third lap at 40:00.3, 107.973 km/h (67.091 mph), and handed over to Rodriguez, who was so far in front he could relax for once. Gendebien was on hand as spare driver since Hill was in disgrace and he took over for the closing stages, bringing the

Above and right Cause and effect demonstrated during practice for the Targa Florio in 1962 when Phil Hill's new 268SP '0802' had its throttle jam into one of the mountain corners. Phil is explaining to Italian journalist Pilogallo how he did everything he could to stop the car, with tyre marks from its brake-locked front wheels bearing silent testimony behind him. Down below road level the locals run a quick valuation on the wreck—the Ferrari crew, however, beat them to it. '0802' had appeared at the press conference with the 286 V6 engine installed, but that overstretched unit was never raced. She would be rebuilt as a 196SP 2-litre two-cam V6 and would finish second in the Targa one year hence
Right Young Ricardo Rodriguez vaults from the cockpit of the 1962 Targa Florio-winning 246SP '0796', which he shared with Mairesse and Gendebien to such great effect during the race. Note the radiator header tank cooling scoop fitted above the long-nose nostril cowl on all regular SP/62s

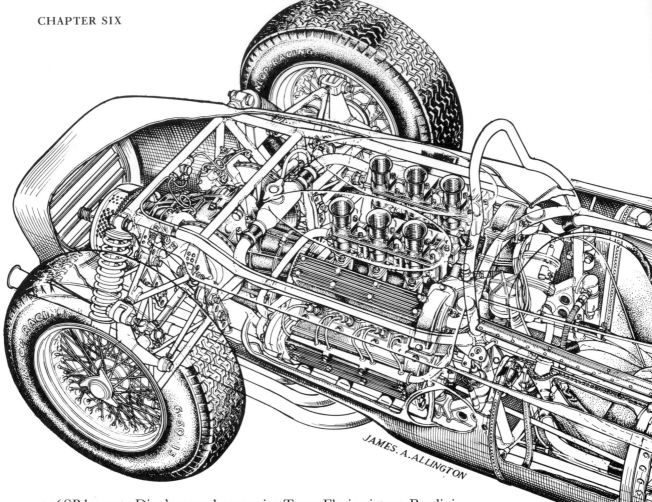

JAMES. A. ALLINGTON

246SP home to Dino's second successive Targa Florio victory. Bandini drove the smaller car faultlessly with Baghetti and they salvaged second place to make it a prestigious Ferrari Dino 1–2.

Three weeks later '0790' (not the Targa car) 246SP appeared at Nürburgring for the ADAC 1000 Km, to be driven by Hill and Gendebien, alongside the second new 268SP (chassis '0806') for the Rodriguez brothers, and the Targa 196SP again for Baghetti/Bandini. As the skies clouded over and rain began falling just before the start, there was a frantic tyre-changing comedy which had drivers running to their cars at the Le Mans-type start to find them jacked-up with wheels off and alive with harassed mechanics. Bandini jumped into the 196SP while its front was still off the ground, and Pedro Rodriguez could not start the big V8.

Jim Clark was driving a little Lotus 23 with a 1500 cc Lotus-Ford twin-cam prototype engine, and he fled away from the established big sports cars to draw out an enormous lead.

On lap 5 the sun appeared briefly, in time to illuminate Pedro Rodriguez's way into a deep ditch with the 268SP, and Hill was fourth behind Gurney's Porsche and Mairesse's experimental 4-litre V12 'GTO'.

The 1962 press conference model Formula 1 Ferrari 156 fitted with finned cam-cover heads said to carry 4 valves per cylinder. Note the modified rear suspension with extra transverse links to control toe-in, and the gearbox between the final-drive and engine. Compare this drawing with that on pages 120–21

When Clark was overcome by cockpit fumes and left the road, Mairesse led briefly before making a scheduled stop to hand over to Mike Parkes, and Hill took the lead in the Dino 246SP. Ending that lap Phil handed over to Gendebien without losing the lead. When Bandini brought in the fourth-placed 2-litre car for refuelling it was retired as the sump was found to be cracked and it sat on the pit apron in a spreading pool of oil. The Dino 246SP was absolutely untouchable, whether Hill or Gendebien was driving, and they won as they pleased from the Mairesse/Parkes experimental coupé. It was only Ferrari's second victory in the ADAC 1000 Km since 1953, when Ascari and Farina won in a big Ferrari 375. Hill's fastest lap was 9 min 31.9 sec, 143.6 km/h (89.22 mph).

After this event the 2-litre 196SP was handed over to the Scuderia Sant'Ambroeus under the aegis of Eugenio Dragoni for Ludovico Scarfiotti to drive in the European Mountain Championship 'hillclimb' series. This was an old-established competition which achieved major significance in the thirties when some events counted towards the European Drivers' Championship title—the World Championship of its day. The FIA had revived the competition in 1957, when Swiss Willy Peter Daetwyler had won in a Maserati. Thereafter it became a Porsche preserve; the property of German and Swiss drivers. Now in 1962 both Abarth and Ferrari brought Italy into the fray. Scarfiotti, the chosen Dino driver, was twenty-nine years old and was well attuned to the smooth, fluent reflex driving required for success on these long climbs, and the Dino V6 proved an admirable mountain climber.

The team missed the first event at La Faucille in Switzerland on 3 June, where the organizers refused to conform to the financial scale of the other Championship rounds. Abarth ran there and found their cars so bad-handling they were withdrawn for the rest of the season. Heini Walter won the climb for Porsche in a works-prepared RS 1700.

Round two was on 10 June over a shortened version of the classical Parma to Poggio di Berceto climb, now cut from its original 17.4 to 8.1 miles to remove sections considered too dangerous for modern cars. Renamed the Fornovo-Monte Cassio climb it remained a formidable venue, and when Scarfiotti's long-distance racing Dino spreadeagled the seasoned opposition it was a sensation. His time of 7 min 50.3 sec, 99.46 km/h (61.80 mph), established the new climb record and beat four Porsches driven by Walter, Sepp Greger and the two Mullers, Herbert and Hermann, none of whom could crack 8:07.0!

The appearance of the quasi-works Sant'Ambroeus Dino awoke works reaction from Porsche, who put a 2-litre flat-8 *Spyder* at Heini Walter's disposal for the French climb at Mont Ventoux on 17 June. Greger's RSK received a works 1700 engine, but still Scarfiotti—known as 'Dodo' to his friends—was quickest in practice on the historic 13.4-mile climb. In the official runs he shattered Maurice Trintignant's existing record, set in 1960 with an F2 Cooper–Climax, by no less than twenty-four seconds. His new figure of 11:28.8 was 12.6 seconds better than Walter's in second place, while Greger was a further 11.8 seconds down, third.

Scarfiotti was set for a hat-trick at Trento-Bondone on 8 July. Walter was better accustomed to his flat-8 Porsche there and he pushed the Dino hard, but still Scarfiotti made it three climbs, three victories: 3.2 seconds faster than the Swiss, having covered the 10.75-mile distance in 12:25.9, an average of 83.44 km/h (51.85 mph). This shattered Edoardo Govoni's existing course record by nearly forty-five seconds, but was attributable in part to resurfacing and eased radii on some corners.

At this point in the competition Scarfiotti and Walter tied for the lead with 27 points each, but the Ferrari Dino driver had scored all his in only three events, having won each outright.

On 22 July the battle moved to the Black Forest in Germany for the Freiburg–Schauinsland climb, where twice-Champion Walter was reckoned to be a match for the Dino's 'extra power'. Here Scarfiotti proved his mettle, clocking 6:47.7 on his first run, a new course record, to which Walter's best of 6:53.0 was good only for second place. After the second climb Scarfiotti's aggregate of 13:36.6 was 10.1 seconds below Walter's.

With two climbs left, Scarfiotti's Championship looked certain, and when Porsche sold their flat-8 *Bergspyder* to America and Walter had to fall back on his faithful RS, a Dino title was assured. But at Ollon-Villars in Switzerland on 25 August, an inexplicable choice of new unscrubbed front tyres for the first run saw Scarfiotti beaten into second place by Sepp Greger, the Swiss Porsche driver's two-climb aggregate of 9:13.9 for the 4.95 miles of twists and hairpins bettering the Dino's by just 0.2 second. Scarfiotti's second climb in 4:34.7 was 1.9 seconds under Greger's best in a Championship car, but was put in perspective by fastest time of the day, which went to Jo Bonnier's Championship-ineligible Formula 1 Porsche in 4:27.8, 107.50 km/h (66.80 mph)—a new climb record....

Ludovico Scarfiotti was confirmed as European Mountain Champion and the sports-racing Ferrari Dino had won itself a major International title at last. Mr Ferrari opted out of the final Championship round, at Austria's Gaisberg on 9 September, and five Porsches were split there by a Lotus 19, third amongst the top six.

Top far right Ricardo Rodriguez takes the V8 car '0798' out of the Le Mans pits during the Le Mans test weekend in April 1962, running the car with a laminated glass screen insert and the first airfoil beam behind the cockpit intended to limit buffeting and turbulence in this area. A contemporary report reads: 'The type 248 was not very fast, nor was it handling particularly well, its tail twitching through the esses: and Bandini's time of 5 min 5.4 sec indicates that all was not well...'

Left Ludovico Scarfiotti takes his 196SP two-cam 2-litre *Tipo* 561 '0804' off the line at the start of the Freiburg Mountain Climb in July 1962. This car, which appears to have been prepared as a stand-by spare—or a possible 2-litre class entry—for Le Mans since it carries the Le Mans running-light modifications. This car fell into the good hands of English enthusiast John Godfrey in 1970

Top and middle centre The 268 V8 engine of the Baghetti/Scarfiotti car '0798' stands revealed during the Le Mans 24-Hours meeting of 1962. Note the carburetter velocity stacks have been removed together with the engine air-box, though the feed trunking is still in place, showing how engine air was drawn from openings on the body sides. The hip intakes just behind the doors fed trunking to cool the inboard rear brakes. The 248 V8 engine was photographed on the floor of Automeccanica Toni in Modena in February 1979, where it had survived with a number of other Dino units, including 246SP four-cam V6s. The V8 was offered for sale at 7.5 million lire

Middle right Ricardo Rodriguez rounds Mulsanne Corner at Le Mans in the works' 246SP/62 '0796', which he shared with his brother Pedro. The car is running with a full-width laminated glass screen insert, a metal bug-deflector on the front access hatch, cross-beam driving lamps in the nose nostrils and with Le Mans regulation side and running lights and rear wheel-arch trailing-edge extensions

Meanwhile the Players '200' sports car race at Mosport Park, Toronto, Canada, on 9 June had seen Innes Ireland running fourth for much of the distance in the tired Nürburgring winning 246SP '0790' entered by the British UDT-Laystall racing team, but in the second heat ignition trouble forced him to retire.

At Le Mans the trials weekend in April had seen the Dino 268SP fitted with a deep-chord fared roll-over structure behind the cockpit in addition to a glass insert in the Perspex windscreen to prevent impact obscuration by heavy rain.

For the 24-Hours race on 23–24 June the winning experimental 4-litre prototype Ferrari inevitably shared by Phil Hill and Olivier Gendebien carried a similar roll-bar structure, while Baghetti and Scarfiotti drove the lone surviving Dino 268SP—chassis '0798'—alongside the Rodriguez brothers' 246SP—'0796'.

The Mexicans drove their car typically hard, lying second behind Hill in the early stages and moving into the lead whenever the big experimental front-engined V12 made its scheduled stops. The

145

Baghetti/Scarfiotti V8 lay third at midnight, but by 4.30 am on the Sunday morning the Rodriguez brothers were out, suffering transmission failure while leading. Then the Baghetti/Scarfiotti car broke its gearbox when second after seventeen hours. But having won all four rounds of the new *Challenge International de Vitesse et d'Endurance* 'La Ferrari' was again World Champion.

Mike Parkes took the Dino 246SP to Brands Hatch on a teeming wet August Bank Holiday Monday for the Guards Trophy races, and after lapping in practice in 1 min 46.4 sec he started from pole and led Innes Ireland's UDT-Laystall Lotus 19 all the way in horrible conditions, winning by 63 seconds after a beautifully smooth drive, and setting fastest lap at 1:50.0, 153.89 km/h (86.73 mph). He won the GT race that day in a Ferrari GTO, and the touring car race in a 3.8 Jaguar....

The sports car season closed with the razzmatazz of the Bahamas Speed Week in December, at which Lorenzo Bandini drove a 268SP reputed to be Phil Hill's Targa Florio practice wreck '0802' rebuilt. He was eighth with it in the Nassau Trophy event, but on his first practice lap had left the road when the throttle reportedly stuck open ... which news amused Phil Hill. In fact it was '0798'. Buck Fulp drove a Dino 196SP '0804' into fourth place in one of the supporting races. Finally, late in the year, 246SP '0796' appeared at Modena and Monza with a V12 engine shoe-horned into its midships section. At the wheel was John Surtees, having his first drive in a sports Ferrari preparatory to joining the team for 1963. He broke Ginther's existing lap record with it; Dragoni was pleased.... The mid-engined V12 Ferrari was now on the Maranello drawing boards.

Below right John Surtees on his first acquaintance with the Ferrari team at Modena in November 1962 heads the rolling experimental car '0796' into one of the Autodrome's tighter turns. The car has been modified with a midships chassis extension to accommodate a 3-litre V12 engine in place of the original 2.4-litre four-cam V6. Body fillets in the front of the engine cover and ahead of the rear wheel-arch are just apparent in this Pete Coltrin picture. Early in 1963 '0796' continued testing with a new letter-box nose in place of the Chiti-signature nostrils. It was used as a hack during training for the Targa Florio, and burned out—apparently beyond repair; the only Dino SP not to survive. During 1963 the mid-engined V12 Ferrari 250Ps became the team's front-line armament. They lacked the nimble surefootedness of the 1962 V6 cars

Baghetti was the elder son of a wealthy Milanese industrialist, and he started racing quite late, in 1956, with an Alfa Romeo 1900TI. In 1957 he drove two Alfas—a 1900 Sprint and a Giulietta—in minor events with some success and in 1958 he drove the Veloce very well with his brother Marco to take second place in the Mille Miglia rally.

In 1959 Baghetti went road racing seriously with a Fiat-Abarth 750 and he was invited by Carlo Abarth himself to join a factory team to tackle some World records—which they did successfully.

In 1960 he turned to Formula Junior racing with a Dagrada-Lancia and he won three important events at Monza; the Crivellari, Fina and Vigorelli Cups. He gained support from one faction in the Italian press and public while another backed Bandini. It was rather like Musso versus Castellotti all over again. When it came to FISA's choice for a driver to put into Mr Ferrari's quasi-works Formula 1 car in 1961, they opted for Baghetti in preference to Bandini. Giancarlo's 1961 record vindicated his selection, but in 1962 this serious-minded, rather bovine character reached a performance plateau and Bandini always had more fire.

In 1963 Baghetti followed Phil Hill to ATS and the experience ruined both drivers' Formula 1 careers. In 1964–65 Baghetti drove Centro-Sud's sadly deteriorating BRMs and occasional Dino outings did little to enhance his tarnished reputation. Sixth place with Biscaldi driving an Alfa Romeo T33 in the 1968 Targa Florio was his last International performance of note. For Baghetti the last straw came in the London to Sydney Marathon when his road book, documents and money were stolen from his Lancia—forcing him to retire on the spot. Many sympathized with the self-effacing, taciturn Milanese when he announced his retirement thereafter from competition driving.

Giancarlo Baghetti
b. 25 December, 1934

Right Mike Parkes driving 246SP/62 '0790' to win the 1962 Guards Trophy race at Brands Hatch, lapping Paul Hawkins's tiny Ian Walker-entered Lotus 23 on the way. This was the car which Innes Ireland had raced unsuccessfully for UDT-Laystall in Canada, but here at Brands Hatch it was perfectly prepared and very well driven in horribly wet conditions. The car is pictured bottoming over the hump on the entry to Paddock Bend: note the extreme negative camber assumed by the rear wheels

In Formula 1 the 1962 season began at Brussels with a non-Championship Grand Prix over the Heysel public roads circuit. It gave Ferrari an opportunity to run Willy Mairesse on his home ground, and to have a close look at the new V8-engined cars from Britain. Race day was appropriately 1 April, for the race was run in three twenty-two lap heats with overall results by addition of placings, not of time.

Mairesse's mount was chassis '0006', featuring a new oil tank in the nose, with air-cooling tubes passing through it vintage Bugatti style, and an overhung six-speed gearbox. During practice Mairesse contrived to send its tacho needle round on a second lap of the dial, having reached 12,000 rpm or more, but the 120-degree engine held together. He qualified fourth quickest on 2 min 04.7 sec, behind Clark's new Lotus–Climax V8 on pole at 2:03.1, Moss's Lotus–Climax V8 and Graham Hill's new BRM V8. The Belgian ran second behind Hill early in the first heat, only to be gobbled up by Moss and displaced to third at the finish. Trying to hold Moss in heat two he spun out of second place after six laps, screamed back onto the track and collected Trevor Taylor's works Lotus, tearing off its right rear wheel without damaging the Ferrari—which was some measure of the cars' respective strengths. When Moss blew up Mairesse had to catch the 4-cylinder cars of Ireland (Lotus) and Bonnier (private Porsche) to win, and he did just that. In the last heat Mairesse drove coolly (for him) and led most of the way, the class opposition having all blown up or fallen foul of the rules, and he won as he liked. On addition of placings he was first overall from Bonnier and Ireland. It was a satisfactory outing, but had proved nothing.

On 23 April the Pau Grand Prix in southern France was graced by a Ferrari entry for the first time since 1955, Ricardo Rodriguez arriving to drive a 120-degree model and Lorenzo Bandini making his works Formula 1 debut with a 65-degree engine in Mairesse's Brussels chassis. Both chassis were identical, with the new six-speed gearbox overhung behind the axle.

Both young drivers tried very hard in practice, Rodriguez occupying the middle of the front row with a 1:32.5 lap compared to Clark's pole in the Lotus 24 V8 of 1:30.6. Bandini was on the inside of the third row with a best of 1:33.1.

Rodriguez led narrowly from Bonnier's Porsche and Clark's Lotus ending lap 1, but on lap 9 the Scot stole by. Bandini was fifth and under so much pressure from Welshman Jack Lewis's BRM V8 that he spun off and appeared late with straw trailing from the car's rear suspension. Maurice Trintignant was charging through the field in Rob Walker's Lotus 4-cylinder and he shouldered his way past Rodriguez and began to harry Clark. By lap 16 he was in the lead as the Lotus 24's gearchange came adrift, and Rodriguez was tiring and falling back. Lewis began to press him and the Mexican inherited second place once more, which is where he finished, while Bandini was fifth, lapped, behind the private BRM V8s of Lewis and Tony Marsh.

On 28 April the similarly non-Championship Aintree '200' was run in Liverpool, venue for the year's British Grand Prix, and Ferrari sent two 1962 V6 cars for Phil Hill and Baghetti, both with 120-degree engines and Hill's using the latest inboard gearbox. The American was suffering from 'flu, and in first practice, as his best time was 0.2 second slower than Baghetti's, he explained that he felt awful and the car was handling worse. Things improved for both in second practice, Hill qualifying on row three with 1 min 57.4 sec compared to Clark's Lotus 24 V8 pole of 1:53.8. Baghetti was one row behind with 1:57.6.

A 1962 120° Formula 1 chassis frame under construction at Maranello

The Brussels GP on the public-road Heysel circuit in April 1962 saw Willy Mairesse victorious in '0006' after the British V8 cars had all struck trouble. Here he harries Stirling Moss's new Walker Lotus V8 through Heysel itself

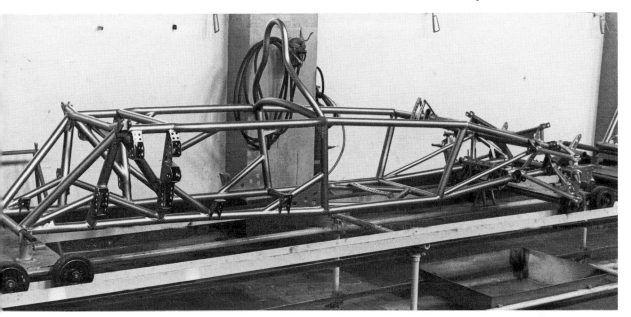

Factory scenes prior to the 1962 season showing the 120-degree Formula 1 chassis frame with its bulged engine bay top rails, extra toe-in location for the rear suspension uprights, meaty tube-wishbone front suspension and leading-edge Dunlop ventilated disc brake with steering behind the axle line, and V6s (a 120-degree in the foreground) on test in the Maranello engine house. Like the original 1957 F2 engines, the Formula 1 V6s in 1961/64 carried 'Ferrari' rather than 'Dino' cambox lettering. They are undeniably, however, part of the V6 Dino story

Hill ran fifth behind the two leading BRM V8s of Ginther and Graham Hill, Clark's Lotus and McLaren's Cooper from the start, with Baghetti eighth. John Surtees's Lola then displaced him and towed the Ferrari past McLaren. When Ginther retired, the number one Ferrari lay fourth at half-distance (twenty-five laps) and Baghetti, driving very well, was sixth just behind McLaren. When Surtees's Lola expired with Climax V8 valve gear trouble, Phil Hill was third only to miss a gear and be repassed by McLaren. Graham Hill's BRM V8 engine then failed, leaving McLaren second far behind Jimmy Clark's winning Lotus, Phil Hill finished third and Baghetti was fourth. The V6 Ferraris had failed to match the new British V8 cars—and that became the story of the season. . . .

The BRDC International Trophy race was held at Silverstone on 12 May, and Ferrari took the unusual step of loaning one of their Formula 1 cars to the UDT-Laystall team for Innes Ireland to drive. It was a 120-degree V6 model and Innes found it something of a tank after the Lotuses he had been driving, but the engine was 'beautifully smooth'. He qualified sixth at 1 min 37.4 sec, compared to Graham Hill's BRM pole of 1:34.6 and he managed to bring it home fourth, happy with the experience but not terribly anxious to try it again.

Mr Ferrari had asked Ken Gregory, UDT team manager, to see him at Maranello and on the Wednesday after the Aintree '200' Gregory and Ireland had lunch with him. Because of his tremendous admiration for Stirling Moss he had been going to provide a 246SP for UDT, but this plan was foiled when Moss had been severely injured in his Goodwood Easter Monday accident. Ferrari wanted UDT to run one car at Silverstone. Ireland was fitted into Baghetti's Aintree car in the Maranello racing shop, and it was duly delivered to Maranello Concessionaires in England for the UDT Silverstone entry, complete with a pale green stripe painted along its sharknose, not at UDT's suggestion but purely thoughtfulness on Ferrari's part . . . all most mystifying.

After driving cars red-lined at 7800 rpm it took Ireland a while to acclimatize himself to revving the Ferrari V6 to 10,000. He later wrote: 'Everything about the car was functional. There was not a slipshod feature anywhere . . . that gearbox was a dream, I honestly think that car had the best gearbox I have ever experienced in a racing machine. The change was absolutely positive and went through just like a knife through butter.' He liked the steering, though not the car's handling. He was disappointed in the engine's power despite its smoothness and willingness to rev (it was giving 189 bhp) and never gained confidence in the brakes, which tended to lock. In rain during the race he found the car gave him enormous confidence (unusually so, because Innes hated racing in the wet): '. . . I was very impressed with the way the Ferrari acted out of the corners. You can screw the power on coming out of a corner . . . though the car was slow on entering one.' Still he could not match the Climax and BRM V8-engined cars and was happy that UDT had V8s on order for him.

Ireland reported to Ferrari, suggesting the car could use a wider track and wider front rims since he was sure the Borrani wire-wheels were flexing and causing a loss of adhesion. 'The power was good from about 7800 rpm — just the point where at the beginning I was trying to slack off! And the power was very controllable, it didn't come in with an almighty bang, as I had somehow imagined. That V6 really started steaming when 9000 rpm came up on the clock, and that was when it sounded really healthy....' Innes's wide track ideas became a great source of irritation to Phil Hill as the season progressed....

The Dutch Grand Prix at Zandvoort opened the World Championship on 20 May, with Phil Hill, Baghetti and Rodriguez reporting for duty with 120-degree-engined cars, Phil's being modified to Mauro Forghieri/Ireland ideas with a wide-track rear suspension. Hill thought the young engineer had probably fought with Chiti over the idea the previous year, and it apparently did little but make his car slow in a straight line. The extra cross-links to limit rear toe-steer had been removed from all three cars. They gave a sorry showing in a race noted for its introduction of the monocoque-chassised Lotus 25, the flat-8 Porsche 804 and a new six-speed transmission lowline Cooper-Climax V8. They qualified ninth, eleventh and twelfth — Hill, Rodriguez, Baghetti — and on the fourth race lap the Mexican spun and was struck by Brabham's private Lotus 24, losing two laps while he kedged his Ferrari out of a sand-trap. Hill drove very hard indeed to run second behind Graham Hill's BRM V8, but late in the race he was caught by Taylor's works Lotus 24 and displaced easily to third. Baghetti was fourth, one lap behind, and Rodriguez after a lurid day was clipped by Taylor (getting

Phil Hill's fighting drive in '0007' — the new centre-gearbox car being apparently '0009' at this race — during the 1962 Monaco Grand Prix was absolutely worthy of the reigning World Champion. He was narrowly beaten at the finish by Bruce McLaren's Cooper

Willy Mairesse

b. 1 October, 1928
d. 4 September, 1969

'Wild Willy' was born in Momignies, Belgium, near the French border. He was only son of a timber merchant and grew up fascinated by fast cars and motor racing. He made his debut in a big-time event in 1953, co-driving a Porsche 1500 with a Dr Missone. They retired after some hair-raising adventures, and the following year Mairesse was back with a blown Peugeot 203, finishing 26th. In 1955 he was a class winner on 'the Liège', and won the Huy 12-Hours outright. This success encouraged him to buy a Mercedes 300SL. With this car he won the 1956 Liège-Rome-Liège beating Gendebien. he won again at Huy.

During 1957 Mairesse spent his time wrecking cars, and in 1958 only help from Jacques Swaters, Belgian Ferrari importer, kept him running. With his help Mairesse acquired a Ferrari Berlinetta, which he drove to several fine placings.

In 1959 he won several of the timed stages on the Tour de France, forcing Gendebien to work harder than ever for his third successive victory in the event. The two Belgians were sincere rivals, having little in common; the aristocratic Gendebien versus the rough tough little man with the wild ways. Mr Ferrari gave Mairesse a test drive in the Targa Florio, sharing with Scarfiotti, and he placed fourth.

After his Ferrari Formula 1 debut in 1960 Mairesse outclassed Gendebien at last on the Tour de France, though Olivier and navigator Lucien Bianchi sportingly pulled his car out of a ditch and gave him a spare wheel to enable him to continue to the finish and win. During this incident neither man spoke to the other....

Following his 1963 German Grand Prix crash Mairesse's F1 career was finished. but in 1965 he won the Spa 500 km in a Ferrari 275LM and in 1966 he won the Targa Florio for Porsche. But he crashed an *Equipe Nationale Belge* Ferrari heavily at Spa in 1967, and at Le Mans in 1968 failed to latch his Ford GT40's door properly at the start. The door flew open on the straight and pitched the car into the trees, and 'Wild Willy' was back in hospital.

He never fully recovered, and died by his own hand in Ostend in 1969.

his own back for Brussels perhaps?) and vanished into the sand dunes for good.

While the main team was having its problems at Zandvoort, Ferrari ran two cars in the non-Championship race at Naples that same day. Mairesse in his Brussels-winning '0006' and Bandini were the drivers, the Italian taking pole position in practice with a lap in 1 min 18.7 sec, 0.2 second quicker than 'Wild Willy'. Bandini led the first twenty-three laps, Mairesse moving ahead to complete the sixty-lap distance, winning his second Formula 1 race of the year while sharing fastest lap, in 1:17.7 115.48 km/h (71.76 mph), with his team-mate.

Hill, Bandini and Mairesse were firm entries for Monaco on 3 June, while Rodriguez was present driving only the training car, fitted with a 65-degree engine. All three 120-degree-engined cars had the Forghieri wide rear track, but retained the original coil/damper top mounts so they were now more steeply inclined. A fifth Ferrari appeared for second practice, ostensibly brand new with a 12-valve 120-degree engine and the inboard six-speed gearbox. Hill drove it in final practice with the Perspex screen's side sections cut away, while Bandini and Mairesse ran their cars with old-fashioned aero screens in place of the normal wrap-arounds.

They qualified fourth, ninth and tenth—Mairesse on 1:36.4 compared to Clark's pole time of 1:35.4, Hill with 1:37.1 and Bandini alongside him with 1:37.2. Phil drove his overhung gearbox car in the race, but Mairesse made the initial impression with a meteoric start from

Right way up and wrong way up, V6 Formula 1 Ferraris in 1962 at Modena (*left*) on 28 July, 1962, with Hill pondering, Bandini fondling and Ricardo Rodriguez leaning, and at Spa (*right* after Mairesse's fearful accident in the Belgian GP from which he escaped with quite mild injuries

the second row, arrived at the Gasworks Hairpin far too fast with everything locked up and sparked a chain-reaction multiple accident, compounded by Ginther's BRM having its throttle jam open. Mairesse then spun totally at the Station Hairpin, while Phil Hill was third behind Graham Hill and McLaren, with Bandini fifth.

Hill dropped back in the first half of the race, but towards the end re-established himself third, and when Graham Hill's leading BRM expired he was in hot pursuit of McLaren's Cooper, which had inherited the lead. Bandini was running very strongly and happily in fourth place, while at ninety-five laps, with five to go, Phil Hill was 12 seconds behind the leading Cooper, the next lap 11 seconds, then $8\frac{1}{2}$, then 7, and the Ferrari was being waved on deliriously by Monaco's usual horde of Italian spectators. Finishing lap ninety-nine there was still five seconds between them, and McLaren had matters well under control, winning by a 1.3-second margin. Bandini was third, on the same lap as the winner after an exemplary and confident performance, while Mairesse drove in very deflated style after his scatterbrained start and had managed to switch off his engine on lap 90 before it burst, being classified seventh.

The Belgian Grand Prix was at Spa on 17 June, where four 156s with 120-degree engines appeared for Hill ('0009'), Mairesse ('0004'), Baghetti ('0001') and Rodriguez ('0003'), while it was Bandini's turn to sit on the pit counter and click stopwatches. All had overhung six-speed gearboxes, and the wide-track rear ends, while only Rodriguez's had a rear anti-roll bar and lacked the new front wishbones offering adjustable base pivots.

Baghetti had a fright in practice when his mechanics forgot to fasten his car's engine cover, and it blew open at Eau Rouge like a huge air-brake and spun its startled driver heavily into the crash barrier. Hill clocked 3:59.6, not as fast as in 1961, and the effort left oil covering the back of his car. His time was fourth fastest, while Graham Hill's BRM V8 took pole at 3:57.0, and Mairesse and Rodriguez were sixth and seventh on 3:59.8 and 4:01.0 respectively.

Security straps were fitted to the Ferrari engine covers for the race, but Baghetti made a long stop with misfiring after only the second lap. Two laps later Mairesse had bustled himself to the front and he became embroiled in a desperate battle with Trevor Taylor's Lotus in which both drivers were in over their heads on this very fast and deceptive course. While they swopped the lead between them, McLaren, Graham Hill and Clark sat close behind and watched. Baghetti retired with ignition trouble after four laps, and eventually Clark took the monocoque Lotus 25 past the Taylor–Mairesse battle and ran away into the middle distance, while his team-mate fought off Mairesse to allow Clark to get clear. Rodriguez and Phil Hill were running sixth and seventh, swopping places much to the American's disgust, but on lap 26 the inevitable happened between Taylor and Mairesse. On the 120 mph Blanchimont Curve above the pits the Lotus and Ferrari touched, the British car felling a roadside telegraph pole as it cannoned into the ditch and the Ferrari rolling to rest inverted and on fire. Both drivers were flung out and escaped miraculously, Mairesse being worse off with burns and cuts. Late-race retirements suddenly elevated the two surviving Ferraris to find themselves racing for third place, and Phil Hill just managed to nose out his 'team-mate' Rodriguez by one-tenth of a second at the line.

That night Hill overheard Dragoni on the telephone to Mr Ferrari in Modena, telling him that his World Champion hadn't done a thing.... His mounting frustration was fuelled by an outbreak of intense industrial unrest in the Italian metal-working unions, which gave Ferrari the excuse to miss the French Grand Prix at Rouen, and the non-Championship events at Reims and Solitude. Phil drove a Lotus 24 for the Swiss Ecurie Filipinetti in the latter events, something Mr Ferrari never liked.

For the British Grand Prix at Aintree on 21 July—after Solitude— Maranello managed to prepare a single car for Hill, this being the Monaco spare 156/62 chassis '0007' with the inboard gearbox and 120-degree engine still retaining 12-valve heads. He qualified twelfth, on the centre of the fifth row with a 1:56.2 lap compared to Clark's Lotus 25 pole of 1:53.6. The car was hopeless, and after struggling around in midfield, running ninth at one stage, he retired at forty-seven laps with ignition problems, one distributor being at fault.

The team returned to full strength for the German Grand Prix at Nürburgring on 5 August, having given itself some breathing space in which to catch up on development and to complete a new experimental car. Going by the chassis plates Hill had his Aintree chassis '0007' with the inboard gearbox, Baghetti a standard 120-degree model and Ricardo Rodriguez a pure 1961 machine with 65-degree V6, and very unhappy about it he was. Bandini was entrusted with the experimental model.... According to Ferrari's records Hill had '0002', his Aintree '0007' being handled by Baghetti. Rodriguez was in '0006'.

Unfortunately the new, experimental car adapted old features of the British F1 cars. It used a new small-tube spaceframe, in which the driver's seat was inclined to reduce overall height and hence the car's cross-sectional area. The steering rack and track-rods were moved ahead of the front axle line to give space for the foot-pedals to pass further

THE 'SPORTS CAR' CHAMPIONSHIP

The World Sports Car Championship was instituted in 1953. Ferrari won it seven times, and Mercedes-Benz and Aston Martin once each until the CSI decided to legislate against 'two-seat racing cars' for 1962 and applied regulations which placed the emphasis on 'normal' road-going capability. Therefore 1962 saw a Grand Touring Car Championship for vehicles of which at least 100 units were to be built in 12 consecutive calendar months. The issue was complicated in the general public's eye by the CSI dividing the championship into three sub-divisions, producing World Champions in the up to 1000 cc, 1001–2000 cc and over 2000 cc classes. The result was really a foregone conclusion, with Fiat-Abarth, Porsche and Ferrari respectively dominating each division.

Meanwile the *AC de l'Ouest*, autocratic organizers of the Le Mans 24-Hours classic, retained extra spectator attraction by running a class for 'experimental prototype sports cars', more or less catering for the open-cockpit two-seaters which everybody knew and loved, and they persuaded the Sebring, Targa Florio and Nürburgring organizers to do the same—creating a sports-prototype championship within 'The Championship'. Ferrari won it, of course....

In 1963 Sebring, the Targa Florio, the Nürburgring 1000 km and Le Mans formed the only significant endurance races of the year, ostensibly run for 'GT cars' with poorly-defined 'GT Prototype cars' also admitted. Ferrari won both GT and GT Prototype titles the following year, but in 1965 Shelby American Cobra-Fords pipped Maranello's cars in the GT category leaving the Prototype Trophy to Ferrari.

By 1966 the CSI had formalized matters, recognizing Group 6 prototype and Group 4 production (50-off) sports cars. The International Championship for Sports Cars was organized in three classes, Group 1 700 cc–1300 cc, Group 2 1301–2000 cc and Group 3 over 2000 cc. These class titles fell respectively to Fiat-Abarth, Porsche and Ford of America, with their GT40s. The Sports Prototype Championship was also Ford's with their 7-litre Mark 2 cars beating Ferrari in Division 1 over 2000 cc, and Porsche beat the Dinos in Division 2, up to 2600 cc.

In 1967 Ferrari won the Constructors' Trophy from Porsche and Ford in Division 1 and Porsche beat Lotus in Division 2, while the Sports Car Champion went to Ford's GT40s beating Ferrari ... and Austin-Healey!

For 1968 the CSI hurriedly invented a World Championship of Makes, open to 3-litre 'pure-bred racing' Group 6 sports-prototype cars and to 5-litre Group 4 'production sports cars' of which a minimum of 25 had to be built in a 12-month period. Porsche astonished everyone by building 25-off their Porsche 917 flat-12 racers, and in 1970 with Fiat backing Ferrari produced their answer, the 5-litre V12 512S.

During the 1970s long-distance racing collapsed and the Group 6 open cockpit sports-racing car virtually died. The law-makers rearranged their groupings, and Ferrari won the Group 5 World Championship of Makes in 1972 with their 312PB 3-litre flat-12 cars. In 1973 Matra beat them off and in 1974, in the absence of Ferrari, Matra-Simca ruled supreme. The World Championship applied to Group 5 sports-prototype cars and Group 4 'Special GTs', and in 1976–77 the Group 5 classification was applied to so-called 'Silhouette' cars based on production GT shapes with very close to 'anything goes' mechanical parts. Thus the Stratos and Dino or 308GTB circuit 'specials' came into being, while Group 6 two-seater racing cars still survived virtually for Porsche's benefit at Le Mans.

forward, and the front disc-brake calipers were shifted behind the axle to make room for the steering arms. An exposed one-piece anti-roll bar was clamped to the chassis replacing the earlier splined-end bar from which heavy forged links picked up the wishbones. Cooling water was carried from radiator to engine and back via the chassis longerons, and lightweight pannier fuel tanks were adopted with their filler necks at the forward instead of the rearward end. This chassis offered extra rigidity at front and rear to support the heavy radiator and gearbox. The front suspension was to the latest standard Dino 156 pattern though with lowered top mounts, while the rear suspension geometry was altered to provide a swept-back planform, altering the car's weight distribution while the wheelbase remained unchanged. The coil/damper units were now mounted ahead of the wishbones instead of behind them, and a one-piece rear anti-roll bar was fitted. The nostril nose was replaced by a single 1960-style air entry. The tail orifice was open without grille bars, while the carburetters were cleared by bulges beaten into the alloy tail cowl, with brake cooling scoops formed behind and partly over them to feed the inboard rear discs. It carried the 1960/61 experimental chassis serial '0008'.

Hill tried the car—sometimes known as the 156/62P—in practice and found he kept sliding down the new inclined seat into the basement, preferring his inboard gearbox car. Meanwhile Rodriguez qualified quite well, tenth on the grid with 9:14.2, while Hill was twelfth with 9:24.7, Baghetti thirteenth on 9:28.1 and Bandini eighteenth with 9:39.7 in the new car. Weather conditions played no part in this sorry leap backwards from 1961, as Gurney's pole time in the flat-8 Porsche 804 was 8:47.2!

Hill made a superb start, passing many people on the outside to run fourth and then third, while Rodriguez was seventh on the tail of the leading bunch ending this first lap. The track was very wet and slippery under leaden skies, and on lap 4 Bandini spun the new Ferrari at the Karussel, damaged its radiator and crawled into the pits to retire. Hill made a stop to change his visor before retiring on lap 9 with defective rear dampers, which made the car undriveable after its fine start. Ricardo Rodriguez drove his ancient car with tremendous fire and skill to finish sixth and score another Championship point, while Baghetti splashed home tenth though on the same lap as Graham Hill's winning BRM—which at Nürburgring means he was less than 14¼ miles behind after 2 hrs 38 min racing....

On 19 August the *10 Gran Premio del Mediterraneo* was held on the very fast egg-shaped Pergusa circuit around the Enna lake in Sicily. Giancarlo Baghetti and Lorenzo Bandini were in search of Italian Driver Championship points and Ferrari entered them in face of ten privateers. Baghetti drove the Dino 156 '0003' used by Rodriguez at Spa and Bandini Phil Hill's '0009'. Bandini took pole with a lap in 1 min 21.5 sec with Baghetti next up at 1:22.9, and in the race they slipstreamed each other for the entire fifty laps, sharing fastest race lap at 1:20.9, 213.90 km/h (132.92 mph), Bandini winning comfortably from his team-mate to average 207.56 km/h (128.98 mph) for the 149 miles. The Sicilian crowd, of course, was overjoyed at a 'superb' all-Italian 1–2....

Lorenzo Bandini yumping the experimental 156 '0008' during practice for the 1962 German GP at Nürburgring. This shot shows off the new car's open nose and the metal induction and brake cooling humps on the engine cover. The narrow-based wishbone rear suspension without radius rod location is also clearly visible. Bandini spun into one of the 'Ring's springy hedgerows on the opening race lap

The year's Italian Grand Prix abandoned the combined speed-bowl and road circuit through the Monza Park, concentrating only on the *Autodromo's* already very fast road course, and the race distance was increased to almost 500 kilometres. Ferrari appeared in force, with Hill, Baghetti, Bandini, Ricardo Rodriguez and Mairesse. The American defending World Champion had the central-gearbox 120-degree car '0002'; Baghetti a standard 120-degree, Bandini the obsolete 65-degree (he must have blotted his copybook by winning at Enna), Rodriguez a 120-degree and Mairesse the experimental 120-degree car '0008' repaired since its radiator-rupturing escapade at Nürburgring.

Mairesse was making his first appearance since his Spa crash, and in practice—trying as hard as ever—he rammed Gregory's Lotus-BRM in the tail under braking for the *Parabolica*, crumpling the lightweight Ferrari's nose. All the cars were understeering, Hill's centre-gearbox model most of all. Mairesse's do-or-die driving placed his experimental car highest on the starting grid, tenth quickest with 1 min 42.8 sec compared with Clark's Lotus 25 pole of 1:40.35. Rodriguez was next up with 1:43.1, Hill was fifteenth on 1:43.4 and Bandini and Baghetti seventeenth and eighteenth with 1:44.3 and 1:44.4—Bandini's greater talent shining in his 65-degree-engined car.

Early in the race Baghetti, Rodriguez and Hill formed a red Ferrari flotilla battling for the lead of the second group, led by Gregory in ninth place overall. Mairesse recovered from a slow start to catch this bunch and join in with its leaders, while Hill lost his tow and dropped back and was lapped by Graham Hill's leading BRM before half-distance.

The mid-field Ferraris fought a torrid running battle with the UDT-Laystall Lotus 24s of Gregory and Ireland, swopping places and bobbing and weaving along every straight, and cornering side by side. Profiting from trouble ahead they climbed the lap chart, Mairesse inches ahead of Baghetti and Rodriguez and all three at close quarters with the McLaren and Maggs Coopers and Gurney's Porsche. On lap 59 a tremendous roar from the crowd announced that Baghetti was leading the bunch and was third overall though far behind the leading BRMs of Hill and Ginther, but next time round he spun violently at the *Parabolica* and fell to the back of the group, who all, mercifully, missed him.

Rodriguez drove into the pits with his engine flat and losing power, while Bandini, who had spent the whole race at the tail of the field caught and passed Hill. When he was lapped by his team-mates he clung onto their tails and slipstreamed through the field. There was a brief shower of rain; Hill brought his car into the pits for fuel, which Dragoni considered unnecessary, and on lap 83, with only three to run, Bandini did likewise. Mairesse was third into the last lap, but McLaren cut him out very easily before the finish line, leaving the Belgian's experimental Ferrari to finish fourth. Baghetti was fifth, Bandini eighth and twice lapped, and Hill eleventh, five laps behind his namesake's winning BRM. Rodriguez had retired his car on lap 64 with incurable ignition trouble.

That result marked the end of Ferrari's 1962 season. Soon afterwards Mr Ferrari wrote to Hill, Bandini, Baghetti and Ricardo Rodriguez announcing his team's withdrawal from competition for the remainder of the season, 'due to the lack of the indispensable collaboration of our workmen, for reasons that have their origin in a national problem and not one that originates in our own organization. . . .' The Italian Grand Prix, which he had twice won, marked the end of Phil Hill's long career as a Ferrari works driver and he and Baghetti signed for Tavoni and Chiti to join ATS's new team for 1963. Ferrari fortunes had reached a low ebb, but through that winter they turned the tide.

Right Luigi Musso opposite—
locks his rebodied interim
F2/F1 Dino around
Modena's *aerautodromo*
during the non-
Championship Grand Prix
race held there on 22
September 1957. The car is
chassis '0011' running an
1877 cc V6 engine. Musso
placed second in both heats
and overall. (Jim Sitz via Joel
Finn)

Below Dino 246 line-up at
Monza, prior to the Italian
GP on 7 September 1958. In
comparative terms these V6
GP cars were wickedly small
and compact. (Edward Eves)

Above Thoroughbred beauty shows in every inch of the Pininfarina-styled production Dino 246GT. (Neill Bruce)

Left Bertone's sober body-style for the Dino 308GT4 2 + 2 attracted considerable adverse enthusiast comment. It proved a production success nonetheless; a refined and practical Ferrari by any standards. (Neill Bruce)

Below left The unmistakable Pininfarina form resurfaced, to most enthusiasts' delight, in the Ferrari 308GTB—not a Dino by name but certainly so by ancestry. (Neill Bruce)

1963   New beginning

During their troubled 1962 season Ferrari's revised engineering staff studied closely what the World Championship-stealing British teams were up to. Only Ferrari and BRM survived as 'proper' Formula 1 car manufacturers, building their own chassis, engines and gearboxes—for Porsche had now withdrawn—while constructors like Lotus, Lola, Cooper and Brabham produced solely chassis, buying engines from Coventry Climax and gearboxes from other outside suppliers. Chassis designers like Colin Chapman of Lotus and Eric Broadley of Lola had refined Formula 1 car suspension and chassis structure to a degree far in advance of contemporary Ferrari thinking. Maranello had no need to study anybody when it came to racing engine design and construction, but they lagged sadly behind in chassis and suspension developments.

However, the 65-degree F1 Dino V6 engine was dead and its close cousin, the Chiti 120-degree V6, was obviously near the end of its Formula 1 life expectancy against the new Coventry Climax FWMV V8 with its good mid-range torque, and the very high-revving BRM P56 V8 with its excellent top end. Consequently, engineers Mauro Forghieri and Angelo Bellei had been briefed to design a new generation of Ferrari Formula 1 engines to replace the V6s; working respectively on a long-term horizontally opposed four-cam 12-cylinder and a shorter-term 90-degree four-cam V8.

During the long and very hard winter of 1962–63 the Maranello design teams were heavily committed in finalizing layouts for their new 250P mid-engined V12 sports cars to defend their endurance racing World Championship image and prestige which sold the production road cars. Delays in testing caused by heavy snowfalls knocked back the Formula 1 programme, and although both new engines ran initial evaluation tests during the season neither was available when it mattered, and both were held over for 1964. Meanwhile the new chassis intended for them ran through 1963 with the faithful 120-degree Chiti V6 nestled into its engine bay, and in the event proved to be just another interim model in the Formula 1 Ferrari's modernization.

The competitiveness of Ferrari's new Formula 1 cars in 1963 would not have happened without the willingness of new team engineer Mauro Forghieri and of the old hands Rocchi, Bussi and Salvarani to learn from the competition and to push through change at Maranello—and Mr

Ferrari's willingness to accept it and follow where he had once led. In part his willingness may be attributed to his unusual rapport with his new lead driver—the Englishman John Surtees.

This serious and single-minded Londoner had been seven-times motorcycle World Champion before turning to cars, riding much of the time for Count Agusta's MV concern, and living and working in Italy. He liked the country and its people and spoke the language fluently. The *tifosi* loved him for his MV-Agusta exploits, and christened him *Il Grande John*—'John the Great'.

In 1959 he had test-driven Tony Vandervell's Vanwalls, finding his feet as a racing driver rather than a racing motor-cycle rider, and he displayed immense sensitivity and skill and tremendous potential. Vandervell was an old-established supplier of bearings to Ferrari as well as a respected Formula 1 adversary, and he and Enzo Ferrari might have come from the same autocratic industrialist mould. Vandervell's evident interest in Surtees heightened Ferrari's, and when John drove for Team Lotus in 1960 in selected Formula 1 events he excelled and underlined his promise. In 1961 he learned the ropes with a full Formula 1 season in an uncompetitive Cooper, and for 1962 Mr Ferrari made him an offer . . . but Surtees refused it.

One suspects this refusal may have increased Mr Ferrari's regard for the man, particularly as Surtees went his own way and established what was more or less his own team to run new Lola-Climax cars designed by Eric Broadley. This independent operation was typical of the man, and during the year he matured into a technically gifted driver of the highest class. Still, Lola could offer little future, and when Mr Ferrari repeated his offer for 1963 John felt he was ready—and he accepted.

He brought with him up-to-date knowledge of British Formula 1 chassis and suspension practice combined with a total dedication and unremitting will to win, which fired Ferrari's technicians from the highest to the lowest with new enthusiasm. At the same time Ferrari signed on full-time the formally qualified British engineer-driver Mike Parkes to undertake development duties on the sports and production-car side. Mike had been with the Rootes Group as project engineer on the alloy-engined Hillman Imp small-car programme and as it successfully entered production he moved to Maranello permanently. Parkes and Surtees were to grow apart rather than together in their Ferrari years, but in the meantime Forghieri, under the eye of the senior engineers like Jano, Bazzi (always on hand) and Rocchi, developed new Formula 1 cars which would match the British 'special-builders' and BRM at their own game. Franco Rocchi is known mainly as an engine man, but Surtees recalls he played a leading part in design of the 1963 chassis.

Surtees flew to Italy in November 1962 for his initial test-drives, first at Modena then at Monza. He found Modena '. . . not a good development circuit—all you can really test there are gearboxes, brakes and driving position. You have to muddle through on the rest.' He drove the latest experimental centre-gearbox Formula 1 156, now fitted with unpainted body panelling with a nose orifice 'waisted' at the centre but lacking the vertical 'septum' of the original shark nose. Its rear

Lorenzo Bandini

b. 21 December, 1936
d. 10 May, 1967

The handsome Bandini was born to Italian parents in Barce, Cyrenaica, North Africa, and moved with his family to Florence in 1939. Lorenzo's father died when he was 15 and he left home to become a motor mechanic in Milan. His employer, a Signor Freddi, encouraged his motor racing enthusiasm, but after five years young Bandini set up his own garage in Milan's Via Bardelli.

He made his competition debut in 1957, driving a borrowed Fiat 1100 in the Castell'Arquato-Vernasca hillclimb. He was placed 15th in class.... Freddi loaned a tuned Fiat 1100 and later an 8V for further minor events, and eventually provided a Lancia Appia in which Bandini and Ciali won their class in the 1958 Mille Miglia rally.

At the end of that year Bandini bought a Volpini FJ and made his debut with it at Syracuse on September 28. He was third in both race heats and drove Volpini and Stanguellini FJs through 1959 into 1960. Mimo Dei, patron of Scuderia Centro-Sud, took him on and he drove Cooper-Maseratis for the team, even taking a 2.9 version to the Tasman Series in 1962. Mr Ferrari took him on for occasional Formula 1 and sports car drives in the European season, and then he was dropped to Centro-Sud once again in 1963, driving their new BRM. Performances in this car and injuries to Mairesse won Bandini a permanent place in the Ferrari team at the close of the season...

He drove hard and often more with his heart than his head, but he never developed the skilled edge which could make a determined driver a genuine winner. He lost his final race at Monaco in 1967, when he tired in his long second-place pursuit of Hulme's Brabham-Repco. His Ferrari 312 tipped the chicane barriers and rolled over. Bandini suffered unsurvivable impact injuries and burns to which he succumbed three days later.

suspension had been modified to comprise an upper wishbone, reversed lower wishbone (with the 'thin end' attached to the chassis frame) and two non-parallel radius arms extending forward on either side to pick-ups in line with the rear cockpit bulkhead. The upper radius rods were attached at hub height on the upright in Lotus fashion, but the car retained Borrani wire wheels. John found the car had done a lot of miles and after acclimatizing himself to the left-hand gear-change he was able to compare its handling to the 1960–61 Coopers he had raced the previous year! He found its suspension too hard for comfort, but the gear-change was delightful and the brakes 'most impressive'. And the engine? 'What an engine it is!' he reported. 'It seems to want to rev for ever and although I only used about 9500 to 9800 rpm—which seemed to give about maximum power I'm told that the 120-degree units are pretty well unburstable, and that's just the impression that this well-used example gave me. I would rate it a very sturdy engine indeed, and I thoroughly enjoyed my thirty-odd laps....'

He was more intrigued by the two sports cars provided, for they gave his first opportunity to handle a sports-racer since his initial trial in December 1959 with an Aston-Martin DBR1/300. One was a works development Dino 246SP with low-tail bodywork, which he was told had completed '3000-odd racing miles... without an engine overhaul, it wasn't surprising to find it down on power'. Still he 'liked it a lot. It was exceedingly well balanced, with a fair amount of understeer, and I soon became accustomed to the extra cockpit noise, the heavier feel and the vast screen, all of which contrasted vividly with the Formula 1 car.... I must admit that I had been nursing some reservations about the two-

seaters before the test, but these were quickly dispelled....' The other sports car was 246SP/62 '0796' fitted with a 250 *Testa Rossa* V12 as a prototype for the 1963 250P, and according to Surtees it was brand new on the day of his test; freshly modified with the V12 engine installation having its first outing in this form. He found it had vicious oversteer initially, but after some juggling with anti-roll bars, springs and tyre pressures it improved, and next day at Monza he drove forty laps at around 1 min 40 sec. He found the car 'a real treat' and admitted his brief experience had given him 'a taste for sports car racing....' He delighted in its steering, which was '... about 60 per cent on the throttle and 40 per cent on the steering wheel'.

Surtees was signed-on with Willy Mairesse for the new season, Mr Ferrari emphasizing at his February press conference that he intended to run fewer cars than previously, and that he had signed on these two as test-drivers first and racing drivers second. 'I want no more drivers who want only to race, never to test,' he declared in what was taken as a jibe at Phil Hill. Lorenzo Bandini had been released to drive a private red-painted BRM for Scuderia Centro-Sud in Formula 1, while being retained for the Ferrari sports-car team; poor Ricardo Rodriguez had lost his life in a Rob Walker Lotus 24 during practice for his home country's first F1 Grand Prix the previous year, and Baghetti of course had gone with Hill to ATS. Team manager Dragoni hated the idea of Bandini, a fellow Milanese, being replaced in his team by an Englishman and a Belgian, and during the season he pressed for the talented young Italian's return.

Meanwhile the finalized V12 250P was unveiled as Maranello's front-line endurance racer, its front end reshaped to erase the Chiti-signature nostril-nose which was replaced by a single 'letter-box' intake. The V6 Dinos were largely replaced in the works team, the surviving 1962 cars in the main being sold into private hands after having new-style letter-box

Above Sebring 1963 with the Buck Fulp/Harry Heuer NART-entered Dino 268SP '0798' on their way to a 34th place classification after twelve hours of toil and trouble. This car shows the letter-box nose standardized in 1963 in place of the original nostrils. It was subsequently raced by Tom O'Brien and Dick Hutchins in the USA

Right Ludovico Scarfiotti hurtles 196SP '0802' round the majestic 45-mile Piccolo Madonie circuit to take a close second place in the 1963 Targa Florio in partnership with Lorenzo Bandini and Willy Mairesse. This was the V8 car crashed by Hill in practice for the 1962 Targa, and already it shows evidence of solid contact with the Sicilian roadside. Mairesse spun it on the last lap and finished with the engine cover broken open and ballooning in his wake

Right The 1963 Targa
second-place car has been
described by some authorities
as a 206S, suggesting it used
the four-cam 2-litre V6
engine. This Geoff Goddard
shot in the Ferrari garage at
Cefalu shows the 'bed-knob'
one-piece cam covers of what
was in fact the two-cam 196S
engine, the induction air-box
fed from an intake on the
right side of the engine cover,
hip-duct-fed brake cooling
trunks, coolant system header
tank on the rear cockpit
bulkhead and hefty transaxle
assembly with the overhung
exposed clutch drum and
robust release support. Rear
wheel camber and toe-in is
still considerable

noses fitted. However, they had a hat-trick of Targa Florio victories to shoot for, and on 5 May the Sicilian classic saw Ferrari entering two of the already successful 250Ps in the 3-litre class and a Dino 196SP— actually Phil Hill's ex-Targa crash ex-V8 '0802'—in the 2-litre division. It was to be driven by Scarfiotti and Bandini, while a privately entered 196SP ran for Lualdi and Bini. According to Denis Jenkinson's *Motor Sport* report the only evident difference between these V6 cars and the 3-litre V12s was that the 'Prototype GT' cars' cockpits were lined with carpet and rubber mats. Practice troubles saw Scarfiotti assigned to a 250P for the start alongside Parkes's sister car, while Bandini had the Dino. The Bonnier/Carlo Mario Abate Porsche flat-8 led after Scarfiotti was slowed by fuel system troubles with one 250P and Surtees crashed the other and split its fuel tank while leading. Scarfiotti managed to force his 250P back into the lead despite bouncing it off the rockery, but the Porsche had made its final scheduled stop while 'Lulu' had one still to go. Mairesse took over the sick Ferrari, soon to abandon it as its fuel feed problem developed into a massive leak, but Scarfiotti was out in the Dino and running very fast indeed. He forced it into the lead, but the Porsche had made its final stop and the Dino's was still to come. Dragoni put Mairesse instead of Bandini into the car at that final stop, which proved to be a mistake, as although he was very fast Mairesse was more likely to 'drop it' than Bandini—who was quite fast enough....

Mairesse was ahead on corrected time only half a lap after leaving the pits, but rain was beginning to fall. Bonnier was outdriving Mairesse on the slippery mountain roads into the last lap, and although the Belgian had the Dino's lights ablaze his lead at Campofelice village was only 4.5 seconds, with seven miles to go.

Bonnier had started six minutes before the Dino, so after arriving safely at the finish he had to wait to see whether or not he had won. Mairesse was driving the Dino absolutely flat out in the rain along the bumpy Buonfornello Straight beside the sea, but in the final swerves before the pits area he spun and clumped a road-side marker stone with the Dino's tail, breaking the retaining catches and safety strap. Time was so precious he picked-up bottom gear and smoked away for the finish line with the engine cover ballooning open like a huge air-brake. He crossed the line 6 min 11.6 sec after the Porsche for second place by just the 11.6 sec, after seven hours' racing.

The other Dino shared by Lualdi and Bini suffered even worse misfortune, crashing on the opening lap and catching fire. Edoardo Lualdi-Gabardi had won the minor Stallavena-Boscochiesuanuova hillclimb with the car before the Targa, and with its fire damage repaired he won the Consuma climb on 2 June. Without works participation in the European Mountain Championship, Ferrari lost their title to Porsche.

Lualdi-Gabardi ran his '0790' in the series, but his performances were a mere shadow of Scarfiotti's splendour the previous year. The car was no match for the new works Porsche *Bergspyder* driven by Edgar Barth, which won five of the seven Championship climbs outright and the East German defector won a sixth in a Porsche-Abarth Carrera. Lualdi's muted Championship challenge began in round two, Mont

What became of the 1961 246SP prototype '0790'? Well, here it is, rebodied as a 1963 196SP and driven in Targa Florio practice by its new owner Edoardo Lualdi-Gabardi. He was to have shared it with Bini in the race, but it caught fire and was forced out on the opening lap. John Godfrey's detailed research revealed the identity of this chassis. It was later hillclimbed before being sold to Leandro Terra for the 1964 season

Ventoux, on 23 June, but his 12 min 21.2 sec climb was good only for fifth place behind three Porsches and a Lotus-BMW — Barth's winning time being more than half a minute faster.

At Trento–Bondone on 14 July, Lualdi was sixth, again thirty seconds slower than Edi Barth, and two weeks later at Cesana–Sestriere the Dino 196SP was placed eighth, in deep trouble and over a minute behind. Lualdi did not feature at Freiburg, but 25 August at Ollon – Villars saw an improvement to fourth and another Championship points score (first six places scoring). His time of 9:27.8 was only twenty-five seconds slower than Barth, but that was the end — his bolt was shot; his six points placing him eighth overall in the Championship behind Edgar Barth's winning total of 45.

While the Targa Florio was the highspot of the Dino sports cars' dying season, in the USA several cars (including the NART 268SP V8, chassis '0798') were campaigned by amateurs. Buck Fulp and William Cooper won the Sports Car Club of America 'E-Modified' Divisional Championships with Dinos, while names like Bob Grossman, Ray Heppenstall and Doug Thiem handled the cars on occasion.

The NART V8 car ran at Sebring on 24 March, shared by Fulp and Harry Heuer, and they lay seventh at half-distance behind four Ferraris (led by Graham Hill/Pedro Rodriguez in the Le Mans-winning

TRI-330LM V12) a Cobra and an E type Jaguar, but later hit trouble. They were classified 34th, forty-nine laps down on the winning Surtees/Scarfiotti 250P.

The big Dino V8 ran again in the third Canadian Grand Prix at Mosport Park on 28 September, when Pedro Rodriguez won in a NART-backed 250P. Lorenzo Bandini drove the Dino and qualified eighth quickest at 1 min 38.2 sec compared to Surtees's 250P pole of 1:33.5. He ran in mid-field until the car threw a wheel and spun harmlessly into a trackside embankment, Bandini vaulting from the cockpit to chase the errant wheel.

Against this background, the Formula 1 V6 cars were far more active and successful. Ferrari passed up six of the early season non-Championship races while finalizing the new cars, and they eventually made their debut in the BRDC International Trophy at Silverstone on 11 May.

The new multi-tubular spaceframes were much lighter and more compact than their 'iron' predecessors, properly triangulated with a centre sheet fuel tank embodying the seat, as in the contemporary Cooper-Climax. Double-wishbone front suspension with outboard coil-spring/damper units was retained, the top wishbones being very short and the lower members very wide based. The rear suspension followed Lotus/Lola practice as seen in the interim Monza/Modena test chassis, with a pair of long radius arms on either side, the upper unit meeting the hub carrier at axle height, while lateral location was provided by reversed wishbones (the narrow end picking up on the chassis, the forked outboard end carrying the hub-carrier foot) and by single top links, which were tubular members threaded to provide rapid camber adjustment. The half-shafts had splined sliding joints and mounted Dunlop disc brakes inboard on the transaxle cheeks, while outboard front brakes were retained. At last Ferrari had dropped the heavy Borrani wire-spoked road wheel and had adopted complex 20-spoke alloy castings of their own design and manufacture, retained by centre-lock eared nuts and located on five drive-pegs.

The 120-degree V6 engine was installed steeply raked in the chassis with a torsional coupling to the primary drive-shaft, which ran through the transmission aggregate as before to the usual Ferrari overhung multi-plate clutch. A concentric shaft then drove forward from the clutch beneath the final-drive to the inboard gearbox, which was now a remarkably short assembly with gears clustered on three shafts providing six forward speeds.

Engine development had seen a Bosch-based high-pressure fuel injection system tailored to the V6 with the assistance of Swiss former Porsche engineer Michel May. The pressure pump was driven by an internally toothed belt from the camshaft drive. There were long induction trumpets within the vee with slide throttles on each bank of three. The injectors were screwed into the cylinder walls within the vee and directed across the piston axes, unlike Mercedes-Benz's Bosch-injected racing engines, in which the injectors had been aimed tangentially to promote swirl. There were two sparking plugs per

John Surtees in the sleek new alloy-wheeled '0001' chases Graham Hill's BRM over the cement dust at Monaco's Station Hairpin, 1963. Surtees found the V6 'nice, but it couldn't compete with the British V8s. It worked best when it was geared to rev, then it sang along nicely, but wouldn't last. If you geared it for safety you lost ten horse and with only 1½-litres to play with ... that was too much'

cylinder, and the unit was rated at 200 bhp at 10,200 rpm with 'increased mid-range torque,' although precise torque figures were never published.

Wheelbase was 2380 mm (93.7 in), which was about $2\frac{1}{2}$ in longer than the last shark-nose cars, and the track at 1380 mm (54.3 in) was nearly $2\frac{1}{2}$ in wider than before. The wheels themselves were 15-inch diameter carrying Dunlop 5.00–15 and 7.00–15 tyres front and rear. Weight, less fuel and driver was 465 kg (1025 lb) and the cars were clad in sleek new aluminium bodywork by Fantuzzi, which was everything a modern Formula 1 car should have, neat, sleek and extremely handsome. These chassis began a new number series, commencing again at '0001'.

Ireland's Lotus-BRM V8 took pole at Silverstone on 1 min 34.4 sec, Surtees qualified seventh on row two with 1:36.2 and Mairesse was ninth one row behind with 1:38.0. Surtees hared into third place behind McLaren and Clark on lap two, but his car was trailing a stream of blue oil smoke from the left side of the engine, where a trivial leak was burning away on the exhaust manifolding. Surtees disposed of McLaren and set off hard after Clark's leading Lotus 25, and with the race being run at record speed it was clear Ferrari were back in touch. Meanwhile Mairesse was still learning the circuit down in mid-field, and being led by Bandini's Centro-Sud BRM, until lap 7, but, having got by, the Belgian misjudged Stowe Corner and spun his brand-new car backwards into the earthworks. Surtees was running a consistent six seconds behind Clark and leading a top-quality field until lap 28, when his smoke cloud had disappeared and it was clear his engine was running out of oil. On lap 31 he switched off past the pits, and coasted to a standstill out on the circuit, his race run—but notice served.... When the V8 engine arrived Ferrari would be up front once more.

The Monaco Grand Prix was on 26 May and Ferrari fielded Surtees in his Silverstone car and Mairesse in a brand-new replacement for the damaged Silverstone machine. They ran with cut-back 'Monaco noses' and tried long and short megaphone exhausts in practice, the long pipes offering better results. They had an early handling problem on the hairpins, understeering violently, but later Surtees got into his stride and battled with Clark and the BRMs of Hill and Ginther for fastest time. Then brake trouble intervened and he hit both sides of the chicane, bending his car's suspension and cracking its chassis frame. While it was being repaired Clark took pole at 1 min 34.3 sec, Surtees's 1:35.2 placing him third on row two of the grid, while Mairesse was seventh at 1:35.9.

Clark and Graham Hill fought for the race lead, while Surtees ran fifth behind Ginther (BRM) and McLaren before attacking and passing them both. He ran right on Hill's tail for second place, but was coated in oil leaking from the BRM. Mairesse lost sixth place when his final-drive failed after thirty-seven laps, and on lap 57 Surtees finally slashed by Graham Hill for second place. But once in front he could see nothing through his oil-covered goggles, and without the shape of the BRM to follow he was lost and flurried into the pits for a replacement pair. He rejoined some way behind the BRM, and found his engine's oil pressure down from 6 kg/cm² to nearer 2 kg/cm² as the lubricant was overheating.

He eased up and allowed Ginther and McLaren to close on him, and got blue-flagged by Race Director Louis Chiron, who thought he was holding them up. This let Ginther by, then McLaren, much to the Italian spectators' vocal disgust, but on lap 79 Clark's race was run and Surtees inherited fourth behind the two BRMs and McLaren's Cooper.

Into the final ten laps McLaren settled back for third and Surtees began a win-or-bust effort as his oil pressure had stabilized. He set a new lap record of 1:34.6 on lap 97 and on the 100th and last time round recorded 1:34.5, 119.809 km/h (74.44 mph), but McLaren beat him to the line by 1.3 seconds; the Ferrari finishing fourth.

On 9 June Spa–Francorchamps saw another Belgian Grand Prix, and Ferrari ran special small-air-entry nose cowls on both cars for Surtees and Mairesse. Practice found them again in hot oil trouble, causing the pressure to drop, and although happy with the car's high-speed handling Surtees remained unconvinced by its brakes. He ended up tenth on the grid with a best lap of 3 min 57.9 sec, while Mairesse was up on the front row alongside Graham Hill and Gurney's Brabham, with 3:55.3 compared to Hill's 3:54.1 pole.

Mairesse lay third early in the race while Surtees was involved with Brabham, McLaren and Gurney in a battle for fourth. Mairesse braked too late for La Source fourth time round and careered straight on towards Spa centre, and after gathering it up he did another lap and peeled off into the pits because the V6 was not firing properly. After two more laps in which the car continued to misfire Mairesse retired, Mr Bosch getting the blame. Meanwhile Clark was leading from Graham Hill, and Surtees established himself third until, on lap 14, he dived into the pits with his V6 misfiring. After a few more laps he gave up.

Two weeks later, at Zandvoort on 23 June, the Dutch Grand Prix found Surtees supported by Ludovico Scarfiotti, having his first single-seater drive in place of Mairesse, who had suffered burns at Le Mans when his leading 250P caught fire. The fuel-injected V6 engines had been developed to give more power and were revving to 10,600 rpm for the first time.

Scarfiotti got off to a poor start by breaking his engine in first practice and Surtees was in the usual Ferrari handling problems on this circuit. After a lot of hard work the grid was decided with Surtees fifth fastest on the outside of the second row with a lap in 1 min 33.0 sec (Clark's pole being 1:31.6), while Scarfiotti was eleventh on the inside of row five with 1:35.6.

Both cars became embroiled in a mid-field battle early in the race, while Clark led from Graham Hill and Brabham. Surtees was fourth before being caught and passed with apparent ease, by Gurney's Brabham, and when Hill and Brabham ran into trouble John finished third behind Clark and Gurney, though the Lotus driver had lapped the whole field. At one stage Surtees had run second, but a spin demoted him once more. Scarfiotti had a regular downfield run punctuated by a wild spin (very out of character) at Tarzan Curve with only ten laps to go, but he lost no places and finished sixth. Things were looking better....

The French Grand Prix was again at Reims, on 30 June, and there the

Giulio Borsari, long-serving Ferrari mechanic and eventually crew-chief in the seventies, in Mairesse's '0002' at Spa during the 1963 Belgian GP meeting. Here the cars ran with lengthened, small orifice high-penetration nose cones. The cast-alloy wheels, replacing the heavier and less rigid Borrani wires to which Ferrari remained faithful for so long, and Lotus-like rear suspension with hub-level top radius rods are noteworthy

The 1963 Formula 1 Dino 156 V6 engine removed from the new-generation space-frame cars, showing the shelved sump pan mirroring the engine's down-turned mounting within the chassis. The idea was to adapt the ageing engine to a modern F1 chassis' low drive-shaft height and also to assist oil scavenging. Note the twin-plug ignition between the cams. It had two-valve-per-cylinder heads. Here at Nürburgring, Carlo Amadessi had something to smile about

two cars from Zandvoort reappeared with new engine covers incorporating eared air scoops feeding the injection from intakes on either side
behind the driver's head. Ferrari said the scoops absorbed 14 bhp, but
that they added more power than they cost. Surtees was quicker in
Scarfiotti's car early on while the engineers played with tuned exhaust
lengths, and on the second practice day — Thursday — the Reims circuit
was soaked by rain. Scarfiotti was running his car late that afternoon
when he went into a slide on the viscid surface at the top of the hill
between Muizon and Thillois and the Ferrari cannoned along a ditch and
hit a telegraph pole, which wrote off its front end and damaged
Scarfiotti's knees. He was very bruised and shaken, and declared he
would not drive in Formula 1 again....

His best time in the dry had been 2 min 27.0 sec, while in the wet
before his accident he managed 2:41.6 compared to Surtees's
wet-weather lap in 2:33.8, which was fastest of the session. John ended
up fourth fastest with 2:21.9 on row two behind Clark's pole of 2:20.2,
and nobody saw which way the Scotsman went once the race began.
Surtees was again embroiled in a high-speed group battling for second
place, including Ginther, Gurney, Brabham, McLaren, Taylor, Graham
Hill and Tony Maggs's Cooper and he had just assumed command when
the Ferrari's fuel pump abruptly failed. He coasted into the pits and
rejoined the race after attention, only to break down for good after
completing thirteen laps. It was a sorry disappointment.

Silverstone and the British Grand Prix followed on 20 July, and
Ferrari made a lone entry for John Surtees with the choice of two cars.
Practice was run at fearsome pace and it was evident that fuel tankage
would be marginal for this eighty-two-lap 240-mile race. The Ferrari
carried nominally 125 litres of fuel, but the night before the race Surtees
stayed up with Forghieri and the mechanics to fit a reserve 3-gallon tank
into the cockpit — just in case.

He had qualified fifth quickest with 1 min 35.2 sec against Clark's
inevitable Lotus pole of 1:34.4 and raced hard with Brabham, Gurney,
McLaren and Hill again for second place behind the fast-disappearing
Scot. This second place battle resolved itself into a three-cornered
dispute between Gurney's Brabham, Hill's BRM and the lone Ferrari,
and when Gurney's engine exploded Hill was second and Surtees close
behind a constant third. On the last lap Hill ran out of fuel and coasted for
the line, but Surtees was by and away into second place, happy that his
reserve tank hunch had saved the day. He also set fastest lap of the race,
before the track became oily, at 1:36.0 on lap 3.

Ferrari as usual missed the Solitude Grand Prix to prepare for
Nürburgring and the German Championship round on 4 August.
Mairesse had recovered from his painful Le Mans burns, and was back in
harness alongside Surtees, while the cars were slightly modified.
Surtees's car had bolt-on wheels in place of the knock-off centre-locks,
and this caused considerable amusement amongst the British teams, who
had adopted this lighter fixing years before. Someone commented that
one day soon Ferrari would also discover the 10 mm spark plug, for the
V6 engines were the last Grand Prix bastion of the 14 mm fitting.

Fulfilled promise — Surtees
and Clark during their fierce
battle in the opening stages of
the 1963 German Grand Prix
at Nürburgring, sweeping
down over the Wehrseifen
bridge towards Adenau
Crossing. For this race
revised Bosch fuel-injection
greatly improved mid-range
punch. The cut-down engine
cover and gauze induction
cowl on '0002' is clearly
visible

Surtees and the engine men had spent several days at Bosch, modifying their fuel-injection metering to improve mid-range torque. Attention was also paid to minimizing air temperatures at the intake trumpets, first by using an aluminium shroud to deflect engine heat downwards away from the centre of the vee, where it had been cooking the injector pump and causing vapour locks as well as mechanical problems inside the pump. Now the engine hatch was fitted with a one-piece wire gauze over the trumpets, and the former suggestion of a head-rest was removed, lowering the car's profile slightly.

Surtees spent much time in practice experimenting with suspension settings and spring/damper combinations which would minimize the length of time the car spent airborne over the Nürburgring's humps and jumps, and was soon down to 8 min 46.7 sec for the 14.2-mile lap. On the second day the Ferrari's chassis cracked, but Surtees finished with second spot on the four-strong front row, with his first session time comparing to Clark's 8:45.8 on pole. Bandini drove his Centro-Sud BRM very well for third spot with 8:45.3, which confirmed growing Ferrari interest in the man, and pleased Dragoni no end. Mairesse was seventh quickest on the outside of the second row with 9:03.5.

Both Bandini and Surtees made poor starts, and while Clark should have run well clear Ginther caught and passed him in the BRM and Surtees had recovered to close on his tail down towards Adenau Bridge. Bandini crashed at the *Karussel*, while Surtees completed the lap second between Ginther and Clark with Mairesse seventh. Lap 2 saw Clark and

Surtees simply leave the rest standing, while over the jump at *Flugplatz* Mairesse leapt high, landed askew and was thrown off course into the ditch, severely damaging his car and hospitalizing himself once more with a broken arm. Unhappily the crashing car struck and killed a medical attendant.

Clark's Lotus continued in the lead, but it was occasionally cutting out on one cylinder and Surtees was not to be shaken off. On lap 4 the Ferrari forged by to take the lead. Surtees drove with majestic calm and pace, setting a new lap record ninth time round at 8:47.0, 155.8 km/h (96.80 mph), and the Dino 156 hammered home to a convincing win over everybody save Clark, whose handicapped Lotus finished second. The 'interim' Ferrari had scored a notable maiden victory on the hardest Grand Prix circuit in the Championship series. The days at Bosch had paid off.

Pergusa, Sicily, on 18 August was the scene for the Mediterranean Grand Prix and Ferrari entered Surtees there in his German Grand Prix winning car, facing works Lotus and Brabham opposition, although Jim Clark was absent. John took pole in practice with a 1 min 16.1 sec lap compared to Bandini's Ferrari pole the previous year of 1:21.5, the Italian driver taking second place in the Centro-Sud BRM 0.3 second slower than the Englishman. Surtees led all the way to win from Peter Arundell's Lotus 25 at an average speed of 221.83 km/h (137.84 mph). His fastest race lap was set at 1:15.9, 227.99 km/h (141.67 mph)—another new record.

With two consecutive Formula 1 race victories under their belt, one major, one minor, Ferrari arrived at Monza on 8 September with three cars for Surtees and Bandini, the latter being invited to rejoin the Formula 1 team in Mairesse's enforced absence; Centro-Sud patron 'Mimo' Dei gladly giving him the opportunity.

Left and above The prototype 'Aero' semi-monocoque Ferrari 156 photographed in the Monza paddock during the 1963 Italian GP meeting. The 120-degree V6 engine hung on mild-steel fabricated brackets at top and bottom with a sketchy support frame passing back around the sump to pick up the rear suspension lower wishbones. The tub itself can be seen panelled around the driver's backrest with a separate seat tank fitted into the cockpit, its filler neck protruding through the flimsy roll-over hoop. Front suspension featured inboard coil-spring/damper units actuated by top cantilever arms. The rivet lines on the tub sides betray the existence of a tube infra-structure. Note the additional long-range fuel tank strapped over the driver's leg space by rubber bungees

Above right Surtees's new 'Aero' smokes its way round the Parabolica turn at Monza on its way into retirement after starting from pole position and establishing an early race lead. This was one of the prettiest mid-engined Formula 1 Ferraris

The hard winter and Ferrari's demanding sports-prototype programme had delayed introduction of the new semi-monocoque F1 chassis which had been planned to carry the V8 and flat-12 engines this season. As time had slipped by its debut was knocked back, first to Nürburgring, then to Enna and finally to Monza for the Italian Grand Prix. Even then the V8 engine was not considered ready, and so the new chassis was modified to accept the 120-degree fuel-injected V6.

Forghieri's interpretation of the Lotus-introduced monocoque chassis comprised two parallel fuel tank pontoons, fabricated and riveted aircraft-style over a sketchy framework of two tube longerons, which were staggered slightly in the vertical plane. The tubes doubled to carry oil and water runs to and from the engine at the rear and cooler matrices at the front. The stressed-skin pontoons were united side-to-side by a stressed floor panel with angle stiffening plates, and at each end were riveted to transverse bulkheads. That at the front was doubled to sandwich inboard coil-spring/damper units actuated by an inboard cantilever extension of a top rocker-arm 'wishbone' member. The dash panel structure amidships provided another lateral chassis stiffener, while the rear bulkhead behind the cockpit was a hefty fabrication in which the whole chassis nacelle terminated, leaving no chassis extension to carry the engine and gearbox. This was most unusual, and was a leap ahead of British chassis practice, for Forghieri and the Ferrari technical team had opted to design their new generation V8 and flat-12 engines with sufficient crankcase rigidity to double as load-bearing chassis members in the rear of the car. The engine would bolt rigidly to the chassis closing plate and would react major rear suspension drive and braking loads from mounting lugs cast onto the engine/transmission aggregate. A similar stressing principle had been adopted by Jano ten years before, when he laid out the Lancia D50 chassis design, which

175

became Ferrari's in the middle of '55, but that was a front-engined configuration in which the V8 engine merely replaced cross-bracing tubes to 'triangulate' the forward chassis bay.

On the new model, christened the Ferrari 'Aero' monocoque 156, the front suspension with its inboard coil/dampers, top rocker arm and broad-based lower wishbone with outboard disc brake in the wheel hub closely resembled Lotus practice. Rear suspension intended to hang on the engine and gearbox mirrored the existing cars' system, but the six-speed and reverse gearbox was new, overhung outboard of the final-drive and with the clutch and flywheel in a conventional bell-housing on the back of the engine. The rear brakes remained inboard on the transaxle cheeks. A sleek nose cowl, simple tray-type engine cover with gauze mesh over the injection trumpets, and engine bay side fairings formed the bodywork, the painted monocoque flanks amidships running exposed.

The new car with a prototype V8 engine installed was tested before the Grand Prix and proved satisfactorily fast, but its reliability was suspect. Consequently the rear end of this prototype 'Aero' chassis was modified to carry a revised 120-degree V6 engine. A new crankshaft was made up specially to accept the inboard clutch and flywheel mechanism, and a crankcase scallop was provided to remount the starter motor beneath the bell-housing. The original casting patterns were used suitably cut about and modified to provide this temporary expedient of an engine, and one can imagine no modern Formula 1 team other than Ferrari having the capacity to do such a thing. Still the basic V6 crankcase was not pre-stressed to the levels required by V8 design analysis, and so a tubular sub-frame was fitted beneath the unit to accept some suspension and chassis loads.

This extraordinary example of a Ferrari Formula 1 'special' had the same 2380 mm (93.7 in) wheelbase of the tubular spaceframe '63 cars, but narrower track at 1350 mm (53.1 in) front and 1340 mm (52.8 in) rear. It weighed-in at 460 kg, 1014 lb, which was a saving of around 5 kg (11 lb) over its predecessor.

The Ferrari engineers had been aiming at a smaller cross-section than the already tiny British Lotus 25s, but Mr Ferrari backed his drivers in asking for improved cockpit space and the 'Aero' nacelle ended up 70 cm (27.5 in) in width, 1 cm wider than the Lotus.

Surtees tried this car—apparently chassis '0004'—in Monza practice, after his Nürburg and Pergusa-winner, while Bandini's similar spaceframe car was running the latest bolt-on wheel modifications. *Il Grande John* was fastest in practice on the combined road and speed-bowl course when the banking caused some suspension failures in other cars and the omnipresent police banned the used of the speed-bowl, to the relief of many drivers and team managers. The race was to be run instead on the pure road circuit through the Royal Park.

When the 'Aero' V6 arrived for Surtees he proceeded to set a new standard in Formula 1, taking pole position with a stunning 1 min 37.3 sec lap, which was fully 1.2 seconds faster than Graham Hill's best for BRM, alongside him on the front row. Bandini was sixth, on row three, with 1:40.1 in the spaceframe car.

The starter kept the field waiting too long with engines running, and Surtees was gesticulating at him when he finally dropped the flag abruptly and the Ferrari was slow away, wheel-spinning furiously as Hill and Clark (from the second row) gripped and sprinted ahead. Hill led while Clark and Surtees ran wheel-to-wheel for second place in the opening laps, and on lap 17 the immense crowd groaned audibly as Hill went by the pits and grandstands followed by Clark alone. The Ferrari had dropped a valve and Surtees coasted into the pits to retire with white vapour puffing from the exhausts. Bandini drove hard but well behind the leaders until lap 38, when his car's gearbox failed, bringing Ferrari's effort to an ignominious halt. Clark won the race, and the World Championship.

Ferrari went to America for the United States Grand Prix for the first time in four years, Surtees having the 'Aero' V6 special and Bandini a standard model, with a second spaceframe car as spare. In practice at Watkins Glen Surtees had the 'Aero's' right-rear lower wishbone break away from the chassis, and Bandini slowed to ask what was the matter, Brabham and Ginther barrelling over a blind brow moments later to find the road blocked by two Ferraris, and skittering by on the verges. John managed 1 min 13.7 sec in his spaceframe car, third-fastest overall behind Hill's pole of 1:13.4, and he raced the older chassis. Bandini was ninth with 1:15.8.

Surtees soared to second behind Hill early in the race, with Bandini ninth, and John was soon in the lead, which changed, Surtees to Hill and back again. The Ferrari lead became established until at lap 80 with thirty still to run Surtees's V6 engine ran rough, and three laps later he stammered into the pits to retire. Bandini ran intelligently home into fifth place four laps behind Hill's victorious BRM.

The season ended with the first World Championship Mexican Grand Prix at Mexico City's Magdalena Mixhuca park circuit on 27 October. Ferrari flew out a second monocoque V6 special to join the Watkins Glen 'Aero' and two spaceframe cars, but only Surtees and Bandini were to drive, John opting for the older monocoque.

Surtees qualified on the two-car front-row with a best lap of 2:00.5, compared to Clark's 1:58.8 on pole, while Bandini was seventh in his monocoque car at 2:02.4. Clark drew away from Surtees off the line, and the Ferrari was relegated to third place by Gurney, the car understeering so much on the fast curve before the pits that blue smoke was pluming back from its outside front tyre. The front suspension was slowly collapsing, and was bottoming out all round the circuit, and after being passed by Brabham, Surtees stopped at the pit to investigate. When he tried to rejoin, the starter would not work, an attempt to push-start was halted by officials and Surtees retired. Bandini ran many laps on the tail of Hill's BRM, climbing through the field to seventh place, then sixth, but on lap 36 his engine stammered onto five cylinders and he pulled into the pits to retire.

The long season was to end in the South African Grand Prix at East London on 28 December, but this 'Springbok' tour began with the non-Championship Rand Grand Prix at Kyalami, outside Johannesburg, two weeks previously. Ferrari fielded one 'Aero' for Surtees, holding back their other for East London, while Bandini drove a spaceframe car. Jim Clark and Trevor Taylor provided main opposition in the works Lotus 25s, the big field being completed by local drivers in their national championship Formula 1 cars. Surtees set the pace in practice, and running the larger-megaphone exhausts he took pole with 1 min 34.2 sec, way below the existing lap record. Taylor was on the centre of the front row with 1:36.0 and Bandini on the outside with 1:36.02. Clark was next up on 1:36.9. The race was run in two twenty-five lap 127-mile heats, Surtees leading throughout the first to win at 152.72 km/h (94.9 mph) average, with Bandini second, by 11.7 seconds. The two Ferraris similarly dominated the second heat to repeat their 1–2 performance, Surtees winning this time at 153.2 km/h (95.2 mph) from Bandini, 1 min 26 sec behind. Both Lotuses struck trouble, but the Ferraris had shown formidable pace in the altitude and the heat.

At East London, down beside the Indian Ocean, both Ferrari drivers ran their 'Aero' V6 specials, but found a lack of low-down torque slowing them out of the tighter corners. They finished practice side-by-side on the second row, fourth and fifth quickest, with Surtees on 1:29.8 and Bandini 1:30.2. Clark was on pole (yet again) with 1:28.9. Surtees was second and Bandini sixth behind Clark ending the first lap, but John was in trouble and was holding up the Brabhams, allowing Clark to get away. After five laps the Brabhams were surging alongside, while Bandini lost three places when he spun. Next time round Surtees signalled the pits he had a problem and dropped back, but Brabham had taken the edge off his engine and the Ferrari moved back into third. On lap 43 Surtees lost the place when his engine failed in a great puff of blue smoke on the downhill curve behind the pits. Bandini ran home fifth, having won a lengthy battle with Tony Maggs's Cooper, but lapped by Clark and Gurney, who were first and second.

It was a slightly disappointing end to the season, but better things were promised for 1964. Rather surprisingly for all concerned, it was going to prove a Champion year....

1964   The quiet year

By 1964 the Ferrari Dino sports cars were virtually dead; long-obsolete and surviving only in private owners' hands. Terra/Toppetti shared the ex-Lualdi 196SP in the Targa Florio and ran ninth on the second lap before falling to thirty-third fifth time round, whereupon they dropped out, while in the USA Tom O'Brien did some winning in the V8 Dino 268SP along with Von Imrey's V6 196SP.

Ferrari's first Formula 1 outing came at Syracuse on 12 April, where Surtees won with a brand-new 'Aero'—thought to be number '0006'—running the full four-cam V8 engine in its debut. With the advent of this engine the Formula 1 Ferrari became known as the Tipo 158, with the forthcoming 12-cylinder it would be the '1512', and with the V6 engine's replacement the honoured 'Dino' tag was dropped, as it had been from the cam-box lettering since the advent of the 120-degree Chiti unit.

Still the V6 engine had some races left to it, and at Syracuse Lorenzo Bandini drove his 'Aero' V6 '0001'. Both this car and Surtees's similar spare were in modified form, with revised suspensions to match new cast-alloy five-spoke 13-inch wheels by Campagnolo, carrying the first of a new generation of wide-tread Dunlop racing tyres. Bandini was in tremendous form, breaking the all-time Syracuse lap record set by Moss's Vanwall in 1958 with a practice lap of 1 min 50.5 sec, 179.185 km/h (111.34 mph), 3.8 seconds under the record. He took position on pole with Surtees alongside, while heavy rain on race-day cut the scheduled fifty-six lap distance to only forty. Bandini led his team leader for the first four laps then ran second, with Peter Arundell in a works Lotus closing on him fast. On lap 27 Bandini's visor was shattered by a flying stone and he hammered into the pits, screaming for goggles. Arundell passed into second place and Bandini lit up his rear tyres in a shower of steam and spray as he took off along the pit road, scattering mechanics and officials in all directions. After setting a row of fastest laps he clocked a new record of 1:53.9 to close on Arundell's tail, and ending lap 37 the Ferrari was ahead again and held off Arundell's Lotus by a tenth of a second at the finish, to give Ferrari a very popular 1–2 before the Sicilian crowd.

Surtees ran one of the 'Aero' V6 specials—'0003'—in the BRDC International Trophy race on 2 May, qualifying seventh on 1 min 34.6 sec, against Gurney's Brabham–Climax pole of 1:33.4. The race was a Silverstone thriller, with Jack Brabham skittering past Graham Hill's BRM round the outside on the last corner of the last lap, but Surtees dropped back from an early fifth place with low fuel pressure, retiring on lap 22 with fuel pump failure.

For Monaco on 10 May, Ferrari fielded the three Syracuse cars, the lone 158 V8 for Surtees with both 'Aero' 156s for Bandini as race car and spare. This third car had the Marelli electronic ignition set-up replaced by a normal Bosch coil system. Bandini was troubled by understeer in his 'Aero' 156, while Surtees took out the spare when his 158 developed transmission trouble, but he raced the repaired V8. Bandini qualified seventh, on 1 min 35.5 sec against Clark's pole of 1:34.0. Surtees ran fifth with the leading group early on, but his gearbox quickly played up once more and he was out after fifteen laps. Bandini ran sixth in his V6, took fifth place from Phil Hill's Cooper after half-distance, but was forced out after sixty-eight laps when his gearbox also failed.

A second Ferrari 'Aero' 158 ('0007'?) was available at Zandvoort, and after spending most of practice in the V6 spare, Bandini took over Surtees's older 158 for the race, while John drove the brand-new car, and the V6 was set aside. Surtees finished second to Jimmy Clark's Lotus, while Bandini retired.

In the Belgian Grand Prix the 158s were raced again, while the V6 spare lay fallow, and both suffered engine failures. The French Grand Prix returned to Rouen, where Surtees's 158 had an oil pipe let go and Bandini finished twice-lapped and ninth after being barged heavily by Dan Gurney's Brabham, which went on to win.

The V6 'specials' returned to the fray in the British Grand Prix at Brands Hatch, Kent, on 11 July, where the 158s were late arriving and Surtees began practice with the spare 156, while Bandini had no car at all. A solitary 158—'0006'—arrived for Surtees in time for the second day's practice, but Bandini had to rely upon the monocoque V6 '0003', and while the V8 car clocked 1 min 38.7 sec in John's hands to qualify fifth on the grid, Bandini could manage only 1:40.2 for eighth quickest time and a place on the third row. The race developed into a classic Jim Clark–Graham Hill confrontation with Surtees third well ahead of Bandini, who was narrowly beaten in a desperate final fling by Jack Brabham, the Ferraris finishing third and fifth at the end of a long and gruelling race.

Ferrari entered both drivers for the non-Championship Solitude Grand Prix near Stuttgart on 19 July, Surtees running a 158 and Bandini the team's 'Aero' 156 special '0003'. Surtees qualified on the centre of the front row with his V8, alongside Clark's 3 min 49.6 sec pole on his favourite circuit, and only 0.2 second slower, while Bandini put the V6 car onto the second row, fourth quickest at 3:54.2. Unfortunately heavy rain delayed the start, and it was eventually made in brilliant sunshine with the track still awash. Early on the opening lap Bandini lost control and as his Ferrari broadsided so four other cars hit it or spun out in avoidance, all five being damaged in varying degrees. Surtees fought a battle of sensitivity and car control with Clark, and lost it narrowly — eventually finishing second 10.4 seconds behind.

Mr Ferrari decreed that Surtees should be supported fully in his

Leandro Terra shaking the goat-shed door in Sicily as he takes '0790', his ex-works ex-Lualdi 196SP, round the Targa Florio course in 1964. He shared the car with Topetti, but their luck ran out after completing six laps of the 45-mile circuit, and the Dino failed them. The podded instrument panel layout of the 1962 car specification is clearly visible here in this Geoff Goddard photograph

World Championship chase and so he had choice of both 158s at the Nürburgring, while Bandini was to run the team's repaired Solitude 'Aero' 156. Surtees was all out to repeat his 1963 victory in this the German Grand Prix, and when the grid formed up on 2 August he was on pole with the 158 on 8 min 38.4 sec, while Bandini was on the outside of that front row, fourth quickest with 8:42.6. Bandini led down into the *Sudkehre* turn, but Clark went by and away behind the pits. Surtees took the lead out in the hills, and fought off Clark to score that second consecutive victory when the Lotus retired, while Bandini ran fifth much of the way before profiting by retirements to finish third, nearly five minutes behind his team-mate. Graham Hill's BRM split them in second place.

The Austrian Grand Prix on the bumpy Zeltweg airfield circuit was accorded Championship status on 23 August, and Ferrari arrived with the Nürburgring cars and Surtees retaining choice of the two 158s. All three cars carried aluminium air scoops feeding the front brakes. Practice proved just how bumpy the concrete surface could be, as several cars suffered suspension and chassis failures, but Surtees got onto the front row and Bandini qualified seventh on the second row with a lap in 1 min 10.63 sec, compared to Graham Hill's pole of 1:09.84. Gurney led away with Surtees second and Bandini third, but Surtees quickly moved past Gurney and they drew away from the V6 Ferrari running third. Then on lap 8, as Surtees braked for the hairpin, the Ferrari 158's rear suspension collapsed and it flurried off course in a shower of sparks and dust. Bandini was now second behind Gurney, but he was soon displaced by a determined Clark, who had been unable to find a gear at the start.

Bandini ran securely third until lap 40, when Clark's Lotus sheared a drive-shaft joint and Gurney was left in a long lead from the Ferrari V6, which he felt he could comfortably maintain. But on lap 44 he was craning out of the Brabham's cockpit to examine its front suspension, and two laps later he was in the pits. So Bandini, much to his own surprise, inherited the lead and he held off a late challenge from Ginther's BRM to maintain it to the finish, scoring what was to be the only World Championship Grand Prix victory of his career. It was the last Grand Prix victory for the Ferrari V6 family.

Surtees collected some tools from the pits, repaired his 158's rear suspension out beside the circuit, and drove back to retire to the paddock. . . .

For the Italian Grand Prix at Monza on 6 September Ferrari produced the prototype Tipo 1512 flat-12 car, considered to be chassis '0008', and in practice it was driven solely by Bandini, who approached within fractions of a 2-minute lap in conditions under which only Gurney and Clark got below that mark. The new car was not hazarded in the race, Surtees and Bandini both driving their 158s, while Ludovico Scarfiotti made his Grand Prix come-back in V6 'Aero' '0001' and Bandini's Austrian Grand Prix winner was set aside after he had practised it briefly.

Surtees put his 158 on pole position with a best lap of 1 min 37.4 sec, while Bandini's sister car was seventh at 1:39.8 and Scarfiotti's V6 sixteenth, on row seven, with a best lap of 1:41.6. 'Lulu's' return to

Much of Il Grande John's story is told in the accompanying text but further detail is worth consideration. He was born at Tatsfield, Kent, son of Jack Surtees—a well-known motorcyclist and garage owner. John's mother, his younger brother Norman and small sister Dorothy were all avid motorcycle racing fans. They were bombed-out of their Beckenham home during the war and John was evacuated to York.

When he was 11 he bought his first motorcycle, and when he left school at 15 he went to work for his father. In 1950 he made his racing debut as passenger on Jack Surtees's sidecar combination. They won the race, then somebody protested that John was under the minimum permitted age.

John worked his apprenticeship at Vincent-HRD and in 1951 he fell off his mount in his first two solo races, at Luton and at Brands Hatch. He won his first race at Brands in 1952; won 27 of 40 races in 1953, and 40 of 55 in 1954. In 1955 he beat the great Geoff Duke for the first time and after winning 68 of his 76 races was offered an MV Agusta works ride for 1956. He won his first 500 cc World Championship that season, and added a double hat-trick of 350 and 500 cc titles in 1958–59–60. He won six Isle of Man TTs and at the end of 1959 Reg Parnell of Aston Martin talked him into a driver trial, in which he shone at the wheel of a DBR1/300 at Goodwood. Tony Vandervell was interested, and Surtees learned about Formula 1 cars in a Vanwall on private test at Goodwood, shattering the lap record. on March 18, 1960, he drove Ken Tyrrell's FJ Cooper in his four-wheel race debut at Goodwood, and was second behind Jim Clark's works Lotus. He raced his own F2 Cooper and was in the Lotus Formula 1 team by mid-season....

After leaving Ferrari in 1966 he won the year's final event, at Mexico City in a Cooper-Maserati, then drove Hondas in 1967–68—winning an epic Italian Grand Prix. For 1969 he built his own Formula 5000 cars, and drove F1 BRMs without joy. In 1970 he introduced his own Surtees F1 car, and built and raced them into 1973, when he retired from driving. His Formula 1 team withdrew from Grand Prix racing at the end of 1978....

John Surtees, MBE
b. 11 February, 1934

Formula 1 was steady and unspectacular; he was lapped on the leaders' thirty-fourth tour and eventually finished ninth. Meanwhile Surtees had broken up the opposition to win and Bandini held off Ginther's BRM by 0.1 second to finish third, though both were one lap behind.

Surtees was now very well placed in the World Championship against Jim Clark and Graham Hill, and the United States Grand Prix followed at Watkins Glen on 4 October. Two 158s were present for Surtees, with the brand-new 1512 for Bandini and a V6 as spare, and since Mr Ferrari had just fallen out with his national club in an almighty row and had surrendered his competition licence (in favour of temporary theatricals) all the cars were painted blue and white American national racing colours and were entered by Chinetti's North American Racing Team. Both Surtees and Bandini tried the V6 car in practice, clocking respectively 1 min 13.32 sec and 1:15.8, but times of 1:12.78 with the V8 and 1:13.83 with the flat-12 placed them on the race grid. Surtees finished second behind Hill while Bandini retired in the Grand Prix.

Into the final and deciding round of the World Championship at Mexico City on 25 October, Surtees, Graham Hill and Jimmy Clark were all in line for the Drivers' Championship title, carrying Ferrari, BRM and Lotus–Climax hopes with them for the Constructors' Championship. This unprecedented battle had become three-cornered only by Surtees's and Ferrari's late-season charge. At Mexico City the team

fielded the Watkins Glen cars, again in NART American livery, two V8 158s for Surtees to choose between and the flat-12 1512 for Bandini, and this time V6 '0003' was to be raced by Pedro Rodriguez on his home soil. The flat-12 seemed to like Mexico City's 7000 ft altitude and thin air, Bandini qualifying alongside Surtees on the second row of the starting grid with a best time of 1 min 58.60 sec, compared to the 158's 1:58.70. Clark was on pole with 1:57.24 and Graham Hill was back on the third row behind Mike Spence's Lotus with a 1:59.80. Rodriguez was ninth fastest qualifier on row five of the two-by-two grid with 2:0.90 in the V6.

Clark led from the start with Bandini third, Surtees slow away in midfield keeping out of trouble and Rodriguez ahead of him, seventh. While Clark drew away on every lap Surtees caught Graham Hill and the pair of them began to climb through the field. Hill displaced Bandini for third place behind Clark and Dan Gurney around one-sixth distance, while Surtees was behind Brabham on Bandini's tail. Bandini was running in very close contact with Graham Hill, and at the hairpin on lap 30 the Englishman shook his fist at the Italian for coming too close. Next time round they drove wheel-to-wheel into that corner, and as Hill pulled in front Bandini's left-front wheel clumped the BRM, spinning it round to brush the guard-rail and fold over its tail pipes. Surtees nipped past the sliding cars to inherit third place, while Hill staggered to the pits to have the closed-up exhaust pipes sawn off. Any chance he had of holding third place, and hence the World Championship if Clark should win, had gone completely. Three laps after the Hill incident Bandini caught Surtees and passed him, while Rodriguez, who had overtaken Spence when the Lotus number two had a spin, was repassed. It looked very much like Clark's race and his second consecutive Championship when a rubber oil line split on the Lotus and its life-blood began to pump away. On the last lap he passed the pits with both hands despairingly in the air, Gurney slammed past to win and, as prearranged, Bandini backed right off, allowing an overjoyed Surtees to move forward into second place. Bandini was third and Rodriguez was classified sixth behind Clark's defunct Lotus, which did not make it round to the flag.

During the Championship season Graham Hill had amassed a total of 41 points, but as only his six best results could be aggregated to provide the total he lost two vital points. Surtees could count all of his and consequently his new total of 40 pipped Hill and his BRM to the World Championship titles by just one point. John had achieved his ambition; a four-wheeled World title to add to his seven on two wheels. For Ferrari it was a sensational end to a variable season, in which the old 120-degree V6 engine had played a noble part. Pedro Rodriguez's Mexican drive was the last race appearance of a works 1.5-litre Formula 1 V6. One story had ended, but an extensive postscript was about to be written....

Lorenzo Bandini in his 'Aero' V6 special '0003' at Nürburgring in 1964 showing off its gauze-cowled induction and the latest-style Campagnolo cast-alloy road wheels. One of the 1962 Ferrari defectors, Girolamo Gardini, had returned briefly to Ferrari, but left again to join Campagnolo in the winter of 1962–63. Campagnolo had recently become Amadori's partner in the cast-wheel, disc brakes, etc., business, and whether by coincidence or design the competition Ferraris began to run Campagnolo wheels in 1964

1965   Dino reborn

Early in December 1964 Mr Ferrari held a press conference to outline his plans for 1965 at Modena's Hotel Real-Fini. He announced his plans for the Formula 1 team to rely on the new Bellei V8 and Forghieri flat-12 engines, while the long-distance races would be contested by new P2 prototypes with 3.3- and 4-litre V12 power. One major surprise then followed, for he made passing mention of a new '168 Dino GT car', and was reticent when asked for further details, merely confirming it would be a '168' or 1600 cc with an 8-cylinder, presumably V8, engine. More details would be published early in the coming year. It was suggested by sources close to Ferrari that the power unit would be used as the production basis required for the new Formula 2 class due to take effect in 1967....

This was the beginning of the Ferrari–Fiat accord that eventually produced the V6-engined Fiat Dino models in 1966–67. Nothing more was heard of the phantom 'Dino 168' and during practice for the Monza 1000 km race on 25 April 1965, it was the delightful little 'Dino 166P' which made its ear-splitting public debut. A few days previously it had been demonstrated to the specialist press and some selected 'friends of Ferrari' at the Maranello works.

Pete Coltrin, describing the car in the British *Motor Racing* magazine 'Coche' column originated by Hans Tanner, wrote: 'At first glance [the new Dino] appears to be a dehydrated 250LM, an impression heightened by the cockpit layout, in which the two seats are inboard of wide side boxes, and the pedal area recessed between two large wheel arches just as in the Le Mans models. But chassis- and engine-wise the Dino is in many respects a closer relative to the Ferrari Formula 1 cars than it is to the more recent GT and prototype models.'

The engine was in fact an endurance racing version of the Fiat–Ferrari Dino V6 engine then being finalized by *Ingegnere* Franco Rocchi. Pete continued: 'The double-overhead camshaft 65-degree V6 engine, derived from the F1 power unit, has been given a bore of 77 mm and a stroke of 57 mm to produce a swept volume of 1592 cc, and has a compression ratio of 9.8 to 1...carburation is by three twin-choke downdraught 38 DCN Webers, and twin ignition is by a pair of 12-volt Marelli distributors. The Dino's dry weight is just under 1300 pounds [and] although no official power output details have been given, other

Lorenzo Bandini shrieks the prototype Dino 166P Coupé down into Nürburgring's Sudkehre turn during the 1965 ADAC 1000 Km on his way to fourth place with Vaccarella. The car was chassis '0834' and this Goddard picture shows off the high greenhouse cabin and separately glazed driving lamps very nicely

than the fact that it is achieved at 9000 rpm, I would personally estimate it to be in the region of 185 to 190 horsepower.' He commented, 'I must say I found this interesting newcomer more pleasing to the eye than the photographs might suggest. The unusually low bonnet and rear deck make the top look disproportionately high, but in fact the Dino is only 37.8 inches tall. . . .'

Wheelbase of this lissome newcomer was 90 in (c. 2280 mm), track 53.2 in (c. 1350 mm), overall length 152 in (c. 3820 mm) and height 37.8 in (c. 960 mm). The chassis was a lightweight tubular framework with riveted-on aluminium-alloy stressed skin panelling, and like its recent Formula 1 forebears the little car carried Dunlop disc brakes, outboard at the front and inboard on the cheeks of an overhung transaxle at the rear. It ran five-spoke cast-alloy wheels by Campagnolo, carrying 5.50–13 front and 6.50–13 rear Dunlop tyres. Maximum speed was announced as 160 mph, and it was explained that the 65-degree Jano-series four-cam V6 had been preferred to the lower but more powerful 120-degree Chiti unit since it fitted more easily within the confines of an enveloping body. This one-off 166P had the chassis number '0834'.

At Monza the car was to be shared by Giancarlo Baghetti and Giampiero Biscaldi, and, while the Parkes/Guichet 275P2 was fastest during practice with a lap in 2 min 46.9 sec, Baghetti blasted his little 1.6-litre bomb round in 3 min 2.3 sec despite all manner of teething troubles, which was twelfth fastest time in a big field and faster than one of the big Cobra Daytona coupés and several 3-litre 250LMs and GTOs. Baghetti lay eleventh, ending the first race lap, but almost immediately the engine blew and the first Ferrari Dino coupé's race debut was finished before it had really begun.

On 16 May at Vallelunga, Baghetti had a second chance, in a sports car race supporting the Formula 2 Rome Grand Prix on the day the main

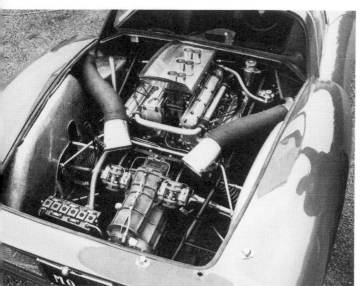

Far left and left Engine bay of the 166P '0834', showing the neat four-cam 1600 cc V6 engine installation in-line with the five-speed and reverse offset-shaft transaxle in unit, carrying Dunlop ventilated disc brakes inboard on the final-drive output shafts. Note brake cooling ducts, twin-plug ignition and battery mount and the hatch-style engine bay access, replacing the one-piece hinged body section of the old 1961–63 works cars. In the cockpit the skimpy lining is visible along with a stubby little gear-change just asking to be used

Below left After its failure at Le Mans the 166P was fitted with an uprated 2-litre engine running much more radical cam-timing than the long-distance engines and with a compression ratio as high as 12.5:1. With this unit installed Ludovico Scarfiotti won first time out in the European Mountain Championship

Above right Immediately after the Trento success the pretty 166P Coupé '0834' was cut down as a *Montagna* Spyder, fitted with a Perspex screen, low-level engine hatch with a blister to clear the carburetter velocity stacks and a roll-over hoop. The car is seen in August at Freiburg with Scarfiotti about to leave the line on the way to another victory and his second Mountain Championship title

Right Spartan cockpit of '0834' in hillclimb Spyder form shows the larger-diameter wood-rim steering wheel and taller gear-change lever favoured by Scarfiotti. Compare with the Coupé cockpit shown opposite

team were contesting the Spa 500 km in Belgium. He won the 1600/2000 cc class with ease to record the new Dino 166P's first victory.

The following week the little car was taken to Nürburgring for the ADAC 1000 km, and there Lorenzo Bandini shared it with Sicilian lawyer Nino Vaccarella. There is no better way of recording their performance than to quote Denis Jenkinson's *Motor Sport* commentary: 'Surtees and Scarfiotti gave a very impressive demonstration' (in the winning Ferrari 330P2) '... but it almost paled into insignificance compared with the relative performace of the 1600 cc Ferrari Dino coupé, driven by Bandini/Vaccarella. This coupé two-seater "Grand Prix" car staggered everyone by its performance and set a new standard. It also made it very obvious that technical progress in GT Prototype racing has been lagging, for the 65-degree 4-cam V6-cylinder engine dates back to 1958 in basic design. This little red coupé with its yellow Grand Prix alloy wheels went so fast that a lot of people refused to believe it was only 1600 cc. As the class limit was 2000 cc it did not matter much to Ferrari whether they were believed or not. On the opening lap it lay 8th overall and then moved up into 6th place where it stayed, headed only by its big brothers and the two Shelby Fords. It was leading all the GT cars, of any capacity, all the LM Ferraris, all the Porsches, both 8-cylinder and 6-cylinder, and was undoubtedly the star of the show. As other cars struck trouble it moved up into third place, was pushed back to fourth place by Whitmore in the open Ford, and then became third again when the Ford retired. For a long while the Ferrari team were on top of the world with their 4-litre prototype in first place, their 3.3-litre prototype in second place, and their 1.6-litre prototype in third place, with Porsches,

---

'Lulu' or 'Dodo' Scarfiotti was a patrician Torinese, grandson of the Agnellis—founders of Fiat. Motor cars and motor racing were in the family, and in 1955 Scarfiotti began his own career with a Fiat 1100 saloon. In 1956 he won his class in the Mille Miglia, and for 1957 aspired to a Fiat 8V in which he won national titles both for hillclimbing and circuit racing. Performances with an OSCA proved him a skilled and capable driver, and in 1960 he made his Ferrari debut with Gonzalez in the Dino 246S at Buenos Aires.

When Ferrari did not call on his services for 1961 he fell back on OSCA, but when Mr Ferrari wanted a hillclimb driver in 1962 he recruited the Fiat boy—from Portorecanati, Maserati—with the results related in these pages.

Scarfiotti became a steady, reliable bastion of Ferrari's driver strength, with the sprint ability vital for effective mountain climb driving. After his brief foray into Formula 1 with the works team in 1963, he returned in 1965 with Centro-Sud's tatty BRMs, and then came 1966 and victory for Ferrari in the Italian GP—the first Italian victor in his home *Grande Epreuve* since Ascari's Ferrari had won in 1952. It was also Firestone's first Grand Prix victory, and Scarfiotti became famous overnight throughout America....

In 1967 he drove one of Dan Gurney's F1 Eagles briefly, while forming a mainstay of Ferrari's sports-prototype driving team, then in 1968 he joined Cooper-BRM, placing fourth in Spain and at Monaco, and Porsche. While practising for the Rossfeld hillclimb in the shadow of Hitler's 'Eagle's Nest' at Berchtesgaten, his Porsche *Bergspyder* apparently had its throttle jam open, and it crashed off the road into stout trees. Poor Scarfiotti was thrown out and died within minutes....

Ludovico Scarfiotti
b. 18 October, 1933
d. 8 June, 1968

Fords, Cobras, Alfa Romeos and everyone else behind them. Then there was a moment of panic when the Dino started to misfire and Bandini came into the pits. There was no undue noise, no smoke, no loss of oil pressure, but the misfire was still there and it remained to the end of the race, so that one of the Porsches was able to take third place and the Dino finished fourth. It transpired that a piece of rubber from a seal in the intake system had gone down one of the downdraught Weber carburettors and partially blocked a jet. But the Dino Ferrari had certainly made its mark. . . .'

After the race Dragoni allowed the scrutineers to tear down the engine and verify its displacement, after which the muttering began about 'thinly-disguised Grand Prix cars'. During the tear-down it was found that a spoke, evidently from a shattered wheel on David Piper's private 250LM, had embedded itself in one of the Dino's Dunlop tyres.

At Le Mans on 19 June poor Baghetti again blew up the little Dino's engine very early in the race, the Milanese driver continuing a career which had become a nightmare, with virtually everything he touched bursting asunder. Certainly second driver Mario Casoni was far from happy, not having a stint at all.

After this misfortune the Dino ran out of 2-litre class endurance races in which to compete, and so it was handed to Ludovico Scarfiotti for another attempt on the European Mountain Championship, which he had won so handsomely in 1962.

He missed the first two events at Mont Ventoux and Rossfeld, but appeared at Trento-Bondone on 11 July with the works prototype coupé, re-engined with an experimental 2-litre (86 mm × 57 mm) Dino V6 producing around 205 bhp at 8800 rpm. Neither the regular works contenders, Porsche and Abarth, could hold the combination of Scarfiotti and his Dino and he set fastest time in 11 min 56.4 sec, an average of 86.30 km/h (53.63 mph), which gives some idea of the course, and 6.4 seconds under Hans Herrmann's best in the works Abarth in second place. Gerhard Mitter's works Porsche *Bergspyder* was third, 14 seconds slower. Scarfiotti was back with a vengeance.

Two weeks later at Cesana-Sestriere on 25 July, Scarfiotti arrived with Ferrari's answer—as if they needed one—to the lightweight Abarth OT 2000 and Porsche *Bergspyder*. It was Dino '0834' cut-down as a 206P with the enlarged 2-litre engine and an open cockpit within a shallow wrap-round Perspex screen. A very flimsy roll-over hoop was fitted behind the car's right-hand driving position, and it was dubbed '*La Piccola*'.

Cesana's 6.44 miles included a mixture of gradients, fast curves and tight hairpins, the 1964 record there standing to Edgar Barth of Porsche in 5:33.1. In practice Scarfiotti blasted his new machine to Sestriere in 5:16.3. The Championship runs were made on a half-wet surface and Scarfiotti clouted a wall on his, but still stopped the clock at 5:12.8, 6.2 seconds quicker than Mitter's ugly flat-8 Porsche, while Herrmann was third in the Abarth another eleven seconds adrift.

At the historic Freiburg climb on 8 August, Scarfiotti rattled Barth's existing record of 6:40.6 down to 6:21.6, 105.58 km/h (65.61 mph), in practice, the new Dino Spyder setting new standards, just as its predecessor had, three years before. His first Championship run shattered the opposition: 6:14.95, 107.50 km/h (66.8 mph). His second of 6:18.96 gave him an aggregate time beating Mitter into second place by a tight 1.9 seconds, for the German had responded magnificently on home ground to the Italian challenge, but could not match it. It was an old score settled on the climb where Mercedes-Benz and Auto Union had once humbled hopeful Alfa Romeos. . . .

Two climbs remained in the Mountain season, Ollon-Villars in Switzerland on 29 August and the Gaisberg in Austria on 19 September. The 4.97-mile Swiss climb's record stood to Jo Bonnier's four-wheel drive Ferguson P99, set in 1963 at 4:23.0. Scarfiotti equalled it on his second practice run with the Dino, and despite being baulked on his fifth run by a slower car he clocked a staggering 4:12.0. Mitter drove his Porsche desperately hard to maintain contact, and on his seventh and last practice run came within 0.6 second of Scarfiotti's unofficial record.

Mitter made his first Championship run in 4:12.4. Scarfiotti wailed up the climb in his pretty little Dino, a pause, his time was announced: as

After his Mosport Park CanAm accident in his own Lola-Chevrolet at the end of 1965, John Surtees proved his recovery by running a virtual Grand Prix distance on test at Modena in what had been intended as his Dino 246 Tasman special for the 1966 'down under' season. Here Giulio Borsari carefully polishes a front rocker-arm, while John the Great checks his rear vision. The car used a Formula 1-style 'Aero' chassis numbered '0006'. The engine installation with belt-driven alternator run off the left-hand exhaust camshaft nose is shown in detail, together with the press agency side-view put out to inform the world of *Il Grande* John's successful rehabilitation. Pete Coltrin was present that day: 'John covered 50-plus laps and at the end of them wasn't even breathing hard. The whole of Modena stood up and cheered. . . .'

4:09.8, a new record and an average speed of 115.87 km/h (72 mph). As other climbs made the hill dirtier the Championship contenders' second runs were slower, but Scarfiotti's aggregate of 8:20.3 beat off Mitter's best for Porsche of 8:25.5 and the Italian and his Ferrari Dino were assured of their second European Mountain Championship title at only their second attempt in a four-year period. Mitter could only equal Scarfiotti's points total at the Gaisberg, and Scarfiotti would take the title on his greater number of victories.

Still Ferrari presented their new Champions in Austria, where the climb was run in pouring rain, sleet and hail dependent on how far one progressed up the mountainside. Near the top there was swirling mist and in these conditions, on a relatively strange venue, Scarfiotti could only place fifth with an aggregate of 10:42.46, behind Porsches driven by

Michel Weber (10:19.67, 99.90 km/h—62.08 mph), Sepp Greger and Rolf Stommelen (all in coupé 904GTS models), while Mitter was fourth in the *Bergspyder* some fifteen seconds faster than the Dino... but it was no day for open cars....

There was no sign of the Dino family V6 engines in Ferrari's single-seater outings during 1965 until, right at the end of the European season, the Maranello racing shop searched along their parts shelves and began to bolt together a *Formule Libre* special, which John Surtees was to take down to New Zealand and Australia immediately after Christmas to contest the 1966 Tasman Championship, in January and February.

They assembled a 65-degree Dino V6 engine basically to the old 2.5-litre Formula 1 specification, though with heads modified in light of recent knowledge. It had bore and stroke dimensions of 85 mm × 71 mm, giving 2417.3 cc as of yore, with two valves per cylinder, twin-plug ignition and a 9.8:1 compression ratio. It was fitted up with Lucas fuel injection and was rated at 280 bhp at 8500 rpm, these figures being suspiciously lower than those claimed in 1960 F 1-guise, but the Tasman circuits were tight and twisty in the main and it was not top-end power which mattered there, but mid-range punch.

The engine castings were modified in the same way as those of the 120-degree 1.5-litre V6 in 1963, when the first 'Aero' special had been constructed, and this larger V6 was hung onto the rear closing panel of what had formerly been a 158 Formula 1 monocoque. Bolt-on attachment was retained on the front wheels, but dropped on the rears, where knock-off centre-locks returned. The wheels themselves were the now standard five-spoke Campagnolo cast-alloy variety.

Dimensions of this potentially very fast Dino special were nominally identical to those of the normal 158-series cars. It used an uprated five-speed and reverse transaxle derived from the sports car spares tray.

Unfortunately Surtees crashed very heavily while driving a Lola-Chevrolet T70 in a sports car race at Mosport Park late in September 1965, suffering serious injuries, which laid him low throughout the winter. Only his fitness and considerable determination pulled him round, and he bounced back for Ferrari in the 1966 Monza 1000 km race, which he won handsomely in terrible conditions. His Tasman special never went south of the Equator, but as a new 3-litre Formula 1 came into being in 1966 it was tailor-made as a standby car should the projected new V12 Tipo 312 Formula 1 cars be delayed.... 'Dino' was about to make its Grand Prix come-back.

1966 V6 renaissance

Early in February 1966 Ferrari introduced their glorious 330P3 prototype to the press at Maranello, this model becoming one of the most mouth-watering evocations of 'sports-racing car' ever produced. In its shadow, but still of great interest, was its little sister—the new Dino 206S. It was Ferrari's intention to run off fifty of these little V6s to qualify them for homologation as 2-litre Group 4 sports cars, as opposed to Group 6 prototypes. However, during that summer Italy's always simmering labour troubles boiled up once again, and they effectively gutted not only Ferrari's production car programme for the year but also his competition projects. In an attempt to maintain adequate pressure in Formula 1 and sports-prototype racing, production of the Dino 206S was allowed to idle, and it appears that no more than eighteen true entities were to leave the plant. They were even-numbered consecutively from chassis '002' to '036', this being a separate series from the works team prototypes. However, the works '0852' became Bill Harrah's '002' allegedly first production model while '0842' may also have been renumbered in the production series on completion of its long hillclimb career.

Several changes were made to the Dino with this new model. Most noticeable was the brand-new bodywork by Piero Drogo's *Carrozzeria Sports Cars* in Modena, which clothed a modified-construction chassis housing a considerably revised 65-degree Dino V6 four-cam engine. This unit adopted the 86 mm bore and 57 mm stroke of the previous year's Mountain Championship engine, giving 1986.6 cc. Its cylinder heads had been redesigned with alterations to port angles and the provision of reduced lenticular form combustion chambers. Compression ratio was reduced from 12.5:1 to 10.8:1 and confidence in better combustion was shown by the reversion to single-spark plug ignition in place of the two plugs per cylinder used previously. The engine carried three twin-choke Weber 40 DCN2 carburetters as in 1965, though reports suggest larger 42 mm instruments were quite rapidly adopted, and fuel-injection experiments were certainly under way. In this form the age-old V6 received another lease of life, and its power output was quoted as 218 bhp at 9000 rpm.

Drogo's Ferrari-styled bodyshell was a scaled-down version of that applied to the big V12-engined P3s. It was attached to a revised semi-monocoque chassis structure formed over a calibrated welded tubular frame stiffened by high-stressed alloy panels riveted into place. Some glass-fibre panels, comprising the floor and some of the flanking sections, were then bonded on to the tubes to form a cellular frame centre-section, with bag-type fuel tanks fitted into the sills. This same basic construction was used for the big P3, and the shared light-alloy body form was a study in flowing curves, its wing lines lowered relative to the 1965 Dino 166/206P, highlighted by subtle crest-lines front and rear. The driving lamps, which resided under separate transparencies from the headlamps in the 1965 models, were taken under single Perspex fairings mounting the two lamps vertically one above the other, with the lower unit stepped forward. While the P3 had quite large brake cooling intakes sunk into its radiator air intake's upper lip, the Dino received a much more pretty treatment, with two subtle slots cut into a similar position.

The rather high roof of the 166P had gone, to be replaced by a

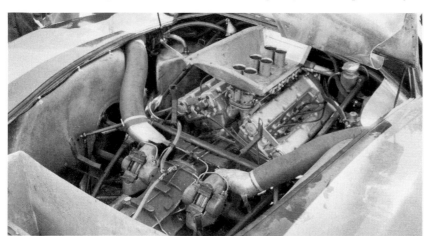

206S single-plug engine and rear end on the type's release also showing the regulation 'luggage space', more carefully shrouded brake cooling ducts and still quite confined hatch access

transparent 'greenhouse' arrangement with marked tumblehome on the side windows merging into a steeply raked almost semi-circular framed windscreen, which was mimicked by a faired roll-over bar behind the cockpit. The effect was that of a coupé with an open sun-roof, and a detachable roof panel was in fact available to enclose it.

Dimensionally the 206S was fractionally longer and higher than the 166/206P, but also slightly narrower. It turned the scales 105 lb heavier, and once again Ferrari quoted a top speed, adequately geared, of 160 mph.

This new Dino 206S—running as a prototype since its homologation had not (and would not) come through—made its racing debut at Sebring in the 12-Hours race on 26 March 1966. The works entered an open model for Bandini and Scarfiotti to share, and in practice they lapped twelfth fastest overall, Bandini's time of 3 min 5.0 sec comparing with Dan Gurney's best of 2 min 54.6 sec in the 7-litre Ford he shared with Jerry Grant. Gerhard Mitter gave Porsche hope, however, by lapping the works Porsche Carrera 6 he was sharing with Gunther Klass in 3:3.6, the only 2-litre car to better the Dino's time.

Scarfiotti actually led from the start in '0842' and was running seventh amongst the big Fords, Ferraris and Chaparrals in the first hour, leading the class by miles. But then the Dino's gearchange began to hang up and at half-distance (six hours) it was still seventh, but behind the Porsches shared by Patrick/Wester and Mitter/Klass. When the works Carrera 6 retired the Dino moved into sixth place, displacing the Americans' Porsche, but then came a long pit stop while mechanics worked on its gearbox.

Three Fords led from the Rodriguez/Andretti NART Ferrari P2/3 and the Patrick/Wester Porsche with the delayed Dino next up but too far behind to challenge. Unfortunately in the early darkness Andretti spun his big Ferrari and struck the Wester Porsche, which careered off course and struck some spectators standing in a prohibited area, killing four of them. But the Dino's rear suspension was now coming adrift, and Mitter was out in the Porsche previously shared by Hans Herrmann/Joe Buzzetta, and there was no way the little Ferrari could catch him. The 12-Hours ended with three Fords victorious, the three-man Porsche fourth and the limping Dino fifth after an arduous debut.

Italy's Liberation Day holiday, 25 April, saw the Monza 1000 km race held in driving rain, and John Surtees's return to racing after his Mosport crash. The works entered two Dino 206Ss for Bandini/Scarfiotti and Vaccarella/Bondurant, the formers' Coupé '0842' running a fuel-injected V6 with twin-plug ignition, while the latter's had the standard Weber V6s and an open top, as did the new private cars of Scuderia Sant'Ambroeus shared by Giampiero Biscaldi/Mario Casoni and the British-entered Maranello Concessionaires' car of Richard Attwood/David Piper. This last Dino was immaculately turned-out in the British distributor's gorgeous Italian-red and pale-blue livery.

On the combined Monza road and track circuit, the works' injection car recorded fifth-fastest practice time with a lap in 3 min 10.7 sec, 1.75 seconds faster that Lucien Bianchi and 'Beurlys' could achieve with their

The works prototype 1966 Dino 206S pictured by Pete Coltrin on a typically misty Modena winter's day by the factory fuel pumps. Note the single-transparency twin headlamps, cast wheels, front and rear access hatches and almost quarter-spherical windscreen with steeply curved side windows matching the fared roll-over bar line

Ecurie Francorchamps P2/3 V12! Clearly the Dino was a potential winner in poor weather conditions and all who drove the little cars had nothing but praise for them. The Sant'Ambroeus car lapped in 3:13.0 and Maranello Concessionaires' in 3:14.7. The second works Dino on carburetters lapped very rapidly driven by both Sicilian Nino Vaccarella and the American Bob Bondurant, but the latter crashed heavily at the *Curva Grande* late in the session luckily emerging uninjured.

Ferrari were to have terrible screen wiper troubles in this very wet race, starting with the Bandini Dino, whose wiper failed at the start and had to make a first-lap pit stop. Surtees's P3 led from three Ford GT40s in the early stages with Biscaldi fifth ahead of the works Porsches. Attwood fell back after a fine start, and on lap 7 Hans Herrmann edged out Biscaldi to place his Porsche ahead of the private Dino. Bandini had been skating furiously around the course to make up for his early delay, but the wiper drive pin sheared again and he had to stop for another repair. This same fault afflicted both other Dinos and the works P3. Eventually, many laps behind, Bandini and Scarfiotti gave the injection Dino everything it had, but still their lap times were a second down on those of the fourth-placed Mitter/Herrmann Porsche Carrera 6. They finally finished ninth behind three Porsches, while the Biscaldi/Casoni car went out with clutch trouble and the Maranello Concessionaires' car finished thirteenth.

Five days later the red and blue British-entered Dino was at Oulton Park in Cheshire for the RAC Tourist Trophy, a race marred in practice when Dick Protheroe crashed fatally in his new V12 330P. Mike Parkes was to drive the Dino, and after lapping at 1 min 44.0 sec in practice (against Denny Hulme's Lola-Chevrolet pole of 1 min 37.4 sec) Parkes heard a grinding noise from the car's transmission. It was diagnosed as diff failure and Col. Ronnie Hoare, patron of the team and long-time

Above left Surtees at Modena again, this time with a prototype Coupé 206S, perhaps the prettiest of all versions. Note the new-design cast wheels on this car, replacing the five-spoke ex-Formula 1 cast design

Above Twin-plug ignition quickly returned to the four-cam 2-litre V6 Dino engine as on this 206S, which is complete with regulation spare wheel and tyre roughly lashed in place

Right The immaculate Maranello Concessionaires-liveried 206S '010' in trouble at the Oulton Park pits during Mike Parkes's brief appearance in the 1966 Tourist Trophy race. The interior trim was quite lavish, though light, one-piece and quickly detachable

British Ferrari importer, telephoned Maranello for spares. These were brought over by air as a factory mechanic's hand-baggage, but on strip-down it was found that insufficient oil flow to the crown-wheel and pinion had caused tooth damage. The car was reassembled and Parkes started the race under instruction from Colonel Hoare to stop if it looked like breaking. Parkes ran just two laps of the first seventy-lap heat and called it a day. Still he was classified 21st, and won £25.

8 May, Targa Florio time, and in Sicily SEFAC fielded a 330P3 for Vaccarella/Bandini and two Dino 206Ss for Parkes/Scarfiotti (open car '004' with injection and dual-ignition engine) and Jean Guichet/Giancarlo Baghetti (coupé '0852' with dual-ignition but carburetters). Scuderia Sant' Ambroeus ran '0842' open—using Firestone tyres unlike the works entries on Dunlop—for Biscaldi/Casoni. In practice Parkes hurtled off the road and wrapped one front fender around a stout tree, but the car was repaired in time for the race.

Scarfiotti, Guichet and Biscaldi took the start in the Dinos, and the Mountain Champion was third ending the first forty-five-mile lap, though behind Mitter's Porsche Carrera 6, while Vaccarella led in the big P3. It was raining, and once again the Biscaldi car was delayed by wiper

failure, and the Guichet car, running sixth, suffered similarly. Parkes took over the injection Dino, but was soon in trouble as its fuel tank had split and he was haring along the mountain roads gushing petrol in his wake. He eventually spun on his own fuel, and crushed the car's tail and shattered a wheel. He fitted the spare, beat the body out and limped into the mountain depot at Bivio Polizzi to pick up a new spare wheel and tyre. Biscaldi also hit something solid and broke a wheel, losing more time, but unlike Parkes not suffering terminal suspension damage. Through all this, and the rain and hail which enveloped the Madonie circuit towards the end, Guichet and Baghetti drove with assured pace and calm, and picked up second place at the finish behind the private Ecurie Filipinetti Porsche Carrera 6 of Willy Mairesse and Herbie Muller. The Sant'Ambroeus car was flagged off a finisher, having completed nine of the ten laps in thirteenth place. The Targa Florio had again been kind— in some measure—to the Ferrari Dino....

The first Spa 1000 Km race was held on the very fast *Circuit National de Francorchamps* on 22 May, and Col. Hoare's Maranello Concessionaires entered Dino '0852' on the works behalf for Richard Attwood and Jean Guichet. It lapped at 4 min 7.3 sec in practice, a half-second slower than the Udo Schutz/Gerhard Koch works Porsche, though on the second day the Dino was some ten seconds slower, and Hans Herrmann/Dieter Glemser clocked 4:05.5 in their fuel-injected Carrera 6. Attwood drove the first stint in the race and was running comfortably seventh overall, leading all the 2 litres and locked in a battle with Peter Sutcliffe's Ford GT40. After the stops Guichet was sixth briefly before being overtaken by Chris Amon's GT40, and all the time the Parkes/Scarfiotti works P3 was running away with the race overall, while the Dino led its class by a similarly huge margin. One key was tyre choice, for both P3 and Dino were on Firestone rubber for the first time,

Above left Sebring 12-Hours 1966 with Ludovico Scarfiotti three-wheeling the prototype works Dino 206S '0842' towards fifth place overall at the finish. The car is running in the Prototype 2-litre class as the type had not—and would not—reach the production quota necessary for sports car homologation

Above centre The mad English have done it again— long faces in the Ferrari pit at Cerda during the 1966 Targa Florio as Amadessi and his fellow mechanics prepare to take Mike Parkes's tattered 206S '004' away

Right One damp day at Modena Coltrin found Ferrari testing a Dino apparently for Le Mans, running timed trials back-to-back, firstly with a coupé roof panel and rear wheel-arch spats fitted, then without them. The high-penetration needle nose remained throughout. Bandini is driving

Above right This beautiful Geoff Goddard shot of the Biscaldi/Casoni 206S '0842' shows it high in the Madonie Mountains approaching the Bivio (fork) Polizzi junction on the way to a delayed 13th place finish in the 1966 Targa. Over the wall is a typical Targa tree—the top 12 feet of a tree 72 feet tall…

instead of Dunlop. The Porsches broke up in pursuit of the Dino, which was most unusual, and while the 330P3 won from four Fords the Dino was next up, sixth overall and well ahead of two surviving Alpine–Renaults!

The scene shifted just across the German border to the Nürburgring on 5 June for the ADAC 1000 km race. Three Dinos faced a fleet of Porsches on their home ground; the works Lucas-injected dual ignition '004' for Bandini/Scarfiotti, a second works car operated by NART for Pedro Rodriguez/Richie Ginther and the Maranello Concessionaires' car for Attwood/Piper. All were running open, the latter pair with Weber carburetters, NART's with dual-ignition. Jochen Rindt was driving a 2.2-litre Porsche Carrera, which he lapped in practice at 8 min 47.4 sec,

while Scarfiotti blared round in 8:48.2, nearly 6½ seconds faster than the Herrmann and Schutz prototype 2-litre Carreras. The NART car recorded 8:59.4.

Scarfiotti made a lightning Le Mans-style start to lead the whole field away, but Surtees quickly established his P3 in the lead and was 17 seconds clear on the charge back past the pits. Scarfiotti was displaced by the Phil Hill/Jo Bonnier Chaparral on lap 3, but kept in touch, miles clear of all the Porsches, including the 2.2. Attwood and Rodriguez were nose to tail in seventh and eighth places behind three Porsches. The big P3 suffered a suspension collapse, and the Chaparral took the lead, relinquishing it to the remarkable injection Dino when it made its scheduled fuel stop. After the Dinos had made their first stops the Chaparral led from Bandini and Ginther, while the Piper/Attwood car was sixth. Bandini could not hold the Chaparral like Scarfiotti, for the Dino had begun to understeer on its Dunlop tyres. Scarfiotti stalled on take-off at the second stop and let the NART car go by, but two laps later Ginther came in and Rodriguez resumed, changing its front Goodyear tyres while Scarfiotti drew closer in third place.

The Maranello Concessionaires car was rubbing its right-rear Dunlop through the bodywork, and then Attwood heard a recurrence of the TT 'grinding noise' and the car was withdrawn before its transmission broke, or locked, which would have been more dangerous. When Scarfiotti stopped again for fuel and tyres in the works' third-placed Dino, Bandini took over again: the NART car ran clear in second place until Rodriguez came in and Ginther rejoined, driving into a rainstorm. Bandini flailed in to have a large sheet of paper removed from his car's radiator intake while the NART car was stationary and went out in second place.

They ran happily home like that to finish second and third behind Phil Hill in the winning Chaparral, ahead of all the Porsches and the Ford GT40s and the larger Ferraris. Nürburgring was tailor-made for thinly disguised Grand Prix cars, and only the sophisticated chassis engineering of the Chaparral and its fine drivers prevented an outright Dino victory.

Differences between John Surtees and Eugenio Dragoni came to a head in practice for Le Mans, and the resolute Englishman walked out, severing ties with Ferrari in what could and should have been another Formula 1 World Championship year for them both. Three Dino 206Ss ran in the 24-Hours race on 18–19 June; two entered by Chinetti's NART organization for Nino Vaccarella/Mario Casoni and Charlie Kolb/George Follmer and one by Maranello Concessionaires for Mike Salmon/David Hobbs. Le Mans had never favoured the Dinos and 1966 was no exception, all three retiring in the third hour with respectively clutch failure, overheating and transmission trouble.

The endurance season being virtually at an end, it remained for the Maranello Concessionaires' car to be driven by Mike Parkes in the Guards Trophy race at Brands Hatch on 16 July, supporting the Ferrari-less British Grand Prix. Parkes finished sixth and won the 2-litre class easily in a race dominated by 6-litre Chevrolet-engined Group 7 cars. On 7 August the *Coppa Citta di Enna* at Pergusa in Sicily saw Vaccarella's Dino 206S dicing furiously and at very high speed with Mario Casoni in a

That faithful *Ferrarista* Edoardo Lualdi-Gabardi ran a 206S in some 1966 and 1967 Mountain Championship climbs and circuit races with some worthwhile amateur-level success. It is thought his 1966 car was the ex-works ex-Maranello Concessionaires' model '010'

GT40—they broke each other up and had to retire, the Dino with an engine fire. The local driver 'Pam' was allowed into the lead and he won in a second Dino 206S at an average of 197.62 km/h (122.8 mph).

Meanwhile Scarfiotti had embarked on the defence of his European Mountain Championship with works-entered fuel-injected Dino '0842', facing Gerhard Mitter's much modified lightweight 8-cylinder Porsche based on the latest Carrera 6 series. The season's Championship commenced on 12 June at Rossfeld in Germany, a fast 3.66-mile climb placing the accent on local knowledge. The Dino suffered fuel starvation in practice, and its output, variously reported as 220 or 235 bhp, could not match the reliable 240 of the Porsche. When Mitter was nearly four seconds faster than Scarfiotti in practice some thought the Italian was sand-bagging. The Championship runs proved he was not, and Mitter won with an aggregate of 6:1.72 against Scarfiotti's 6:6.46, for second place. The Rossfeld climb's GT class fell to a young Swiss named Peter Schetty, handling a brutish Shelby Mustang 350GT. Three years later he would become Mountain Champion in the Ferrari 2-litre flat-12 '212E' and would go on to become their best-ever team manager.

At Le Mans Scarfiotti's P3 Ferrari rammed a Matra-BRM and he ended up in hospital and missed the second European Championship climb at Mont Ventoux on 26 June. He was fit for the third round at Trento–Bondone on 10 July, but the Tuesday before the event Mr Ferrari announced that, '...because of continual strikes by the metal-workers in the racing department—at the moment working only three of their six days per week—we are forced to suspend all racing activities for an indeterminate period....' In Italy many felt that the decision might have been avoided if Bandini had won the French Grand Prix, the works Ferraris had not collapsed at Nürburgring and Le Mans and the latest Dino 206S had proved itself the sensation the original 166P had promised in 1965. There was also a wave of resentment by the *tifosi* in Italy against Dragoni's much-publicized attitude against Surtees. Scarfiotti did not run at Trento, leaving Mitter to win handsomely from four other Porsches and Lualdi's private carburetter Dino 206S.

The Mugello sports car race on 17 July had entries from Ferrari for a P3 to be driven by Scarfiotti and a Dino 206S for Bandini, but after both drivers had spent six days practising on the long Apennine road circuit they were informed no race cars would be available.

At Cesana–Sestriere on 24 July, Scarfiotti and his Dino returned to the mountains, Mr Ferrari having announced the preceding Monday that industrial problems within his racing department had been resolved. The Dino Spyder had been lightened, and on his home ground Scarfiotti tested at the hill before the meeting began, his two mechanics sorting out ratios, damper and spring settings and choice of Firestone tyres.

In his first run Scarfiotti clocked 5:17.1. Mitter bettered it at 5:15.0. If Mitter won here the Championship was his, if Scarfiotti could cheat him the title would remain open a little longer. On the second runs the yellow-wheeled, flame-red Dino hurtled towards the chic Italian ski resort: 5:09.6, a new record. Mitter clocked 5:14.7 to take second place behind Scarfiotti, by 5 seconds. The Championship remained open.

The following week at Freiburg–Schauinsland Mauro Forghieri was on hand to supervise the rather tatty Dino's running, and it had experimental 3-valve-per-cylinder heads fitted as a development exercise for the forthcoming Formula 2 engine. Both Ferrari and Porsche ran on Dunlops, though carrying a spare set of Firestones for emergencies. The tyre war had spread to the mountains. Scarfiotti was quicker than Mitter in practice by 1.8 seconds, but on his first official climb he misjudged the *Gieshübel* hairpin near the summit and thumped the inside kerb. His time was 6:06.05—Mitter was faster on 6:05.8. Scarfiotti was first to go on the second runs: 6:04.32. Mitter responded—a shattering 6:02.49—the Championship was his and Porsche's.

Two rounds remained, at Sierre–Montana in Switzerland on 28 August and the Gaisberg in Austria on 4 September. At Sierre Scarfiotti beat Mitter again with an aggregate time of 12 min 59.4 sec, an average of 101.79 km/h (63.25 mph). The new Champion's time was 3.8 seconds slower. Scarfiotti and the Dino did not go to Austria for the final round.

Team engineer Mauro Forghieri stands hands in pockets alongside Italian journalist Adriano Cimarosti to see Scarfiotti leave the start-line at Freiburg 1966, during his unsuccessful (interrupted) defence of the Dino's European Mountain Championship title. The car is '0842' partially stripped and lightened, for example with one pair of lamps removed. Here 'Lulu' placed second, beaten by Porsche

He spent that day instead in a Formula 1 312 V12 at Monza, where he won the Italian Grand Prix for Ferrari; the ultimate success for any Italian racing driver. It was the zenith of his career. Two years later he would die in a Porsche on the mountain climb at Rossfeld. . . .

Meanwhile, in the USA the season had seen NART's ancient Dino 268SP revived to finish fifth in the SCCA Nationals meeting at Vineland, New Jersey, and in the late-season American events Charlie Kolb began a busy Dino story by placing sixth overall and second 2-litre at the United States Road Racing Championship Buckeye Cup event at Lexington, Ohio, on 28 August. He was edged out of the class victory by Joe Buzzetta's Porsche Carrera 6. On 4 September at Elkhart Lake, Wisconsin, Kolb dropped out with brake failure after lapping a second faster than Buzzetta in practice. In September at Bridgehampton both Kolb and Pedro Rodriguez ran Dinos, but they retired respectively with engine problems and a thrown wheel. At Laguna Seca on 16 October Rodriguez drove Bill Harrah's troubled Dino to fourteenth place in the first heat and twenty-fifth in the second. He was ninth in a twenty-lap Consolation race; determined little Pedro would have needed some by that time. . . .

Back in Europe on 11 October, in the Austrian Tulln–Langenlebarn airfield circuit inaugural meeting, Edoardo Lualdi-Gabardi was second in his 206S, splitting the Porsche Carrera 6s of Hans Herrmann and Swiss driver Dieter Spoerry . . . and that ended the new Dinos' busy year.

Ferrari had completed a new 3-litre V12-engined monocoque Formula 1 car in preparation for the start of the new season and the new Formula. It made its debut on May Day at the Syracuse Grand Prix, driven by John Surtees, and after starting from pole position with a practice lap in 1 min 42.3 sec it won easily against new or lashed-up opposition. Running second all the way, after qualifying second-fastest with 1:43.9, was Lorenzo Bandini in the hitherto unraced Surtees 'Tasman Special' Dino 246 '0006', which finished twenty-three seconds behind Surtees.

Maranello completed a second V12 car in time for the Monaco Grand Prix, opening the 1966 World Championship series at Monte Carlo on 22 May. The Dino 246 special was taken along in support and Bandini drove it in the race. The new V12 car was just too new to be raceworthy, while the torquey V6 was ideally suited to the winding street circuit with its steep gradients and slow hairpins.

Surtees qualified his V12 on the front row with 1 min 30.1 sec, against Clark's pole in a 2-litre Lotus–Climax of 1:29.9, while Bandini was fifth quickest on row three at 1:30.5. Surtees led the race with Stewart's 2-litre Tasman BRM on his tail, while Bandini was caught in a battle for third place. On lap 13 the Ferrari V12's transmission failed, and it was then up to Bandini. He closed rapidly on Hill's BRM to take third place behind Rindt's Cooper–Maserati and the leading BRM, and on lap 20 he shouldered past the Austrian to run second. Bandini was running around eighteen seconds behind Stewart for much of the race, but made a tremendous effort to close the gap towards the end, setting fastest race lap on the ninetieth tour in 1:29.8, 126.080 km/h (78.34 mph), which

Below left Bandini didn't reckon much to racing in the rain at Spa. Here he splashes '0006' carefully towards third place in the 1966 Belgian GP. The massive transaxle with its side-slung battery mount dominates the car's rear end

Left and middle left Lorenzo Bandini hurries his Dino 246 Formula 1 special '0006' into the left-right harbour-front chicane at Monaco during his brave drive into second place in the 1966 Monaco Grand Prix. One year later he suffered fatal injuries at this point. The engine installation had been modified from its winter Tasman trim, now with fuel-injection replacing carburetters and a new high-level exhaust system. Surtees would have preferred 'my V6' to the brand-new 3-litre V12 for the start of the 1966 season and the new 3-litre Formula. 'That V6 was as much as two to three seconds a lap faster than the first V12 most places. Everybody thought the V12 had a lot of power. Wasn't true. It had less power and twice the weight of the Repco-Brabham. The first one I had delivered 270 horsepower, the first time we had a genuine 300 was at Spa and with revised heads we got about 308.' Undoubtedly John and his Tasman V6 are another of motor racing's might-have-beens. The potential was there, and the honest workman Bandini could not quite fulfil it

broke the previous record. He closed to within twelve seconds before his effort was spent, and then settled back and ran home securely second, forty seconds behind the winning BRM. There was life in the Dino yet.

The Belgian Grand Prix followed, at Spa on 13 June, and Surtees and Bandini had the Monaco cars again. Bandini opted to use the 246 in the race as rain was imminent and he was not yet fully confident with the powerful new V12. Surtees was on pole with a 3 min 38.0 sec lap, and Bandini was fifth quickest on row two with the Dino 246's 3:43.8. Surtees led with Bandini fourth at Malmedy, but there the field ran into a rain squall and cars slithered in all directions, while Stewart crashed very heavily in the Masta Kink a little farther on. Surtees had a long lead from Brabham and Bandini at the completion of that lap, and then Brabham fell back and Rindt took his place between the two Ferraris. Bandini had little taste for this type of racing and fell farther back, a very lonely third, and as Surtees had the measure of Rindt in second place so they finished, with the Dino 246 special having achieved two second places and a third in its three races thus far.

That Belgian Grand Prix proved to be Surtees's last race for Ferrari, and V12 cars were provided for Bandini and Parkes at Reims for the French Grand Prix, labour troubles then keeping the team away from the British event. Bandini and Parkes reappeared with the V12s in the Dutch Grand Prix, and then on 7 August the German Grand Prix at Nürburgring saw the return of the Dino 246, entered for Ludovico Scarfiotti to drive as team number three alongside the V12s of Bandini and Parkes.

Scarfiotti had performed so well in the Dino 206S during the ADAC 1000 km race that this entry made all kinds of sense, and despite his relative inexperience with single-seaters the patrician Italian was third quickest for much of practice and ended up fastest of the Ferraris, in fourth position on the outside of the front row with a best lap in 8 min 20.2 sec against Clark's pole of 8:16.5. Bandini and Parkes were sixth and seventh quickest on the second row with their V12s, on 8:21.1 and 8:21.7 respectively. The cars ran on Dunlop tyres instead of the Firestones they had been using hitherto, and as the race developed Scarfiotti could not repeat his practice form, and they all ran down the field, Parkes leading Bandini and Scarfiotti; eighth, ninth and tenth. Starting their tenth lap the Dino 246 began to pop and bang, and while Parkes went slithering off into the bushes, Scarfiotti had his engine cut out completely due to an electrical fault. Bandini finished a distant sixth, while John Surtees was second now driving for Cooper-Maserati—which may have hurt Mr Ferrari....

For the Italian Grand Prix at Monza on 4 September, while Bandini, Parkes and Scarfiotti all drove V12s, Dragoni arranged to lend the Dino 246 to Tim Parnell's private team as an entry for Giancarlo Baghetti, the luckless ex-Ferrari team driver having broken the gearbox of the 2-litre Lotus-BRM which Parnell had intended him to race. The Ferrari V12s didn't really look like being beaten, although Clark's suspect prototype Lotus 43 with H16 BRM engine took third fastest time and Surtees's Cooper-Maserati fourth fastest, to split Bandini (on

1 min 32.0 sec) from his team-mates; Parkes on pole with 1:31.3 and Scarfiotti on the middle of the front row with 1:31.6. Baghetti was down on the seventh row, sixteenth qualifier with 1:35.5 in the Dino 246.

Baghetti fought a long duel with Mike Spence's Lotus–BRM, actually his Parnell team-mate, and got the better of him to run strongly in fifth place, while Scarfiotti led from Parkes. Bandini had been delayed, so Ferraris were racing 1–2–5 before a deliriously happy Italian crowd. But on lap 55 the Dino's throttle linkage vibrated apart, and the luckless Baghetti drew into the Parnell pit, finally rejoining last. He finished in this position, tenth on the road but eleven laps behind the winning V12s and having completed insufficient distance to be classified.

The next time a Dino single-seater would race was to be in Formula 2.

Scarfiotti became something of a Nürburgring specialist during the sixties and at the 1966 German GP he qualified '0006' fourth fastest on the outside of the front grid row, only to hit trouble in the race. The car is owned today by Pierre Bardinon

1967 Time for change

Engineer Franco Rocchi's 'civilianized' version of the 65-degree four-cam Dino V6 engine made its debut in the new 2-litre Fiat Dino Spyder and Coupé production cars in November 1966 at the *48e Salone dell' Automobile Torino*. This prestige Fiat sports car in turn provided Ferrari with a licence to go ahead and 'develop the production engine' for the new 1600 cc Formula 2 category taking effect in 1967.

While the Rocchi-developed V6 in its Fiat-developed chassis received an enthusiastic press, competition Dino 206S production at Maranello had tailed off sadly. After showing such promise in their 1966 outings, the cars had a dreadful year in 1967.

At Sebring early in April, Dan Gurney was listed originally to share the NART-entered Dino 206S with Pedro Rodriguez, but tyre contracts intervened and Jean Guichet took the ride. The Porsches were quicker in practice, and Dinos shared by Herbert Muller/Gunther Klass and Charlie Kolb/Ed Crawford both failed to feature in the results. The Rodriguez/Guichet machine, of which much had been expected, was abandoned after 101 laps with incurable overheating.

Ferrari had taken on two newcomers this season. One was the German ex-Porsche driver Gunther 'Bobby' Klass, who showed tremendous potential, and the other was the reliable rather than meteoric English Formula 3 driver, Jonathan Williams. In the Monza 1000 km race he shared the works Dino 206S open car with Klass. The new Herrmann/Siffert Porsche 910 was fastest 2-litre in practice, with a 3 min 7 sec lap, while Williams was next up on 3:08.8 — on the combined road and track circuit of course. The Dino was one of the works' 1966 chassis, updated with an 18-valve V6 engine with fuel injection between the cam-boxes rather than in the vee. Carlo Facetti crashed Antonio Nicodemi's Dino during practice when he lost control and flipped coming off the speedbowl banking. Although he was trapped beneath the wreck his injuries were mild. Williams blared around seventh early in the race, leading all the 2-litre cars, but the effort proved too much and after Rindt forced his Porsche ahead the Dino succumbed to overheating, just after Klass had taken over.

For the Targa Florio on 14 May, it appeared that Ferrari did not want to make works Dino entries while the cars were not winning, and their Mario Casoni/Bobby Klass 18-valve injected model was entered by

Casoni, and the older carburetter model of Jonathan Williams/Vittorio Venturi by Scuderia Nettuno. NART nominally entered a third car for Ferdinando Latteri and Ignazio Capuano, and the Dinos were faced by three works Porsches, four new V8-powered works Alfa Romeo T33s (designed by Carlo Chiti) and three works Renault Alpines. In practice Klass showed his great potential with a 38 min 13 sec lap, which made Porsche regret his move to Ferrari, but on the second race lap he clouted a marker stone and tore out a suspension corner when lying sixth overall. The Williams/Venturi car climbed to sixth, dropped back as Porsches and Alfa Romeos moved by, and finally profited by retirements to finish fourth behind the winning 2.2-litre and two 2-litre Porsches. It was a fine and consistent drive in what had suddenly become an outdated and under-developed car.

At the Nürburgring 1000 Km late that month Ferrari made a single works entry in place of the promised 330P4. It was a fascinating Dino 246P special, actually the old works 206S chassis '004' carrying the Formula 1 Dino 246 engine, which had last raced at the 'Ring the previous August in Scarfiotti's Formula 1 car. Scuderia Filipinetti from Switzerland ran their new 2-litre Dino 206S '026' for Jean Guichet/Herbert Müller, while the big-engined works special was to be handled by Scarfiotti and Klass and should have done very well.

As it was, the 2.4-litre engine broke a piston in practice, damaging itself too badly for the car to race, and as if this wasn't bad enough, the Filipinetti car caught fire down in the *Hatzenbach* woods. After Jean Guichet scrambled clear, thirty-five minutes elapsed before fire extinguishers were brought to the scene from the pits and by that time the Ferrari Dino was just a carbonized heap of scrap. Ironically the team had lost a brand-new Ford GT40 in the same way at the Monza 1000 Km.

There were no Dinos at Le Mans and so their sad endurance racing season stammered to a halt. Meanwhile Mario Casoni had run his Dino

Above left Williams again, this time in the 1967 Targa Florio in which he finished fourth, sharing this Dino Spyder with Vittorio Venturi. Single headlamps were becoming standard among the relatively few and typically individual Ferrari 206s built

Right Another version of *La Piccola*, the works' pet name for their cut-down Mountain Championship Dino Spyders, appeared at Trento–Bondone in July 1967, this being the flat rear deck lightweight-bodied 206SP Group 7 car seen here storming the hill in Scarfiotti's experienced hands. It recorded second fastest time

206S '010' in the opening round of the year's European Mountain Championship at Montseny, a ten-mile climb just outside Barcelona in Spain, on 21 May. He was third behind the Porsche 910 *Bergspyders* of Gerhard Mitter and new boy Rolf Stommelen, twenty-eight seconds slower than the winner. It was rumoured that he would appear in a Group 7 'two-seater racing' Dino at Mont Ventoux, but this did not transpire and Stommelen beat Mitter there.

The Italian climb at Trento–Bondone was held on 9 July, and there SEFAC Ferrari appeared with a 4-valve-per-cylinder Dino Group 7 car for Ludovico Scarfiotti, and a 1967 Group 6 206S for Gunther Klass. These chassis were respectively '0842' and '004'. Casoni's similar Group 6 car was entered for him by Scuderia Brescia Corse, and Edoardo Lualdi-Gabardi reappeared with his 1966 Dino.

In Saturday practice Scarfiotti was fastest early on in the new lightweight Group 7 Dino with a climb in 11 min 56.3 sec, but Mitter was faster that afternoon, clipping the Italian's second climb time of 11:44.3 by 11.2 seconds.

In the official runs on Sunday Klass jumped the start and was docked ten seconds penalty, which put him right out of the running, his steady climb actually clocking 11:45.3 in what was, by 'mountain-special' standards, a very heavy car. Mitter reached the finish in 11:17.53, Stommelen was faster in the foothills before landing upside down in a field fifteen feet below road level, and Scarfiotti achieved 11:29.44—a fine time, but just too slow in 1967. Casoni non-started with transmission failure, both Scarfiotti and Klass complained of poor selection in the works cars and Lualdi's climb was abortive as the car's fuel pump failed. Scarfiotti was runner-up in the one-climb competition behind Mitter.

Cesana–Sestriere was next, on 16 July, but Maranello was hard-

Above centre Monza 1000 Km 1967 with Williams leading Porsche 910, three GT40 Fords and an LM Ferrari into the Curva Parabolica in works Dino 206S '004'. He shared the car with the German works driver 'Bobby' Klass. Today '004' is owned by Dudley Mason-Styrron in England

The prototype Formula 2 Ferrari Dino 166 was displayed to the public at the Turin Racing Car Show in February 1967. Here it is on Firestone tyres with the fuel-injected twin-plug F2 horizontal exhaust pipe runs and bulky but quite light Ingegnere Salvarani-designed five-speed and reverse transaxle

pressed preparing Formula 1, Formula 2, sports-prototype and the new Group 7 Dino cars. Something had to go, and it was participation in the Cesana climb. One car, they said, would be ready for Klass at Freiburg on 30 July. Meanwhile Casoni ran the Brescia Corse 206S at Cesana and was fifth with 5:30.8 compared to Stommelen's winning time for Porsche of 5:02.3. Casoni's first run on five cylinders had been declared void and he was allowed a re-run after being baulked by yellow flags at the scene of an accident to Dieter Quester's works Lola-BMW.

It had been intended that Klass should drive Scarfiotti's Group 7 light-weight Dino in the Freiburg mountain climb a week after the Mugello Championship sports car race on 23 July. At Mugello Ferrari entered two Dinos for this Targa Florio-like event on a 66.2 km Apennines circuit, which took in part of the old Mille Miglia course, including the famous Futa Pass. One car was the 4-valve-per-cylinder

'004' for Scarfiotti and Vaccarella, and the other the three-valve '010' for Williams and Klass. A carburetter Dino was to be driven by private entrants Antonio Maglione and Corrado Ferlaino. After Williams had lapped very quickly at 33 min 57.9 sec, Klass took out the Group 7 hillclimb training car and about 15 km from the pits area he entered a left-right ess-bend at very high speed. The road was bumpy and Klass apparently flew from one of these bumps, got both nearside wheels on the verge and half-spun, careering off the road and hitting a tree broadside-on just behind the cockpit at about 60 mph. The car was almost cut in two and although a first-aid helicopter was quickly on the scene, and took Klass to hospital, he died on arrival. SEFAC Ferrari withdrew its two entries immediately.

Understandably there were no Ferrari Dinos at Freiburg the following weekend and none ran in either of the year's remaining Mountain Championship events at Ollon–Villars and Gaisberg.

Meanwhile the long-awaited new Formula 2 Dino 166 had made its debut at the Turin racing car show in February, revealing itself as a neat and pretty scaled-down version of the 'Aero' 1.5-litre Formula 1 monocoques though with the 65-degree V6 engine slung in a tubular sub-frame at the rear, contributing only partially to the chassis structure unlike the fully stressed 1.5-litre F1 V8s and flat-12s. The engine had bore and stroke dimensions of 86 mm × 45.8 mm, providing a swept volume of 1596.3 cc. One-piece cam covers with cast-on 'Dino' lettering

Christopher Arthur Amon
b. 20 July, 1943

Chris Amon, born in Bulls, New Zealand (North Island), came from a well-to-do farming family. Father bought him an ancient 1.5 Cooper-Climax in 1961 when he was 17 and he placed it second first time out. In 1962 he drove a front-engined Maserati 250F and won two races, and in the 1963 Tasman Series he ran a 2.5 Cooper-Climax under the Scuderia Veloce banner. Reg Parnell, Lola team manager, spotted his potential and at 19 Amon found himself the youngest driver on the Formula 1 circuit. He had a mixed 1963 Grand Prix season in Parnell's Lolas, crashing heavily at Nürburgring and Monza, and when Reg died of peritonitis late in the year it was a heavy blow.

His son, Tim Parnell, took over the team, and Amon drove their Lotus-BRM 25s in 1964–65, when fellow Kiwi Bruce McLaren helped provide Elva-BMW, Ford GT and occasional Cobra drives. He was intended as Bruce's number two in the 1966 McLaren Formula 1 team, but the car never materialized and he had a single outing in a Cooper-Maserati at the French GP. In Group 7 he did very well with big American V8-engined McLaren sports cars, and proved beyond doubt his ability; winning Le Mans with McLaren in a 7-litre Ford GT Mark II.

Mr Ferrari signed on the 24-year-old for 1967 long-distance and Formula 1 races, and after Bandini's death and Mike Parkes's Belgian Grand Prix accident—which ended his Formula 1 career—Amon rose nobly to carry the Prancing Horse's honour alone for much of the year. Into 1969 Amon's bad luck was becoming legendary in Formula 1, and fate or something in his own make-up seemed to cheat him repeatedly when victory looked imminent. When he left Ferrari at the end of 1970 he left a down-and-out team about to bounce back with a winner—the flat-12 312B car—and with March he won one F1 race, at Silverstone. In 1971 he went to Matra, and won the non-Championship Argentine Grand Prix, but nothing else. His Grand Prix career fizzled out in 1977....

Left On the F2 Dino's debut at Rouen-les-Essarts in July 1967 the diminutive English racing driver Jonathan Williams explains how things are to Mauro Forghieri. Firestone engineers check the situation behind. The car failed early in the race and was not raced again that year

housed two chain-driven overhead camshafts to each cylinder bank, actuating three valves per cylinder, two inlets and one exhaust, set in Heron heads. It used Lucas fuel injection and Magnetti Marelli transistorized twin-plug ignition, and was rated at 200 bhp at 10,000 rpm.

The 'Aero'-style chassis carried inboard coil/damper front suspension with faired top rocker arms and cross-braced wide-based bottom wishbones, while at the rear the single top link, reversed lower wishbone, twin radius rod system was revised in light of recent developments with a tall extension of the hub carrier placing the top radius rod's outboard pick-up high above hub level. The Turin show car was fitted up with short high-swept exhaust megaphones passing over the rear suspension. Transmission was via an overhung five-speed and reverse Ferrari transaxle, Campagnolo cast-magnesium five-spoke wheels were used with Firestone 5.50/9.50-13 front and 6.00/12.00-13 rear tyres, and chassis dimensions included a wheelbase of 2200 mm (86.6 in), front track of 1405 mm (55.3 in) and rear track of 1425 mm (56.1 in). Weight was quoted as 425 kg, around 937 lb.

The car did not make its first race appearance until 9 July, when Jonathan Williams ran it at Rouen-les-Essarts. It was his first single-seater appearance for Ferrari, although he had made his name in Formula 3 cars. The car had been considerably modified from its original guise, running new cylinder heads as already seen in the works development Dino 206S with the fuel injection tracts entering the heads between the camshafts rather than within the vee, and with the exhaust stacks now passing below the half-shafts through the rear suspension instead of over it.

Right Talented works engineer Piero Lardi, second from left wearing dark glasses, presiding at June, 1967, Modena tests with the Rouen Dino 166 prototype car '0002'. Jonathan Williams is on the pit counter at the right. This engine has between-cam injection and through-the-suspension exhausts

At Rouen Williams's new car looked bulky and unusual amongst its 4-cylinder Cosworth FVA-engined British opposition, and he qualified thirteenth amongst company including Jim Clark, Graham Hill, Jackie Stewart, Jack Brabham, Denny Hulme and Jochen Rindt with a time of 2 min 6.6 sec, compared to Rindt's Brabham pole time of 2:01.9. The Ferrari handled and braked well, but for a change was some 15 bhp down on its rivals. Williams ran briefly in the race before engine trouble put him out after seven laps.

The car did not race again that season, although it was often to be seen on test at Modena, as in August, when a 24-valve V6 was tested with an airbox shrouding the injection intakes, and Williams lapped in 54.8

Below This version of the Formula 2 Dino 166—the second car '0004'—appeared at Modena in 1967 and set the type's best lap-time yet running the vestigial air-box seen here. The engine has injection between the cam-boxes and single-plug ignition

seconds, the quickest Formula 2 lap of Modena thus far with this set-up. In October another 24-valve engine variant appeared in the F2 Dino 166, this time with single-plug ignition in the head centre between separate cam covers, while the injection equipment was resited within the vee. This was closer to the finalized 1968 Dino 166 layout in which one-piece twin-cam covers were refitted, with housings for single-plug ignition and the fuel injection air intake assembly with its tall trumpets and slide throttles nestled into the vee.

Meanwhile New Zealander Chris Amon had become well established in the Formula 1 team after Bandini's untimely death and once again a Tasman Championship foray was planned, and the Maranello technicians hunted along their parts shelves to see what they could produce. The result was another Tasman Dino 246, but this time using the Dino 166 Formula 2 chassis nacelle with an 18-valve, dual-ignition V6 engine installed. This unit had been revised internally to increase its bore in relation to the stroke, the bore going to 90 mm from the 1966 special's 85 mm and the stroke shortening to only 63 mm from 71. Swept volume was 2404.7 cc. With an 11.5:1 compression ratio this unit produced around 285 bhp at 8900 rpm with meaty mid-range torque. With Firestone 6.00/12.50-13 rear tyres the standard Dino 166 track was reduced to 1400 mm (55.1 in) from the F2's nominal 1435 mm, and the car weighed in at 440 kg, 970 lb.

Ferrari's youthful *Ingegnere* Gianni Marelli accompanied Amon and the car to New Zealand and Australia in January and February 1968, and they proved yet again that the 11-year-old Jano V6 could still be a winner in the right circumstances.

Photographed by Pete Coltrin at Modena in October 1967, yet another Dino variant, this time with induction within the engine vee and single-plug ignition between the cam-boxes

1968–1970s F2, Tasman and Lancia-Ferrari V6

On 6 January 1968 the faithful old 65-degree Ferrari Dino V6 returned successfully to International motor racing in the stern of Chris Amon's Formula 2-chassised Tasman special, as it began its Australasian tour by winning the New Zealand Grand Prix at Pukekohe.

The car was the centre of attraction in the Auckland circuit paddock, despite the presence of two BRM V12s, a Lotus 49T for Jim Clark with a 32-valve 2.5-litre Cosworth DFW V8 engine and a beautifully presented Brabham special fitted with Carlo Chiti's sports car Alfa Romeo V8. Running temporarily on Goodyear tyres, Amon clocked a fastest practice lap in 59.9 seconds, 0.8 second slower than Clark's eventual pole position time. The Ferrari led off the line in the race but was quickly overhauled by Clark's Lotus, and then ran a close second until lap 46 of the scheduled fifty-eight when the Scot's Cosworth engine dropped a valve. Amon inherited the lead with a comfortable forty seconds in hand over Frank Gardner's Brabham-Alfa Romeo, and he won as he pleased. He set fastest race lap at 59.3 seconds and became only the second New Zealander to win his home Grand Prix in the race's fifteen-year history—Bruce McLaren having been the first, in 1964.

In the Levin International on 13 January Amon ran regular Firestone GP125 tyres and set practice alight with an early lap at 46.9 seconds, 146.30 km/h (90.19 mph), but then he spun and cracked a front upright. As was the custom in New Zealand a fourteen-lap preliminary race was held, in which Clark narrowly beat Amon to the line before the cars formed up again for the main event. Clark was on pole, with Gardner and Amon ranged alongside him, and when early leader Frank Gardner spun out, Amon took the lead with Clark chasing him until the Lotus struck a course marker and damaged its suspension. Amon never set a wheel wrong, and won handsomely, setting fastest race lap again at 46.8 seconds, 145.46 km/h (90.385 mph).

The Lady Wigram Trophy race followed outside Christchurch, and on the airfield circuit there Amon appeared with his spare engine fitted on decree from Maranello. He clocked 1 min 20.2 sec, 166.148 km/h (103.24 mph) in practice, two-tenths slower than Clark's now Gold Leaf-liveried Lotus, and was beaten by it by one second in the preliminary. In the forty-four lap 101-mile main race the story was the same; Clark led all the way with Amon second. They shared the record

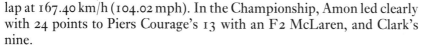

lap at 167.40 km/h (104.02 mph). In the Championship, Amon led clearly with 24 points to Piers Courage's 13 with an F2 McLaren, and Clark's nine.

Invercargill was the next stop, for the Teretonga Trophy race on the world's southernmost circuit. The first preliminary heat was run in blinding rain and the Dino 246 collected so much water in its electrics on the warm-up lap it refused to fire on more than three cylinders, and was wheeled off the grid. Since the rain had so affected these races, which had been intended to decide grid places for the sixty-lap, ninety-six-mile main event, the organizers fell back on practice speeds, and this gave Amon pole with a 154 km/h (96 mph) lap. He was running a distant second behind Clark until lap 39, when he spun and lost a lap. Clark went off at around 140 mph over a bump soon after, and Bruce McLaren was left to win for BRM with Clark recovering second, Gardner third and Amon fourth. He now had a nine-point Championship lead over Clark and the Lotus.

Top left This prototype 24-valve Dino was photographed at Modena in November 1967, and had one-piece cam-covers enclosing 24 valves, in-vee injection and single-plug ignition. It is also running an old 1.5-litre Formula 1 car nose-cone from *c.* 1964–65

Above left The Swedish 'Team Bam-Bam' Dino 206S of Hans Wangstre/Evert Christofferssen hammers through Cerda's main street during the 1968 Targa Florio in which it finished 22nd — not bad for a private entry

Above centre The 1968 prototype Dino 246T business end showing the injection between the cam-boxes, ignition coils in the vee feeding a 12-plug distributor driven off the tail of the right-hand inlet camshaft and exquisite workmanship on the transaxle, inboard brakes and drive-shafts. This appears to have been chassis '0004'. Pete Coltrin took the photograph in November 1967

The circus travelled to Australia to continue the Championship series, starting at Surfers' Paradise, Queensland, on 11 February. The Ferrari ran with a new 24-valve V6 installed, this unit having its injection stacks within the vee rather than between the cams on either bank, and with single instead of dual ignition. It was claimed to offer 20 bhp more than the development 18-valver employed in New Zealand. Amon ended practice fastest with 1:09.7, compared to the two Lotus 49Ts of Clark and Graham Hill on 1:09.9 and 1:10.3. He drove Scuderia Veloce's special ex-Jonathan Williams CanAm Ferrari P4 sports car in the supporting event, but was put off course by a back-marker and finished second.

He then won the Tasman Formula preliminary by 3.1 seconds from Gardner and in the fifty-lap, 100-mile main race he was able to challenge Clark's Cosworth V8 very strongly until a head seal blew and the Ferrari came boiling into its pit after twenty-four laps. Clark closed to three points behind Amon in the Championship chase.

Their battle was resumed at Sydney's Warwick Farm circuit on 18 February, where Jack Brabham joined in with a Repco V8-engined car. Amon had to run an 18-valve engine again, and in practice it began blowing oil and water. He was third fastest in practice with 1:28.0, a fifth slower than Graham Hill and 0.8 slower than Clark on pole. Overnight before the race his crew rebuilt the 24-valve engine, and with this installed he chased Clark and Hill hard, but was caught by Courage and Brabham. On lap 30 Hill had a moment and Amon spun in avoidance, allowing Courage to go by followed by Hulme's Brabham, Jack having made a stop. Amon displaced Hulme—the reigning World Champion—but could do nothing about Courage and finished fourth. Clark won and took the Championship lead by 33 points to the Ferrari Dino driver's 30.

The Australian Grand Prix was held at Melbourne's Sandown Park course on 25 February. The first New Zealand 18-valve engine had been flown to Maranello for rebuilding and was now returned as spare, while the 24-valver remained in the car. Brabham took pole with a 1:06.7 lap, while Amon was next up on 1:06.8, then Clark 1:06.9.

Chris ran second behind Clark from the flag and drew alongside the Lotus on the back straight, only to be outbraked and forced to tuck in behind again. Brabham's engine was off song early on, then chimed-in properly and he began taking a second a lap off the leaders, closing on the Ferrari's tail on lap 14. These three were then twenty-five seconds clear of the rest in a very hot race, and Amon repeatedly drew alongside Clark only to be outbraked into the corners. Brabham retired abruptly with engine failure, while lap 33 saw Amon lead across the timing line only to be forced back again into second place. This wheel-to-wheel battle had the enthusiastic Australian crowd shouting themselves hoarse and it ran to the line, with Amon diving out of Clark's slipstream and surging almost alongside—his Dino's front wheels level with the Lotus's cockpit—as the chequered flag swept down. The timekeepers split the pair by one-tenth of a second, Clark averaging 101.9 mph for the fifty-five-lap 106-mile race, while Amon took fastest lap at 1:07.0, 166.72 km/h (103.6 mph). Jim Clark extended his Championship lead to six points with this victory—which sadly was to prove his last in a 'Grand Prix'.

The Tasman Championship decider followed at Longford, Tasmania, on 4 March, a public road circuit with daunting swerves and 150 mph straights. Clark lapped at 2:12.8 in practice, while Amon had trouble starting the Dino and did just one flying lap after Clark set his time— 2:13.8—which was subsequently bettered, narrowly, by Graham Hill.

Amon needed to win the main race with Clark finishing no better than fifth to take the Tasman Championship for Ferrari Dino, but in the preliminary race on Saturday, 3 March, he had just taken the lead when another head seal failed and the Ferrari retired. Chris then drove the Scuderia Veloce CanAm P4 to victory in the sports car race.

On the Sunday the heavens opened and Longford was awash. Amon ran second behind Clark from the start of the main race, but shot down the escape road at Newry Corner, rejoining seventh. The high-powered cars were all in trouble finding traction on the slick surface and Courage's 1600 cc McLaren took the lead and danced away to win. Amon's ignition began to drown around the tenth lap, and he finally finished seventh, while Clark was fifth and took the Championship for Lotus by 44 points to 36.

Back in Italy, meanwhile, Mr Ferrari had announced a new Sport 2000 model, allegedly using the chassis and body of Scarfiotti's Group 7 Trento–Bondone *Montagna* '0842' with a 2-litre flat-12 engine installed, derived from the 1965 Formula 1 engine. This car did not actually run until 1969, when as the further-developed 212E it carried the Swiss

---

This tall, friendly driver was born in Trieste and began motor racing while studying law. He first made his name in 1963–64, running a Formula Junior Lola with an early Novamotor-tuned engine. He rallied an Alfa Romeo Giulia TI Super, winning the Fiori and Portogallo events, and in 1965 he won the Italian FJ Championship in a Lola-Novamotor-Ford.

Autodelta, the quasi-works Alfa Romeo competitions concern under Carlo Chiti, hired his services for their touring car team and he won at Monza and Nürburgring. At the end of that year his close friend Bruno Deserti was killed while testing a sports Ferrari at Monza, and it was only after some soul-searching that De Adamich continued racing in 1966, when he won his European Touring Car Championship division with an Alfa Romeo GTA. He handled the new T33 sports car in endurance racing but found they wouldn't last the distance, and handled a Brabham in Formula 3.

The 1967 season saw him placed fifth in the Nürburgring 1000 km, second at Rossfeld and first in both the Tourist Trophy and Budapest Grand Prix in GTAs and these performances earned him a Ferrari Formula 1 debut in the non-Championship Madrid Grand Prix at Jarama. He crashed in the 1968 South African Grand Prix, without injury, but during practice for the Race of Champions at Brands Hatch he crashed his Ferrari 312 very heavily, and injured his neck. He rejoined the fray with the F2 Dino 166s right at the end of the year, then in 1969 signed with John Surtees for F5000 and Alfa Romeo for sports-car racing. 1970 saw him back in Formula 1 with a McLaren-Alfa V8 and in 1971 his Alfa Romeo T33/3s were winning endurance events. He retired when sports car racing lost significance and his Brabham crashed in the infamous British GP multiple collision of 1973—having broken his leg rather badly. Andrea de Adamich was never a top-line driver, but he was an excellent sporting ambassador for Italy.

Andrea Lodovico de Adamich
b. 3 October, 1941

The NART-entered 206S Coupé driven by the Frenchmen Chevalier and Lagier at Le Mans in 1968 true to Dino form failed to last the distance. The Coupé cars were always amongst the most pretty of an attractive breed

Wheel-spin at the start of the 1968 Surfers' Paradise Tasman Championship race in Queensland, Australia, as Chris Amon's privately campaigned Dino 246T — probably chassis '0004' — scrabbles for grip alongside Jim Clark's newly Gold Leaf-liveried Lotus 49T, which has its rear Firestones well and truly alight. Here Amon was running the four-valve-per-cylinder, in-vee induction Dino engine for the first time, and after starting from pole position he ran second until a seal failed and the engine overheated

Chris Amon in the 246T at Melbourne's Sandown Park circuit in 1968, where he finished fourth. The 24-valve single-plug engine had been repaired since Surfers' and was fitted in haste the night before the Sydney race at Warwick Farm, when Amon had also finished fourth

Left One of the author's rare worthwhile efforts at photography captured Brian Redman's Dino 166 '0008' two-wheeling round the Nürburgring *Sudschleife* in the 1968 Eifelrennen on the way to an heroic fourth place and new lap record. Brian's goggles had been smashed by a flying stone, and he is driving here with Ickx's spare dark-tinted pair. What he could not see the very pleasant Lancastrian did not worry about...

Left Howling downhill into one of the Barcelona Montjuich Park circuit's slow hairpins, Chris Amon leads Jack Oliver's Lotus 48 in the Formula 2 Dino 166 '0008'. This was the opening round of the 1968 European Formula 2 Championship, and the New Zealander finished third behind the Matras of Jackie Stewart and Henri Pescarolo

Below centre 7 April, 1968, was a foul day at Hockenheimring, damp and misty for the Deutschland Trophy F2 race. It claimed the life of Jim Clark. Here a disconsolate Amon tours home to a fifth on aggregate finish in '0006'

Below right Ickx's sister car '0010' appeared for the Eifelrennen with pressed-aluminium coarse screen gauzes over the nose-top exit ducts for exhausting radiator air and within the front suspension cut-outs. The car retired early on. It was in this race that Englishman Derek Bell impressed the Ferrari team with his driving of a Brabham-Cosworth F2. He was invited to test a Dino 166 at Modena and subsequently made his debut for the team in the Monza Lottery GP

driver Peter Schetty to the European Mountain Championship title with a series of magnificent outright victories and climb records.

Meanwhile the Dino 166 Formula 2 cars were being prepared for the full F2 season they had missed in 1967. The V6 engines were now developed with in-vee injection, two inlet and two exhaust valves per cylinder and single-plug ignition, and with the narrower bore and lengthened stroke of 79.5 mm × 53.5 mm they displaced 1593.6 cc and produced 225 bhp at 10,600 rpm.

In this new 166/68 trim wheelbase was lengthened slightly to 2250 mm (89.8 in) instead of 2200 mm as in 1967, and rear track was 10 mm wider at 1435 mm (56.5 in). Weight was quoted as 430 kg, 948 lb. The new Dino 166s looked a very competitive proposition, particularly since the season began with the prospect of Chris Amon and new Formula 1 recruit Jacky Ickx driving.

The 1968 European Championship Formula 2 season began at Barcelona on 31 March, where Amon and Ickx arrived in company with Mauro Forghieri and two Dino 166s. Handling problems and tyre doubts slowed them in practice, Ickx being fifth and Amon seventh fastest behind Jackie Stewart on pole with a Matra-Cosworth. Ickx had trouble stopping his Ferrari on lap 2 of the race and rammed Clark's Lotus, putting it out of the race and rupturing one of the Dino's water-lines, which forced the Belgian to retire. Amon finished third behind the Matras of Stewart and Pescarolo. The Dinos were chassis numbers '0008' and '0010'.

The Deutschland Trophy at Hockenheim on 7 April was the scene of Jimmy Clark's fatal accident. Amon was there with a choice of his Barcelona Dino and a brand-new chassis, brought instead of Ickx's damaged car. He was sixth quickest in practice and finished sixth in heat one and seventh in heat two, his aggregate time giving him a tardy fifth place. He drove '0006', the newer chassis.

Brian Redman tested a Dino 166 at Modena the following week, since the title of European Champion was intended only for a non-Graded driver, and neither Amon nor Ickx was eligible. It was intended to run three cars for these drivers at Thruxton on Easter Monday, but Ferrari

did not make the trip. On 21 April there were Formula 2 races at Pau and at Nürburgring on the little-used South Circuit, where the Eifelrennen saw Redman make his Ferrari debut alongside Ickx in Dino 166s, Ickx in his Barcelona chassis and Redman in the latest one.

Ickx took pole with a 2:44.0 lap with Redman on the outside of the front row with 2:44.6. Ickx stormed into the lead with Redman fourth, but Kurt Ahrens's Brabham flung up a stone which pierced the Lancastrian's goggles and damaged his eye. He pulled into the pits, where the only spare goggles available were Ickx's dark-tinted pair. Brian hared away wearing them. When Ickx was displaced by Ahrens another stone tore a gash in his Dino's radiator and he was out. Redman tore into the opposition to make up his lost time and stormed home fourth at the finish with a new lap record to his credit at 2:47.0, 167.0 km/h (103.76 mph). This drive could have won him a regular Ferrari ride, but he crashed heavily in the Belgian Grand Prix soon afterwards when his Cooper-BRM's suspension failed, and a broken arm put him out of racing for the rest of the season.

Ferrari were 'off' Formula 2 again as they missed the Jarama race late in April, but returned with Ickx and Amon driving in the Limbourg Grand Prix at Zolder in Belgium on 5 May. The race was run in two twenty-four-lap sixty-four-mile heats, and Amon was second quickest in practice on sticky Firestone rubber behind Rindt's Brabham. These two finished heat one in that order, with Ickx eighth, his engine off-song. At the start of heat two, Rindt was struck by another car and the Dinos powered away, running 1–2, with Ickx's revived machine leading Amon, and since the overall race result was to be decided by addition of places all that Ferrari had to do was to ensure that Amon finished ahead of Ickx, and with Rindt out of touch the New Zealander would have to win. Unfortunately Ickx was Belgian, racing on his own circuit, and he later claimed he had not seen the signal which was shown. So he won, beating Amon into second with Rindt third. Rindt's first and third places gave him precedence over Amon's two second places, and so Ferrari lost a race victory they should have scored, Amon being classified second on aggregate and Ickx fourth. The New Zealander was justifiably unhappy....

For the Crystal Palace meeting in London on 3 June Ferrari cabled three late entries, but only Ickx was accepted. He crashed in practice on this tight circuit, but was placed fifth in the first twenty-two-lap heat despite gear-selection problems, and then collided with two other cars at the start of the ninety-lap 125-mile final, breaking the car's rear suspension and trailing round to retire. He was classified fifteenth overall.

Hockenheimring hosted its second Formula 2 race of the season on 16 June, the Rhein Cup, where Ferrari presented two cars for Amon and Ickx, one reporter writing that they were 'MO53' and 'MO36' respectively, mistaking their temporary Modena test-plate registrations....

They went well in practice on this high-speed slipstreaming circuit, Ickx third and Amon fourth quickest behind two Matras. The thirty-lap race was all about maintaining a 'tow' and Ickx finished fifth and Amon eighth, the New Zealander not being too fond of this kind of racing on the track where Jim Clark had been killed.

Tragically, the previous weekend the Rossfeld hillclimb had been run in Germany, where Ludovico Scarfiotti crashed his new works Porsche into a tree, and was killed. It was a sad fate for the gentleman driver who had played such a part in our Dino story.

One week later the Monza Lottery Grand Prix was the promised Formula 2 slipstreamer, with SEFAC Ferrari entering Englishman Derek Bell in their only official Dino 166 entry, while three sister cars were fielded under AC Milano auspices in the individual names of Giancarlo Baghetti, Mario Casoni and local Monza driver Ernesto 'Tino' Brambilla. Bell fulfilled the promise he had displayed in his private Brabham–Cosworth earlier in the year by sitting the Dino on pole position with a 1 min 33.3 sec lap, Casoni (the endurance racer-cum-hill-climber) was fourth, Brambilla fifth and Baghetti eighteenth....

The first heat produced the expected slipstreaming dogfight, with Bell amongst the leaders and Baghetti and Casoni at the back. On lap 22, leaving the *Parabolica*, Bell spun and cars exploded in all directions. Baghetti and Brambilla crashed beside Bell's crushed car, while Casoni hit something solid and stopped at the pits for the tattered nose cowling to be torn away. Jaussaud's Tecno caught fire and ignited the track surface, which caused a terrible bottleneck for some time. The race ended its forty-five laps with Casoni seventh in the sole surviving Dino, while Jonathan Williams, dropped by Ferrari, won in a private Brabham.

By this time Maranello reportedly had six available Dino 166 chassis, of which three were badly damaged in the Monza collision. On 14 July at Tulln–Langenlebarn in Austria two cars were presented for Amon and Bell. The F2 team was managed by Franco Gozzi, later Ferrari's long-serving press chief, since Forghieri was now happy for the cars to run without top-level technical presence. The race was run in two thirty-five-lap heats and in the first Bell was nudged early on and flurried into the straw bales. Amon ran third on the leaders' heels until gear selection trouble put him out on lap 13. Bell recovered after his early bale-bashing and finished twelfth. In the second heat Amon's engine quickly went onto five cylinders and he was placed a distant eighth, behind his team-mate. Perhaps Forghieri had been overconfident. On aggregate the two Dinos were placed seventh (Bell) and twelfth.

The Zandvoort Formula 2 round on 28 July decided the European Championship in Matra driver Jean-Pierre Beltoise's favour, but was marred by a fatal accident to British privateer Chris Lambert. Three Dino 166s were entered for Bell and Brambilla, and for Andrea de Adamich, but he had not yet fully recovered from crashing a Formula 1 Ferrari 312 at Brands Hatch early in the year. Bell put his car on pole position with Brambilla third for the first twenty-lap heat, and Derek won from Beltoise, with the Italian Dino driver third and setting fastest race lap—a new record—at 1:26.52, 174.466 km/h (108.408 mph).

In the fifty-lap final Bell led, Brambilla having steering trouble and retiring after sixteen laps. Bell was exchanging the lead with Courage's Brabham in a tight duel until the Dino's gearbox abruptly froze in fourth.

After a long stop the disappointed Bell finished fourteenth.

Amon had surrendered any Formula 2 aspiration he may have nursed, and on 25 August the Mediterranean Grand Prix at Enna was run for Formula 2 cars, with Ferrari fielding four of their Dinos, for Bell, Ickx, Casoni and Brambilla. Ickx scraped a barrier heavily at high speed in practice and in the fifty-lap race Casoni discovered a fuel leak while on grid and set off nine laps after the rest. After twelve laps there were ten cars in the leading slipstreaming bunch, including Bell, Brambilla and Ickx, and they battled to the finish, with Rindt winning, Brambilla outfumbling his team-mates for third, Bell fifth and Ickx a moody sixth. Casoni came home sixteenth.

Ferrari were too busy preparing CanAm cars to take the Dinos to Reims, but on 13 October the Formula 2 team made its third trip of the year to Hockenheim for the Preis von Wurttemberg. Bell had the latest car Dino 166 '0010' and Brambilla '0004'—apparently the second and fifth cars in an even-numbers-only system—and they qualified eighth and tenth in reverse order. It was a thirty-five-lap race and Bell was well placed in the leading slipstreaming bunch for much of the distance, until the very last lap. Brambilla had closed on the group with a record lap in 1:59.0, 204.77 km/h (127.23 mph), faster than his best practice time, and coming down the final straight into the twisty stadium section before the finish line he came careering into contention as if from nowhere, all four wheels on the grass at near 150 mph. As he careered back onto the track he forced Bell across to clip wheels with Pescarolo's Matra, and as

Left Temporada Formula 2 tour, 1968, with Brambilla leading de Adamich in the opening Argentinian race series round at Buenos Aires

Centre above Dinos victorious: the Rome GP in October 1968 saw 'Tino' Brambilla (number 4) win handsomely from his senior team-mate Andrea de Adamich (following) with Derek Bell a troubled sixth on aggregate. By this time the Dino 166s wore tiny nose tabs and strutted rear fins mounted on the chassis. Bell was a little disappointed to be beaten, but he was running against Italians in an Italian team: 'I knew that in Formula 3 I had consistently beaten both of them . . .'

Above right 1968 Argentine Temporada Champion—the tall and friendly former law student Andrea de Adamich in his works Dino 166 '0012'

Brambilla lapped a back-marker in the process he was clean away and had scored Ferrari's first Formula 2 victory since Solitude in 1960! Bell was a rather shaken third, 0.2 second behind a very angry Pescarolo, and the pretty little Dino 166 was a winner at last. . . .

Ferrari passed up the Albi Formula 2 race in favour of the Rome Grand Prix at Vallelunga on 27 October, final Formula 2 fixture of the European season, and there Bell appeared in '0010', Brambilla in '0004' and the tall de Adamich made his Ferrari F2 debut in '0012', a modified long-cockpit car which had been based on that which Bell raced at Enna. Brambilla and de Adamich were 1–2 in practice with 1:16.4 and 1:16.46, while Bell was seventh quickest at 1:16.96—1600 cc Formula 2 was that close.

The race was run in two forty-lap heats, Brambilla and de Adamich finished the first heat 1–2, separated by 1.7 seconds with Bell sixth, perhaps feeling rather an outsider in this all-Italian atmosphere. Brambilla set fastest lap at 1:16.2. In the second heat de Adamich led initially until Brambilla and then Peter Gethin in a Brabham went by, and they finished in that order, Brambilla's fastest lap being set at 1:16.4 this time. Bell was troubled by understeer and fluctuating oil pressure, and he was sixth again. On aggregate the result gave Ferrari Dino 166s 1st, 2nd and 6th, having won two representative Formula 2 races on the trot . . . and more followed.

The Argentine *Temporada* race series had been revived, initially for Formula 3 cars and now in December 1968 for Formula 2. Ferrari

225

despatched Dinos '4 and '12 for Ernesto Brambilla and de Adamich, who was being nursed towards rehabilitation in the Formula 1 team. The race series commenced in the Buenos Aires Autodrome on 1 December, and while Jochen Rindt's inevitable Brabham took pole at 1:18.9, 155.76 km/h (96.79 mph), de Adamich and Brambilla completed the front row with 1:19.0 and 1:19.4. De Adamich, the law student, led Rindt for the first three laps, before the Austrian found a way past, and on previous form that would have been the end of the matter, but Brambilla was moving forward. He first displaced his team-mate, then on lap 14 of the seventy scheduled he overtook Rindt for the lead. De Adamich was second ahead of Rindt when a wing strut broke on the Brabham, and the Ferraris were left with an unassailable lead, Brambilla winning from de Adamich by 0.2 second on the line. Brambilla's fastest lap of 1:19.5 established the Formula 2 lap record.

The Oscar Cabalen Autodrome at Cordoba saw round two of the series the following weekend. Brambilla had problems with his car, while de Adamich shared the front row with Clay Regazzoni's Tecno, on the same lap time. Rindt and Beltoise held early leads before de Adamich slammed the Dino 166 through, leading the rest of the seventy laps to win by 4.4 seconds from Rindt's Brabham. Brambilla was plagued by power loss and retired near mid-distance. Courage's Brabham set fastest lap, at 194 km/h (121 mph). Right at the end de Adamich's engine began to stutter; a soft cam lobe had worn down.

On 15 December the circus tackled the Championship's round three at the *Autodromo Zonda* at San Juan, 2500 ft above sea-level around the crater of a long-extinct volcano. Both Dinos were fitted with new engines at this midway stage, but de Adamich reverted to his original V6 in practice when the replacement went onto five. Practice was rather unconventionally disrupted by a sand storm and ended with Jo Siffert's Tecno on pole and de Adamich alongside 0.4 second slower. Brambilla was on the second row a further 0.4 second down.

De Adamich took the lead halfway round the opening lap, was displaced by Brambilla on lap 5 and then both were hustled out of the way by Beltoise's Matra, the European Champion driving luridly. Brambilla pushed back and took the lead, with de Adamich on his tail, and when the Monza garage owner had a slide de Adamich retook the lead. On lap 13 Brambilla spun at the hairpin, delaying Beltoise, and de Adamich was clear in a lead he held to the end of the seventy laps, although the Dino's battery was flapping along retained only by its leads. Brambilla drove furiously to regain second place, but on lap 37 he missed a gearchange and rattled in to retire with his tachometer tell-tale off the clock and the engine blown. Andrea de Adamich was Temporada F2 Champion for Ferrari Dino with the last race still to run, but despite Brambilla's furious drive fastest race lap went to Rindt at 170.25 km/h (105.79 mph).

Buenos Aires provided the venue for the final round on 22 December, using a different circuit combination from the first round. The Ferrari Dinos dominated practice, with Brambilla on pole 0.1 second faster than his Champion team-mate. The race was run in two twenty-five-lap heats, and in the first Brambilla built a big lead from de Adamich, until with five

---

THE DINO 206S

One of the nice things about Ferrari for those who enjoy mysteries is the endless scope for further research into one specialised area of their activity. Such an area concerns the Dino 206S and so-called SP models—since they were never homologated as 'sports cars' they should all retrospectively be termed 206SPs. I have used the SP tag to identify the cut-down hill-climb prototype cars as opposed to their fully-equipped long-distance racing sisters. This factory-originated chassis listing has been extensively amended, but the story has yet to be comprehensively unravelled . . . It asks more questions than it answers.

CHASSIS NUMBER	FIRST AND SUBSEQUENT OWNERSHIPS
002*	Bill Harrah (via Chinetti), Bally Manufacturing, Carpenter, Steve Mitchell, Mistretta, Ed Niles *Schanbacher/Bill Schworer (USA)*
004	SEFAC Ferrari, Tony Dean, Alain de Cadanet, Bamford, Crawford, *Dudley Mason-Styrron (UK)*
006	Maranello Concessionaires UK, Gustav Diedens, Hans Wangstre (Sweden), *Claes Jung, Sweden* reputedly fitted with Volvo B20 engine
008	Chinetti, Schroeder, Fred Baker for Kolb and Cutler, Cluxton, *Walter Medlin (USA)*
010	SEFAC Ferrari, Lualdi, Ecurie Francorchamps, Alain de Cadanet, Bamford, Zcuner, *Michael Vernon (UK)*
012	Maranello Concessionaires '66 Le Mans Coupé, Scuderia Bear (USA) Bill Conte, Cluxton, Kirk White, Sam Brown, John McGary reputedly at *Grossman's Fort Lauderdale, Florida*, summer 1979
014	Chinetti, Harrah, Chinetti for Kolb and Rodriguez, re-skinned, to Simmers, *Frank Weinberg (USA)*
016	Lado (Verona), Group 6 cut-down spyder-bodied, Hofer (Austria), reputedly stolen and not yet recovered . . . summer 1979
018	Latteri . . .
020	Works listed as 'Incommunicato' . . .
022	Ravetto, Pietro lo Piccolo, Group 6 cut-down spyder-bodied almost identical to 212E flat-12 engined *Montagna* in original form, to *Pierre Bardinon (France)* with 2.4 Tasman 18-valve V6
024	Brescia Corse, reputedly 'Pam' (Marcello or Marsillio Pasotti), Alain de Cadanet first car, crashed and re-chassised by Arch Motors, rebodied by Wilkinson's of Derby, to Jeff Edmonds, Bamford, Cluxton, De Friece, *David Seibert (USA)*
026	Filipinetti car, burned-out Nürburgring 1967—reincarnated, to *Pierre Bardinon (France)*
028	Lualdi, Guglieminetti rebody *a la* 312P plus 2.4 24-valve engine for *Gelles Bros (USA)*
030	Antonio Nicodemi, Bamford, Messersmith, Cluxton, Kerry Payne, *Mark Tippetts, (France)* modified with carburettors by Mason-Styrron for road use
032	*Pierre Bardinon, (France)* via Corrado Cupellini, Italy
034	Allegedly to Pininfarina for styling exercise coachwork

*Originally works team car '0852'

Prototype Dinos included: '0834' 1965 166P Coupé cut-down as hill-climb spyder; '0842' Sebring and Monza 1966 first works car, raced Targa Florio, subsequently cut-down as hill-climb spyder through 1967; '0852' works 206S second at Targa Florio 1966 as Coupé, subsequently reworked and renumbered as first prototype 206S '002'

NB—This listing is intended purely as a general guide to the individual histories of each car—100 per cent verification has not, in every case, been possible

laps to go his Dino began to run short of brakes. De Adamich closed rapidly, but on the last lap Brambilla's engine ejected a puff of blue smoke and died as a con-rod broke, leaving the Champion to win.

At the start of heat two de Adamich hesitated at the flag and surprised Courage behind him, whose Brabham was promptly rammed up the tail and catapulted into the Dino. De Adamich found himself bundled broadside off course, striking a group of spectators before smashing the nose cone on the pit wall. Six people were injured in this sorry incident, two sustaining broken legs, but after losing some forty-five seconds de Adamich flurried away into the race. He had an early spin, and was sixth at the finish. On aggregate he was awarded fifth place behind Courage's winning Brabham. In the final Championship scoring Andrea de Adamich took the title with 36 points to Jochen Rindt's 21, Courage's 14 and Brambilla's 13.

It was a highly successful tour for the Dino 166s, but although they won three of the four Championship rounds and established a record of five consecutive Formula 2 race victories they were not really as dominant as has since been suggested. When the cars returned to Europe to commence their 1969 season they were a shadow of their former selves, and the story has gained currency that the Temporada cars had run 2-litre engines. This seems highly unlikely for two reasons. Firstly I doubt very much if Ferrari would have risked their international reputation on such a series (though scrutineering might be expected to be slack there), but secondly the race statistics do not show the Dinos to have out-powered their rivals. They were beaten for pole positions, they were beaten for fastest laps, and both de Adamich and Brambilla were well attuned to this type of racing, so it was not a case of totally indifferent drivers inexplicably beating the established 'King'—Jochen Rindt.

The F2 Dino 166s in fact combined usable power with fine handling and they were running Firestone YB11 compound tyres, which in Formula 1 had brought lap times tumbling down, while the opposition were on Goodyear and Dunlop. Reporting on the Cordoba race, *Autosport* magazine's correspondent Dr Vicente Alvarez commented: 'The Ferrari's roadholding could best be seen at the entry to one of the

Yorkshireman Tony Dean, who had made his name as a member of the British Kart Team, then in various Lotus, Brabham and Porsche cars, made a great impact on the British national scene in 1968 with his ex-works Dino 206S '004'. Here he three-wheels under acceleration up The Mountain at the twisty Cadwell Park course in Lincolnshire. This car used a sand-cast Ferrari block and was later sold to Alain de Cadanet who had two other cars both with Fiat cast blocks. All had 18-valves and injection between the cam-boxes

corners, where Rindt, Courage, Beltoise and the others were dabbing their brakes, whereas de Adamich only had to lift off; or at another, where the others lifted off momentarily, but the Ferrari went through flat. . . .'

It was not 'bent' engines which brought Ferrari their Formula 2 Championship in Argentina in 1968; it was the combination of competitive engines and chassis, fine tyres and adequate drivers.

While the Formula 2 season had progressed from disappointment and disaster to achieve domination, the Dino 206S sports cars did little else but disappoint during 1968. Tony Dean did quite well with his car in Britain, where Alain de Cadanet ran an ex-Casoni 206S, which he eventually painted purple and crashed very heavily at Crystal Palace, and in Italy several cars were raced without conspicuous success, though the Sicilian Lo Piccolo was fourth in the *Coppa Citta di Enna* around the lake at Pergusa.

Tony Dean in Britain spent a lot of money on his motor racing and his ex-works 206S '004' was consistently the best-prepared and best-performing Dino in captivity. In direct contrast to the tight-lipped Leeds garage owner was self-described 'gent racer' Alain de Cadanet. The Chelsea-based young man about town was son of General de Gaulle's wartime Free-French *aide de camp*, who had married into English society. During 1967 de Cadanet had raced a Porsche 904, and early in 1968 he was told of a 'P2, or possibly P3 Ferrari' lying disused in Italy.

He found the car lying in a tumbledown shack in the middle of a field near Brescia. It was an ex-Brescia Corse Dino 206S, chassis '024', which had been extensively raced and hill-climbed. It had the 18-valve engine with fuel injection. Alain was overexcited, and did a bad deal. He arranged to take delivery in Geneva, flew home, telephoned an entry in the Nürburgring 1,000 km and set off for Geneva in an American station wagon towing a four-wheel trailer to collect his Ferrari.

At Nürburgring he and prospective co-driver Anthony McKay towed the 206S literally for miles trying to start it. A cheery injection fire and many plug-cleans later they surrendered, never having attempted a lap of the circuit.

Prior to the RAC Tourist Trophy at Oulton Park he rebuilt the engine

The 1969 Tasman tour was a two-car team effort, and here at Melbourne's Sandown Park circuit Derek Bell in '0010' leads Amon in his title-winning '0008'. Derek loved driving the little Ferraris, both Formula 2 and Tasman models: 'They were beautifully balanced little cars with, in 2.4-litre form, a superb power-to-weight ratio. The gear-change was magnificent generally, but if you tried to change too fast you could catch-up the gate in the top of the gearbox — that's what happened to me at Zandvoort in 1968 and I had to stop to have it freed-off.' In the Tasman tour a piston let go at Levin, leaving Derek with just one engine, rev-limited 1000 rpm below his team leader's. Bell was always a good team man, and just enjoyed his racing with a thoroughbred racing car

ancillaries and set fire to London's Gloucester Road when a high-pressure fuel injection line burned through on an exhaust primary. After finishing a tardy twelfth in the TT de Cadanet towed the car to Vila Real in Portugal, where Mario Cabral drove it home eleventh. At Crystal Palace in August de Cadanet began practice after a heavy night, never having seen the circuit before, and crashed heavily at the first corner, crushing the now-purple Dino's left side very badly.

Fellow amateur Jeff Edmonds offered a straight swop; his Porsche for the shattered Dino and de Cadanet agreed, first having the car re-chassised by Arch Motors and rebuilt. Tony Dean, meanwhile, had been cleaning up the British 2-litre class and even Formula Libre club races with his immaculately prepared '004', and that November saw him shipping the car to the Springbok Series in South Africa, where he shared its driving with local ace Basil van Rooyen; placing an excellent second in the Rand 9-hours at Kyalami and fifth in the subsequent Cape 3-hours at Killarney. On his return home, Dean sold this car to the enthusiastic de Cadanet for 1969.

De Cadanet shared the car briefly early in the season with Tony Beeson, but suffered various mechanical problems—not all self-inflicted. At Monza for the 1000 km in April he and Mike Walton failed to qualify after a practice marred by ignition and injection trouble, and Alain approached Porsche to buy a 907. To his amazement they offered him one of their current 3-litre 908 *Spyders*, which he accepted. At Spa in May Léon Dernier crashed and burned Ecurie Francorchamps' ex-Lualdi ex-works 206S '010' and de Cadanet bought the wreck as a source of Dino spares, having it slowly rebuilt between times.

In July at Vila Real David Piper/Chris Craft won outright in the debut race of de Cadanet's Porsche 908, while he and Mike Walton brought '004' home sixth. He tried repeatedly to buy four-valve heads from Maranello, but was told every time that they did not consider the F2-based components suitable for use in private hands.

In August de Cadanet took the now glass-fibre bodied, cut-down screen 206S '004' to the Nordic Cup series in Scandinavia, where Jo Bonnier took him quietly to one side and advised him to acquire a 2.4 Tasman V6 engine for it. 'But Jo,' he responded, 'it's a 2-litre class, that would be illegal.' The Swede looked at him patiently; 'Really Alain, you surprise me—don't you know we all run 5.6 Chevvies in our Lolas?...'—and that was a 5-litre class. Even in the late sixties motor racing could be fun....

Into 1970 de Cadanet concentrated on his Porsches and a Lola GT, and all his Dino chassis engines and spares subsequently found their way to Anthony Bamford's collection before moving on amongst Ferrari enthusiasts. The best of them all, '004', is owned today by Dudley Mason-Styrron in England, who has rebuilt and rebodied the car to decidedly *concours* condition.

The single-seater cars were achieving Ferrari's continuing success, and while the Formula 2 team was doing so well in Argentina two Tasman Dino 246 specials were on their way to New Zealand. This was once more a private operation organized by twenty-six-year-old Chris

The private 206S of 'Cinno'/Barbuscia finished 26th in the 1969 Targa Florio after an enjoyable Sunday drive around the sunsoaked Madonie. Here their car is leaving Collesano, setting out on the tricky descent to Campofelice and the Tyrrhenian Sea. Having safely negotiated the mountain section, many drivers relaxed at this point—and that was often an error which gave them a splendid vantage point down in a ditch, or up in a tree

Pietro Lo Piccolo was one of the Italian national Dino stalwarts in the late sixties and early seventies. Here in the 1970 Targa Florio he placed his cut-down Group 6-bodied 206S a very worthy 11th overall, sharing its driving with Calascibetta. Pierre Bardinon owns a very similar '212E-bodied' Dino, today powered by an 18-valve ex-Tasman Formula 246 engine. Its chassis number is 022, supplied originally to Ravetto in Italy

The cut-down Dino 206S raced in the 1969 Monza 1000 km by 'Matich'/'Meo' (Lado) showing its abbreviated standard bodyshell. It was apparently this car which was sleekly rebodied later in the season, in time for the Mugello 500 km. See page 234

Amon, who had come so close to the preceding Tasman Championship. He had begun his planning in August. Jim Clark had gone, the Championship should be an easier plum to pick. 'Since our car had been raced a lot and had been successful during 1968 it was going to be better developed. We had about 300 bhp from the V6, with a stronger power curve than we had [in the first series], and the handling was very good, but we didn't count on the large developments that other people had made with aerofoils; I think that if we had all come out without wings, nobody would have seen which way the Ferraris went....'

Brabham and Ferrari had tied in introducing strutted 'wings' on their Formula 1 cars at the Belgian Grand Prix and this method of adding down-load on the tyre contact patch without a commensurate increase in mass to be accelerated and braked caught hold like a forest fire. Within weeks enormous strutted wings were appearing on the Lotus Grand Prix cars, and in the Formula 2 race at Tulln–Langenlebarn in July Rindt's

Brabham had appeared with a tall rear wing and trim vanes on its nose. At Zandvoort the Dino 166s ran chassis-mounted wings balanced by triangular-planform tabs attached each side of the nose cone. These aerofoil aids mirrored Ferrari Formula 1 practice, in which hydraulically actuated variable incidence wings soon followed. On the high-speed Hockenheim circuit, where minimum drag was important for maximum straight-line speed, the Dino 166s discarded their wings in the season's final meeting. For the Tasman tour Amon had a second Dino 246 built up by the factory around another 166 Formula 2 chassis, and chose Derek Bell as his team-mate.

In the 1968 series Amon had lost money and he treated this 1969 tour very seriously. Ferrari again provided the cars free of charge in return for a percentage of their gross earnings. Amon recalled: 'I greatly appreciate what Ferrari did for me because it's a helluva long way from them, they air-freighted out any parts we needed and they supplied all the information we asked for. Financially they couldn't hope to make much out of it, and commercially there isn't much hope of doing anything with sales of production cars, so it was extremely good of them to supply us with the Tasman cars.' In response he realized his duty. 'I was supposed to be their number one driver, so it was a responsibility to do well every time I got in the car....' Each car made the trip accompanied by two 24-valve engines fitted with revised head seals and reputedly some 20 lb lighter than the 1968 286 bhp variants, while producing a genuine 300 bhp. The team included Roger Bailey (Amon's long-serving personal

1969 Tasman Champion—popular New Zealander Chris Amon made the most of his second Ferrari-borne Tasman tour and won the Championship in a great battle notably with Jochen Rindt's works Lotus 49. The car ran with an hydraulically adjusted chassis-mounted tail fin (the ram-cylinders being visible halfway up the support struts) trimmed-out by roughly extended triangular nose tabs

mechanic and one of the few British technicians ever to be employed by Ferrari) and New Zealanders Bruce Wilson, David Liddell (ex-Scuderia Veloce) and Peter Bell.

The seven-race Championship commenced at Pukekohe on 4 January with the New Zealand Grand Prix. Amon ran chassis '0008' and Bell '0010'. Chris's engine was changed in practice after losing power and he was regretting he had not driven the 166s more since he was too inexperienced to be confident in setting-up the car. Still he qualified on pole with a 58.2 second lap alongside Rindt's new works Lotus 49 T, with Bell on row three at 59.6 seconds. Amon led the first lap, was displaced by Rindt on the second and then took the lead when the Austrian spun off on spilled oil. He led to the finish to score his second consecutive New Zealand Grand Prix victory for Ferrari, while Bell drove comfortably home fourth, though lapped.

At Levin on 11 January, Bell won the fourteen-lap preliminary from Amon ahead of the Rindt and Graham Hill Lotuses—Derek's first race win in a Ferrari. For the sixty-three-lap main event Rindt was on pole at 45.2 seconds, Amon alongside with 45.6 and Bell third with 45.8. Rindt led Amon until lap 3, when he spun, spinning again later and this time overturning his car. The Ferrari number one then led all the way to win from Courage's Brabham-Cosworth DFW V8, averaging 142.74 km/h (88.7 mph), 5.7 km/h (3.6 mph) faster than in this race the previous year. Bell had inherited second place when Gardner spun his Mildren-Alfa Romeo V8 special, but spun himself on lap 14. He continued with an exhaust megaphone adrift, lost third place in a stop to have it removed and finally retired when a piston collapsed, badly damaging the engine.

The Lady Wigram Trophy at Christchurch saw the Lotuses win the eleven-lap preliminary from Amon with Bell fifth, and the Ferraris side by side on the second row of the main event grid. Amon had clocked 1:19.5 and Bell 1:20.1, compared to Rindt's pole of 1:18.8. Once again the Lotuses won, while Amon fought a close battle with Courage, beating him off and closing hard on Hill's heels to finish third. Bell was fifth. In the Championship scorings Amon led with 22 points to Rindt's 15, and Bell was fifth with his 5 points. Chris shared the Wigram lap record with Rindt at 1:18.8, 169.109 km/h (105.08 mph).

On 25 January the Teretonga Park race at Invercargill closed the New Zealand series, Amon and Bell finishing third and fourth behind Rindt and Courage in the ten-lap preliminary for places on the first and second rows of the main event grid. At the start of the sixty-two-lap race Rindt's car broke a half-shaft and Bell struck it, damaging his Ferrari's nose and stopping to have one front fin excised. Amon led until lap 3, when Courage tore ahead to win and the Ferrari fell back. The Dino 246s were still running Formula 2 springs, which could not cope with the enlarged engines' greater torque. They allowed the cars to squat under power, and as wing incidence was increased so the springs bottomed out. The cars were oversteering tail-waggers throughout the New Zealand tour until Bell knocked off his nose spoiler and found excessive understeer. Amon came home third at Teretonga, with Bell handling his problem very well for fourth.

The Sicilian pair Latteri and Capuano in their NART. Dino 206S during the 1967 Targa Florio, from which they retired

Pietro Lado is listed by the works as being the owner of Dino 206S '016'. Here in the Mugello race of 1969 he shared this very special cut-down Dino with a driver using the pseudonym 'Matich'. The car has a body apparently based on that of the Dino 'Sport 2000' model, which in turn spawned the flat-12-engined European Mountain Championship car used by Peter Schetty that season of 1969. The 'Matich'/Lado car is very much a Group 6 one-off prototype 'special'. If this was '016'—confirmation has not been forthcoming at the time of going to press—it was sold to an Austrian, then stolen and has not been seen since

On the trip to Australia for the Australian Grand Prix at Brisbane's Lakeside circuit, Amon still led the Championship, with 26 points to Courage's 22 and Rindt's 15. Bell was still fifth, with 7 points.

Uprated springs and hydraulically variable rear wings were fitted before the Lakeside race, and for the first time that year the Dino 246s adopted stable understeer. The cars were transported and entered in Australia under the banner of David McKay's Scuderia Veloce.

Amon took pole at 52.3 seconds from Courage on 52.5, while Bell was on the second row alongside Hill, with 53.0. Amon led the race from start to finish, averaging 100.18 mph, and after Courage collided with Hill, Bell took second place and made it a Ferrari Dino 1–2. Amon's fastest lap in 52.8 seconds, 164.59 km/h (102.272 mph), was a new circuit record.

At Sydney's Warwick Farm on 9 February Bell ran Amon's Australian Grand Prix winning engine in his '0010' chassis, while Amon used a fresh engine in '0008'. Bell dented his monocoque in a practice incident, and while Rindt took pole with a 1:23.8 lap, Amon was alongside him with 1:24.5 and Bell fifth on row three with 1:26.3. The race was run in torrential rain on a flooded track, and only Courage could now challenge Amon for the title. Rindt led the first-lap charge from Amon and Courage, and on the causeway between the circuit's two lakes Courage shot ahead, only to spin at Polo Corner when his engine misfired. Amon tried to dodge by, but the cars hooked wheels and crashed. With both cars out, Chris Amon and the Ferrari Dino 246 became 1969 Tasman Champions.

Derek Bell finished second behind Rindt, and in the final Championship round at Melbourne's Sandown Park on 19 February, Amon again qualified second alongside Rindt, with Bell sixth, and he held off Rindt to win by 7.3 seconds at a record average of 106.1 mph. Amon's record lap was 64.5 seconds, 173.16 km/h (107.6 mph), and Bell finished fifth with a very tired V6 engine, taking fourth place in the final Championship order.

After this fourth outright win of the tour Amon was approached by New Zealand driver Graeme Lawrence, who was interested in buying one of the cars. They met at Sydney's Kings Cross, and Chris considered it might be possible, but Lawrence would have to contact Ferrari. Both Dino 246s were returned to the works, while Lawrence interested Shell Oil in the deal, and eventually he had a letter from Maranello which he took to Waikato University for translation. The gist of it was 'yes'.

The price was high, but with Shell's help chassis '0008' was acquired along with a spare engine and gearbox, a dozen wheels, thirty-two ratios and many other parts. Ferrari rebuilt the car in its entirety before delivery, and by the time it was ready the 1969–70 summer season was under way in New Zealand and it had to be air-freighted out to save time. It cost Lawrence's little team $2164 for the freight charge alone.

At first he was puzzled by the car's tachometer, which ran to 12,000 rpm with no red line. He finally figured that he could use 11,000 rpm safely. It was just as well that Bruce Wilson was available to tell him the limit was 8000 rpm with short bursts permissible to 8500 rpm.

Lawrence's first race in '0008' was at Bay Park, and he was beaten by Graham McRae's 5-litre McLaren M10A. Next time there McRae spun, Lawrence led and spun, and finished second. The 1970 Tasman Championship was run essentially for Formula 5000 cars with 'old' 2.5-litre cars also admitted. Lawrence shone with the Ferrari Dino and won the Levin round, going on to clinch the car's second consecutive Tasman Championship at Sandown Park.

A rare photograph showing the multi-tubular base-frame of the Ferrari Dino 206S model, shorn not only of bodywork but also of its stressed-skinning aluminium and glass-fibre appliqué panels. This is actually the frame of Dudley Mason-Styrron's famous ex-works car '004'

Above 1970 Tasman Champion—Graeme Lawrence, the New Zealander, in his extremely successful ex-Amon Dino 246T '0008' in which he beat off a Championship challenge from 5-litre Formula 5000 cars. This machine is now in Pierre Bardinon's collection at Mas du Clos, Aubusson, France

Left Targa veterans 'Cinno'/Barbuscia again, this time in the 1970 event. This car was possibly the ex-Ferdinando Latteri chassis '018'

After this major success he took the car to the South East Asia series, winning at Singapore and again at Batu Tiga in Malaysia 'in the wettest race I have ever run it in'. They moved on to the Japanese Grand Prix at Fuji, giving the Japanese their first sight of a full-blooded single-seat Ferrari, but it bottomed badly on the banked circuit and Graeme did well to finish fourth.

He won the New Zealand Gold Star series with the car in the 1970–71 season, but in the 1971 Tasman Championship the Formula 5000 cars this time ruled supreme, and Lawrence had continual problems with his ageing but beautiful Ferrari. He had his only crash with the car at Levin when running second, but notched his first-ever finish in the Wigram race, which was dear to him, placing third.

After that Tasman series the car was sold to French Ferrari collector Pierre Bardinon for his private museum at Mas du Clos. It was apparently his fourteenth Ferrari and it carried by coincidence Lawrence's New Zealand race number, '14'. Lawrence kept the steering wheel and nose badge as mementos, and writing in the Auckland Car Club Bulletin of May 1976 he recalled some of the car's idiosyncracies: 'It had a five-speed gearbox which had to be split in half to change the ratios—a two-hour job at best.... The engine was a darling, but any work on it was a major undertaking. There were no head gaskets. Instead there was solid rubber tubing and copper "O" rings for sealing. The head nuts were under the valve springs, and to get at them you had to take the

237

Abarth employed an aerodynamicist during the early seventies named Guglieminetti. He turned his attention to the Dino sports-racing car and produced this Ferrari 312P-like body-shell on an allegedly ex-Lualdi chassis '028'. It was fitted with another of the ex-Tasman Formula 246 engines and is owned today in America by the Gelles brothers. This Pete Coltrin picture shows it first time out, unpainted, at Modena

springs out and secure the valves to stop them dropping through. Putting it all back together keeping the "O" rings in place was a cow of a job, and taught us a few things about patience and a few new words. One good point was that the tappet adjustment was similar to the Fiat 125 system, with steel pads of different thicknesses, making adjustment very easy. But setting the valve timing was a long and difficult task. . . .

'Fortunately the only engine trouble we ever had was two split cylinder liners, which resulted in collapsed pistons. Luckily I got it switched off both times before any major damage was caused, and all we had to do was press in new liners. One of the failures was in practice for the final Tasman round at Sandown, and we did an overnight engine swop. . . . Overall we only had two did-not-finishes in the car and with the Tasman and Gold Star titles we had a lot of success in it.

'But best of all was just getting into the car and driving it. It was a real Ferrari. . . .'

After Amon's victorious Tasman Championship early in 1969, the Formula 2 Dino 166s were expected to build on their Temporada title and go equally well in the new year's European Championship Formula 2 events, but it was not to be. That 1969 season generally was the worst Ferrari had experienced for many years, and the Dino 166s were withdrawn at mid-season as continuing labour troubles hampered their preparation, and most of Maranello's competition effort was being put into development and prototype production and testing of the new 312B flat-12 Formula 1 car, and the 512 series of Group 4 5-litre sports cars.

The season opened at Thruxton on 7 April, Easter Monday, where Ferrari fielded a full team of three Dinos, the 1968 chassis '0012' for Bell and what were claimed to be two new cars, numbered '0004' and '0014', for Brambilla and ex-Tecno driver Clay Regazzoni. All had bigger wings than in Argentina, with hydraulic adjustability using gearbox oil. The Dino 24-valve V6 engine, however, was still producing only 230 bhp—if that—and the 1969-series Cosworth FVA 4-cylinder was now giving 235 or more. Brambilla finished sixth and Regazzoni tenth, while Bell retired with a fuel pressure problem.

After this poor showing the same cars were taken to Hockenheim for the Deutschland Trophy on 13 April, Regazzoni driving '0012' and

The sensational 1969 24-valve stagger-head Dino 166 on test at Modena in May 1969 showing off its diagonally disposed injection trumpets, one to each inlet port, with one exhaust primary per exhaust port emerging both within the vee and low from the underside of each head. With the car are Piero Lardi, 'Tino' Brambilla, Gianni Marelli and—leaning over the engine—Giulio Borsari. Out in the paddock is photographer Pete Coltrin's Porsche

Brambilla '0004'. This was a shambles for Ferrari, as Regazzoni was towed onto the circuit in an attempt to start his car, which contravened the regulations, and he was disqualified despite energetic opposition from Ing. Marelli, the Formula 2 team manager-cum-engineer. Brambilla was in engine trouble, so started in the spare '0014' and had its engine promptly fail in the first heat.

Ferrari passed up Pau, but went to the Eifelrennen on the Nürburgring North Circuit (the Grand Prix course) on 27 April, with Dinos for Bell, Brambilla and Regazzoni. They were blown off in practice by the big-winged opposition from Matra, Lotus, Brabham and BMW, and in the circumstances Bell did well to finish fifth. Brambilla had eaten too well before the race and retired out on the circuit after vomiting in the tightly confined Dino cockpit, and Regazzoni retired when an exhaust stack fell apart after a stop to jury-rig the throttle linkage.

Gozzi and Marelli took the same team to Jarama for the Spanish round on 11 May and all three drivers complained of poor power and had camshaft problems in practice. Brambilla salvaged a lapped sixth place, Bell was eighth, and Regazzoni eleventh after a pit stop. This relative débâcle decided Ferrari not to go to Zolder in June, but they could not opt out of the Monza Lottery Grand Prix on 22 June, fielding cars again for Bell, Brambilla and Regazzoni.

In May a wild version of the 24-valve V6 engine had been tested at

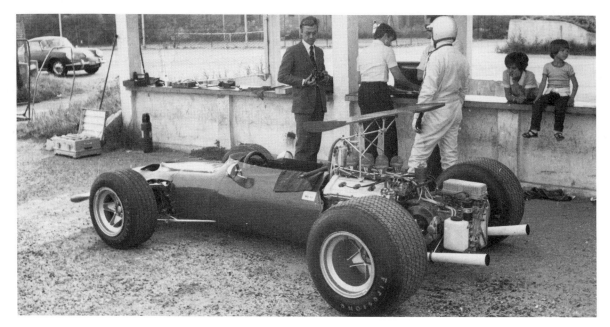

Modena, with individual injection trumpets staggered between the camshafts for each of the twelve inlet ports, and exhaust pipes both within the vee and down below the heads on either side to service each exhaust port. This complex fully cross-flow system showed sufficient promise to be taken to Monza for testing on the day before official Lottery Grand Prix practice commenced, but was quickly returned home, as Marelli explained, 'for further development....'

Brambilla was the best Dino qualifier, fourth fastest with 1:34.13, compared to Galli's Tecno pole of 1:33.5, while Bell was behind the local Monza man with 1:34.7 and Regazzoni eleventh with 1:35.83. Brambilla and Bell ran second and third from the start, Ernesto leading on lap 4, but after falling back he pulled into the pits with smoke pouring from one exhaust bank. He was told to rejoin, but could not last long, and retired for good after thirty of the forty-five laps. Regazzoni's engine had already let go after twenty-one laps and Bell was left to salvage fifth place after a Dino showing which had promised more than hitherto this season, but which displayed Ferrari fragility far too publicly on their home ground. Mr Ferrari decreed that the cars should be withdrawn from competition until they could be made competitive. In fact it was the end of Ferrari's involvement as a Formula 2 works team.

In 1970 one of the cars, the last chassis '0014', which indicates there were seven Dino 166 'entities' constructed, was loaned to Ernesto Brambilla for the European Formula 2 Championship, Tino having failed sadly the previous season as a Ferrari Formula 1 prospect. The 1.6-litre 24-valve V6 was still no match for the 16-valve 4-cylinder opposition from Cosworth nor from BMW, whose Formula 2 engines had begun to achieve some success, though on the faster circuits its top-end performance still matched them well.

Brambilla's 1970 season with the Dino 166 is quickly recorded: nine

Engineers Marelli and Forghieri at Modena with the winged 24-valve Dino 246T for 1969. Tasman racing success presaged a terrible season for the company; so bad it would have broken a less resilient concern, with less stature, and fewer friends willing to assist...

early-season races entered, five non-arrivals, retirement at Thruxton and Barcelona, fifth amongst the slipstreamers at Hockenheim and then third at Monza, where he was beaten by Giovanni Salvati's Tecno and Gerry Birrell's Brabham—neither of which could be considered top-line opposition. After this failure, Ferrari withdrew their engines, and Brambilla took to running a pair of Brabhams with home-brewed Cosworth engines for himself and his hard-charging brother Vittorio.

A new 2-litre Formula 2, still demanding production-based power units, came into effect in 1972, but for 1977 the regulations were relaxed and pure-bred racing engines were allowed into the fray. With this opportunity before them, Ferrari decided to re-enter the Formula for the first time since 1969, though only as engine suppliers—offering power units to 'approved' customers for installation in whatever chassis they should choose. Mr Ferrari announced the new project at his press conference in November 1976, saying that he had '...suggested to Mr Fusaro, the person who runs the factory, a change within our technical outlook and of our International standing. To these ends I suggested a Formula 2 engine in view of the demand that existed and I took it upon myself to have such an engine projected by our research department. This engine has now been built and tested....'

Tino Brambilla in one of his rare 1970 Formula 2 appearances with the works-loaned Dino 166 running engines prepared back home at Monza by his brother Vittorio—soon to become a Formula 1 driver of note if not notoriety. The venue is Thruxton, on Easter Monday; 'Tino' retired. The 24-valve engine is shown in close-up in the Hampshire circuit's paddock

Former long-serving Formula 1 team chief mechanic Giulio Borsari was put in charge of the project, and he was handed for development an all-alloy 65-degree Dino V6 with 24 valves and chain-driven twin overhead camshafts per bank! The bore and stroke dimensions were 86 mm × 57 mm, using the 1965 Dino 166P short-stroke with the big 86 mm bore of the unlamented Dino 166 1.6-litre Formula 2 engine. This achieved a displacement of 1986.61 cc. The unit ran a compression of 12.0:1, used dry-sump lubrication, 10 mm Champion spark plugs and, according to Ferrari's original press-release, titanium con-rods. They quoted 300 bhp at 10,500 rpm and a rev-limit of 11,000. Weight was 120 kg, 264.5 lb. Renault-Alpine had been having much success with their V6 Formula 2 engines, and this doubtless attracted Ferrari's attention.

Rather surprisingly this 206/F2 V6 unit was very long, longer than the contemporary Hart and BMW 4-cylinder Formula 2 engines, partly because its alternator and oil filter were mounted on the crankcase front and so had to be sandwiched against the monocoque of whatever non-Ferrari chassis were specified by the customer. The engine was also very tall, for although dry sump its pressure and scavenge pumps occupied much space, and the sump itself was deeper than modern practice thought proper. The engine was outdated before it had begun to race, and was to prove no true match for the V6 Renault-Gordini Ch1B unit which eventually found its way into Formula 1 as a turbocharged 1.5-litre.

Plans were laid initially for Ron Dennis's Project 4 team in Britain to run the V6s in his March chassis for Vittorio Brambilla—while Ernesto was to prepare the engines in his Monza workshop. That did not come about, and instead Signor Minardi's Scuderia Everest and Italian Chevron car importer Pino Trivellato's team acquired the prototype units for their British-built Ralt and Chevron chassis. They were driven by the young Italians Lamberto Leoni, Elio de Angelis and Gianfranco Brancatelli. Only towards the end of the season did the Dino V6 make any serious showing, due to early-season lubrication difficulties and handling problems caused by the unit's relatively high centre of gravity.

Things might possibly have improved more quickly had not Ferrari become very upset when Chevron developed their own dry sump system in order to fit the V6 lower in Trivellato's Chevron development chassis, so he went to BMW for engines for his fast-rising star Riccardo Patrese. Ferrari took five months to produce their own modifications, using the Chevron-Ferrari with the Bolton company's self-modified V6 variant for most of their testing.

Leoni was the most successful driver to use the 206/F2 engine during the 1977 season, taking eleventh place in the European Championship. He drove a Ralt-Ferrari Dino RT1 in seven of the first nine Championship meetings, failing to qualify three times, retiring twice and finishing seventh at the new Mugello Autodrome on 19 June and ninth at Nogaro on 10 July. He then opted out of the Minardi Ralt and tried Trivellato's Chevron-Ferrari Dino B40, running in three of the last four Championship rounds and finishing eighth at Enna on 24 July, then giving Ferrari their first Formula 2 victory since San Juan in 1968 at Misano–Adriatico on 7 August. By that time the V6's lubrication system had been extensively revised and the engine was a more viable proposition.

In his final outing of the season at Estoril in Portugal on 2 October, Leoni could finish no better than ninth.

Brancatelli ran his Minardi Ralt-Ferrari Dino in ten of the season's thirteen Championship F2 rounds, non-started once, failed to qualify at Estoril and retired from five events. His finishes yielded a worthwhile fourth at Rouen on 26 June, eighth at Mugello and a poor thirteenth at Vallelunga on May Day.

Elio de Angelis ran in a Minardi Ralt in the final three events, placing eighth at Misano, retiring at Estoril and finishing tenth in the final round at Britain's revived Donington Park circuit on 30 October.

This encouraging if minor flourish at the close of the season set some observers bubbling with optimism that the 65-degree Ferrari Dino V6 could match the modern 90-degree belt-driven cam Renault-Gordini V6 and perhaps produce a turbocharged variant for Formula 1.... The 1978 Formula 2 season soon dispelled much of that optimism.

Renault withdrew their raucous V6 2-litre F2 engines to concentrate upon turbocharged preparation for Formula 1 and the all-important Le Mans 24-Hours sports car classic (which they finally won), and the 4-cylinder power units from BMW and Brian Hart came into their own. As one Formula 2 enthusiast observed: 'Whether the 4-cylinder would have survived against another year of the Renault is open to debate, but one thing swiftly became apparent: the other V6, the Ferrari Dino variant, was a dead loss. This vintage design was just too big and too heavy even though it possessed plenty of horsepower at the top end of the rev range, torque is what it lacked and torque is what the 4-cylinders had....' And torque is what the modern vogue of artificial autodrome circuits with short straights and chicane corners is all about....

Pino Trivellato ran Chevron B42 chassis once again with the Dino V6 installed, as did Minardi. Elio de Angelis was equal-fourteenth in the European Championship final standings, with Giuseppe Gabbiani the other regular Chevron-Ferrari driver equal-nineteenth. De Angelis ran only five races with the 206/F2 engine before jacking it in and using a Hart 420R. His Ferrari-powered outings included two initial retirements at Thruxton and Hockenheim, tenth in the Eifelrennen on 30 April, fourteenth at Mugello on 28 May and tenth again at Vallelunga on 4 June. Gabbiani ran at eleven of the twelve qualifying meetings, failing to qualify three times, suffering three retirements and finishing fifth at Vallelunga, seventh at Thruxton, eleventh at Hockenheim, twelfth at Misano and fifteenth at Nogaro. Not the stuff of which the Ferrari legend is made.

The Argentine driver Miguel Angel Guerra drove one of the Chevron–Ferraris in the last five events, once failing to qualify (at Misano), once retiring (at Nogaro) and finishing seventh on his debut with the car at Donington Park on 25 June, eighth at Enna on 23 July and finally twelfth in the last Championship round at Hockenheim on 24 September.

By that time a factory development turbocharged V6 engine intended in part for Formula 1 — details of which are still classified at the time of writing—was bringing a muffled new exhaust note to the Ferrari test-beds at Maranello. Just how closely it is related to the Dinos of yore we must wait and see.

The Dino story in endurance racing, meanwhile, virtually came to its end in 1969, as the surviving 206S cars receded into obscurity. The production Dino 206GT and 246GT did not lend themselves to competition at any level against the increasingly specialized cars being run through the mid-seventies, in which period the once so attractive concept of the open cockpit sports-racing car virtually died. The same was true of the Dino 308s so far as most Europeans were concerned, until NART entered in the 1974 Le Mans 24-Hours, a competition variant based on the 308GT4, which they called the 308GTC. The car was run on behalf of owner Bill Schanbacher and was extensively modified with wider wheels and racing tyres, voluminous wheel-arch blisters, additional brake cooling ducts, an under-nose air dam and an end-fin-supported rear wing.

It was to be shared by Franco-Italian pair Jean-Louis Lafosse and Giancarlo Gagliardi and lapped the Sarthe in practice at 4 min 25.3 sec, some six seconds slower than the quickest 'cooking' 3-litre Porsche 911. Early in the race Lafosse made a long stop to cure overheating brakes and soon after rejoining abandoned out on the circuit with a broken clutch.

NART returned to Le Mans with the 308GTC in 1975, accompanied by their mouth-watering competition Boxer Berlinetta, which had run in 1974, and a special Michelotti-bodied Daytona. Unfortunately the Dino was too heavy and too slow and the organizers considered it had not qualified. Chinetti considered it had, and when the organizers became insulting he withdrew the entire NART entry, making it an expensive trip for the team, which had supported the 24-Hours race for so many years.

During the autumn of 1976 and into 1977 several spy photographs were published of competition-modified Ferrari 308GTB variants either emerging from the factory gates at Maranello or running on their Fiorano test circuit nearby. It would appear that this was a succeeding series of modifications all made to one hack test chassis in an attempt to perfect a competitive Silhouette Formula long-distance car to combat the all-conquering Porsches. According to the Italian magazine *Autosprint*—never the most reliable of sources—what they termed a 'Ferrari GTB4' was being developed with twin Garrett AiResearch turbochargers for

Giampiero Moretti and actor Paul Newman to share at Le Mans in 1977. Moretti had reportedly commissioned former Ferrari aerodynamicist and chassis engineer Giacomo Caliri of *Smartauto*, Milan, to produce the car. Little concrete result emerged, but photographs and news leaks continued, until late in 1978 a Group 5 'Silhouette' 308GTB was announced, developed by Carlo Facetti (building on his turbo Lancia Stratos experience) and Martino Finotto, who had been driving a single-turbo Porsche 935 for some time. Facetti and Finotto reserved a Le Mans entry for the car, which was said to have been engineered in part by the veteran Gioacchino Colombo—designer of the very first Ferrari V12s. With its twin turbos the 3-litre V8 was said to develop up to 710 bhp.

Yet still another chapter in the long Dino story was being written, in a rather unusual branch of motor sport. It had all begun in 1970 at the Turin Show, when the Bertone styling house displayed an incredibly low, wedge-profiled coupé into which they had shoe-horned a Lancia Fulvia engine-transaxle package amidships. The car was so unusual and striking in appearance that one of the Bertone men considered it 'looked like something from the stratosphere', and that remark christened the car 'Stratos'.

It was criticized at the time for being utterly impractical, and therein lay a cautionary note for all would-be motor show reporters. During that year in International rallying Alpine–Renault had been growing ever stronger against Ford and Fiat and Lancia, and Porsche were coming in as well. In 1971 Ford of Dagenham introduced a short-lived mid-engined GT70 coupé, but the threat was enough to send Lancia scurrying to the drawing board. Their beautiful little Fulvia 'Hi-Fi' coupés were becoming obsolescent as front-line rally cars, and Competitions Manager Cesare Fiorio and his President Piero Gobbato addressed themselves to the problem of finding a replacement.

They tried the Ferrari Dino 246 made by their parent company and its prestige satellite, but it was too long and heavy for high-speed use on loose-surfaced special stages. Fiorio polled his staff and drivers for features they considered important in a rally car, and established a set of basic parameters on which to work. Then thoughts turned to finding capacity to build a special car, and it was decided to approach the specialists—Bertone. Lancia had been interested in the original Stratos styling exercise since it had used their power unit, and while Nuccio Bertone and his chief designer Gandini tugged and pulled and moulded the original shape to offer a little more practicality, Lancia President Gobbato tackled the power unit problem. He had served formerly as the Fiat plant executive at Ferrari, and he negotiated the use of the 65-degree Dino 246 V6 engine and transmission for his rally team's new weapon.

Bertone's Grugliasco plant outside Turin completed the first Lancia Stratos HF prototype, complete with Ferrari-Fiat Dino power, in time for the 1971 Turin Show, at which it appeared sprayed brilliant matt-finish red. It was the first car for which Bertone had designed and built the entire structure, based on an all-new sheet steel frame with a centre coupé monocoque. In this original form it carried double wishbone independent suspension at front and rear, but when the Lancia team

Pininfarina somehow destroyed the beautiful lines of their 308GTB when they executed this 'racer' exercise for the 1977 Geneva Salon

Right The Targa Florio Stratos's engine bay, showing a lot of engine and not much chassis behind the car's rear cockpit bulkhead, although what there was of the chassis looked very robust. The car is on Dunlop racing tyres

Left A new shape in the mountains; Sandro Munari/Jean-Claude Adruet shared this early prototype Lancia Stratos sponsored by Marlboro cigarettes in the 1973 Targa Florio—the last to be given World Championship of Makes status—and their Dino V6-engined mount carried them home into a fine second place behind the winning Martini-Porsche

engineers and drivers came to grips with the car in the summer of 1972 a MacPherson strut rear end was quickly adopted.

Meanwhile, although Alpine-Renault had won the World Rally Championship in 1971, Lancia had fought back with its well-tried Fulvias in 1972 and had taken the title back to Italy. Right at the end of that season, shortly after an announcement of Marlboro cigarette brand sponsorship for the Lancia rally team, the prototype Stratos with a 12-valve Dino V6 amidships beneath a Formula 1-style induction air ram made its competition debut driven by Sandro Munari in the high-speed *Tour de Corse* rally in Corsica. Ford's short-lived GT70 ran in the same event, but both exciting mid-engined coupés failed to last the pace.

Development of the Stratos hung fire during 1973 after Sandro Munari and navigator Mario Manussi won the International Firestone Rally in Spain to give the newcomer its first victory. They took the lead early on when the Pinto/Bernacchini Fiat-Abarth Spyder had rolled and held it handsomely to the finish.

Munari and Jean-Claude Andruet took a works Stratos to the last World Championship-qualifying Targa Florio held that spring, and despite trouble with a broken seat mounting they hammered home into a fine second place behind a works Martini–Porsche.

In September Munari and Manucci Dino-powered their way to victory in the gruelling nine-day *Tour de France Automobile*, including many miles of special stages, hillclimbs and circuit work.

Through the winter of 1973–74 Bertone began production at Grugliasco using the iron-block Fiat-Ferrari V6 engine, the road-going Lancia Stratos coupé selling in Italy for slightly less than the contemporary Ferrari Dino models, and being less habitable though arguably even more fun to drive.

Still its reason for living was rally competition and in 1974 it was Munari/Manucci once again who gave the Stratos its first World Championship Rally victory at San Remo in October. Their points score

247

for that event brought Lancia within striking distance of the works Fiat team for the World title, and although the companies are related they fostered a healthy atmosphere of internecine competition. Next round was Canada's Rally of the Rideau Lakes, and Munari/Manucci won again in the Stratos to lead the Championship chase. The Press-on-Regardless Rally in the USA remained, but there police interference brought the competition shambling to a halt, and amid protest and counter-protest a Renault-Gordini R17 was given victory, after the Stratos entry had retired. Britain's RAC International Rally, with its miles of rough unsurfaced forestry stages, was considered utterly unsuited to the 'fast tarmac' Lancia, but Munari achieved a brilliant third place for the Stratos, navigated this time by Piero Sodano. The *Tour de Corse* is virtually the modern equivalent of the legendary Mille Miglia, a flat-out blind from beginning to end, and it was won by Jean-Claude Andruet's Stratos navigated by pretty Michele Petit, who rallied under the pseudonym 'Biche'. Munari ran a 24-valve Stratos carrying Tasman cylinder heads and developing some 275 bhp at 8800 rpm as compared to the normal big-valve big-port rally V6's *circa* 240 bhp at 7800. In Corsica this unit gave trouble and Munari was forced to retire, while the third car of Ballestriere stopped charging and dropped out when the battery ran flat.

The following season, 1975, was a Lancia Stratos year, as these astonishing wedge-shaped coupés with apparently more track than wheelbase and so much visible power went from strength to strength. Munari/Manucci won the Monte Carlo and Acropolis Rallies, and led the San Remo Rally until their car lost a wheel, whereupon Bjorn Waldegaard/Hans Thorszelius took victory in their sister car. Waldegaard led the Greek Acropolis Rally easily until his distributor blew apart. The privately entered 12-valve Stratos of Frenchmen Bernard Darniche/Alain Mahé won the *Tour de Corse*, and using a turbocharged model took the *Tour de France* as well.

Lancia won the World Rally Championship title, with the Dino-powered cars creating enormous interest and excitement wherever they ran. Fiorio considered their best performance came when they did not win—in the East African Safari Rally over a totally unsuitable course. Still Munari and local navigator Lofty Drews brought their car home second despite the rear body section coming adrift, while Waldegaard/Thorszelius finished second.

Not only was the Lancia Stratos body/chassis assembly immensely strong, but the Dino engine provided reliable power while enduring phenomenal torture. And Munari was an exceptional driver. He had won the Targa Florio with Arturo Merzario in 1972, stepping straight into a 3-litre flat-12 Ferrari 312PB prototype from a 2-litre rally Fulvia, and he was magic in a Stratos. Likewise the Swede, Waldegaard, as witness his drive in the RAC Rally, when he was disqualified for a technical infringement of the regulations after setting a string of fastest times on loose-surfaced forest stages.

Mike Parkes, ex-Ferrari engineer and driver, was Lancia's technical competition engineering manager at this time, and with Carlo Facetti's tuning company a Stratos was developed for circuit racing. It ran

248

Top Bernard Darniche achieved great stature as a gifted rally Champion in the Dino V6-powered Lancia Stratos cars provided for him by André Chardonnet, the French Lancia distributor. According to Bertone's records they built 502 production Stratos between 30 October, 1973, and 8 April, 1976. Several passed to

and fro for modification according to the first delivered production number '3', and the last '177'
Above An outstanding competition driver by any criteria—Sandro Munari, backbone of the works Lancia rally team in his Stratos in the 12e Rallye San Remo, with co-driver Mario Mannucci

Kugelfischer fuel injection on a 24-valve Dino V6 and developed around 335 bhp while weighing in at 900 kg. This project developed into a turbocharged Stratos-Dino V6 programme, with help from Michel May, and late in 1975 Parkes was talking of 385 bhp at 8000 rpm from this 12-valve 7.5 : 1 compression engine, with a target of 490 bhp for 1976!

In the new year Facetti shared this Marlboro-liveried Stratos turbo with Vittorio Brambilla for endurance racing, but first time out at Mugello the car ignited in practice and was badly damaged by fire. Some rally Stratos proved susceptible to fire, including the Chequered Flag team car run in Britain and that of the Italian privateer Pregliasco, who was severely burned in a rally crash with his car, which killed his co-driver, Alberto Garzoglio. Facetti/Brambilla ran the turbo very strongly amongst the Porsches in third place at Vallelunga, but at Osterreichring later in the season the turbo V6 set itself on fire for the last time, blazed furiously for an hour and all that remained was taken home in a sack.

That year's rally season was much more successful than the Lancia–Ferrari's circuit career. Stratos were first, second and third on the Monte Carlo Rally—the Alitalia-liveried works 24-valvers of Munari/Silvio Maiga and Waldegaard/Thorszelius finishing ahead of the blue Darniche/Mahé 12-valve model, entered by French distributor Andre Chardonnet. Munari/Maiga won the Portugal Rally and the Stratos' third consecutive *Tour de Corse* (from Darniche/Mahé), while it was Waldegaard/Thorszelius's turn at San Remo, and they beat off Munari/Maiga by four seconds, with other Stratos third and fourth crewed by Pinto/Bernacchini and Fassima/Mannini. Darniche and Mahé won the San Martino di Castrozza Championship rally and with second place in the Spanish Rally to add to their other fine placings, Bernard Darniche was declared European Champion Driver.

The toughness of the Lancia Stratos and its Dino V6 engine was proved again in the European Rallycross Championship, in which Austrian Franz Wurz misused and abused the beautiful car to tremendous effect, and carried off the title.

The Stratos carried Sandro Munari to another FIA Cup for Drivers' victory in 1977, when he also won the Italian Championship. Bernard Darniche repeated his European Championship success and Pregliasco (recovered from his Stratos fire) won the less important International Italian title, both in the Dino V6-powered coupés.

Munari and Maiga won the Monte Carlo Rally again, achieving Sandro's Stratos hat-trick in that event, and he added victories in the South African Total Rally (decided later in a Paris courtroom) and San Martino di Castrozza Rally. Darniche's European title was achieved with a pair of Chardonnet-entered Stratos, and included a staggering run of nine important victories, including four Internationals in four different countries in four weeks.

But the liberal Group 4 regulations extended for two years in 1975 expired at the close of the 1977 season, and from 1978 the Stratos had to run standard 12-valve heads (the 24-valve being outlawed), a standard-type clutch and a Dino production gearbox casing. These changes were relatively minor, since the 12-valve engines had already acquitted themselves extremely well, but the Stratos somehow was not the same car during that year and it certainly suffered a plague of gearbox problems. Tony Carello, son of the Carello lamp manufacturer, won the European Championship in a works Stratos, now Pirelli-liveried, and when Saab (responsible for Lancia distribution in Sweden) agreed to their driver Stig Blomqvist handling a Stratos in the Swedish Rally, he placed it fourth amidst all the snow and ice and set more fastest times on the special stages than any other entry. When Marku Alén was hungry for FIA Cup points late in the year he handled a works Stratos in the San Remo Rally and won, and soon afterwards ran a Group 5 24-valve 335 bhp car in the *Giro d'Italia* with veteran racing driver Giorgio Pianta and won again, adding more points towards his FIA Cup victory. On the RAC Rally Alén led for a long time before the Lancia's gearbox succumbed. Meanwhile the Fiat–Lancia management had taken a decision to phase out the Stratos 'special' in favour of the mass-production Fiat 131 *Mirafiore*. The Stratos had performed nobly its task of adding glamour to international rallying machinery, and now was the time for the bread-and-butter cars—though highly modified—to build on its prestige. Still the Lancia–Ferrari of the seventies was still far from dead, and as I write Bernard Darniche and Alain Mahé have added a fourth Monte Carlo Rally victory to the remarkable Stratos record.

Stig Blomqvist stood the Swedish rally establishment on its ear with his performance in the 1978 Swedish International event. The works Saab driver, used to front-wheel-drive saloons, showed himself equally at home in the powerful mid-engined coupé, as shown here on one ice-bound stage with Escort and Fiat in hot, if that is the right word, pursuit

The production cars

Enzo Ferrari made his first contact with the Fiat car company in the winter of 1918–19, when he presented himself at their Turin offices in search of a job. He tells us in his memoirs that the Colonel of his Army regiment had given him a letter of introduction to Fiat on his discharge. As Mr Ferrari tells the story: 'I was full of hope when I entered the mahogany-furnished, green velvet-curtained office of Ing. Diego Soria, a stalwart man with close-cropped, reddish hair turning grey. But it was an abortive interview. As Soria explained to me courteously, Fiat was not a sufficiently big concern to take on all the ex-servicemen who were applying for jobs....'

The story of how Ferrari became an Alfa Romeo man has already been told, and of how he was instrumental in stripping Fiat's racing department of its established engineers and attracting them to Portello. But by and large he tells us that his relations with Fiat always remained good, '...even though they were sporadic on account of the simple fact that Fiat took no direct interest in my world, the world of motor racing.' He explains that he had been a constant admirer of the company, personified in its early days by the dynamic figure of Senator Giovanni Agnelli, despite popular criticism of the concern '...as a predatory swallower of smaller firms'. If Ferrari had a hero in the motor industry, it would appear to be Senator Agnelli: '...a giant. He foresaw the development of the automobile and possessed a boundless faith in it. He founded a works that is the finest in Italy and one of the greatest in Europe, and created institutions for social assistance that only a government could equal....'

Agnelli's successor as President of Fiat, Professor Vittorio Valletta, was a diminutive man with enormous drive and an intellect to match. He was pointed out to Ferrari at the Milan Motor Show of 1922 as a fast-rising star in the Fiat firmament. He tells us they met rarely in later years, it would seem only once every ten years or so, but one time in August 1956, soon after Dino's death, stuck in his memory. It was in Professor Valletta's office at Mirafiore, where he was given '...a cordial—I might almost say an affectionate—welcome. He said to me: "Behind this desk there sits a friend, and that friend represents Fiat. You know you may always count on us and that you have my personal affection because you have always believed in the work we are both doing...."'

Thus Ferrari's regard for Fiat was fully reciprocated, and it outlived Valletta and imbued his successor, Gianni Agnelli.

Ferrari has always been by inclination a motor racing man, pure and simple, and his company's prestige production models were to him little more than a source of extra income which enabled him to go racing the way he wished—which was first class. 'The productive development of my business', he wrote, '. . . can be of interest to me only if it is run by others. . . .'

Before 1953 the road Ferrari was usually a hair-shirt machine bodied independently by any one of several outside *Carrozzeriere*, almost invariably to the individual order of a wealthy client with sporting instincts. Then in 1951 the courtship had begun between the Italian industry's two most celebrated autocrats—Mr Ferrari the car constructor of Modena, and Pininfarina, the stylist and body-builder of Turin. The *cognoscenti* said it would never come to anything, but in Pinin's words they combined 'like a pair of clasped hands'.

An agreement was reached which founded Ferrari's *Gran Turismo* series-production car division, and their prototype Pininfarina-bodied Ferrari 212 starred at the Brussels Salon of 1953. From that point forward the Ferrari road cars became numbered amongst the world's best and most sought after.

In the sixties Gianni Agnelli's deft touch was guiding Fiat's multiple industrial interests towards new heights. When Ferrari wanted a production tie-up to rubber-stamp his Dino racing engine for a new production-based Formula 2 starting in 1967, it was to Fiat that he turned. Like so many productive industry deals both parties had much to gain. Fiat could associate closely with the prestige and glamour of *La Ferrari*, while Ferrari could slip a four-cam race-bred engine around the rules of what was strictly a production-based category. So the Fiat Dino was evolved, using Rocchi's de-tuned version of the 65-degree four-cam V6 engine.

Two new models were planned, one a classically styled open sports car and the other a more conservative and practical coupé. Both made their debut at the Turin Show, in November 1966.

Fiat mounted the engine in a unitary chassis-body structure available either as a soberly attractive Spyder* by Pininfarina, or as a fastback 2-plus-2 coupé by Bertone. The largely light-alloy engine was fitted with three downdraught Weber carburetters and in touring tune and fully silenced it developed 160 bhp at 7200 rpm. Bore and stroke were familiar at 86 mm × 57 mm, providing a swept volume of 1986.61 cc.

This tamed racing engine drove via an hydraulically released diaphragm-spring clutch to a five-speed all-synchromesh gearbox, thence through a divided propeller-shaft to a rigid hypoid rear axle. The suspension was derived from Fiat's 125 model, with two long underslung rear semi-elliptic leafsprings (only a single leaf in fact on each side) pivoting direct on the chassis structure at the front and on orthodox

This Pininfarina styling exercise, which they released as a show car at the Paris Salon of October 1965, was a street version of the newly announced Dino 206 S, with in-line V6 engine/transaxle amidships, reverse-curve rear screen and an impossibly low roofline. The full-width Plexiglas nose treatment attracted much interest—the whole car looked stunning, if not wholly beautiful

This Turin Show 1966 Dino 206 GT show car by Pininfarina was the recognizable prototype of the 1968 production model, and set chins wagging as it was set against a backdrop of Fiat's Dino release. All the elements of the beautiful 206 GT final shell were there

Pert, saucy, undignified, silly, downright ugly—all were used to describe the rather capricious 206 GT show car confected by Pininfarina for the 1967 Frankfurt Show. This is thought to have been based on 206 S chassis '020', but its five figure chassis number does not fall into a 206 S series

---

*Although rendered 'spider' in Italian—normal usage prefers the Germanic form 'spyder'

shackles at the rear. Radius arms picked up on the chassis above these shackles, running forward to joints on top of the axle tube, thus forming in effect a Watt link location to control torque reaction. The leaf spring mountings provided lateral axle control. At the front more orthodox coil-and-wishbone suspension was used, with a hefty anti-roll bar. Servo-assisted disc brakes were carried at front and rear, and 14-inch diameter cast elektron wheels wore 185–14 Michelin XAS tyres as standard. At around 2500 lb it was a very heavy sports car, but a top speed of close on 130 mph and 0–60 mph acceleration around 8 seconds, 0–100 mph in 19.9 seconds, made it a very Ferrari-like Fiat.

The Spyder's Italian launch price was quoted as 3,485,000 Lire, and as will be gathered from the road tests reproduced later it represented good value for the Dino, which was the most complicated Fiat since the '520' of 1922, and though it was quite noisy, with the inevitable camshaft clamour of a race-bred engine, the Dino V6 was hailed as being 'turbine smooth' and its suspension location was sufficiently firm for independent testers to enthuse. 'If one did not know that the car had a live rear axle', they wrote, 'one would think it had a very good all-independent system.'

In 1968 the Fiat Dino series adopted easy maintenance transistorized ignition on its latest models, and the 1969 Fiat Dino 2400s saw the introduction of 2.4-litre engines as standard, using the cast-iron V6 cylinder block adopted by Fiat to ease production methods preparatory to introducing their new executive-class Fiat 130, which mounted single overhead-camshaft heads on this new block. Notwithstanding the enthusiasm for the original live-axle system of those early road testers, Fiat also adopted strut-type independent rear suspension on the 2400s.

The Dino Coupés were priced at 4,100,000 Lire and the Spyders at 3,930,000, in comparison to Ferrari's own new Dinos at 5,500,000 Lire, Isos at 6,300,000, Maseratis up to seven million and Lamborghinis much, much more. Fiat Dinos were never produced with right-hand steering.

Meanwhile, the new year of 1968 had seen Ferrari preparing to launch his own up-market version of the production Dino, aiming at a slice of the

The Fiat Dino two-door hard-top Spyder on display at the Turin Show soon after the type's public release in late 1966. The flowing body-style was executed by Pininfarina, the cast wheels were by Compagnolo—the Ferrari heritage was all there

2-litre market already enjoyed by Porsche. Various Dino styling exercises had already appeared on the International Salon circuit beginning with the pilot 206GT *Berlinetta Speciale* of 1965 and Mr Ferrari relied upon his old partner Pininfarina for the styling of his transverse mid-engined production model, the Dino 206GT Coupé. It was designed around the Rocchi-developed Fiat–Ferrari 65-degree V6 engine in a more advanced state of tune than Fiat had adopted, with a 9.2:1 compression ratio and three Weber 40DCN twin-choke carburetters. It was rated at 180 bhp at 8000 rpm from those 1987 cc, and was mounted in unit with a five-speed gearbox, transfer case and final-drive assembly ahead of the rear axle line 'east-west' across the chassis' longitudinal axis, nestled up against the rear cockpit bulkhead. This mounting provided space for a modest luggage space in the tail.

The chassis was a composite platform structure of welded elliptical section steel tube, carrying all-independent suspension by pressed-steel double wishbones with outboard coil-spring/damper units at front and rear. The Dino was the only contemporary Ferrari production car with rack-and-pinion steering, and it carried voluptuously curved Pininfarina-styled bodywork produced by Scaglietti. Most remarked feature of this beautiful if rather bulbous body was the concave rear screen set between long quarter buttresses leading the roofline down into the rear wings. A panel just behind the rear screen on the flat tail deck gave engine access—though in truth not much of it—and behind that was the baggage hatch. A spare wheel consumed most of the available space in the car's nose.

Dino was launched as a separate marque from Ferrari, though it could never be divorced from its parent. Further details of the car and its performance are published in a later section, but when Fiat effectively absorbed Ferrari's production car operation in 1969 the Dino link became closer than ever.

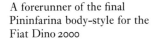

A forerunner of the final Pininfarina body-style for the Fiat Dino 2000

When Dino Ferrari died, his father was already 58 years old. Without an heir the future of his immense creation must have weighed heavily on

those broad shoulders. The attempted take-over by Ford, whose rebuff by Ferrari triggered the Le Mans Ford GT programme, has been well documented. Reputedly there were other approaches, possibilities explored, with his first love—Alfa Romeo—and with Lancia and Chrysler and—unthinkable?—with General Motors.

But Fiat was always the natural partner; the Italian motor industry giant whose products sold worldwide, where Ferrari prestige proved that Italy made fine motor cars.

It would appear that the late nineteen-sixties were hard years for Ferrari; 1968 in particular, perhaps 1969 more so. On 18 June that year Mr Ferrari—then 71—journeyed to Turin, the mountain going to Mahommed, and there on the eighth floor of the Fiat offices at Corso Marconi 10 he met alone with *Avvocato* Gianni Agnelli. In the latest limited edition of his memoirs Mr Ferrari says of this meeting: 'I was able to express the depth of my feelings as never before. Then Agnelli spoke. Younger than me by over twenty years. I felt in him the force of the modern man, of the politician and the diplomat of the business world, of the vital and all-perceiving observer. The questions he put to me were concise and precisely to the point, those of the man who wants only to know and to understand. At the end he called in his aides and concluded, "Well, Ferrari, couldn't we have done this a long time ago?" And then, turning to his own men, he said, "Gentlemen, perhaps we have lost time. Now we have to regain it. . . . " '

Fiat took 50 per cent of Ferrari SpA's stock and effectively absorbed its *Gran Turismo* production division. Mr Ferrari was President of the company, while Fiat appointed under him a general manager and managing director. The company was divided into two self-contained concerns, the *Riparto Corse* or racing division, which was 100 per cent Mr Ferrari's and the *Riparto Industriale*, which was the production GT division for which Fiat, through its two board members, became entirely responsible. Fiat's appointees to the board were thirty-six-year-old Ing. Giuseppe Dondo, and the veteran former general manager of the Fiat-owned Weber carburetter company, Francesco Bellicardi.

These curvacious lines belong to Maranello Concessionaires' demonstrator 246GT, shot here by Neill Bruce photographic contributor to *Automobile Quarterly*. While these cars cannot be described as fragile they do need taking care of particularly in a wet climate

Pininfarina was justifiably proud of the 246GTS—on this car he has added his badge to the panel just in front of the rear wheel. This 1972 car was photographed on the body builder's familiar 'turntable'

There seems little doubt that Agnelli's interest in Ferrari had, as Griffith Borgeson has put it, '... decided to reach out and keep a worthy tradition alive', and certainly Mr Ferrari had found a worthy heir and generous partner. For his accord with Fiat was made *in vitalizio*, a legal form under which the would-be purchaser pays the vendor a fixed annuity as long as he lives in return for the use of his property. If Mr Ferrari had died in 1970 Fiat would have won the company cheaply, as it is ... *La Ferrari* is extremely valuable ... and in the meantime the Dino production cars had played a vital part.

The Ferrari Dino 246GT with the enlarged 92.5 mm × 60 mm, 2419.20 cc V6 engine had been announced in the spring of 1969, replacing the 2-litre original production Dino GT of which, according to Maranello, only 150* were built. This enlarged power unit employed the simplified Fiat cast-iron V6 block, which departed from the Dino 206GT and former Ferrari practice of an alloy block casting with shrunk-in steel liners. The crankshaft ran in four main bearings, of course, and light-alloy cylinder heads still carried double overhead-camshafts on each bank, driven by chain from the crankshaft nose. The two valves per cylinder were inclined at an included angle of 45 degrees. The European version offered 195 bhp, giving the 2.4-litre Dino a top speed of around 146 mph. The US version, this being the first Dino to achieve quantity sales in America, ran Weber 40DCNF 19 twin-choke carburetters, and was rated at 175 bhp, producing a maximum of 140 mph.

The handling of the Dino 246 was more than a match for its deadly German rival, the Porsche 911S, but its performance could not compare, and in 1972 the first prototypes of a new V8-engined variant took to the road, while at the Geneva Salon that year the open Dino 246GTS made its public debut. This version matched the Pininfarina lines of the Coupé, except that the small quarter windows of the Coupé were replaced by three upright louvres. Scaglietti produced this version, with its fixed

*According to Maranello. The chassis books, however, suggest a figure nearer to 500.

'roll-over' structure behind the cockpit and detachable roof panel, in small quantity alongside the established Coupé until they were both discontinued—to the regret of most discerning enthusiasts—in 1973. At that time 2732 Dino 246GTs had been produced, plus a total of 1180 of the Dino 246GTSes.

Meanwhile the Fiat Dinos had been assembled in the company's Rivolta plant, drawing Spyder bodies from Pininfarina, the Coupés (more of them) from Bertone at Grugliasco outside Turin and engines direct from Maranello. When the original 2-litre models were discontinued in 1969, production totalled only 1163 Spyders but 3670 Coupés. The 2400 variants were produced in less quantity over a longer period, just 420 2400 Spyders and 2398 2400 Coupés emerging between 1969 and 1973. Fiat record the first and last chassis numbers for the Dino Spyder as '000026' to '0001583' and (strangely) for the Dino Coupé as '000026' to '0006068'. That dual-bodied '026' must be a real collector's item.

Towards the end of the Coupé production run Fiat had transferred the Dino line in its entirety to Maranello, and Bertone delivered their bodyshells there. From this liaison grew a respect amongst Ferrari personnel for the way Bertone went about things. Pininfarina were fully committed as the Fiat and Ferrari V6 Dino programme neared its end, and Bertone was asked to produce a replacement. Thus the Ferrari Dino 308GT4 2-plus-2 came into being with a sober Bertone body-style, and from its release at the Paris Salon in October 1973 Nuccio Bertone shared with Battista Pininfarina the honour of being coachbuilder to the house of Ferrari.

Their new Dino carried the first non-Pininfarina bodyshell to appear on a production Ferrari in almost twenty years. Its new, perhaps too-sober body form was criticized for lacking the sporting flair and panache of its predecessor and was certainly much more conservative though still

Production road cars on the race track even when they are Ferraris are not all that rare in Italy. The Dino 246GT was never used in the quantity that say the Porsche 911, its direct rival, was used on the race tracks of the world perhaps because its modification was thought to be too expensive and probably not worth it in the end. It's on the road that this car excels

Although there are reports over the years suggesting that the Ferrari workforce can be as militant as any other Italian engineering employees, there is no doubt that they do have pride in their work. This Dino V6 engine builder appears to have something to smile about while the machinist and his foreman discuss the day's production of V8 crankshafts

246GTS instrument panel and cockpit. The driver faces some eight dials two of which tell him, together with the steering wheel boss, that he is driving a Dino

French photographer Jean-Francois Marchet took this photograph of a 1976 308GT4 2+2 at the factory. There is little to tell you that it has Dino connections. Even the wheel hub caps feature the prancing horse. This car has been built to North American specification with side marker lights and extended bumpers, and in America they wanted a Ferrari, not a Dino

Six factory mechanics attend this early GT4 as it undergoes testing. It has been somewhere pretty fast if the spattering of dead flies on the side lights is anything to go by

undeniably attractive. It was a confined 2-plus-2, though with slightly more space and certainly a little more rear-seat headroom than the competitive Lamborghini Urraco and Maserati Merak. The new V8 engine formed a distant derivation of the Bellei Formula 1 158, having the cylinders arranged at the classic 90-degree angle, and bore and stroke dimensions of 81 mm × 91 mm to displace 2926 cc.

The crankcase was cast in light-alloy with shrunk-in liners and carried a five-main-bearing crankshaft. Double overhead camshafts on each cylinder bank were driven by internally toothed flexible belts (a sign of the times) operating inclined valves through thimble tappets. It used wet-sump lubrication with a gear-driven oil pump and an oil cooler in the system, and ignition was via two Marelli distributors. Cooling was handled by a nose-mounted radiator with expansion tank and automatic electric fans. The engine breathed through four twin-choke Weber 40DCNF carburetters, had a compression ratio of 8.8:1 and produced a nominal 255 bhp at 7700 rpm.

Back on the turntable at the Pininfarina works in Turin is this handsome 308GTS with its black roof panel removed. This photograph shows a striking resemblance to the early 246GTS although the Dino badge has been replaced by the Ferrari prancing horse on the front

Compare this photograph of the 308GTB interior with that on page 259 of the 246GTS. There is again a strong resemblance but this time the pedals do not have rubber covers, there are fewer dials and four times over you are told you are driving a Ferrari

This impressive unit was mounted transverse amidships, as the original 65-degree V6 had been in the earlier production Dinos, mated to a five-speed transmission. The chassis was based on a 100.8 in wheelbase (over eight inches more than the 246GT), weighed 2866 lb in European trim with a top speed quoted as 152 mph. The de-toxed US version offered 240 bhp at 6600 rpm, weighed 3235 lb and could not better 138 mph, but in most respects it could out-perform such rivals as the Lamborghini Urraco and the Maserati Merak.

Again at Geneva, in 1975, Ferrari responded to 'the Oil Crisis' by announcing an 'economy' version of their road-going Dino, this being the 2-litre 208GT4, which in most respects was identical to its 3-litre big sister other than having a 66.8 mm bore × 71 mm stroke 1991 cc V8 engine delivering some 170 bhp at 7700 rpm. Top speed for the European version was down to 137 mph, it ran a lower final drive and skinnier tyres than the 308 and was distinguishable externally by a silver instead of matt-black painted grille and louvres, and the lack of long-range lamps below the front bumper.

Still many would-be owners clamoured for a more sporting evocation of the Dino theme, and in 'September 1975 the Pininfarina-styled Scaglietti-built Ferrari—not Dino—308GTB made its bow, being launched internationally at the Paris Salon in October. This classically styled newcomer was a pure two-seater and it carried the first full glass-fibre body to be carried by a production Ferrari, beautifully formed by Scaglietti and virtually indistinguishable in finish and appearance from their metalwork shells.

The new V8 GTBs were derived technically from the Dino GT4 but it was emphasized that these cars were to be known as Ferraris, the marque 'Dino' being played down as a matter of Fiat management policy. There had been some would-be customer reaction suggesting that a Dino 'was not a proper Ferrari'—which reaction was as nonsensical as it was ignorant, as this story has sought to show. However, all the usual 'Dino' idents were replaced by prancing horses and 'Ferrari' logos on the new plastic-bodied cars, and it was only the prospect of having to re-certify the existing GT4s for sale in certain markets which saw them retain one 'Dino' logo on the bootlid after summer 1976, when they too were officially named 'Ferrari' and the Dino marque died. It could be argued that the 308GTB has no place in these pages, but its use of the established Dino V8 engine alone makes mention necessary to give proper perspective, whatever the marketing policy might be. My contention is that 'Dino' is not a name to be ashamed of....

This 'proper Ferrari' used the well-proven tubular chassis format and engine/transmission aggregate of the Dino GT4 2-plus-2 though returning to the 246GT's 92.1-inch wheelbase. The 255 bhp engine was modified from its 308GT4 application in having dry-sump lubrication instead of wet-sump, and average fuel consumption from its twin-tank capacity of 16.3 Imperial gallons was anticipated 'in average touring conditions' to be between 18 and 22mpg, reality reducing this to 15–16mpg. Speeds at 7000rpm running a 17/63 back axle ratio and 205/70 VR 14XWX Michelin rear tyres were quoted as 41 mph in first, 59 mph in second, 83 mph in third, 112 mph in fourth and 151.6 mph in top. Maximum speed was 156.6 mph at 7250 rpm.

At the Frankfurt Show in 1977 the Pininfarina-styled 308GTS Spyder was reintroduced at last, restoring to the Dino-based 'little Ferrari' all the masculine panache and muscle suggested by the original 206 and 246 models, though with a more elegant beauty and less overstatement.

By that time it had become obvious to the Ferrari *Riparto Industriale* that the Scaglietti glass-fibre bodies, though beautifully finished, offered little advantage over steel and were certainly more time-consuming to make. Since steel 308GTBs were in any case being produced for the American market, the line was rationalized in June 1977 and all-steel Ferrari 308GTBs took over. The last right-hand-drive 308GTB was chassis '21253' and the first steel-bodied right-hand-drive model chassis '21333'.

The US-specification cars meanwhile differed from their European counterparts in running twin Marelli distributors instead of a single, plus

Michelotto, an Italian tuning company, used this 308GTB in a number of Italian rallies during 1978. On the San Remo, Rafaele Pinto showed great promise. Power output was quoted as 288 bhp with a weight of 1020 kg

normal emission-control equipment and different body trim standards. Though the four Weber twin-choke 40DCNF carburetters and 8.8:1 compression ratio were common, the European-standard 308s developed (nominally) 255 bhp at 7700 rpm, while the American variants were strangled to 240 bhp at 6600.

As of November 1978 production figures stood at: '308GT4 2+2 2301*; 308GTB 1944 and 308GTS 767 ...'

At the time of writing, the 1979–80 *Produzione Ferrari* list includes the Italy-only 208GT4 and the 308GT4 as the last bearers of that rightly honoured name – 'Dino'.

*Again chassis books suggest a figure nearer 3500 units built. Once again Ferrari fox the world.

The road tests

All the tests published here are the copyright material of the journals concerned. All are published in full with their permission

1 Fiat Dino Spyder-Autosport, GB

Sheer enchantment

No engine has such glamour as a thoroughbred racing unit, built regardless of cost. It is therefore a privilege to be able to test a new high-performance car which literally has a "productionized" version of a genuine racing Ferrari engine, and the privilege is all the greater when the test is on the roads of Italy.

The V6 Ferrari engines trace their line from 1957, when Enzo Ferrari initiated the type and named it after his son, who had died in 1956. The first Dino engines had a 60 deg cylinder angle*, which was increased almost at once to 65 deg. Various sizes of Dino were made, both for racing and sports-racing cars, and one version of the engine was a Grand Prix unit of 120 deg cylinder angle, but in general the 65 deg conformation was retained, in sizes from 1.5 to 2.9 litres.

We first met the 2-litre engine of 86 mm × 57 mm, which has been adapted for the new Fiat, in the front-engined Modello 206 Dino. This was the car with which Scarfiotti won the European Mountain Championship in 1962*, and it developed 218 bhp at 9000 rpm on a compression ratio of 10.8 to 1. The Fiat derivative is a refined version of this very engine, embodying the latest thinking of the Ferrari technical department. Fully silenced and in touring tune, it develops 160 bhp at 7200 rpm on a compression ratio of 9 to 1, which permits it to run on any reasonable petrol.

Constructed largely of light alloys, the power unit has

*Some background history in these magazine articles does not bear close scrutiny. They are reproduced here for their text content, which is excellent.

detachable cylinder heads and wet sump lubrication. The extremely rigid crankshaft is on four main bearings and carries a vibration damper. It drives the four camshafts through a pair of reduction gears and one length of duplex roller chain, supported by an idler sprocket and a spring-loaded jockey sprocket. In accord with modern racing practice, the angle between the valves is only 46 deg, and they are opened through hardened-steel inverted piston tappets. The rigidity of the crank case is ensured by its great depth below the crankshaft centre line, and the main bearing caps are extremely rugged and positively located. Three twin-choke downdraught Weber carburetters supply the gas on which this delectable piece of machinery runs.

The diaphragm-spring clutch has hydraulic operation. It drives a five-speed, all synchromesh gearbox, which in turn supplies the power to the rear axle through a divided propeller shaft.

Of great technical interest, the rear suspension is based on two long, underslung semi-elliptic springs which have only a single tapered leaf each. They pivot directly to the chassis in front and move on orthodox shackles behind. Above these shackles, radius arms have their rear pivots, their front ones being above the axle, so with the front halves of the springs they form what is, in effect, a Watt's linkage. This looks after torque reaction very effectively and the springs themselves locate the axle laterally, though they are attached to it in such a way that they cannot be twisted. Both ahead of the axle and behind it are telescopic dampers, four of them altogether.

Fiat Dino Spyder, handsome from any angle

The front independent suspension is of orthodox layout, with a hefty anti-roll bar. Disc brakes of Girling derivation have cooling slots and a diameter of 10.6 ins in front and 10 ins behind, reinforced with an Italian Bonaldi servo. The 14 in light-alloy wheels are of the centre-locking type with 6½-in rims, the suspension having been designed in conjunction with Michelin high-speed cross-ply tyres.

Curiously enough, the appearance of the car out on the road is much more attractive than it was on the Fiat stand at the Turin Show. The wide doors give easy entry and the driving position is excellent. The compact little engine allows the bonnet to be short and it slopes well down, giving the driver an excellent view. When the hood is up, a full width transparent rear panel zips into place, giving the mirror a fine panorama to survey. To raise or lower the hood is easy, and it has a neat cover behind which it disappears, leaving an unobstructed space in addition to the normal boot.

I had the hood erect for the timed speed tests on an autostrada which had been suitably marked out. I must at once say that this is about the only hood I have ever met which is quiet and totally without a tremor at speeds over 120 mph. It would be unthinkable that any wind noise should be allowed to spoil one's enjoyment of the superb music of the engine!

The Dino engine is smooth beyond belief and there is no mechanical tap or clatter at any speed up to 8000 rpm, which was my normal changing-up point. Yet the song of that little beauty is too sweet for words. It is the pure hum of mechanism running perfectly, and no engine without a racing pedigree can make such a sound.

Though the Dino is flexible, it does its best work above 4000 rpm. The ratios of the five-speed gearbox are sufficiently close for the high-revving power unit to be exploited to the full. Bottom gear is ideal for hairpin bends and can approach 40 mph, while second and third cope with the faster bends and instant overtaking. Fourth is good for 120 mph and then in goes fifth, which is as silent as all the other gears. It gives a timed 127 mph at an indicated 7500 rpm or so, and this is a speed which the car is happy to maintain.

The unusual rear suspension is 100 per cent successful in absorbing the torque of a racing start. Wheelspin there is, of course, but no sign of patter or tramp can be detected. The car is also extremely steady at speed, and I drove for many miles with one hand while grasping a stopwatch in the other, my usual timing equipment not being available. Fiat claim a 16 secs quarter-mile, and I was able to equal this exactly by reaching a full 8000 rpm on the three lowest gears. To change up at 7500 rpm resulted in an appreciably longer time, and one can quite believe that the racing version was habitually used at 9000 rpm. The car is luxuriously equipped and extremely solid, weighing 22½ cwt, which is heavy indeed for a 2-litre.

After the timed tests, I put down the hood, making for the open country and the mountains. The car handles well on fast corners, even when the road is bumpy. On sharper corners, the rear-end can be made to break away, and when the surface is wet it is necessary to apply opposite lock fairly smartly, for which purpose the steering is suitably quick. On open bends, the Dino is tremendous fun, and the occasional rear-end breakaway adds to the pleasure of handling this high-spirited animal.

I was lucky enough to conduct my test in beautiful

SPECIFICATION AND PERFORMANCE DATA

Car tested: Fiat Dino Spider. Price not announced at time of test.

Engine: Six cylinders in 65 deg. Vee, 86 mm × 57 mm (1987 cc). Inclined valves operated through inverted piston tappets by four chain-driven overhead-cam-shafts. Compression ratio 9 to 1. 160 bhp at 7200 rpm. Three downdraught Weber twin-choke carburetters. Coil and distributor ignition.

Transmission: Single dry-plate clutch. Five-speed all-synchromesh gearbox with central remote control lever, ratios 0.87, 1.0, 1.35, 1.82 and 3.01 to 1. Divided open propeller shaft. Rigid hypoid rear axle with limited-slip differential, ratio 4.875 to 1.

Chassis: Combined steel body and chassis. Independent front suspension by wishbones, helical springs with telescopic dampers and torsional anti-roll bar. Recirculating ball steering gear. Rear axle on single-leaf semi-elliptic springs with radius arms pivoting at rear and two pairs of telescopic dampers. Disc brakes all round with vacuum servo. Electron wheels with three-eared knock-on hub caps and 6½ ins rims, fitted 185-14 Michelin XAS tyres.

Equipment: Twelve volts lighting and starting with alternator. Speedometer, rev counter, oil pressure, oil temperature and fuel gauges. Clock, heating, demisting and ventilation system. Windscreen wipers and washers. Flashing direction indicators. Radio (extra).

Dimensions: Wheelbase, 7 ft 4¼ ins; track (front), 4 ft 6¼ ins, (rear) 4 ft. 5¼ ins; overall length, 13 ft 6 ins; width, 5 ft 7¼ ins; turning circle, 34 ft 6 ins; weight, 1 ton 2¼ cwt.

Performance: Maximum speed, 127 mph; speeds in gears: fourth, 123 mph; third, 90 mph; second, 65 mph; first, 38 mph; standing quarter-mile, 16 secs; acceleration: 0-60 mph, 8.1 secs; 0-100 mph, 19.9 secs.

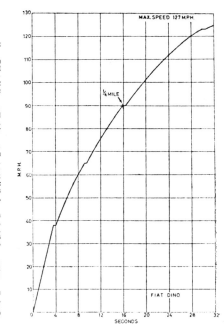

Coupé and Spyder, two exciting Fiats

sunshine, and it would have been a crime to put the hood up in the glorious mountain scenery. With the windows raised and the powerful heater going full blast, my companion and I were perfectly comfortable without a roof, even above the snow line. With a superb luxury car such as this, one feels that only the very best hotels are good enough, so lunch was taken at the Duc d'Aosta at Sestriere, where the pleasures of the table can be experienced while one watches skiers breaking their legs. I had no opportunity to try the four iodine vapour headlamps.

The farther I travelled in the Dino, the better I liked it, for it is a driver's car *par excellence*, yet it is also a luxury coupé of delightful appearance, thanks to Pininfarina. Slow work in towns makes the engine feel 'fluffy', but a short speed burst soon cleans the plugs again and there is never any fear of oiling up.

No car is perfect, especially a brand-new model. I found that the brake pedal was too light, and for fast driving on winding roads it would be better if the servo were less powerful. A fairly firm brake pedal is best, especially when heel-and-toe is being constantly employed in the mountains or on winding roads. The accelerator pedal, on the other hand, would be improved if it were less sticky at the initial opening. Also, with the car open on bad roads, there was a trace of scuttle shake. These are all things that are likely to be eliminated from the regular production models.

The Fiat Dino is a car which is sheer enchantment for the enthusiast to handle. Small enough to be driven fast on narrow roads, it is also sufficiently large to be very comfortable. We understand that a fixed-head coupé version is about to be unveiled at the Geneva Show, and certainly the demand for both models will be tremendous, even if the price proves to be fairly steep. Unlike any previous sports car of advanced racing design, the Dino will have the world-wide service organization of Fiat behind it, so it can be regarded as thoroughly practical transportation rather than a pampered status symbol.

2 FIAT DINO COUPÉ—Autocar, GB

10 days on the Continent with Fiat's mini Ferrari

Above all she was a lady. Like a lady she arrived late, breathless, full of apologies and looking like a billion *lire*.

For almost half the morning we had been cluttering the marble lobby of the Parco dei Principi in Rome with our assorted test gear, roped-up holdalls, ski boots and clip-boards. After the first hour the doorman began looking at us sideways and whispering with the desk clerk. We assured them that our car would be there

subito. Just as I was about to make the third phone call there was a yelp of tyres, a thrash of camshaft chains and the zoom-zoom of six Weber throats.

Blood red and gleaming in the winter sunshine our Dino arrived, complete with Italian driver *and mechanic*, who both leaped out and began explaining. Our rating with the hotel staff immediately rose 500 points.

We threw all the luggage in the back, scrambled in and roared away, swept up in all the excitement but not really in a hurry to go anywhere. I was there behind the

wheel, armstretch and snug, everything to hand. In no time at all we had threaded through the suburbs north and were blasting up the *Autostrada del Sole* at a steady 120 mph.

She sounded like an orchestra. At the top were the treble chords of her four cams, whining and whirring up to 5,000 and screaming like a circular saw on to 7,500 or 8,000. From 2,000 she would pull like a lion with a deep throaty growl which hovered and burbled, then picked up to rise in a crescendo with all the other sounds—gearbox, wind and exhaust—joining in with a double *forte*.

Not that she was noisy, she just liked to sing. At 130 mph it was possible to talk with raised voices; and every note she sounded was the purist music, harmonious and always true to key.

I had met her sister, the Dino Spider, last year when the car was announced and fallen in love at first sight. That car had an open two-seater body by Pininfarina, this one was the 2 + 2 by Bertone, not quite as slim, not quite as curvaceous, but every bit as chic. Under the bonnet they both have a vee-6, 2-litre ohc engine designed by Ferrari and developing 160 bhp net at 7200 rpm.

High speeds going North

It took us a while to work out the symbols for the row of switches across the centre console, but we found the out-of-town air horns and squeezed 100 miles into our first hour of *autostrada*. Strong winds were corkscrewing down some of the cuttings giving us a choppy ride and suddenly the high-speed kinks became bends. With a perfectly spaced five-speed gearbox it was possible to keep the engine right up in the meaty part of its range, whatever the conditions. We timed one flat-out kilometer at 131 mph and although we had all the gear with us to measure all the performance, we did have to be in Nice by the next afternoon and I for one did not want to stop driving. After all, I thought, this time we could take the performance on trust (it was certainly all there) and it would be wrong to insult the lady by putting a tape measure round her.

Our journey slowed as we crept round the arch of the Italian Riviera, bogged down by heavy traffic and distracted by a glorious red sunset across the bay towards Santa Margarita. The Hotel Regina Elena seemed pleased to see us, and when you arrive in a Dino the attendant even moves his own car out of the covered porch to give you pride of parking place. Obviously it raises the tone of the place and may tempt even a lone Maserati to stop.

Next morning we cruised to the frontier at Ventimiglia only to be delayed two hours, while the French customs returned from lunch, to clear our gear. It was then an exhilarating thrash along the *Grand Corniche* with stirring echoes off the rock face and the deep azure of the Med (yes, even in January) down to the left.

From Riviera to the Alps

By 10 a.m. the following day Martin Lewis had vacated the passenger seat to Neil Harrison (of *Flight*), who was joining me for a week's ski-ing in Switzerland. We rushed over the Col de Tende, through the old railway tunnel, and down to Cuneo, watching carefully for the patches of *verglas* which at this time of year really do exist just beyond those familiar skidding car signs. Often loose grit was more of a hazard than the ice itself, but we survived without bumping the rocks and feeling like a team in the old Mille Miglia.

At 7200 rpm the speedometer read the equivalent of 31, 62, 86, 104 and 130 mph in each of the five gears and there is spring loading towards the central, third and top plane with fifth round the corner forwards to the right. The lever is a stout vertical rod with a large ball-shaped knob which is ideally placed to be tossed between each position, and the throttle pedal has a great big pad that makes it natural to heel-and-toe as one changes down.

So I was up and down through the box the whole time, playing tunes on the engine as we burst up to each twist and hairpin, braking late and throwing the car round as it was built to be driven, fast and furious just for the fun of it all. Considering the rear suspension uses only a live axle on single leaf half-elliptics (plus radius arms), the way the power could be turned on in bottom out of tight bends was truly amazing. On gravel or even a dusty dry road the tail would twitch this way or that just to show it had some spirit of its own, but the wide Michelin XAS tyres never let this get out of hand. Slow turns called for a lot of steering effort, so it was often easier to steer with the throttle a bit.

Both of us were keen to get to the Alps, so we dispensed with lunch and kept going up the Aosta valley. Dry roads turned to packed snow when we emerged from the St. Bernard tunnel, but the Dino did not seem to mind. I took things steadily, going in the downhill non-priority direction and suddenly feeling the responsibility of manipulating £3,500 worth of somebody else's machinery.

At noon on a Saturday I watched the little twin-engined Beechcraft soar out of Nice, turn over the sea and head back to England. I began to feel the end of a beautiful friendship looming as I turned the Dino once again to Turin and headed for Savona and the tortuous *autostrada* to Fossano.

It was a lonely drive and I swear I treated her more gently than ever before. Together we had covered 1,300 miles and being possessive with my treasures no one else laid a hand on her leather steering wheel while she was in my charge. Apart from a touch of temperament when she would not start after a night in a blizzard, and the day she refused a climb in fresh snow, she had behaved perfectly. At only 17 mpg overall she had cost me a lot of money, but I could forgive her almost anything because of the way she ate up the *autostrada* and stormed the mountain passes.

Like a true lady, she was the best possible company.

3 DINO 246GT—Ferrari, GB

A thoroughbred in all respects

I have been asked to give my experiences as the owner of a Dino 206 GT for the interest of owners who have this model and especially for an American member who has just acquired one.

It seems that many people, including those who own the Dino 246 GT, do not realise that there are considerable differences between the two models. For example the 206 GT's chassis is some 2½ inches shorter and the dry weight is at least 3 cwt (150 Kg.) lighter—the lightness being achieved by the all alloy engine castings, light alloy body built around a steel-welded frame. The 206 also has knock-on wheel as standard.

Ferrari gives Vittorio Jano the credit for designing the original V6 engine and it should be understood that there have been three separate series but we are concerned with the third development of the engine which was designed by Ing. Rocchi. Fiat had a hand in the construction of the engine so that it could be used as a Formula 2 power-plant; it also powered the 206 SP series, the Fiat Dino GT cars and then the Ferrari built 206 GT.

1968 Ferrari Dino 206GT, bird's eye view

The 65° V-6 four-camshaft engine has a bore/stroke of 86 × 57 mm giving a cubic capacity of 1986cc and develops 180 bhp at 8000 rpm against the 2418cc and 195 bhp of the 246 GT. Compression ratio is 9.2:1 and there are three Weber 40 DCN carburettors. The engine is mounted in unit with a transmission, transfer case and differential assembly and located forward of the rear wheels centreline immediately behind the seats.

The coachwork is elegant and aesthetically right, the design being pure Pininfarina but executed by Scaglietti. There is a small boot and the spare wheel is carried under the front bonnet (hood).

With four forward speeds and reverse the gearbox is delightful being light and positive after the first two or three miles to warm up the engine and transmission unit and once 4000 rpm is reached the final surge up to the maximum is sheer delight with a musical high pitch exhaust to accompany one and one's passenger! In fact the mechanical noise, although near to the ear, is not particularly noticeable even on quite long trips. The gearbox makes most of the power available giving an excellent overall performance as 8000 rpm is there on all the intermediate gears. I must admit that general road conditions, even before the present speed restrictions, have never allowed me to see the maximum claimed

(146 mph) but 140 mph has been touched on a few occasions.

I purchased my car when it was twelve months old in 1970. It had had very little use and was in showroom condition and I have to admit it 'sold itself' to me for its 'just-right' appearance. After some four years of use the paintwork is still pristine even though the chrome on the bumpers (fenders) and wheel caps need some replating.

Comfort is a byword and even after runs of 300 or 400 miles one arrives as fresh or even fresher than after driving a Bentley Continental over the same type of 'going'. The compactness and utter stability no doubt being the reason for this, in fact driving on the Motorways is rather like sitting in a comfortable chair at home. The roadholding is literally the best I have ever experienced and even on black-ice conditions with awkward situations set-up by other road users I found a response to every twitch of the steering wheel. It has a 'flat-iron' feel with no semblance of either under or oversteer.

The major troubles over 20,000 miles have been :-

1. A replacement alternator. This is a bothersome job which entails the removal of the exhaust pipe and even the replacement of a drive belt takes some time and isn't a job to be 'lightly' undertaken on the road side!

2. The Dinoplac ignition unit gave trouble without warning, in fact it had always run noticeably hot and on dismantling it was discovered it had run some of the internal soldered joints. Although made serviceable by resoldering the fault again occurred; a later type unit has now been fitted with a cowl from the lower side of the body to deflect cool air around the unit.

A coil system is fitted so you can switch over if trouble does arise but I found that the plugs do need resetting to get a tick-over and the loss of revs (on the coil) amounts to some 600/800. The plugs leads need to be watched as a short to the engine through a faulty lead can damage the Dinoplac unit.

Hints

The tyre size on the 206 GT is 185 × 14 but after accidental damage to one rear tyre which made the replacement of two necessary I found that the 185 was no longer available so the size fitted to the 246 GT (205-70 VR × 14) was used and found satisfactory.

It should be emphasised that at no time the 'choke' control (between the driver/passenger seats) needs to be used. A double stab on the accelerator pedal being necessary even on the coldest day and when warm do not touch the pedal until the engine has fired-up.

The battery is somewhat inaccessible being under the spare wheel but do not be put off by this since a frequent 'top-up' is required.

The chassis frame of the 206 (the Daytona has the same 'fault') has had very little attention paid to it by the 'paint shop' when under construction or at least the paint doesn't remain for very long. Use a wire brush to remove any remaining paint and rust and then treat with an anti-rust preparation and also paint. A tedious but worthwhile chore.

The exhaust system has a 'soft spot' (don't most?) at the right-angle bend from the rear block where it joins the silencer burning through the pipe. The removal and replacement of the silencer is no easy task, two people are really required to hold the 'box' in position whilst the awkward suspension bolts are fitted. The small pipe can be replaced by welding in a new section.

The outside door levers operate through a long shaft in a long steel tube and there is no obvious means of lubrication. It, therefore, pays to 'ease' back the door trim and oil from time to time.

To complete the story, at the time of writing, the fuel consumption is around 22 imperial gallon pm on average but I am finding that with the various speed limits now in operation, viz. 50 mph on 'two-way' roads, 60 mph on 'dual-carriageway' roads and 70 mph on Motorways that an overall average of 26 mpg is readily obtainable. Oil consumption is nil between services when the oil should be changed.

To sum up Kay and I think the Dino 206 GT is beautiful, predictable and has the 'feel' of a thoroughbred that requires the careful selection of the right gear at the right time to get the most out of the slightly under 2-litre engine as there is little power until you reach the 2000 rpm mark!

It has the brakes and precise steering of its larger race-bred models of this famous breed.

P.S.: Do tell your friend NOT to lean on the body panels, remember it is alloy and is readily dented!!

---

4 DINO 246GT—Motor, GB

The first is beauty...

Perfection is an absolute quality found only in nature or that part of it we call genius: it is rarely applicable to the collection of compromises known as the motor car. Occasionally, however, we do test cars that closely approach perfection, missing it only in details of execution or performance. Into this rare category comes the 2.4-litre transverse mid-engined Ferrari Dino 246 GT.

It attains this elevated classification not only because its designers and stylists have got virtually all their sums right—it cannot be faulted in any area of importance— but because they have endowed it with two additional virtues. The first is beauty—at least in the eyes of everyone at *Motor* who beheld it. The second is the car's forgiving and controllable behaviour when its limit of adhesion is finally exceeded, an important advance for a mid-engined vehicle which has revived our wavering faith in the concept for roadgoing cars. But few drivers will ever manage to lose the Dino, for it has the tremendous grip characteristic of this configuration. Unlike some other mid-engined cars, however, it has adequate threequarter rear visibility (excellent everywhere else) and a boot which is as capacious as the airy cockpit. Such spaciousness follows from an overall length almost as great as that of the latest Ford Cortina, yet with an overall height of only 54in. Pininfarina's graceful styling contrives to make it look a tiny jewel of a car, as miniscule as is claimed in the sales literature.

Then there is the superb engine, the equally superb gearbox, the exceptionally comfortable ride, the excellent driving position and the well laid out controls. Perhaps the Dino's only significant fault is its fuel consumption, which is rather heavy for its performance; apart from this we had no more than one or two minor complaints about such matters as ventilation and the location of the instruments. Nor is the Dino an unattainable dream: you have to be rich to own one but you needn't be a millionaire, for it is the 'cheap' Ferrari, costing only £5486 in Britain—it has been available in

rhd form since October. At this price demand should greatly exceed supply and the car constitutes formidable opposition to the Porsche 911S.

Performance and economy

The original transverse-engined Ferrari Dino announced at the 1967 Turin Show was powered by a 2-litre light alloy 65° V6 with four chain-driven overhead camshafts built by Fiat to a Ferrari design for the Dinos of both companies. Two years later this engine was replaced by another of the same configuration but with a cast-iron block and capacity increased to 2.4 litres; it is now built—again for both Dinos—by Ferrari at Maranello. For the Ferrari Dino it develops 195 (net) bhp—15 bhp more than does the Fiat Dino version—at no less than 7600 rpm, and 155.5 lb. ft. of torque at 5500 rpm.

Ignoring the choke lever between the seats we found that it always started easily from cold, as is usual with Weber carburetters (of which there are three) by simply depressing the throttle pedal a few times to make the

Prettiest in red or yellow, 246GT

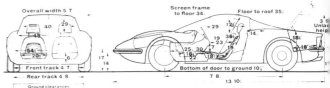

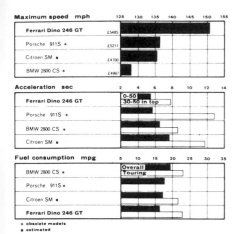

Maximum speed   mph

		125	130	135	140	145	150	155
Ferrari Dino 246 GT	£5485							
Porsche 911S ∗	£5211							
Citroen SM ■	£4700							
BMW 2800 CS ∗	£4997							

Acceleration   sec

	2	4	6	8	10	12	14
Ferrari Dino 246 GT	0-50 / 30-50 in top						
Porsche 911S ∗							
BMW 2800 CS ∗							
Citroen SM ■							

Fuel consumption   mpg

	5	10	15	20	25	30	35
BMW 2800 CS ∗		Overall / Touring					
Porsche 911S ∗							
Citroen SM ■							
Ferrari Dino 246 GT							

∗ obsolete models
■ estimated

Make: Ferrari. **Model:** Dino 246GT. **Makers:** Ferrari Automobili S.p.A. SEFAC, casella postale 589, 41100 Modena, Italy. **Concessionaires:** Maranello Concessionaires Ltd, Egham-by-pass, Surrey. **Price:** £4,200 plus £1,285.63 purchase tax equals £5,485.63. Electric window lifters £83.55 extra with tax

Performance tests carried out by *Motor's* staff at the Motor Industry Research Association proving ground, Lindley.

Test Data: World copyright reserved: no unauthorised reproduction in whole or in part.

Conditions

Weather: Warm and dry
Temperature: 64-68°F
Barometer: 29.85 in Hg
Surface: Dry concrete
Fuel: 101 octane (RM) 5-star rating

Maximum Speeds

		mph	kph
Max. speed		148	238
4th gear		110	177
3rd gear	at 7,800	81	130
2nd gear	rpm	59	95
1st gear		41	66

Acceleration Times

mph	sec.
0-30	2.6
0- 40	3.6
0- 50	5.5
0- 60	7.1
0- 70	9.2
0. 80	11.4
0- 90	14.5
0-100	17.6
0-110	22.0
0-120	28.5
Standing quarter mile	15.4
Standing kilometre	27.8

mph	Top sec.	4th sec.	3rd sec.
10- 30	—	—	5.2
20- 40	8.4	6.0	3.6
30- 50	7.8	5.0	3.3
40- 60	7.8	4.5	3.6
50- 70	7.2	5.3	3.6
60- 80	7.3	5.4	4.1
70- 90	8.2	5.5	—
80-100	8.9	6.2	—
90-110	9.5	7.2	—
100-120	11.8	—	—

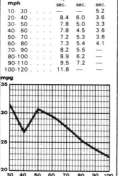

Fuel Consumption

Touring (consumption midway between 30 mph and maximum less 5% allowance for acceleration) . . . . 23.0 mpg
Overall . . . . 16.1 mpg
(= 17.5 litres/100km)
Total test distance . . . 1.294 miles

Brakes

Pedal pressure, deceleration and equivalent stopping distance from 30 mph

	lb.	g.	ft.
	25	0.34	88
	50	0.71	42

75	0.86	35
1-0	0.92	33
135	0.98	31
Handbrake	0.31	97

Fade Test

20 stops at ½g deceleration at 1 min. intervals from a speed midway between 40 mph and maximum speed (= 95.5 mph)

	lb.
Pedal force at beginning	35
Pedal force at 10th stop	35
Pedal force at 20th stop	35

Steering

	ft.
Turning circle between kerbs:	
Left	37
Right	36
Turns of steering wheel from lock to lock	3.1
Steering wheel deflection for 50ft. diameter circle	1.25 turns

Clutch

Free pedal movement = ½in.
Additional movement to disengage clutch completely = 2½in.
Maximum pedal load = 43lb.

Speedometer

Indicated	10	20	30	40	50	60	70
True	10	19	27½	37½	47½	57½	67½

Indicated	80	90	100
True	77	87	97

Distance recorder 3% fast

Weight

Kerb weight (unladen with fuel for approximately 50 miles) 23.3 cwt.
Front/rear distribution . . . 43/57
Weight laden as tested . . . 27.1 cwt.

Engine

Block material	Light alloy
Head material	Light alloy
Cylinders	6 in V
Cooling system	water
Bore and stroke	92.5mm (3.64in.)
	60mm (2.36in.)
Cubic capacity	2418 cc (148.1 cu.in)
Main bearings	4
Valves	Dohc
Compression ratio	9.0:1
Carburetters	Three Weber 40DCN F/7
Fuel pumps	Two Bendix electric
Oil Filter	Full flow
Max. power (net)	195 bhp at 7600 rpm
Max. torque (net)	165·5lb.ft. at 5500 rpm

Transmission

Clutch sdp diaphragm mechanically operated

Internal gearbox ratios

Top gear	0.857:1
4th gear	1.125:1
3rd gear	1.524:1
2nd gear	2.117:1
1st gear	3.075:1
Reverse	2.667:1
Synchromesh	All forward ratios
Final drive	4.44:1 spur transfer gears

Mph at 1,000 r.p.m. in:

Top gear	19.0
4th gear	14.1
3rd gear	10.4
2nd gear	7.5
1st gear	5.2

Chassis and body

Construction Steel tubular and sheet construction with aluminium body panels.

Brakes

Type . . Servo assisted ventilated discs operated by split hydraulic system with pressure relief valve in rear line.
Dimensions 10.6in. dia.. front and rear

Suspension and steering

Front	Independent by wishbones with coil springs and an anti-roll bar
Rear	Independent by wishbones with coil springs and an anti-roll bar
Shock absorbers:	
Front } Rear }	Telescopic, double-acting Konis
Steering type	Cam gears rack and pinion
Tyres	205/70 VR 14X Michelin.
Wheels	14in.
Rim size	6½ in.

Coachwork and equipment

Starting handle	No
Tool kit contents	Reflective triangle, jack, brace, pliers, Philips and ordinary screwdrivers, plug, carburetter and open-ended spanners.
Jack	Screw pillar
Jacking points	One each side
Battery 12 volt	negative earth 60 amp hrs capacity
Number of electrical fuses	12
Headlamps	Halogen type
Indicators	Self-cancelling flashers
Reversing lamps	Yes
Screen wipers	Electric, self-parking, variable speed
Screen washers	Electric
Sun visors	Two

Locks:

With ignition key	Do
Interior heater	Fresh
Upholstery:	
Floor covering	Carp
Alternative body styles	N
Major extras available	Electric wind lif

Maintenance

Fuel tank capacity	15.5 g
Sump	12 pints SAE 10W
Gearbox and final drive 8 pints S	EP
Steering gear	035 Shell Spirax EF
Coolant	30 (2 drain ta
Chassis lubrication	Every 3000 m to 4 po
Maximum service interval	3000 mi
Ignition timing	6° b
Contact breaker gap	0.012-0.01
Sparking plug gap	0.16-0.2ε
Sparking plug type	Champion N6
Tappet clearance (cold)	
	Inlet 0.00
	Exhaust 0.01
Valve timing:	
inlet opens	40° b
inlet closes	52° a
exhaust opens	53° b
exhaust closes	31° a
Rear wheel toe-in	
Rear wheel camber	0° 50' ± 1°
Front wheel toe-in	
Camber angle	0° +
Castor angle	
King pin inclination	9°
Tyre pressures:	
Front	27
Rear	31

1 glovebox catch. 2 footwell fan. 3 left-hand heater distribution control. 4 heater temperature. 5 right-ha heater distribution control. 6 screen fan. 7 ammeter. 8 lights stalk. 9 speedometer incorporating trip a total mileometers. 10 oil temperature gauge. 11 water temperature gauge. 12 trip zero. 13 oil press gauge. 14 fuel gauge. 15 rev counter. 16 clock. 17 cigarette lighter. 18 indicator stalk. 19 hazard warn switch. 20 horn button. 21 wash/wipe stalk. 22 ignition lock. 23 instrument lighting rheostat. 24 wipe rheostat.

accelerator pumps squirt neat petrol into the cylinders. Once started it idled easily and pulled without hesitation at once. To produce nearly 200 bhp from 2.4 litres the Ferrari engine has to be very highly tuned by production standards, yet it pulls extraordinarily well from low speeds. For demonstration purposes it can be made to do so from 1000 rpm in fifth by carefully feeding in the throttle, though if the pedal is floored at around 1500 rpm the engine will hesitate, maybe die. But from 1800 rpm onwards the engine pulls with real vigour, gathering particular strength at just under 3500 rpm and continuing to deliver a surge of power right up to the 7800 rpm limit—surely the highest of any car currently in series production. And throughout this rev range the engine is utterly smooth and unfussed, so much so that care must be exercised to prevent over-revving. All this to the accompaniment of a mellow baying from the four exhaust pipes combined with a whine from the camshaft chains and a faint excited gnashing from the valvegear. Everyone liked this exciting noise, but a few of our test staff thought it just a little too loud and found it tiring on long journeys, even though it reduces to a contented burble when cruising at 100–110 mph, at which speed there is very little wind noise provided the doors are properly shut—they need a good slam.

Despite the handicap of considerable weight for a sports car—23.3 cwt. unladen—and by absolute standards relatively modest capacity and power, the Dino is a very quick car. It gets to 60 mph from rest in 7.1 sec., to 100 mph in 17.6 sec. and will comfortably pull maximum revs in top gear giving a maximum speed of 148 mph. The engine is so torquey that this gear often feels lower than it actually is, inducing an initial underestimation of speed. The Dino's excellent performance in the upper part of the speed range follows largely from its excellent aerodynamics as demonstrated by its flat fuel consumption curve which remains comfortably above 20 mpg at 100 mph. The shape also has other important aerodynamic qualities, for the car feels impressively secure and stable at very high speeds and proved to be virtually impervious to side winds.

Unfortunately the low drag factor does not seem to have counterbalanced the disadvantage of considerable weight—and perhaps of rich-running Webers—for the fuel consumption is rather poor and once or twice plunged below 15 mpg during particularly fast runs, though the final overall figure was 16.1 mpg of 5-star fuel. But owners will probably find, as we did, that after the novelty of the Dino's high performance has worn off, it is possible to get along almost as quickly as before with rather less use of the revs and gears; the fuel consumption then improves to the 17–19 mpg level, giving a range from the 15.5 gallon tank of around 260 miles.

Transmission

Following the Ferrari tradition there is a gate at the base of the Dino's floor-mounted gearlever to define the positions of the five speeds which are arranged Porsche-fashion: first and reverse are to the left of the upper four gears laid out in the usual H. No spring loading is used except for reverse, obtained with a downward push. At a casual glance the presence of the gate might seem to introduce navigational inhibitions, and indeed our testers did need a little practice to get used to the change from first to second. But after a time the presence of the gate is forgotten and the first-second movement becomes as easy and natural—though perhaps a little slower—as, right from the start, do the movements between all the other gears. The gearbox then reveals itself as being superb with unobtrusive but effective synchromesh which allows lightning changes to be sliced through. The lightness and feeling of precision is remarkable in view of the distant location of the transmission behind and beneath the engine to which it is coupled by three spin gears.

On our test car, the quicker the changes the more easily they went through, as the rather heavy clutch did not always disengage completely when depressed slowly. Like the throttle, however, it was very progressive in action so smooth changes are easy once the driver has allowed for the fact that although the engine revs rise quickly enough when the throttle is blipped, they tend to die slowly, perhaps because of a heavy flywheel.

Well-spaced maxima of 41 mph, 59 mph, 81 mph and 110 mph are possible in the four indirect gears. The engine's excellent torque at low revs made it rarely necessary to use bottom gear for anything other than starting off. Only in fourth was some transmission whine audible.

Handling and brakes

When it comes to getting round corners the Ferrari Dino has all the advantages—and makes use of them. One such is racing-style double-wishbone suspension at both ends. Another is the location of the engine just behind the driver which puts more weight on the rear wheels for good traction in slippery conditions and less on the front wheels to allow the use of fat tyres with direct manual steering. Both these last two ends have in particular been admirably achieved on the Ferrari: it has monster 205 XVR Michelin radials guided at the front by superbly precise, direct steering which gives good feel with little kickback and is one of the joys of the car.

The inevitable result of all this is an ability to go round corners, which makes ordinary cars seem wholly inadequate. Only when trying a normal saloon after the Dino does a driver realize just how effortlessly and quickly he has been going. Terms like understeer and oversteer are generally pretty academic: the car just steers. Further acquaintance reveals that taking a corner under power tends to create not so much gentle oversteer as a useful tightening of the line.

So much for impressions on the road—we needed the relative security of a closed test track to learn more about the Dino's phenomenally high limits. Unlike many mid-engined cars it does not always understeer with power, and oversteer without it. On fast bends the gentle oversteer tendency was confirmed; on slow bends we were able to make the front end plough outwards with power. Equally, a vicious bootful of throttle in second could break the tail away though in an easily catchable way.

But there is a much more important question to be answered. Even the Dino must run out of grip eventually—what happens when it does? For the practised anticipation and lightning responses of the professional racing driver, mid-engined cars may be fine, but with their centrally located masses they do tend to spin rapidly when all is finally lost, an unsatisfactory characteristic for the more ordinary mortals likely to drive Dinos on the road, one that has made us hesitate to endorse the concept for practical roadgoing sports cars.

Such hesitations are swept aside by the forgiving nature of the Dino. To begin with, helped by a limited-slip differential, it retains a large measure of its traction and cornering power in the wet, though it does have one vice: a tendency to plane outwards at the front on puddles and rivulets perhaps a little more than would a front-engined car. But if you lift your foot sharply off the accelerator in a corner the car responds with nothing more than a slight twitch that calls for little steering correction. Even if this is done when cornering nearly on the limit, the tail breaks away in a gentle and controllable way, a response to which we had reason to feel gratitude as fuel surge tended to make our test car cut out when entering a corner under the combination of deceleration and turning. It is this safe behaviour in extreme conditions that makes the Dino so outstanding.

To match this handling are brakes of equal calibre. The four huge outboard ventilated discs are operated with servo assistance through a front/rear split hydraulic system. Surprisingly, in view of the 43/57 front/rear weight distribution, there is a pressure relief valve in the rear line, showing how much weight can be transferred to the front wheels during heavy braking. In mid-engined cars this may not be enough to prevent front wheel lock up under heavy braking—especially in the wet—but of this vice the Dino was completely free. Though the pressures required were rather higher than is usual nowadays—the maximum 1g deceleration being achieved with a force of 135 lb.—the brakes felt immensely progressive and reassuring in their action. As might be expected from their racing heritage, they did not fade either on the road or during our test, nor were they affected by a thorough soaking in the watersplash. But a really strenuous pull on the handbrake gave a deceleration of no more than 0.31 g.

Comfort and controls

Few saloon cars other than Citroens—let alone sports cars—ride better than the Dino. Firm, rather than harsh at low speeds, the suspension simply smothers the biggest bumps and soaks up undulations without pitch, float or bottoming. The comfort provided contributes greatly to the feeling of security so characteristic of the car. Unfortunately, the ride is not matched by the seats, which could only suit midgets and have rolls across the tops of their backrests which dug into the shoulder blades of even our shortest drivers. These backrests incorporate adjustable headrests but do not recline—there wouldn't be room for them to do so anyway. In partial compensation for these defects the range of fore-and-aft adjustment is enough to satisfy the legroom requirements of human beings at the other extreme of size as represented by our resident 6 ft. 5 in. giant. And the seats do provide good lateral support, helped by the rest for the left foot which constitutes an excellent bracing spot.

Sports cars tend to have cramped cockpits; Italian cars to have the steering wheel too far away and the pedals too close. Though the Dino is both sporting and Italian, its small steering wheel (which has a leather-covered rim) and its pedals are so well located that everyone was able to achieve a comfortable driving position, regardless of size. Gearlever and handbrake, too, could be reached without effort by all our test staff when wearing seatbelts. Fingertip control over all the services completes the feeling of unity with the machine that the Dino imparts. On the left there is an indicator stalk with behind it a longer stalk controlling all the modes of side and headlamp operation, while in conformity with another of our preferences the horn is operated by a button at the centre of the wheel. A right-hand stalk controls the washers and the wipers which have no intermittent action but can be varied in speed by a rheostat mounted on the facia near the stalk. The wiper arms have an overlapping "clap hands" action which allows them to clear the screen close to both edges, though the wiped area should extend further up the screen for tall drivers. These arms also accelerate as they move from their central positions and even at their lowest speeds make a loud and wearing thump as they contact the frame at the sides of the windscreen. At medium to fast speeds they flick over the frame completely and can be seen through the quarterlights.

The deep, wide and steeply raked screen gives excellent forward visibility over the low bonnet. This falls away towards the ground between the wheelarches out of the driver's sight so that there is more car in front than is at first realized, calling for extra care during parking manoeuvres. In contrast the blunt Kamm-type tail is easily seen from the cockpit. It is seen through the rear window which is one of the Dino's most striking features; nearly vertical and no more than 8 in. high, it curls backwards through 90° at each end to meet the rear quarterlights set into the flanks of the car. In this way it provides a fair measure of the important three-quarter rear vision so lacking in some mid-engined designs while helping to isolate the occupants from engine noise, and in its protected location at the forward end of the rear deck, remains virtually untouched by dirt or rain. At night the halogen headlamps were good both when dipped and when on main beam so long as their plastic covers were kept clean.

There is virtually no wind noise below 100 mph—it builds up gradually thereafter. Road noise is moderate despite the tautness of the steering and suspension which suggests minimum compliance. Radial tyres notwithstanding, it is more high-frequency roar than low-frequency thump.

Hot and cold air is admitted into the interior through four swivelling "egg-slicer" vents, two in the footwells and two on the facia, close to the screen but a long way from the occupants. These are controlled by independent distribution levers for each side of the car which flank a central temperature control lever. This is progressive in action but without the two booster fans (one for the footwells and one for the screen) the throughput is small. With the heater shut off, the screen booster provided just enough cool air in town for the warmish days of our test, and the volume can be increased without introducing much extra noise at speed by winding the side windows down a little.

Fittings and furniture

Betraying a desire to match the graceful exterior and the curved plan-form of the windscreen—which is delineated by the deep shelf of the facia—the stylists have given the cowled instrument cluster an elliptical shape. Like the facia it is covered with a black velvety material. Neither the shape nor the material were popular with our staff despite their functional attributes in minimising obstruction to the base of the screen and in eliminating unwanted reflections. Less popular still were the locations of the speedometer and rev counter towards the ends of the major axis of their elliptical enclosure, just where they are dangerously obscured by the wheel rim to all but very short drivers—dangerous because the engine is so smooth and unfussed that even its very high 7800 rpm limit could easily be exceeded.

On the other hand at no time did it show the slightest signs of rising temperature or falling oil pressure, yet the relevant gauges have been given pride of place, right in front of the driver.

Also covered in the velvety material, and retained by a cheap-looking catch but no lock, is the lid of the moderate-sized glove compartment. Together with the boxes built in to the doors this provides most of the oddments space, though there is room for small packets, newspapers and the like behind the seats. A vanity mirror in the passenger's sun visor, an ashtray and a cigarette lighter complete the cockpit fittings. The front compartment is filled by the spare wheel and toolkit, but the conventional rear boot is large for a sports car, taking 5.6 cu ft of our Revelation suitcases.

The Dino is very well equipped electrically. It has, for example, reversing lights, red warning lights in the door edges and lights for all three compartments. In the front compartment there are boxes of fuses each of which is clearly marked in three languages with the services it protects, while in the boot at the rear is the transistorized ignition system with its spare coil. Our test car was additionally fitted with the optional (£83.55 extra) electric window lifters.

Servicing and accessibility

When an engine is located in the centre of a car it is not easy to get at. The Ferrari's unit is not too bad in this respect except for the long dipstick which requires careful threading into its tube in the forward bank of cylinders under the hinged engine cover. Even minor repairs, however—like replacing blown exhaust gaskets—could prove expensive as the bulkhead in front of the engine cannot be removed so the complete engine/transmission unit may have to be removed for attention of this sort, though it is accessible through a removable panel at the rear of the boot and through detachable panels in the wheelarches.

Servicing, which includes some chassis greasing, is required every 3000 miles and there are 7 Ferrari dealers and distributors in the UK. There is a good toolkit which includes a reflective triangle, and an informative and well-illustrated three-language handbook. We found the pillar jack rather stiff in its action.

5 DINO 246GT—Road & Track, USA

Ferrari's version of the 6-cylinder business coupé

Ferrari's junior car, the Dino, has taken so long to reach the U.S. market that it might look old-fashioned by now but for its handsome Pininfarina body. Named for Enzo Ferrari's deceased son Dino and derived from earlier racing cars carrying the same name, the first road-going Dino prototype appeared at the 1966 Turin show as the Dino 206 Gt. It was closely related to an earlier 2-liter racing car with its 1987-cc 65° V6 engine residing amidship in a longitudinal position and driving a typical racing transaxle behind it. The engine with its light alloy block and heads, four overhead camshafts and three Weber carburetors also made its debut that year in another Dino: Fiat's production car of that name, an entirely different car with front engine and rear drive. Fiat produced these engines and they were tuned for 160 bhp vs the Ferrari's 180, but they shared their dimensions and basic design with the Ferrari unit.

The Dino shown at 1967's Turin show was better detailed and, more importantly, rearranged to provide more space for passengers and luggage. The engine had been turned 90° to become a "sidewinder" and now drove down from the clutch through a transfer drive to a gearbox located in its own casing under the sump. This car gave every indication of being a definitive production version; and indeed it was just that, as production began not long after that. When it did begin, Fiat produced the main engine parts but Ferrari did the assembling. And it should be noted that the production car, like the prototypes, did not carry the *name* Ferrari. Dino is a separate make, as far as Ferrari is concerned.

At the 1969 Geneva show Ferrari showed an updated Dino with its engine displacement increased to 2418 cc by bore and stroke increases, power raised from 180 bhp @ 8000 rpm to 195 @ 7600, and name changed to 246GT to correspond with the new displacement. Since then there have been detail modifications to the gearbox, interior and exterior but the 246GT remains essentially the car it was at the 1967 Turin show: Ferrari's idea of a fullbore sporting 2-seater on a scale smaller than that of the 12-cylinder Ferraris, in price as well as specification.

It's not an easy job to conform such an exciting car to the American safety and smog regulations, and these are the reasons we had to wait so long for the Dino. This is the first published test of the U.S. version. Particularly difficult was modifying the high-output engine for 1972's federal emission limits: 80 net bhp per liter (that's 1.34 bhp/cu in. for English-system thinkers) is a lot for a road car in anybody's terms. Ferrari engineers tried fuel injection but were not satisfied, and they finally settled on the same solution applied to their 12s—an air injection pump to supply fresh air to the exhaust ports, all the plumbing that goes with it, and an electromagnetic clutch that disengages the pump above 3500 rpm or so to minimize peak power loss. The safety and smog alterations to the car add to its weight and cost and detract from its performance: Coco Chinetti of Chinetti motors, who loaned us our test car, estimates the price increase to be about $2000, and our test car weighed some 50 lb more than the European version. Peak power is cut about 10% by the smog equipment; throttle response and fuel economy undoubtedly are degraded too.

Mid-engine cars are reminiscent of early sports cars in that they usually make rather blatant sacrifices in habitability to achieve a very high level of roadholding. That sports cars offering great comfort, quiet operation,

*US-specification 246GT
shells at Scaglietti*

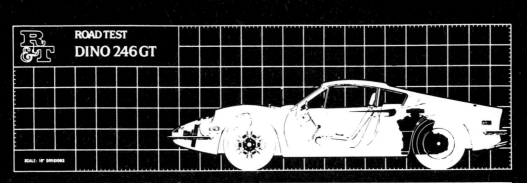

ROAD TEST
DINO 246 GT

SCALE: 10" DIVISIONS

PRICE

List price, east coast	$14,500
List price, west coast	$13,885
Price as tested, east coast	$14,740
Price as tested includes electric windows ($240), dealer prep	

IMPORTER

Chinetti Motors, Greenwich, Conn.
Modern Classic Motors, Reno, Nev.

ENGINE

Type	dohc V-6
Bore x stroke, mm	92.5 x 60.0
Equivalent in	3.64 x 2.36
Displacement, cc/cu in	2418/145
Compression ratio	9.0:1
Bhp @ rpm, net	est. 175 @ 7000
Equivalent mph	127
Torque @ rpm, lb-ft	est. 160 @ 5500
Equivalent mph	100
Carburetion	three Weber 40DCF14
Fuel requirement	premium, 98-oct
Emissions, gram/mile:	
Hydrocarbons	3.25
Carbon Monoxide	22.68
Nitrogen Oxides	n.a.

DRIVE TRAIN

Transmission	5-sp manual
Gear ratios: 5th (1.05)	3.80:1
4th (1.38)	5.01:1
3rd (1.86)	6.75:1
2nd (2.59)	9.38:1
1st (3.76)	13.65:1
Final drive ratio	3.62:1

CHASSIS & BODY

Layout	midship engine/rear drive
Body/frame	unit steel, all steel panels
Brake system	vented disc, 10.6-in front & 10.0-in rear; vacuum assisted
Swept area, sq in	n.a.
Wheels	cast alloy, 14 x 6½
Tires	Michelin XVR 205/70-VR14
Steering type	rack & pinion
Turns, lock-to-lock	3.2
Turning circle, ft	37.5
Front suspension: unequal-length A-arms, coil springs, tube shocks, anti-roll bar	
Rear suspension: unequal-length A-arms, coil springs, tube shocks, anti-roll bar	

ACCOMMODATION

Seating capacity, persons	2
Seat width	2 x 20.5
Head room, front/rear	35.5
Seat back adjustment, degrees	0

INSTRUMENTATION

Instruments: 170-mph speedo, 99,-999 odo, 999.9 trip odo, 10,000-rpm tach, oil press, oil temp, water temp, ammeter, fuel level, clock

Warning lights: oil press, brake failure, low fuel, lights on, high beam, directionals, hazard flasher, seatbelts

MAINTENANCE

Service intervals, mi:	
Oil change	6000
Filter change	6000
Gearbox & diff oil	6000
Minor tuneup	3000
Major tuneup	6000
Warranty, mo/mi	12/12,000

GENERAL

Curb weight, lb	2770
Test weight	3100
Weight distribution (with driver), front/rear, %	41/59
Wheelbase, in	92.1
Track, front/rear	56.2/56.3
Length	165.4
Width	67.0
Height	44.6
Ground clearance	4.7
Overhang, front/rear	40.3/33.0
Usable trunk space, cu ft	6.7
Fuel capacity, U.S. gal	18.6

CALCULATED DATA

Lb/bhp (test weight)	15.9
Mph/1000 rpm (5th gear)	18.2
Engine revs/mi (60 mph)	3200
Piston travel, ft/mi	1250
R&T steering index	1.20
Brake swept area, sq in/ton	n.a.

RELIABILITY

From R&T Owner Surveys the average number of trouble areas for all models surveyed is 11. As owners of earlier-model Ferraris reported 7 trouble areas, we expect the reliability of the Dino 246GT to be better than average.

ROAD TEST RESULTS

ACCELERATION

Time to distance, sec:	
0–100 ft	3.2
0–500 ft	8.5
0–1320 ft (¼ mi)	15.9
Speed at end of ¼-mi, mph	87
Time to speed, sec:	
0–30 mph	3.3
0–40 mph	4.5
0–50 mph	6.2
0–60 mph	7.9
0–70 mph	10.1
0–80 mph	13.1
0–100 mph	21.5

FUEL ECONOMY

Normal driving, mpg	12.7
Cruising range, mi (1-gal. res.)	224

SPEEDS IN GEARS

5th gear (7800 rpm)	141
4th (7800)	112
3rd (7800)	83
2nd (7800)	61
1st (7800)	41

BRAKES

Minimum stopping distances, ft:	
From 60 mph	140
From 80 mph	273
Control in panic stop	very good
Pedal effort for 0.5g stop, lb	33
Fade: percent increase in pedal effort to maintain 0.5g deceleration in 6 stops from 60	nil
Overall brake rating	very good

HANDLING

Speed on 100-ft radius, mph	35.4
Lateral acceleration, g	0.836

INTERIOR NOISE

All noise readings in dBA:	
Idle in neutral	67
Maximum, 1st gear	89
Constant 30 mph	77
50 mph	85
70 mph	83
90 mph	86

SPEEDOMETER ERROR

30 mph indicated is actually	29.0
70 mph	66.5
80 mph	76.0

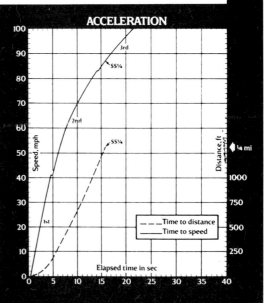

ACCELERATION

Legend: - - - - Time to distance; ——— Time to speed

Speed, mph / Distance, ft / Elapsed time in sec

generous passenger space, etc. outnumber the more "ultimate" type today reflects the fact that today there is less need or justification for these sacrifices. Traffic conditions, speed limits and roads are such that cars of even moderately high capabilities can seldom be used to their limits. Yet it is a thrill to drive a car like the Dino, one whose capabilities are far beyond what even an expert driver can use in most real-world motoring, and that is the Dino's reason for being.

The Dino's most obvious sacrifice affects the human ear. It is noisy in the extreme. The sounds are exciting, to be sure: busy tappets, whining cam chains and transfer drive, a raucous exhaust system. All combine to give driver and passenger sensations just short of those of a race car, and even on a slow run to the corner drugstore the Dino seems to be working, snarling, racing. The exhaust note at low speeds gives away its 6-cyl configuration, but as the engine climbs into its effective rev range (little happens below 3000 rpm, and the unit is decidedly unhappy at low speeds, bucking and misfiring to prove it) it takes on the characteristic Ferrari sounds despite having only half the number of cylinders.

For an extended trip in the Dino we'd recommend taking a pair of earplugs along. Above 65 mph everything smooths out and the wind noise is low, so the Dino is no noisier at 70 mph than a Capri V-6 is at 90. But between 50 and 65 mph (2600–3500 rpm in 5th) the exhaust system resonates badly in the body cavity and the interior is actually louder at 50 than at 70.

Running up through the gears is quite another thing; this is when we relish the sounds, and the potent V-6 hitting 7800 rpm, the redline, is real music. Zero-to-60-mph acceleration, however, is not the Dino's forte, as the somewhat disappointing time of 7.9 sec shows. We tested the car at Lime Rock, Connecticut, where a particularly grippy new track surface absolutely prevented wheelspin getting off the line. The alternative is to slip the clutch, which we did, but we were reluctant to slip it enough to hold the engine at its 5500-rpm torque peak for the first couple of seconds; thus the engine spent an inordinate amount of time in lower rev range on the 0–60 run. The clutch did take what punishment we dealt it with no complaint whatsoever, but in any case the Dino isn't as quick as its Porsche competition. No problem explaining why: with approximately the same displacement, it weighs nearly 300 lb more than the Porsche even in the latter's heavier Targa form.

Another common sacrifice in mid-engine cars is in gearshifting: so far it's been unusual to find satisfactory shift linkage in mid-engine cars and the Dino is no exception. The 5-speed gearbox is behind the engine, which complicates things and is typical of midship layouts whether longitudinal or transverse. On the Dino the shift pattern puts 5th over to the left and back, the other four gears in H-pattern—like the earlier Porsche 911s. This is a good layout for road work in which 1st is seldom used, but in everyday driving it's

most inconvenient. It's often difficult to get the recalcitrant, gated shifter into 1st and sometimes it didn't want to go from 4th to 5th either; the acceleration runs were further hampered by the necessity of quite deliberate motion to get from 1st to 2nd.

A manual choke gave almost instantaneous cold starts at ambient temperatures around 30°F during our test, and the engine would restart quickly when hot when the accelerator pedal was held all the way down while cranking. There's always a backfire or two after shutting off, just to remind us of that air injection, and an additional symptom of the emission control is a very slow return to idle.

If engine behavior isn't the most exhilarating thing about the Dino, then its chassis is; the real joy of a good mid-engine car is in its handling and braking and the Dino shone as we expected it to. The steering is light, wonderfully precise and quick without being super-quick in the sense of the Citroen SM, and it transmits by what seems a carefully planned amount of feedback exactly what is going on at the tires. Thanks to the layout's low polar moment of inertia, the car responds instantly to it. The Dino's cornering limits are very high and we thoroughly enjoyed lap after lap at Lime Rock, finding its limits and improving our times. Though the sharpest lefthand turn brought on some fuel starvation, all was well otherwise and even if the throttle foot was lifted in the middle of an overdone turn, the only consequence was a gently drifting tail. A bumpy surface, of which there are many in rural New England, revealed even more: it takes a big disturbance to upset the Dino's equilibrium.

Braking is just as good, as the stopping distance of 140 ft from 60 mph indicates. An anchors-out stop may lock the front wheels, but the stopping power is simply phenomenal and should impart enough confidence that any driver will be able to modulate pedal effort and unlock them. Only one detraction from this impressive brake performance, achieved with big ventilated discs all around: in light, low-speed braking one notices a bit of nonlinearity in the vacuum booster's action.

Rough road surfaces also bring out a finely engineered ride. Despite being a very low car the Dino has plenty of suspension travel (those wheel arches mean something!) and other than a creak from the left rear suspension the car was at home on any paved road surface we subjected it to. The body also feels strong and solid, but the only way to tell if it's squeaking or rattling is to throw out the clutch and let the engine idle. It is, as it turns out, creaking a bit but the engine and drivetrain din covers this completely.

Seating is another area of mid-engine compromise and the Dino comes off better than most in this respect. Headroom isn't what you'd call generous, but a male of average height can sit comfortably, the big windshield doesn't brush his forehead, and he can see out—even to the rear, where the concave wraparound window is a good solution to a problem that is seldom well solved. The driver's legs necessarily aim toward the car center because of intruding wheel-wells. Seatbacks are not adjustable and the seats don't rock on their mountings, but there is adequate fore-aft travel for a fair range of drivers and the brake and throttle pedals are well positioned for simultaneous use.

Some aspects of the ergonomics design are crude. Though a nice set of instruments is set into a panel right in front of the driver, the steering-wheel rim obscures the speedometer (which clicked loudly despite an attempt at repairs) badly. And that otherwise satisfactory rear window's center section reflects whatever is seen through the windshield, quite a problem at night. Heater controls are confusing, even after careful study of the owner's manual which, wonder of wonders, is a trilingual affair with very good specifications tables, drawings, photographs and minor service instructions. The heater has only a 1-speed blower; but its fresh-air intake is good and heat output powerful.

The Dino's interior, in standard form, is nicely put together but not fancy: about the grade of a Fiat 124 Spider. Leather can be ordered for $275 extra, cloth seat inserts for $65. Our test car had the standard all-vinyl coverings.

Ironically, this Dino was our first exposure to full results of the new 1972 seatbelt regulation, which requires a visual or audible warning if the ignition is on, the handbrake off and the transmission in gear, and if the passenger seat is occupied, without the belts being fastened. It sounds terrible but is actually little bother to those already in the habit of using belts. If you fasten the belt before putting the car in gear (which is natural anyway) you'll never hear the buzzer or see the light. As for your passenger, it can help get her or him to use the belts.

The transverse engine allows a sizable, usable trunk—6.7 cu ft, larger than a Camaro's—and it is nicely finished with carpeting on five of its six surfaces. The spare tire, quite a bulky thing, lives up front behind the radiator. Fuel is stored in two "saddlebag" tanks flanking the engine and fed by a single filler. Clever space utilization is what makes the Dino such a satisfactory mid-engine package.

Ferrari name or no, the Dino is a Ferrari and the mystique plus the exciting shape plus the sounds plus the great chassis all add up to a lot of car. Looking at it another way, in direct comparison to the Porsche 911 E or S, it's difficult to justify the Dino's extra cost because the Dino isn't as quick, doesn't shift as well, uses more fuel, and offers less passenger space. Only in handling does it have a clear advantage over the Stuttgarter and this is akin to comparing a New York steak to a Spencer—both are very good but one is just a bit better.

The conclusion? If you must have a mid-engine car, you can do a lot worse than the Dino. But don't expect to wallop your neighbor's 911 S with it.

---

6 DINO 308GT4 2+2—Motor, GB

For: excellent performance, road holding and handling by normal standards; smooth torquey engine; powerful brakes. Against: very poor fuel consumption; "dead" steering; indifferent gearchange; poor lock; inefficient heating and non-existent face-level ventilation; poor finish.

Nearly all Ferraris are classics but, even so, some are more memorable than others. The Dino 246 GT was one of the memorable ones. That combination of stirring performance, almost unequalled handling and extreme beauty combined to produce not just a national hit, but a worldwide, all-time great, by which all subsequent GT cars have been judged. Inevitably, any car that now bears the name Dino must be compared with the 246 and if it proves impossible to measure its qualities in superlatives, then there will be no match.

Like Maserati and others Ferrari have given in to the demands of customers and the 308 GT is their first mid-engined V8 2 plus 2

In every other respect it is similar in concept to the 246. Its new all-alloy dohc engine is mounted across the frame ahead of and driving the rear wheels. The gearbox is the familiar five-speed Ferrari unit and the double wishbone suspension all round bears more than a passing resemblance to that of the old car.

The new engine is of three litres capacity and is a 90-degree V8. It therefore demands more room longitudinally as well as laterally than the previous 65 deg V6, and the body of the 308 is a full 5 in longer than that of the 246. Like the Berlinetta Boxer's the body is built by Scaglietti, but the styling was done by Bertone rather than Pininfarina.

It is difficult to see how any better use could have been made of the available space, but it is hard to treat the "plus 2" with any seriousness and those extra seats can only be considered of use for small children or extra luggage for there is no real space for adult legs.

Whatever body it might be clothed in, it is impossible to imagine a Ferrari without performance. Certainly the 308 is not lacking here, reaching 60 mph in an impressive 6.4 seconds and 100 mph in a mean of 16.7 secs. But it is from here on that it really impresses, bounding up to its maximum of over 150 mph with astonishing rapidity. In tune with this exhilarating performance is the handling, which though perhaps lacking the precision and agility of the 246's is outstanding by ordinary standards. The brakes are powerful and reassuring and the ride remarkably smooth.

In other ways the new generation Dino disappoints. Its finish is indifferent for a car of this price: our test

Two-tone glass fibre bodied 308GT4 2 + 2

model suffered from a leaking floor, a sticking clutch, doors that dropped on their hinges and a light switch that failed after 3800 miles. Far more serious than these niggling faults was the overall consumption, a hefty 14.1 mpg, and a tricky gear-change which was by far the worst of any Ferrari we have tried. The turning circle, too, is infuriatingly poor at around 40 ft and the wheels rubbed on the wheel arches whenever the car was on full lock.

By absolute standards the 308 is in many respects a very fine car. But if you have been lucky enough to have sampled its predecessor (now, sadly, unobtainable) you might be faintly disappointed. We were.

Performance

Though not startlingly different to the V6 unit of the original Dino, the 308's engine breaks new ground for Ferrari. Their eight-cylinder engines have been seen on the race track but this is the first time the configuration has been used in a Ferrari road car. It is also the first time Ferrari has used toothed belts for the camshaft drives.

The alloy engine has a five-bearing crankshaft and eight cylinders set in a 90-degree V. Toothed belts drive four overhead camshafts, two per bank, which in turn operate inclined valves via bucket tappets. The capacity of this oversquare unit is 2926 cc and its compression

ratio is 8.8:1. Breathing is by four twin-choke 40DCNF Webers and ignition by twin Marello distributors.

Maximum power is 255 bhp (DIN) and torque a full 210 ft lbs. The torque curve is beautifully flat and the engine will pull cleanly from as little as 1000 rpm in fifth. Its 30–50 mph time in this gear is in fact better than that of the 3.0CSi BMW in fourth, and vastly superior to that of the Maserati Merak and Lotus Elite.

Standing start accelerations are impressive partly because it is easy to spin the wheels despite the tail-heavy configuration. With the benefit of a wheelspin start we reached 60 mph in an average of 6.4 seconds and 100 mph in a mere 16.7 secs. These impressive times could undoubtedly have been bettered had the clutch pedal not tended to stick down during fast changes.

As the power keeps on coming right to the maximum of 7700 rpm (and probably well beyond) the Dino is shatteringly quick over 110 mph and will comfortably reach the red line in top gear. Even allowing for an optimistic rev-counter this still gave a mean of around 152 mph, some way off Ferrari's claim of 156 mph. So easily does it attain such speeds that you frequently find yourself travelling 10–15 mph faster than you realise.

Though a choke is supplied, starting of the Weber carburetted engine is best done in the traditional manner—with three or four pumps of the throttle. The engine warmed quickly and pulled cleanly almost immediately. Its sound is seldom harsh and its extreme smoothness throughout the rev range calls for a wary eye on the rev counter when pressing on through the gears.

Economy

Our 14.1 mpg overall fuel consumption can only be described as poor. It is slightly inferior to that of the heavier larger-engine Jaguar E type, considerably worse than the consumptions of other more comparable machines like the Porsche Carrera and Lotus Elite. Even at a steady 30 mph it recorded no better than 27.2 mpg and by 100 mph it had already fallen to 18.6 mpg.

The car ran happily on four star fuel and will hold 17.2 gallons in its twin tanks. With a touring consumption of 18.7 mpg the Dino has a range of some 320 miles between fill-ups.

Transmission

Like the original Dino, the 308 has Ferrari's own five-speed gearbox which, together with the final drive, is mounted behind and beneath the transverse engine. A limited slip differential is included as standard.

The traditional Ferrari change features a slotted "gate" with first back and to the left and the remaining four ratios spaced in the conventional "H" pattern. Reverse is obtained by pressing the lever downwards, then to the left and forward. The gearchange on our test car was not like that of other Ferraris, though, being notchy and baulky and even lacking synchromesh. Hopefully, its faults were peculiar to this car.

Maranello-built boxes always need warming, but on this car the first to second movement remained awkward even when the oil was hot. All the gears were mildly obstructive and the synchromesh, particularly on fifth, proved weak. A heavy (42 lb) long-travel clutch and forward positioning of the gearlever made fast changes difficult until you'd acquired the kack of perfect timing and co-ordination.

The ratios are rather low with first giving no more than 45 mph. Second, third and fourth are all quite close and at full bore top is engaged at little over 120 mph. In practice, the extreme torque of the engine disguises any "holes" and the car's ability to re-start on a 1 in 3 slope as easily as it pulls from 25 mph in top proves there is little wrong with the chosen spacing.

Handling

For their mid-engined cars, Ferrari opt for rack and pinion steering rather than the worm and peg systems of their front-engined models. Even so, the 308 suffers mildly from that dead feel found on the Daytona and some other Ferraris before it. For a sports car, it is also disappointingly low geared and the 3.25 turns required

to swing from lock to lock would be 4.0 or more if the lock were not so extraordinarily poor. At low speeds it is very heavy, and parking the Dino is hard work for anybody. Once you are on the move though, the steering lightens considerably and is pleasant enough at high speed, despite its inherent lack of feel. Ruts and ridges cause the steering wheel to kick back violently in your hands, but most of the time it remains free of such irritation. The Dino is only mildly affected by crosswinds.

The 308's suspension is very similar to that of the preceding Dino; independent all round with unequal length wishbones, wire coil springs and hydraulic dampers. Anti-roll bars are used front and rear.

There is quite strong initial understeer under power, followed on tighter corners by a gradual transition to oversteer as yet more power is fed in. On faster bends increasing throttle merely causes the car to adopt a more neutral, stable attitude. Sudden lift-off results in nothing more than a slight tightening of line—just as it should be. Though the handling is hard to fault by normal standards we found the 308 lacked the feel and confidence-inspiring neutrality of the old 246.

Like the 246, the 308 comes on 6.5 in Ferrari-made all-alloy rims, which are shod with Michelin XWX high-speed radials. Their cornering power in the dry is excellent, but on damp patches you soon learn to treat the throttle with extreme respect.

Brakes

High speeds demand powerful brakes and the Ferrari certainly has them. Servo assisted, ventilated disc brakes on all four corners arrest the car without effort from any speed and, more importantly, will do so repeatedly without drastic fade. At all times they retained their feel, though there was always a tendency to self-servo.

Our initial tests, carried out at only 30 mph, showed how the pads need to be warmed for maximum efficiency. At this speed, a pressure of 25 lb was required to give a 0.34 g stop. In the fade test however, conducted at 98 mph, 27 lb was, initially, all that was required for a 0.5 g deceleration. Six stops, though, were sufficient to cause very detectable fade and a consequent smell of cooking linings. The required pressure rose to 41 lbs, but it remained at that level without further increases until the end of the test. The water splash had virtually no effect on braking efficiency.

The handbrake of our test car may well have required adjustment, for it failed to hold the car on a 1-in-3 slope even when placed on the last notch of its rachet. In the same position it produced a 0.24 g deceleration from 30 mph. The legal requirement is 0.25 g.

Accommodation

A 2 plus 2 the 308 may be, but only when the additional couple are children—and young ones at that. Entry to the back is straightforward enough, but adult-

MOTOR ROAD TEST 2/75 — Ferrari Dino 308GT4

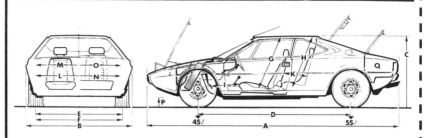

		ft	in	cm				ft	in	cm
A	overall length	14	1.25	429.9	K	front to back				
B	overall width	5	7.25	170.8		seat max	1	11.25	59.1
C	unladen					min	1	3.75	40.0
	height	3	11.5	120.7	L	front elbow			
D	wheelbase	8	4.25	254.6		width	5	0	152.4
E	front track	4	9.75	146.7	M	front shoulder			
F	rear track	4	9.75	146.7		width	4	9.25	145.4
G	com. seat to				N	rear elbow			
	roof front	3	0	91.4		width	4	9.5	146.1
H	com. seat to				O	rear shoulder			
	roof rear	2	7.75	80.6		width	4	7.25	140.3
I	pedal to seat				P	min ground			
	max	1	9.75	55.2		clearance		4.5	11.4
	min	1	2.75	37.5	Q	boot capacity	5.0 cu ft		
J	kneeroom								
	max		8.25	20.9					
	min		125	3.2					

GENERAL SPECIFICATION

ENGINE
Cylinders	V8
Capacity	2927 cc (178.6 cu in)
Bore stroke	81/71 mm (3.2/2.8 in)
Cooling	Water
Block	Light alloy
Head	Light alloy
Valves	dohc

Valve timing
inlet opens	34° btdc
inlet closes	46° abdc
ex opens	36° bbdc
ex closes	38° atdc
Compression	8.8:1
Carburetter	4 twin choke Weber 40 DCNF
Bearings	5 main
Fuel pump	Corona electric
Max power	255 bhp (DIN) at 7600 rpm
Max torque	209.8 lb ft (DIN) at 5000 rpm

TRANSMISSION
Type	5 speed manual
Clutch	Mechanically operated,

sdp, diaphragm spring

Internal ratios and mph/1000 rpm
Top	0.952:1/21.0
4th	1.244:1/16.1
3rd	1.693:1/11.8
2nd	2.353:1/8.5
1st	3.418:1/5.8
Rev	3.247:1
Final drive	3.53:1 ratio

BODY/CHASSIS
Construction	Tubular steel frame

SUSPENSION
Front	Ind by wishbones, coils and anti-roll bar
Rear	Ind by wishbones, coils and anti-roll bar

STEERING
Type	Rack and pinion
Assistance	None
Toe-in	0.08-0.157 in
Camber	0°-10'—0°-30'
Castor	4°

King pin	9°-30'

BRAKES
Type	Disc all round
Servo	Yes
Circuit	Divided front/rear
Rear valve	Yes
Adjustment	Automatic on all four wheels

WHEELS
Type	Ferrari light aloy 14 x 6.5 in
Tyres	Michelin 205/70 VR14 XWX; Spare, Michelin 105 R18X
Pressures	To 95 mph F26; R29; over 130 mph F31; R37; Spare, 21

ELECTRICAL
Battery	12 volt, 66 ah
Polarity	Negative earth
Generator	Alternator
Fuses	18
Headlights	4 x 55W Halogen

STANDARD EQUIPMENT

Adjustable steering	No	Head restraints	Yes	Parcel shelf	No
Anti-lock brakes	No	Heated rear window	No	Petrol filler lock	No
Armrests	No	Laminated screen	Yes	Radio	No
Ashtrays	Yes	Lights		Rev counter	Yes
Breakaway mirror	Yes	Boot	No	Seat belts	
Cigar lighter	Yes	Courtesy	Yes	Front	Yes
Childproof locks	No	Engine bay	Yes	Rear	Yes
Clock	Yes	Hazard warning	Yes	Seat recline	Yes
Coat hooks	No	Map reading	No	Seat height adjuster	No
Dual circuit brakes	Yes	Parking	No	Sliding roof	No
Electric windows	No	Reversing	Yes	Timed glass	No
Energy absorb steering col	Yes	Fog	Yes	Combination wash/wipe	Yes
Fresh air ventilation	Yes	Locker	Yes	Wipe delay	No
Grab handles	No	Outside mirror	Yes	Vanity mirror	Yes

IN SERVICE

GURANTEE
Duration .... 1 year or 10,000 miles

MAINTENANCE
Schedule	Every 3000 miles
Free service	At 600, 1200 miles
Labour for year	Approx £220

DO-IT-YOURSELF
Sump	16.0 pints, SAE 10W50
Gearbox/ Differential	0.88 pints, SAE 90
Steering gear	0.35 pints, SAE 90
Coolant	31.6 pints
Chassis lubrication	
Contact breaker gap	0.012-0.15
Spark plug type	Champion N6Y
Spark plug gap	0.020-0.024
Tappets (cold)	
inlet	0.008-0.010
exhaust	0.012-0.014

REPLACEMENT COSTS
Brake pads (front)	£7.19
Clutch unit	£36.35
Complete exhaust system	£149.50
Engine (new)	£4250.00
Damper (front)	£18.50
Front wing	£69.00
Gearbox (new)	£2350.00
Oil filter	£6.91
Starter motor	approx £106
Windscreen	£114.08

Make: Ferrari
Model: Dino 308GT4
Makers: Ferrari Automobili SpA SEFAC, casella postale 589, 41100 Modena, Italy
Concessionaires: Maranello Concessionaires Ltd, Egham by-pass, Surrey
Price: £7128.00 plus £594.0 car tax plus £617.76 VAT equals £8339.76. Electric windows, £114.66; Leather/cloth interior, £253.89; Air conditioning, £374.40; heated rear window, £30.42 gives total as tested of £9113.13

MOTOR ROAD TEST 2/75 — Ferrari Dino 308GT4

GAM 9IN

PERFORMANCE

CONDITION
Weather   Dry;
           wind 0-18 mph
Temperature   38-42° F
Barometer   29.5 in Hg
Surface   Dry tarmac

MAXIMUM SPEEDS
	mph	kph
	See Text	

Terminal speeds:
at ¼ mile   94   151
Speed in gears at (7700 rpm):

	mph	kph
1st	45	72
2nd	65	105
3rd	91	146
4th	123	198

ACCELERATION FROM REST
mph	sec	kph	sec
0-30	2.5		
0-40	3.4	0-40	2.0
0-50	5.1	0-60	3.1
0-80	6.4	0-80	5.0
0-70	8.7	0-100	7.0
0-80	10.3	0-120	9.3
0-90	13.7	0-140	12.5
0-100	16.7	0-160	16.7
Standing ¼	14.7		

ACCELERATION IN TOP
mph	sec	kph	sec
20-40			
30-50	7.9	60-80	4.4
40-60	7.2	80-100	4.8
50-70	7.2	100-120	4.2
60-80	6.9	120-140	4.5
70-90	7.1	140-160	5.0
80-100	8.2		

ACCELERATION IN 4th
mph	sec	kph	sec
20-40	5.9	40-60	3.2
30-50	5.1	60-80	3.1
40-60	4.8	80-100	2.9

50-70	4.6	100-120	2.8
60-80	4.6	120-140	3.2
70.90	4.8	140-160	3.5
80-100	5.6		

FUEL CONSUMPTION
Touring*   18.7 mpg
         15.1 litres 100 km
Overall   14.1 mpg
         20.0 litres 100 km
Fuel grade   98 octane (RM)
         4 star rating
Tank capacity   17.2 galls
         78.0 litres
Max range   322 miles
         518 km
Test distance   1186 miles
         1908 km

* Consumption midway between 30 mph and maximum less 5 per cent for acceleration.

BRAKES
Pedal pressure deceleration and stopping distance from 30 mph (48 kph)

lb	kg	g	ft	m
25	11	0.34	88	27
50	23	0.68	44	13
75	34	0.87	34	10
100	45	1.00+	30	9
Handbrake		0.24	125	38

FADE
20 ½ g stops at 1 min intervals from speed midway between 40 mph (64 khp) and maximum (97 mph, 156 kph)

	lb	kg
Pedal force at start	27	12
Pedal force at 10th stop	48	22
Pedal force at 20th stop	45	20

STEERING
Turning circle between kerbs

	ft	m
left	39.4	12.0
right	40.2	12.3

Lock to lock   3.25 turns
50ft ¼ diam circle   1.3 turns

CLUTCH
	in	cm
Free pedal movement	0.75	1.9
Additional to disengage	2.75	7.0
Maximum pedal load	42 lb 19 kg	

SPEEDOMETER (mph)
Speedo   30 40 50 60 70 80 90 100
True mph 28 37 46 56 66 75 85 94
Distance recorder: 3.2 per cent fast.

WEIGHT
	cwt	kg
Unladen weight*	25.3	1282
Weight as tested	29.0	1471

* with fuel for approx 50 miles

Performance tests carried out by Motor's staff at the Motor Industry Research Association proving ground, Lindley.

Test Data · World copyright reserved; no reproduction in whole or in part without Editor's written permission.

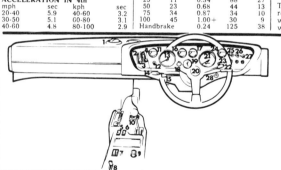

1 Screen demisters	14 lights
2 heater distribution	15 indicators
3 temperature control	16 oil pressure gauge
4 heater distribution	17 water temp gauge
5/6 electric window switches	18 generator light
	19 clock
7 rear demist	20 horn button
8 choke	21 rev-counter
9 cigar lighter	22 wash/wipe
10 air conditioning	23 trip zero
	24 oil temperature gauge
11 fuel gauge	25 fog lights
12 instrument lights rheostat	26 hazard warning lights
13 speedometer	27 heater blower
	28 ignition switch

COMPARISONS

	Capacity cc	Price £	Max mph	0-60 sec	30-50* sec	Overall mpg	Touring mpg	Length ft in	Width ft in	Weight cwt	Boot cu ft
Ferrari Dino 308 GT	2927	8340	152†	6.4	7.9	14.1	18.7	14 1.3	5 7.3	25 3	5.0
Porsche Carrera	2687	9000	150†	5.5	**	16.7	—	14 1	5 3	21.2	4.3
Maserati Merak	2965	7821	140†	7.5	9 4	13.2	22.1	14 2	5 10	27.3	6.6
Jaguar E Type	5343	3743	146.0	6.4	6.0	14.5	—	15 4	5 6.75	28 8	3.8
Lotus Elite 502	1973	6255	125†	8.1	11.6	18.6	26.9	14 7.5	5 11.5	23.0	6.6
Jensen Interceptor	6276	8334	138.5	7.3	3.4	11.3	15.0	15 8	5 10	33.0	8.5
BMW 3.0 CSi	2985	7657	138	7.5	8.2	20.2	—	15 3.3	5 11	25 4	6.2
Alfa Romeo Montreal	2593	6085	135.2	8.1	8.8	13.8	—	13 10	5 5.8	25.1	3.2
Citroen SM EFI	2671	6691	142†	8.3	12.9	14.9	—	16 0.5	6 0.5	29.5	9.0

*Kickdown for Jensen; top for other cars.
†Maker's claimed maximum on estimate.
**not recorded.
—Touring consumption not computed as fuel-injection prevented the measurement of steady speed consumption figures.

sized legs cannot be accommodated unless the front seats are pushed well forward—usually an impractical proposition. Even for children, the seat proved upright, hard and totally lacking in thigh support. Surprisingly, there is a reasonable degree of head room, though the head restraints, like the seats, were definitely built with children in mind.

Front seat accommodation is far more generous and the uncluttered facia and console and hollow doors allow plenty of elbow room. Quite bulky oddments can be stored in the flip-back glovebox, the generous door pockets or handy little bins beside the rear seats. A further tray is located in their divide. More substantial items have to be housed in the rear luggage compartment which is located immediately behind the engine bay. We squeezed 5.0 cu ft of our test luggage into its rectangular space. Yet more oddments can be laid around the space-saver tyre at the front of the car—cases, however, are out of the question. Five cu ft is in fact poor by any standards—less, in fact, than we found room for in the 246 GT.

Ride comfort

Though the Dino's ride is firm it is excellent for a car with such handling and cornering powers. It borders on the knobbly over really poor surfaces but is smooth enough on all other types of road. Though it never feels soft, neither is it harsh.

At the wheel

Unlike some other Italian companies Ferrari are reasonably adept at building their cockpits to accommodate people of various shapes and sizes. There is a hint of the long-armed short-legged Italianate character about the driving position but this can be virtually eliminated by careful positioning of the reclining seats. Far more disconcerting to most of our testers were the heavily offset pedals, the heavy, long travel clutch being particularly awkward—though we discovered after a time that clean changes could be made with only a short stab on the clutch.

The remaining controls are well positioned with three stalks looking after most of the minor facilities. The larger of the left-hand ones is a compound light switch operating side-lamps, and the automatic pop-up headlamps as well as main beam and the flash for the fog lights. A smaller one in front controls the indicators. The remaining one to the right of the column works the powerful electric washers and two-speed wipers. To the right of the facia, angled towards the driver, are a row of toggle switches and associated warning lights which together take care of the blower fan, and hazard warning and driving lights. The potent air horns are worked by the "Dino" button in the centre of the leather-covered Momo steering wheel and the controls for the electric

windows, heated rear screen and redundant choke are on the console.

All our testers complained about the Klippan seat belts which are particularly awkward to adjust, the tensioner being on the diagonal rather than the lap strap, and which, far worse, tend to slip off the shoulder in use.

The driver's seat is of the reclining bucket type and offers excellent support to all key areas of the body. Both the thigh and lumbar regions are comfortably located and a well-curved backrest ensures good lateral support. A handy footrest is built into the edge of the console.

Several drivers complained that the heater and ignition switches were awkward to reach when they were belted in. Another found reverse gear hard to engage for the same reason.

Visibility

Poor visibility is a failing of many mid-engined designs and has made some a dubious pleasure for road use. Though open to improvement the 308 is an exception. The slope of the nose, however, puts it just out of sight from the driving seat, despite the high, forward seating position. Rearward vision ends with the far edge of the engine cover as far as reversing is concerned, so one has to memorise the remaining length of stubby tail.

But the thickish rear pillars aren't as obstructive as one might imagine though their painted inner surfaces do cause reflections in bright sunlight. Due to its sheltered position, the rear screen never required wiping or use of the heated element. A good wiper pattern results in no real blind spots of the front screen either and the wipers seemed to work well at speeds much in excess of 100 mph. The headlights were no more than adequate on dipped beam, but impressive with all four in action.

Instruments

Ferrari owners no doubt expect a full array of instruments. The Dino has a more than adequate selection which includes a matching speedometer and rev-counter sandwiching a trio of smaller dials in the form of oil pressure and water temperature gauges and a clock. Completing the layout are yet more gauges for oil temperature and fuel. Though impressive in quantity, the instrumentation is far from perfect. The dials are all on the small side and the calibrations of both speedometer and rev-counter unnecessarily mean. As the outer gauges are frequently obscured by the rim of the steering wheel, we feel it would make more sense to locate one of them, probably the oil temperature gauge, where the less vital clock is. Subtle, rheostat-controlled green lighting illuminates the cluster at night. Both a trip and total mileage recorder are included in the speedometer head.

Heating

The heating system is inadequate and suffers from several major faults. First, it is of the old-fashioned water mix type and is therefore slow to react to changes of adjustment and is very inconsistent in its operation. Secondly the distribution, with its separate controls for left and right, allows either full flow to the screen or air split between screen and floor—never full flow to the floor. In consequence, the volume of air to the footwells is frequently insufficient. Even the noisy, single speed fan does little to remedy matters.

Ventilation

Other than by aiming cold air from the three screen outlets, the Dino has no ventilation system. The alternative to opening windows—a sorry state of affairs in this class of car—is the purchase of the optional air-conditioning unit. This was fitted to our test car and works well, though the lack of face level vents means the air is still poorly distributed.

Noise

A Ferrari would not be a Ferrari unless the music of the *motore* was dominant. Even though it is sited well behind the driver's ears, the uncharacteristic purr of the Dino's high-revving V8 is always with you. Unlike the chain driven V12 units the Dino's belt-driven cams do not jangle and clatter and the sound is merely the complete one of the busy and potent all-alloy engine. Induction noise is high and the gasp of the twin-choke Webers, through their intake on the rear quarters which is noticeable with closed windows, becomes obtrusive when driving with them open. Road noise is commendably low and wind roar, which is quite preceptible at 80 mph, rises surprisingly little with speed and is only marginally worse at 150 mph.

Finish

Ferrari's "baby" car is a strange mixture of the quality coachbuilt vehicle and low volume "special." The doors dropped on their hinges, the interior handles (easily mistaken for ashtrays) had sharp edges and the facia trim didn't fit properly. Even the door mouldings with their projecting screw heads smacked of the kit-car market. In contrast, the neatly trimmed Momo steering wheel and beautifully upholstered seats did project the sort of image one would expect of a car costing £8340. Still more impressive is the finish on the Bertone body which is protected by rubber inserts in the full-width bumpers and enhanced by the familiar Ferrari alloy wheels first seen on the 246 GT. The boot is trimmed in coarse-weave material which assists in keeping luggage fixed under hard driving conditions.

Though the brakes were little affected by our customary water splash test, the body was, and a good gallon of water was mopped from the mats afterwards.

Equipment

The Ferrari's equipment is sparse for an expensive car. If, however, you believe that one buys a Ferrari solely for its performance and are happy to add the extras yourself then you will most probably be satisfied with the basic article plus a handful of options. It comes with a five-speed gearbox, full instrumentation, reversing fog and hazard warning lights, courtesy and engine lights, head restraints, seat belts front and rear and air horns.

Obvious omissions include face level ventilation, the only alternative to which is full air-conditioning at £374.40, and a heated rear window which is also available for an extra £30.42. The electric windows cost £114.66 and a mixture of leather and cloth trim is a further £253.89. All leather is a full £301.86. Even the radio is extra.

In service

The engine compartment is opened by a lever set into the driver's door pillar. It is alongside that for the boot and the pair can be locked in position. The bonnet is self-propping and tilts forward to reveal a pretty full compartment, dominated by the large black crackle-finish air filter. Access to the rearward bank of plugs is good, as it is to the oil filter, both distributors and the quartet of Webers (once the air-filter is removed). Working on the forward bank, however, does not look so easy.

The bootlid opens the same way, and hides a most comprehensive tool kit, jack and spare set of drive belts for the engine. The bootlid has a catch at each corner and one usually has to apply a little weight to each side when closing. For the same reason, a good pull is required on the release for the front compartment, the lever for which is found under the facia on the driver's side. Under the self-propping lid are four distinct sections, the first of which is solely for the exit of air from the radiator. Behind that sits the space-saver spare tyre which is said to be safe to speeds of around 95 mph. To its left are the controls for one set of pop-up headlamps as well as the washer bottle and compressor for the air horns. The other side houses the battery and the other set of headlamps. The lockable glovebox contains a comprehensive, leather-wrapped handbook and a well labelled bank of fuses.

7 DINO 308GT4 2+2—Autocar, GB

Bargain basement . . .

When the Ferrari Dino 246 was announced, it was the first "cheap" Ferrari and it demonstrated that even a company of Ferrari's reputation still needed volume sales to survive. A timeless design, the first production Dino was rightly lauded as a very significant contribution to the world of sports cars, pioneering as it did a mid-engined configuration. But even sheer good looks are not safe from competition, especially when rivals can boast a higher degree of practicality. Thus it was that the Dino 308 GT4 was launched to compete head-on with the similar offerings from Lamborghini and the archetype of them all—the Porsche 911.

As is Ferrari's wont, the new car was not just to be as good as the opposition, it had to be better, especially in those areas that the marque had previously been pre-eminent. To exceed the performance of its rivals, the new car had to have a more powerful and tractable engine than the then-2.4 litre engines of its closest two competitors. Thus a new 3-litre V8 engine was introduced, benefiting from technological advance in adopting cogged belt drive for its expected twin overhead camshafts, thereby meeting one of the few criticisms of its predecessor, that of excessive engine noise.

Having designed a chassis for the 246 that gave splendid handling, there was clearly little point in changing for the sake of it and the 308 therefore uses the base pan and suspension layout of the earlier car, though with a wider track and greater body width.

It is now some 18 months since the Dino 308 GT4 first appeared and in this time it has nearly, but not quite, taken over the mantle of the Dino 246 as one of the best all round sports cars that money can buy. Not quite, because firstly, the 2 + 2 configuration does not permit such flowing looks and secondly, inflation has meant that although the 308 GT4 is the cheapest Ferrari its price has never been low in absolute terms. But what do you get for the bargain basement price of only a little under £9500 or £8000 less than the most expensive Ferrari?

First, immense performance that only a handful of contemporaries can match, accomplished with a smoothness and willingness that is a real tonic to the owner. Secondly, you have a practical layout that allows good all round visibility without any of the gimmickry to which at least one of its rivals subscribes. You get also an interior layout that allows plenty of room for two adults and two young children, or three adults if the accommodation is considered as 2 + 1. In relation to the performance, you get quite reasonable fuel consumption too, though using all the car's very considerable performance can reduce the figure to nearer 16 mpg than our overall figure of 19.8 mpg. You get a quality of finish both inside the car and outside that is a sheer joy to behold and you have a car that turns heads wherever it is seen. But there are some things that you do not get and in relation to the price, this is a pity.

The low-geared steering for a turning circle of over 40 feet is perhaps the car's worst feature, making any manoeuvre in tight confines a needlessly time and also energy-consuming business, since at low speeds the wide tyres mean high steering effort. You also have a poor heating system as both extraction of air and the control of heated air are bad.

Ready for delivery, Bertone's metal: 308GT4

As with most mid-engined designs, access to the engine is not good, helping in part to explain the lengthy time allowances that are required for routine servicing.

Having dealt in essence with the car and what it has to offer, specific details of the design will show how it accomplishes its design requirements.

Engine and transmission

The 90 deg V8 engine is set transversely well behind the car's centre line, giving a weight distribution of 43/57 per cent front to rear. To avoid excessive height of engine and transmission, the gearbox is set behind, not below, the engine and it shares the sump though a vertical partition keeps the two different lubricants from each other. The two-rail all-synchromesh gearbox drives to a helical spur-type final drive which has a limited slip differential and in turn, drive to the rear wheels is taken via solid drive shafts with constant velocity joints, sliding inner ones allowing for suspension movement. The generous dimension of the gearbox casing permits substantial Porsche synchromesh. The gearbox ratios are chosen admirably, allowing the revs to drop by progressively smaller amounts as each upward change is made in the gate Porsche-pattern gearchange.

Performance and economy

Though turning the scales at 28 cwt as tested, the Dino's 250 bph and good aerodynamic shape promise high performance. The maximum speed of 154 mph corresponds with an engine speed of 7,300 rpm which, though high, is surprisingly still some 400 rpm lower than the speed at which maximum power is produced. While this may suggest that the car is overgeared, the choice of top gear ratio does make it a very useful gear at any time and it need not be used merely as an overdrive. At the car's maximum, it runs straight and true with surprisingly little build up in wind noise which is, itself, only noticed at speeds over 80 mph.

With intermediate gear maximum of 123 mph (4th), 90 mph (3rd), and 64 mph in 2nd, there is a gear for every occasion and it is sheer delight to make full use of the gearbox. Sheer delight that is, away from town, for the clutch pedal effort of 50lb becomes wearing when used continually and often. Since the substantial synchromesh would slow any change attempted without full clutch release, it is essential on every change to use the full travel of the clutch, further aggravating the position.

We were fortunate on the day on which the performance was measured to have a damp surface, for this enabled rapid standing starts to be accomplished with mechanical sympathy. Only 2,250 rpm was needed at the moment the clutch was dropped to give just enough wheelspin to keep the engine in the heart of the torque curve. Once the wheels had gripped fully, the car just hurtled away, recording a series of figures that are extremely good in any company. They beg close

comparison with the Jaguar XJS car that is surprisingly similar to the Dino in many respects; accommodation, price and appeal. The respective times to accelerate from rest to 100 mph show the Ferrari just 1.2 sec behind and indeed, the faster initial step-off is shown by its quicker ¼-mile time (14.9 sec compared with 15.2 sec).

Though the Dino's maximum power is developed at 7,700 rpm the rev counter is marked with a cautionary segment starting at 7,600 rpm. This rev limit was respected after the rev counter had first been calibrated and found to be reading 350 rpm too high at a true 7,000 rpm.

Fortunately such performance that the Ferrari is capable of is not gained at the expense of exorbitant fuel consumption. True, it is possible to drive the consumption down to below 14 mpg, the figure we obtained during performance testing but under more normal driving, an owner may expect to exceed 20 mpg with ease. The overall consumption worked out at 19.8 mpg which is all the more laudable, for prolonged cruising on the Continent at three figure speeds was an unusual aspect of this particular car. Of the fuel tank contents, the last 3.3 gal form a reserve, a warning light flashing when this is reached. Thus allowing for an average return of 20 mpg, a safe range approaching 300 miles is given by the 17.2 gal tank.

Handling and brakes

A classic arrangement of wishbone independent suspension all round promises good handling and this is the case. The characteristics are initially neutral with no tendency for either end of the car to run wide. Provoked further, the front wheels begin to understeer and ultimately, full lock poses the situation. However, it is necessary to exercise great caution over lifting off the accelerator in mid-corner since the transition to power-off neutral or oversteer condition is very sudden. On wet roads, it was found to be most difficult to sustain a full power drift once the initial understeer had been "induced" by lifting off and indeed once any degree of power oversteer had been set up, sudden lifting off would cause the car to spin. However these are circumstances which one is most unlikely to repeat on the road and when driven at any speeds short of absolute, the Dino has go-where-you-point-it accuracy that is most reassuring. There would appear to be slight interference between the suspension and steering geometry for there are conditions of roll and lock that produce "dead" patches in the feel at the steering wheel. These might lead the unwary to think that the front wheels had gone light at the onset of understeer. This is not the case as once through the patch, steering feel through the rack and pinion system returns. Further presence of this phenomenon is shown by the "threepenny bit" position of the steering as the lock returns to the straight-ahead position.

Straightline stability is good in still air right through

Maximum Speeds

Gear	mph	kph	rpm
Top (mean)	154	248	7,300
(best)	154	248	7,300
4th	123	197	7,600
3rd	90	144	7,600
2nd	64	103	7,600
1st	45	72	7,600

Acceleration

True mph	Time secs	Speedo mph
30	2.5	31
40	3.6	41
50	5.4	52
60	6.9	62
70	9.1	72
80	11.4	82
90	15.2	92
100	18.1	102
110	22.4	112
120	30.3	123

Standing ¼-mile:
14.9 sec, 89 mph
kilometre:
27.6 sec, 117 mph

mph	Top	4th	3rd
20-40	—	6.1	3.7
30-50	8.4	5.1	3.4
40-60	7.9	4.9	3.4
50-70	7.6	5.1	3.7
60-80	7.7	5.3	4.3
70-90	8.0	5.7	—
80-100	8.7	6.3	—
90-110	10.5	8.0	—
100-120	13.0	—	—

Consumption

Fuel
Overall mpg: 19.8
(14.3 litres/100km)

Constant speed: Fuel system incompatible with test equipment

Autocar formula
Hard driving, difficult conditions
17.8 mpg
Average driving, average conditions
21.8 mpg
Gentle driving, easy conditions
25.7 mpg
Grade of fuel: Super, 5-star
(98 RM)
Mileage recorder: 6 per cent under reading

Oil
Consumption (SAE 10W/50)
1,000 miles/pint

Brakes
Fade (from 70 mph in neutral)
Pedal load for 0.5g stops in lb

	start/end		start/end
1	25-15	6	25-15
2	25-20	7	25-15
3	25-20	8	25-15-20
4	25-20	9	25-15-20
5	25-15	10	25-15-25

Response (from 30 mph in neutral)

Load	g	Distance
20lb	0.32	94ft
40lb	0.56	54ft
60lb	0.80	37.6ft
80lb	0.95	31.7ft
Handbrake	0.23	131ft
Max gradient	1 in 4	

Clutch Pedal 50lb and 5in

Test Conditions
Wind: 5-8 mph
Temperature: 8 deg C (46 deg F)
Barometer: 29.4 in. Hg
Humidity: 70 per cent
Surface: damp asphalt and concrete

Test distance 2,000 miles
Figures taken at 2,600 miles by our own staff at the Motor Industry Research Association proving ground at Nuneaton, and on the Continent

All Autocar test results are subject to world copyright and may not be reproduced in whole or in part without the Editor's written permission

Regular Service

Interval			
Change	3,000	6,000	12,00
Engine oil	Yes	Yes	Yes
Oil filter	Yes	Yes	Yes
Gearbox oil	No	Yes	Yes
Spark plugs	No	No	Yes
Air cleaner	No	No	Yes
C/breaker	No	No	Yes
Total cost	**£42.30**	**£79.50**	**£128.**

(Assuming labour at £4.30/hour)

Parts Cost
(including VAT)

Brake pads (2 wheels) — front	£9.0
Brake pads (2 wheels) — rear	£7.1
Silencer(s)	£149.5
Tyre — each (typical advertised)	£60.7
Windscreen	£114.0
Headlamp unit	£7.9
Front wing	£69.0
Rear bumper	£69.0

Warranty Period
12 months unlimited mileage

Weight
Kerb: 26.1 cwt/2,923lb/1,327kg
(Distribution F/R, 43/57)
As tested, 28.5 cwt/3,290lb/1,492k
Boot capacity: 10 cu. ft.

Turning circles;
Between kerbs
L. 41ft. 7in.; R. 41ft. 1in.
Between walls
L. 43ft. 5in.; R. 42in. 11in.
Turns, lock to lock 3⅓

OVERALL LENGTH 14'1·3"
OVERALL WIDTH 5'11"
OVERALL HEIGHT 3'10·5"
GROUND CLEARANCE 5"
WHEELBASE 8'4·4"
FRONT TRACK 4'9·5"
REAR TRACK 4'9·5"

Test Scorecard
(Average of scoring by Autocar Road Test team)

Ratings: 6 Excellent
5 Good
4 Better than average
3 Worse than average
2 Poor
1 Bad

PERFORMANCE	4.6
STEERING AND HANDLING	4.0
BRAKES	3.8
COMFORT IN FRONT	3.1
COMFORT IN BACK	2.5
DRIVERS' AIDS	4.1
(instruments, lights, wipers, visibility, etc.)	
CONTROLS	3.6
NOISE	4.5
STOWAGE	3.6
ROUTINE SERVICE	2.9
(under bonnet access dipstick etc.)	
EASE OF DRIVING	4.1
OVERALL RATING	**3.6**

Comparisons

Car	Price £	max mph	0-60 sec	overall mpg	capacity c.c.	power bhp	wheelbase in.	length in.	width in.	kerb weight	fuel gall.	tyre size
Ferrari Dino 308GT4	9,442	154	6.9	19.8	2,927	250	100	169	67	26.1	17.2	205/70 VR
Porsche Carrera 3 (Sportomatic)	10,997	141	7.3	21.0	2,956	200	89½	169	65	22.1	17.6	185/70-215/60 VR
Jaguar XJ-S	9,608	153	6.9	15.4	5,343	285	102	192	71	34.8	20.0	205/70 VR
Lotus Elite 503	8,135	124	7.8	20.9	1,973	155	98	176	72	22.8	14.8	205/60 VR
Lamborghini Urraco P250	9,434	143	8.5	18.7	2,463	220	97	167	69	25.8	17.6	205/70 VR

Specification

ENGINE

Cylinders	8 in 90 deg vee
Main bearings	5
Cooling	Water
Fans	Electric
Bore, mm (in.)	81 (3.19)
Stroke, mm (in.)	71 (2.79)
Capacity, cc (in.)	2.927 (178.6)
Valve gear	dohc
Camshaft drive	Toothed belt
Compression ratio	8.8-to-1
Octane rating	98 RM
Carburettor	Weber, quadruple 40 DCNF
Max power	250 bhp (DIN) at 7,700 rpm
Max torque	210 lb ft at 5,000 rpm

TRANSMISSION

Type	5-spd, all synchromesh	
Gear	Ratio	mph/1,000 rpm
Top	0.95	21.1
4th	1.24	16.1
3rd	1.69	11.9
2nd	2.35	8.4
1st	3.42	5.9
Final drive gear	Helical spur (std. l/s differential) 3.71-to-1	

SUSPENSION

Front-location	Upper and lower wishbones
springs	Coil
dampers	Telescopic
anti-roll bar	Yes
Rear-location	Upper and lower wishbones
springs	Coil
dampers	Telescopic
anti-roll bar	Yes

STEERING

Type	Cam Gears rack and pinion
Power assistance	None
Wheel diameter	14in.

BRAKES

Front	ATE 10⅛in. dia ventilated disc
Rear	ATE 10⅛in. dia ventilated disc
Servo	Bonaldi vacuum

WHEELS

Type	Campagnolo light alloy
Rim width	6.5in.
Tyres — make	Michelin
— type	XWX steel-braced radial, tubeless
— size	205/70 VR 14

EQUIPMENT

Battery	12 volt 66 Ah
Alternator	55amp
Headlamps	110/220w halogen
Reversing lamp	Standard
Hazard warning	Standard
Electric fuses	18 fuses, 13 relays (not incl. air conditioning)
Screen wipers	2-speed
Screen washer	Electric
Interior heater	water valve
Interior trim	Suede/leathercloth seats, pvc headlining
Floor covering	Carpet
Jack	Screw parellelogram
Jacking points	1 each side
Windscreen	Laminated
Underbody protection	Grp floor, mastic in wheel arches

MAINTENANCE

Fuel tank	17.2 Imp. galls (80 litres)
Cooling system	31.6 pints (inc. heater)
Engine sump	16 pints SAE 10W 50
Gearbox and Final drive	7 pints SAE 90
Grease	No points
Valve clearance	Inlet 0.008-0.010in. (cold) Exhaust 0.012-0.14in. (cold)
Contact breaker	0.012-0.015in. gap
Ignition timing	18 deg BTDC (static) 36 deg BTDC (stroboscopic at 5,000 rpm)
Spark plug — type	Champion N6Y — gap 0.020-0.024
Tyre pressures	F26, R29 psi (normal driving)
Max payload	850lb (385kg)

to the maximum speed but in a crosswind or in buffeting caused by other traffic, there is a small tendency to move sideways but this is self-correcting while only a light pressure need be put on the steering wheel rim.

Limited wheel travel and fairly hard springing mean a poor low speed ride and any severe road imperfection results in considerable kickback through the steering. At speed, the ride improves greatly and there is no tendency to self-steering from either end of the car even over severe camber or road surface changes. The seats are a shade too hard to help in damping fulfilment of the car but serious disturbance is only felt at low speeds.

The suspension is resistant to dive or squat under braking or acceleration and the impression for the driver or passengers is of faithful and reassuring following of the road surface, with no tendency to pitch or float over undulations. Substantial anti-roll bars at both ends control the roll well and the car corners flatly; under what little roll there is, some fouling in the front wheel arches on more than half lock can be heard and felt.

Though the steering is heavy at low speeds, once the speed picks up, the effort lightens and the gearing is seen to be more designed for high speed than low. The absence of lost motion in the steering allied to good response from the Michelin tyres gives direct reaction to any steering inputs and the car is easy and satisfying to place accurately on the road.

The rearward weight distribution, generous tyre sections and a limited slip differential all combine to give excellent traction on dry and wet roads alike and only sensible caution need be used to avoid wheelspin from rest or in tight low speed manoeuvres.

Noise

Current 308 Dinos have a revised air cleaner arrangement that reduces intake noise considerably compared with earlier examples. There is still some engine noise, however, which does not reduce appreciably until the car is cruising on a light throttle at speeds over 80 mph. An annoying reverberation occurs at a true 70 mph though it is absent 10 mph either side of this speed. Under hard acceleration, the exhaust note is a beautiful sound starting as a deep burble and ending as a muted shriek as the revs rise over 7,000 rpm. The noise is more noticeable to bystanders than to the car's occupants, however, and some caution may be necessary at certain times to avoid drawing too much unwanted attention to the car.

Brakes

Ventilated discs all round with servo assistance and a pressure regulating valve in the rear of the split circuits adds up to the requirements for braking in keeping with the Dino's performance. In practice, they proved well up to the task with an ability to claw the car down from high speeds repeatedly. Our normal fade test proved only that the brakes are speed sensitive and that their action is mildly over-servoed. On the road, this fact takes a minimum of time to come to terms with and pedal efforts are low. The performance of the brakes is progressive with a need for 80 lb to give an optimum stop at 0.95 g limited by front-wheel locking.

As frequently happens, the handbrake was good enough to hold the car on a 1-in-4 slope yet only capable of producing retardation on its own of 0.23 g (illegal in cars over three years old).

There is the slightest of tyre whine and some bump-thumping over cat's eyes and lateral road imperfections, this effect increasing if the recommended high speed tyre pressures are used. At those recommended for speeds up to 95 mph, the noise is perfectly acceptable.

The transmission does not give off any noise that can be discerned from the inside of the car.

Fixtures and fittings

The four seats are trimmed in a combination of suede-like material for the centre sections and leather-cloth for the edges and bases. This combination is repeated in the doors where the backs of the useful map pockets in each are trimmed in the suede material.

A full set of instruments are clearly in view to the driver through the handsome Momo leather-rimmed steering wheel. Taking pride of place are matching speedometer and rev counter, the former having total and trip mileage counters. Flanking these are individual gauges for petrol tank contents and engine oil temperature while between are gauges for water temperature, oil pressure and also an accurate clock. Tall drivers will find the top sections of the rev counter and speedometer are out of sight and when driving in the recommended "ten to two" position for the hands on the steering wheel, the engine oil temperature gauge is partially obscured.

The end panels of the instrument binnacle are angled in towards the driver and have on them the switchgear for the heater towards the centre of the car and the switches for the foglamp, hazard warning and the single speed heater fan on the outside.

On the facia top are three directional air outlets that double as demist and fresh air vents. Closing these gives more air to an equivalent pair of vents beneath the facia that supply air to the footwells. Running down the centre of the car is a tunnel whose height and width are governed by the pipes for the front-mounted radiator that are within. On the top of this tunnel are mounted the switches for the electric windows, the cigarette lighter, the heated rear window switch (with telltale), the ashtray (lit at night), the choke and (when fitted) the radio/cassette unit which has a separate switch for elevating the electrically-driven radio aerial.

The pedal layout is near ideal with one reservation. The accelerator has a treadle pedal and its action is so smooth that it is easy to release toe pressure on it while

leaving the heel still in contact. The result can be that the speed is not reduced as much as might be expected and this effect is exaggerated by some modern shoes with higher heels. To the left of the clutch pedal there is a welcome rest for the left foot—a good conversion detail to right hand drive.

Also converted to right hand drive are the windscreen wipers and also the releases for the front bonnet (below the facia on the right outside edge), and also the releases for the engine cover and boot which are positioned in the driver's door jamb and can be locked.

The roomy glovebox is also lockable and its bulky lid folds back through 180 deg. to reveal the fuse boxes and a vanity mirror which is press-studded to the inside of the lid. On the right hand side of the glovelocker is a socket for a useful map/wander light but try as we might, we could not get the plug into the socket of the test car.

All 308 Dinos are fitted with static front and rear seat belts that are comfortable to wear but fiddly to put on and adjust. The absence of a B-post makes the fitting of inertia reel belts difficult but they are an unfortunate omission for such a car these days. A further safety consideration is the fitment of head restraints on both front and rear seats, those on the front seats being adjustable for height.

The powerful four-headlamp system is operated by the left hand of the two steering column stalks, the first rotary movement of which turns on the sidelights, the first vertical downward movement bringing up the electric-motor elevated headlamp units and a further downward movement giving main beam. For daylight flashing, a pull towards the wheelrim of the lights stalk flashes the underbumper foglights.

Living with the
Ferrari Dino 308 GT4 2+2

All stock Dino 308GT4s come into the UK with electric windows, heated rear window and tinted glass as "standard" extras, as it were. You can have a car without these, but to special order only. The total cost of these items comes to £195.34 and to this extra cost can be added air conditioning for £374.40; a charge for metallic paint of £152.10; an all leather interior may be specified at an extra cost of £301.86 to which might be added a sunroof for £265.59 and wide wheels for £222.30. The total of these items comes to over £1,500 which could take the new price on the road to over £11,000.

However, even in base form, the Dino is well equipped and even the heated rear window is of questionable value and was never needed during our test period. The electric windows are a good idea if only that the extreme width of the car puts the passenger's window winder out of reach of the driver.

For two adults, there is room and comfort in plenty with generous rearward adjustment for the front seats and infinite rake adjustment for the seat backs.

Considered as more than just a two seater, the position is not as rosy and front and rear seat passengers must compromise considerably if all are to travel in any comfort. It is worth recording that we used the car as a four seater on several occasions during the test period, albeit for short journeys only.

The driving position of a Ferrari is unique. It is typically Italian with the pedal positions closer to a point directly below the steering wheel than usual. It is also necessary to sit closer to the steering wheel than usual because its relatively flat angle requires more of a "push-pull" action. However, even with a minimum of familiarisation, a comfortable seating position can be found and it is a tribute to this and to the undoubted comfort of the seats that long distances can be covered without aches and pains being experienced afterwards.

From the outside, the rear quarter pillars give the impression of limited visibility but in practice there is only a problem at some angle junctions. The view forwards through the steeply raked windscreen is commanding and all but the last foot or so of the nose is in sight. To the rear, the driver can just see the top edge of the tail panel and the car is as easy to manoeuvre as the dreadful turning circle allows.

At night the powerful headlamps give good performance on dipped and main beam and the low-mounted fog lights are very effective as we had good reason to find in foggy, misty Germany while waiting to complete the maximum speed runs.

The long windscreen wipers leave few important unwiped areas though the small windscreen washer reservoir needs frequent replenishment if the washers are used continually. There is little need for a means of washing the headlamps as in their stowed position they keep clean and dry. Adjustment to the headlamps requires screwdriver attention from the front and to remove the headlamps requires prior removal of the bezel. In the event of a headlamp lift motor malfunction, the headlamps can still be raised by manual operation of the electric motor.

The same is true of the motors for the electric windows which can be cranked up manually once a grommet is removed from the door trim.

On-journey stowage inside the Dino is generous with map pockets and the glovebox in the front and three pockets in the rear of the car in which the unused seat belts can be stowed as well.

The low build of the Ferrari makes getting in and out difficult, especially since a normal sitting position leaves the front seat very much at the front of the door opening. It can help to slide the seat right back on its runners when getting out to make the task of getting back in easier. The backs of the front seats fold flat onto the seat cushions and allow tolerable access to the rear of the car but again, the low build makes the operation difficult for those who are not too agile.

The heating system is far from matching the performance of the rest of the car in that it is slow to give heated air when the car is started from cold and the extremely sensitive water valve results in control being possible over only ½in. of the 3in. travel of the control lever. As there is no fresh air venting system as such, it is not possible to have warm air for the foot wells and cool air at head level and the ease with which the side windows mist up proves that the extraction is lacking too. There are individual controls for air distribution for each side of the car and some or all of the ventilation flaps can be closed as necessary. Having tried a car with the optional air conditioning system it should be said that this gives great improvements, though naturally the difficulties of fine control over heated air remain.

Reasonable accommodation for luggage is given by the deep, regular-shaped and fully-trimmed boot. It is deep enough to accept a large-size suitcase standing on end and a set of golf clubs can be stowed with ease. Supplementing the rear boot is a limited amount of space beneath the bonnet where tools or lightweight over-clothing might be stowed. Also beneath the bonnet is the skimpy "get-you-home" spare wheel which is legal as it is of radial ply construction. Though the recommended maximum speed on this tyre is 90 mph, its narrow section limits roadholding and braking on that corner of the car on which it is fitted.

Access to the power unit is good enough for items requiring routine attention, other more serious items are not so easy to reach. The alternator particularly is buried away deep in the engine bay and any attention to the gearbox or transmission will require above-average time allowance. However, you do not pay nearly £10,000 to have mechanical anxieties and it should be recorded that at no time did the power unit or its ancillaries give the slightest cause for worry. Though it needs several seconds of churning to bring it to life when it is hot, the engine always started and ran smoothly though we were warned to avoid using choke from cold on pain of death (or a prolonged and contorted session at plug-changing).

Conclusions

In the respects that you would expect a Ferrari to be good, the Dino impresses greatly. The smoothness and lack of temperament of the power unit belie the high specific output that it produces. With slight reservation over the choice of steering ratio the handling and roadholding are of the highest order.

The design and execution of the details of the car are good though it was disappointing to notice signs of rusting on the nave plates and rear bumper of the young test car.

Who can say whether it is worth its high price?

To anyone who values performance (at quite reasonable prime running cost) the Dino can sell itself but to those looking for value for money, there are a number of strong rivals, as the comparison table clearly reveals.

Beauty is in the eye of the beholder and there is little doubt that most people approve of the neat good looks and the test car's bright yellow paintwork looked resplendent. But beauty is not everything and there are areas notably of heating, ventilation and manoeuvrability, where the car disappoints and where development appears to have been hurried or inadequate. This is in contrast to our own Jaguar XJS which does everything that the Ferrari can, and more, yet costs less to buy. It is nonetheless encouraging that there are still really good cars available in this exclusive corner of the market.

8 DINO 308GTB—Autocar, GB

Ultimate Grand Touring car for two very lucky people. Fast, obviously; economical, surprisingly; comfortable, thankfully; quiet, usually; infuriating, sometimes; satisfying, most times; self-expressive, always. Outrageously appealing—outrageously expensive but still the best Ferrari yet.

A Ferrari is on most people's list when the disposal of a big Pools win is under discussion. The stuff of which such reputations are made is, in the sports car world anyway, a combination of high performance, superb roadholding, a cossetting interior, and the best of good looks. On each of these counts, the Ferrari Dino 308 GTB scores most of the points that are there to be won.

Of course, there are shortcomings. The price, for a start, is enough to ensure that the Pools win must be a big one. There are others. Like the mistaken choice of facia covering that allows bad reflections in the windscreen, and the fact that the beautiful lines spell out "design triumphs over engineering" to the extent that there is not room for a proper spare wheel. But let us see the car in context:

Two-seater cars in the class of the Ferrari are ultimate expressions of hedonism. Most of the time, circumstances—speed limits and sensible caution—keep the car well among the herd where something less exotic would do the job just as well. But it is when the open road beckons, when a touch of adrenalin is wanted and the spirits need to soar, that a car like this particular Ferrari is the best tonic available. We should not support that aspect of the pursuit of pleasure that seeks for flattery but there is no mistaking the admiring looks of passers-by of any age and the questioning yet furtive look inside the car to query, "who is the lucky so-and-so who owns that?"

About the Dino 308 GTB

When the Ferrari Dino 308 GTB 2+2 coupé was brought out to succeed the Dino 246 GT, not all enthusiasts approved. Admittedly, the presence of two reasonable short-journey rear seats widened the appeal of the successor, but in finding space for them, some of the unmistakable goods looks of the first Dino were inevitably lost. Morale among the disappointed Ferrari

fans was boosted with rumours of a two-seater version, and boosted still further when it became known that the design would be executed by Pininfarina, the architect of the first much-loved Dino production mid-engined car. Sneak pictures from Italy at the beginning of last year revealed a long, low, dart-shaped body with a below-nose spoiler and just the hint of a tail-end spoiler on the engine lid. Not surprisingly, when the 308 GTB was shown at the Paris and London Shows a year ago, it was swamped with admirers.

The 308 GTB is the first production Ferrari to feature glass-fibre for the complete construction of the body. The standard of finish is superb, with little or no hint that the material used is out of the ordinary. The glass-fibre body is constructed by Scaglietti who, as well as producing the "Lightweight" light-alloy versions of earlier Ferraris also makes all the bodywork for the Ferrari Formula 1 racing cars as well as the glass-fibre sections used on other road cars in the range (the Boxer has the nose underside constructed in plastic).

Very much of two-seater design, the 308 GTB has little room even for discarded coats in the cockpit, and requires a wide central tunnel to take water cooling pipework to the front of the car and the gearchange and handbrake linkages to the back. Naturally, the overall height of the car at only 3 ft 10 in. could pose problems, but the very reclined seating position, wide door opening, and minor intrusion of the roof into the door opening in the vertical plane all combine to allow entry, exit, and the seating position, to be comfortable.

Suspension details of the Dino 308 GTB parallel those of the GT4 2+2, with double wishbones and coil springs front and rear as well as substantial anti-roll bars at both ends. The low body lines do not permit very much suspension travel, and the need to control roll is very important.

The familiar 3-litre V8 dohc engine is mounted transversely in the middle of the car, and the drive is taken from the left end of the engine via the clutch to a set of drop gears that reverse the direction of drive from right-to-left back to left-to-right towards the five-speed all-synchromesh gearbox. The gears sit in their own separate sump partitioned off from the engine sump. The final drive has a limited-slip differential as standard.

Both the 308 GT4 2+2 and 308 GTB Dino engines produce the same power output of 255 bhp (SAE net) at 7,700 rpm. In the case of the GTB, however, dry sump

308GTB at speed but steady as a rock

oil lubrication is employed, taking the oil capacity up from 16 to 19½ pints. The reasons for the adoption of dry sump lubrication are legion but added oil cooling capacity, a reduction in engine height, avoidance of oil surge, and greater possibilities for racing development are just a few that influenced the change. As well as the high specific output of the Ferrari's engine, it should not be forgotten that the V8 configuration, at 3-litres capacity, in a car only weighing 25.6 cwt, allows the benefits of considerable torque to be enjoyed. The maximum torque given is 210 lb. ft. at 5,000 rpm, and such a high figure means that one is not always changing gear to sustain rapid progress.

A significant difference between the GT4 2 + 2 and the GTB is the wheelbase, which is 8½ in. shorter in the two-seater. However, most of this shortening in the chassis is recovered by the longer nose and tail, and the overall length of the two cars is within 2¾ in. The GTB is ½ in. wider than the 2 + 2 and no less than 3½ in. lower. Suspension details are shared, with unequal length wishbones, coil springs, telescopic dampers all round, and anti-roll bars front and rear.

The body shape of the 308 GTB demands that it can only be a two-seater, but the long tail does permit reasonable luggage accommodation. To get at the boot, one must first raise the engine cover and, with this out of the way, a neat, zipped, pvc cover can be opened to reveal a deep, full width, carpeted area in which the jack, wheelbrace and toolkit also live. There is additional minimal luggage space beneath the front bonnet and again, the contents of the luggage area are kept clean beneath a zipped cover

Performance and economy

Favourable weight distribution, good aerodynamic shape, excellent gearing and the unusually high power-to-weight ratio ensure that the Ferrari gives exceptional performance. The speeds that it can attain are deceptively fast since there is little or no wind and road noise. For this reason, one could be forgiven for imagining subjectively that the noisier GT4 2 + 2 is quicker. To dispel this thought, the performance figures for the bigger car are given in brackets in the details that follow.

Wide tyres, the limited slip differential, and inherently good traction ensure that the step-off from rest (even when searching for ultimates) is without drama. Dropping the clutch sharply with the engine revs at 4,500 rpm gives enough immediate wheelspin to give the clutch an easier time. While the revs stay approximately the same, the wheels catch up within 20 ft or so, when all slack is taken up and the car rockets forward towards the maximum engine speed allowed of 7,700 rpm. First gear takes you to 44 mph, passing 30 mph in just 2.3 sec (2.5 sec) and 40 mph in 3.3 sec (3.6 sec). First gear is out to the left and back in the gated six-position gearchange, but there is enough strong spring centring to ensure that the change up to second gear can be as fast as the hand can move. The improved synchromesh cannot be beaten, and the only considerations that can slow the change are the need for full clutch clearance for each upward (or downward) change and the inertia of the long linkage. 2nd gear takes you onwards to 65 mph with the magic 60 mph mark coming up in 6.5 sec (6.9 sec), when it is time to snatch the gearlever hastily back into 3rd gear to rush the car onwards to 92 mph. 80 mph is reached in the amazing time of 10.8 sec (11.4 sec) and the better shape and lower weight of the 2-seater begin to be noticeable. The change to 4th gear is again a dog-leg forward and out to the right, taking care to push deliberately against the spring pressure. 100 mph comes up quickly in just 17.0 sec (18.1 sec), the ¼-mile mark having passed in

14.8 sec (14.9 sec) at 93 mph (89 mph). 4th gear is good for 124 mph, 120 mph passing in just 25.0 sec (30.3 sec)—perhaps half the time it has taken you to read this paragraph.

Acceleration in each gear reveals the useful spread of torque, as well as the absence of snatch in the driveline or holes in the torque curve. One can accelerate from as low as 10 mph in third gear, and there is no feeling that fifth gear should be used as an overdrive, since you can pull away strongly in this gear from 30 mph. As one would hope in this sort of car, the gear ratios are ideally chosen, the gaps closing up progressively the higher you go to overcome aerodynamic resistance.

When measuring the maximum speed, a long run in was needed before the car would settle on 7,050 rpm (7,150 rpm on the test car's slightly optimistic instrument), equivalent to 154 mph. This is some 4 mph less than Ferrari's claim. (It should be pointed out that our figures were found with overnight luggage and other test gear aboard which, in a car with a rear boot, can be enough to bring the nose up and to knock off the last few mph.) Such a speed is only attainable in quite still air, the slightest cross wind leading to very disconcerting weaving at speeds in excess of 130 mph.

Naturally, one pays a penalty for such performance in fuel consumption. The overall figure of 19.2 mpg is, however, good for the class, and results from a more-than-average amount of open road driving and would not be matched if much urban running was included. The best return was a laudable 25.6 mpg over 270 miles while keeping pace with returning holiday traffic in Germany, when more than 80 mph was out of the question. By contrast, the worst result included the performance testing at MIRA, which increased the consumption to little over 17 mpg. The *Autocar* economy formula gives an excellent guide to the economy potential of this particular test car, and one would expect careful owners to better 20 mpg regularly. Thus, with $16\frac{1}{4}$ gal available in the balanced, twin fuel tanks, the range between fuel stops could be as high as 300 miles; there is no excuse for running out as there is a reserve of 3.3 gal whose use is indicated by a warning lamp in the fuel gauge face. When filling the twin tanks only one filler is used, its screw cap and thoughtful anti-spill bib being hidden behind a louvred flap on the left-hand quarter panel; only the last one-third of a gallon takes extra time to get in.

Though the handbook suggests that an oil consumption of 600 miles per pint may be expected, the test car did not use a measurable amount of multigrade.

Ride, handling and roadholding

The aesthetically satisfying lines of the 308 cannot promise very much wheel travel, and the suspension settings for both springs and dampers are necessarily hard. At low speeds on less than smooth surfaces, the 308 GTB's ride is very bumpy, with potholes giving rise to much crashing and banging. However, once into the mid-range of the car's performance the ride improves greatly, and only the worst of undulations are not soaked up adequately. At very high speed the ride gives great confidence, with no tendency to pitch, and not a trace of float. Under most conditions the handling is reassuring too, though there is a strong tendency to follow camber changes, especially at the front of the car and a strong grip on the steering wheel should be avoided. There is some kickback evident through the steering, and Ferrari argue that some is necessary to give the necessary feel to the steering. One can accept this—the steering gives all the right messages to the hands to tell what the front wheels are doing. Since the predominant characteristic is extra understeer with extra speed, the feeling of increased weight in the steering felt at the steering wheel rim is very pleasantly *pro rata*. Though 3.3 turns of the wheel from lock-to-lock might suggest high-geared steering, one must not lose sight of the dreadful turning circle of around 40 ft. The steering ratio could well be higher still without making parking-speed manoeuvring impossibly heavy.

On the move, the steering is about right, the slightly low gearing helping to avoid any suddenness in the steering reaction. Provided that the air is still high natural stability is not affected. The behaviour in crosswinds was criticised earlier.

While the handling has been praised generally, it would not be right to leave the subject without reference to throttle open/throttle closed response. While the natural tendency is to understeer, if the accelerator is released in mid-corner the resultant weight transfer does lead to an immediate tightening of the line. This is, of course, no penalty under most conditions (and can be used to advantage) but some caution is needed on wet or slippery roads. Once the natural understeer has been killed by lifting off the accelerator, immediate application of power can be used to set up a very satisfying four-wheel drift which will please the skilled and determined driver immensely. However, the relatively short wheelbase and low polar moment of inertia of the design means that extreme angles of drift cannot be held despite the quickness and accuracy of the steering.

Michelin XWX radial ply tyres, of 70 per cent profile and 205 section, give excellent roadholding and splendid traction on wet surfaces. They are guilty of mild bump-thumping which suspension compliance does not completely isolate from the car's occupants, but it is not possible to make the tyres squeal. There is only one recommended tyre pressure setting for all speeds and load conditions, and owners may wish to play around with slightly lower pressures to improve the ride—having little effect on roadholding through maintaining the same differential between front and rear settings. The gains to be made by trying this are marked since the recommended settings are a compromise, leaning towards the full performance potential rather than that which road conditions generally permit.

Brakes

Ventilated disc brakes of generous diameter and thickness are used for all four wheels, and the hydraulic circuit to them is split front-and-rear. A single in-line servo serves for both circuits, the rear of which has a pressure-limiting valve. The handbrake warning light doubles as an indicator of fluid loss from either circuit. The handbrake operates a rather ineffective mechanical linkage to the rear inboard pads.

Though at low speeds there is a feeling that the braking system is over-servoed, this is only to ensure bite from the hard linings and well-cooled discs. At speed such feelings disappear, and the system gives reassuring performance through close progression in efficiency with increased pedal effort, coupled to total resistance to fade. A pedal pressure of 80 lb is needed to produce an optimum 1.00 g, while only just under half this is needed to give 0.50 g when the brakes are cold. As they warm, the pressure required reduces slightly, levelling out at 20/25 lb for 0.50 g and 60 lb for 1.00 g. The handbrake could only hold the car on a 1-in-4 incline and returned an entirely inadequate 0.22 g when used on its own as an emergency brake.

Noise

Such evident refinement as the comfort of the interior of the Ferrari and its eye-catching exterior would be spoilt by an excess of noise. Suffice it to say that the noises the GTB makes are all pleasant ones. The exhaust note is well subdued at most speeds and only full acceleration in confined surroundings could annoy anyone. The note itself is very close to that of the Big Valve Ford Twin-Cam, particularly as installed in the Lotus Elan Sprint. There is just the slightest increase in wind noise at speed and this is not enough to require the radio volume to be turned up.

Only the lowest fan speed of the optional air conditioning is acceptably quiet but higher fan speeds for the system are only required for strictly limited periods.

Equipment and accommodation

As one should surely expect at the price, the Ferrari is well-equipped. Electric windows, tinted glass, a laminated windscreen with tinted top section, heated rear window and leather upholstery are all standard. The options list is confined to air-conditioning, metallic body paint, and wide-rim wheels (carrying tyres of the same size).

Once in the seats the occupants are comfortably positioned, with generous rearward and backrest rake adjustment. Ahead of the driver, there is a very full complement of clear, round instruments, including a speedometer with inset trip and total mileometers (but no kph equivalents), rev counter, and three smaller dials

for oil pressure, fuel contents, and water temperature set between them. Set in the binnacle that houses the main instruments is the warning lamp for the hazard warning flashers, as well as a matching warning lamp for generator charge. Set low down to the right of the facia are two further instruments—an oil temperature gauge and a clock.

Major function controls are operated by three fingertip stalks, with wash/wipe to the right of the steering wheel and indicators and lights controls to the left. The splendid air horns are operated by a horn-push in the centre of the Momo leather-trimmed steering wheel. The steering/ignition lock is conveniently positioned to the right of the steering column (on the facia edge).

On the facia-top, there are three rotating air vents that have flaps which allow the air to be directed. These air vents are supplemented by two vents on the central console that can be used for conditioned air only. In normal Ferrari practice, the air distribution to each side of the car via the car's heating system is individually adjustable though there is only one fan to boost either or both sides. There is a single temperature control for the car's water-valve heating system and two rotating controls for the air-conditioning, one to select temperature and the other to control air-flow speed. All the controls for heating, ventilation, and air-conditioning are positioned on a panel between the seats formed by the top of the central tunnel. At its front, the tunnel has the gated gear change, an illuminated ashtray, a cigarette lighter, and the choke control lever. The front three of the centrally-mounted switches on the tunnel control the heated rear window, the heater fan, and the speed of the windscreen wipers—intermittent and continuous wiping being available on high or low speeds.

On rhd Ferraris, the releases for the front and rear compartment lids are both brought to the driver's side of the car—both releases have an emergency pull should the main one break. Also unique to Ferraris sold in the UK is a Maranello-converted circuit for the electric windows, which allows them to be operated with the ignition switched off.

Other sensible details that show care for rhd owners includes windscreen wiper conversion, a footrest for the left foot alongside the clutch pedal, and transfer of the operating switches for both side windows to the padded roll that forms the top of the driver's door trim.

The big foot pedals are arranged to allow heel-and-toe action with an organ pedal-type accelerator. The driving position is typical Italian with a steering wheel set fairly flat and the need to adopt a knees-up/arms stretched driving position.

Living with the Ferrari 308 GTB

Cars with high cruising speed potential are wasted if they are not used for long journeys. Too often, such potential is spoilt by inadequate comfort, noise, and tiring controls. In the Ferrari's case, only two serious

Maximum Speeds

Gear	mph	kph	rpm
Top (mean)	154	248	7.050
(best)	154	248	7.050
4th	124	200	7.700
3rd	92	148	7.700
2nd	65	104	7.700
1st	44	71	7.700

Acceleration

True mph	Time secs	Speedo mph
30	2 3	28
40	3 3	40
50	5 1	50
60	6 5	61
70	8 7	71
80	10 8	81
90	13 8	91
100	17 0	102
110	20 4	112
120	25 0	124

Standing ¼-mile:
14.8 sec, 93 mph
Standing kilometre:
26.9 sec, 124 mph

mph	Top	4th	3rd	2nd
10-30	—	—	5 1	3 3
20-40	—	6 4	4 1	2 7
30-50	9 5	5 5	3 5	2 6
40-60	8 4	5 0	3 6	4 8
50-70	7 8	5 1	3 6	—
60-80	7 2	5 1	3 9	—
70-90	7 7	5 5	4 4	—
80-100	8 8	6 0	—	—
90-110	9 2	6 7	—	—
100-120	10 2	8 0	—	—

Consumption

Fuel
Overall mpg: 19.2
(14 7 litres/100km)

Constant speed: No figures; system incompatible with Test equipment

Autocar formula
Hard driving, difficult conditions
17 mpg
Average driving, average conditions
21 mpg
Gentle driving, easy conditions
25 mpg
Grade of fuel: Premium, 4-star
(98 RM)
Mileage recorder 2 5 per cent over reading

Oil
Consumption (SAE 10W/50) Negligible

Brakes

Fade (from 70 mph in neutral)
Pedal load for 0.5g stops in lb

	start/end		start/end
1	25-30	6	30-25
2	25-30	7	20-20
3	30-35	8	20-20
4	35-35	9	20-25
5	30-30	10	20-25

Response from 30 mph in neutral

Load	g	Dist.
20lb	0 25	120 0ft
40lb	0 50	60 0ft
60lb	0 75	40 0ft
80lb	1 00	30 1ft

Handbrake 0 22   137 0ft
Max. gradient 1-in-4

Clutch   Pedal 60lb and 7in

Test Conditions

Wind 0-5 mph
Temperature 18 deg C (65 deg F)
Barometer 29 4 in Hg
Humidity 20 per cent
Surface dry asphalt and concrete
Test distance 2,400 miles

Figures taken at 9,400 miles by our own staff at the Motor Industry Research Association proving ground at Nuneaton, and on the Continent

All Autocar test results are subject to world copyright and may not be reproduced in whole or part without the Editor's written permission

Regular Service

Interval

Change	3,000	6,000	12,000
Engine oil	Yes	Yes	Yes
Oil filter	No	Yes	Yes
Gearbox oil	No	Check	Yes
Spark plugs	No	Check	Yes
Air cleaner	No	No	Yes
C/breaker	No	Check	Yes
Total cost	**36.13**	**54.53**	**110.07**

(Assuming labour at £4 30/hour)

Parts Cost

(including VAT)
Brake pads/shoes (2 wheels)
— front   £10 60
Brake pads/shoes (2 wheels)
— rear   £8 80
Silencer(s)   £223 56
Tyre — each
(typical advertised)   £66 12
Windscreen   £198 72
Headlamp unit   £18 00
Front wing (nose section
complete)   £358 60

Warranty Period
12 months unlimited mileage

Weight

Kerb. 25 6 cwt/2 870 lb/1 300 kg
(Distribution F/R 41/59)
As tested 28 7 cwt/3 220 lb/1 460 kg
Boot capacity: 8 6/1 4 cu ft
Turning circles:
Between kerbs L. 40ft 8in, R. 40ft 6in
Between walls L. 42ft 6in, R. 42ft 4in
Turns, lock to lock 3.3

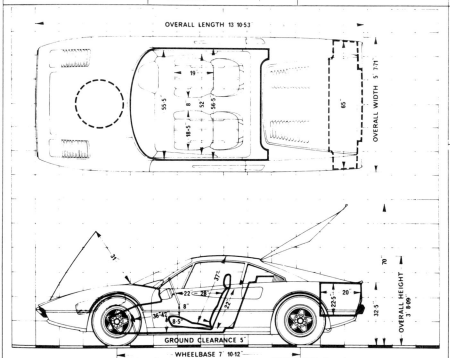

GROUND CLEARANCE 5"
OVERALL LENGTH 13 10·53"
OVERALL WIDTH 5 7·71"
OVERALL HEIGHT 3 8·09"
FRONT TRACK 4 9·87"
WHEELBASE 7 10·12"
REAR TRACK 4 9·48"

Test Scorecard

(Average of scoring by *Autocar* Road Test team)

Ratings:
6 Excellent
5 Good
4 Better than average
3 Worse than average
2 Poor
1 Bad

PERFORMANCE	4 83
STEERING AND HANDLING	4 58
BRAKES	4 00
COMFORT IN FRONT	3 75
DRIVERS AIDS	3 75
(instruments, lights, wipers, visibility etc.)	
CONTROLS	3 75
NOISE	4 83
STOWAGE	3 00
ROUTINE SERVICE	3 10
(under-bonnet access, dipstick etc.)	
EASE OF DRIVING	4 00
OVERALL RATING	**3.97**

Comparisons

Car	Price £	max mph	0.60 sec	overall mpg	capacity c.c.	power bhp	wheelbase in.	length in.	width in.	kerb weight	fuel gall	tyre size
Ferrari 308 GTB	**11,997**	**154**	**6.5**	**19.2**	**2,927**	**255(SAE)**	**94**	**156½**	**67¾**	**25.6**	**16¼**	**205/70x14**
Lamborghini Urraco S	9 434	143	8 5	18 7	2 463	200	96½	167¼	69½	25 8	17½	205/70x14
Jaguar XJS	10 507	153	6 9	15 4	5 343	285	102	191¾	70½	34 8	19	205/70x15
Porsche Turbo 3 0	17 500	153	6 1	18 5	2 993	260	89½	169	69	22 4	17½	205-225/50x15
De Tomaso Pantera	11 500	159	6 2	13 0	5 763	330(gross)	99	168	72	27 8	19	185-215/70x15
Maserati Merak	9 430	135	8 2	17 4	2 965	190	102¼	171	70	28 5	18½	185-205/70x15

Specification

ENGINE

	Rear; rear drive
Cylinders	8, 90deg V
Main bearings	5
Cooling	Water
Fan	Electric
Bore, mm (in.)	81 (3.19)
Stroke, mm (in.)	71 (2.79)
Capacity, c.c. c.c. (in.)	2,927 (178.6)
Valve gear	Dohc
Camshaft drive	Toothed belt
Compression ratio	8.8-to-1
Octane rating	98RM
Carburettor	4 x Weber 40 DCNF
Max power	255 bhp (SAE) at 7,700 rpm
Max torque	210lb. ft. at 5,000 rpm

TRANSMISSION

Type	5-speed all synchromesh
Clutch	single dry plate

Gear	Ratio	mph/ 1,000 rpm
Top	0.918	21.8
4th	1.244	16.1
3rd	1.693	12.0
2nd	2.353	8.4
1st	3.418	5.8

Final drive gear	Helical spur (lsd standard)
Ratio	3.71-to-1

SUSPENSION

Front—location	Unequal length wishbones
springs	Coil
dampers	Telescopic
anti-roll bar	Yes
Rear—location	Unequal length wishbones
springs	Coil
dampers	Telescopic
anti-roll bar	Yes

STEERING

Type	Rack and pinion
Power assistance	None
Wheel diameter	14 in.

BRAKES

Front	10.8 in. dia. ventilated disc
Rear	11.0 in. dia. ventilated disc
Servo	Vacuum, direct-acting

WHEELS

Type	Cast light alloy
Rim width	6½ in
Tyres—make	Michelin XWX
— type	Radial ply tubeless
— size	205/70 VR 14 (105 R 18)

EQUIPMENT

Battery	12 volt 60 Ah
Alternator	55 amp
Headlamps	110/110 halogen
Reversing lamp	Standard
Hazard warning	Standard
Electric fuses	18 fuses, 11 relays
Screen wipers	2-speed + intermittent
Screen washer	Electric
Interior heater	Water valve
Interior trim	Leather seats, pvc headlining
Floor covering	Carpet
Jack	Screw parallelogram
Jacking points	2 each side
Windscreen	Laminated
Underbody protection	Grp body, mastic in wheel arches

MAINTENANCE

Fuel tank	16.3 Imp. galls. (74 litres)
Cooling system	31.6 pints (inc. heater)
Engine sump	19.4 pints SAE 10W/50
Gearbox	7 pints SAE 85W/90
Grease	4 points
Valve clearance	Inlet 0.008-0.010 in. (cold) Exhaust 0.012-0.014 in. (cold)
Contact breaker	0.012-0.015 in. gap
Ignition timing	6 deg BTDC (static) 33 deg BTDC (stroboscopic at 5,000 rpm)
Spark plug type	Champion N7Y
gap	0.024-0.028
Tyre pressures	F 28, R 34 (normal driving)

drawbacks take the pleasure out of long-distance touring. The least serious of these is the clutch pedal effort which, at 60 lb, is very much in the heavyweight class, and is made more wearing because full clutch travel of 7 in. is needed to engage the gears smoothly and quickly, and to avoid grating them when selecting reverse. The worst drawback concerns the choice of covering for the facia top. In either strong overhead lighting at night, or when heading towards the sun during the day, the reflections in the windscreen are bad enough to warrant being called a hazard.

All other aspects of comfort, like seats that do not cause aches, good visibility (except at angled junctions), and a wealth of on-board stowage space, may be taken for granted. The optional air-conditioning really spoils the occupants and, by mixing warmed air from the heating system, it is possible to get that elusive combination of warm air to the feet and cool air to the face.

Only short sections of the front and rear of the car are out of sight when manoeuvring, and the GTB is only slightly worse than its more prosaic GT4 2 + 2 brother in this respect. The wipers are not fast enough on the higher of their two speeds, and the contents of the washer bottle are soon used up. The halogen headlamps give splendid light on main and dipped beam, and are well up to the performance of the car. However, since the headlamps are stowed in electrically-retractable pods, they cannot be used for daylight flashing, there being no auxiliary lamps.

Starting the Ferrari's stirring engine should present no difficulties, provided some simple rules are observed. The choke need only be used in the coldest of weather, three dabs on the accelerator usually sufficing when starting from cold. When the engine is hot, just a third of the accelerator travel should be used to get started, being careful to avoid further movement of the accelerator before the engine has fired up. Despite its lengthy run, the accelerator linkage is excellent, giving smooth, progressive response that helps to avoid jerkiness in driving. Until the engine is warmed thoroughly, and especially when it has just come off the cold-start accelerator mechanism, full throttle at low revs should be avoided as there can be a sudden gulp and some hesitancy. There is a lesser, similar effect noticeable even when the engine is hot, when some hesitancy occurs in the transition from idle to main jets.

One imagines that engine access will not be too much of a problem to most owners of this rather expensive car. This is as well since the access is not good. To change the plugs on the front bank of cylinders would take all day, and there seems to be twice as much of everything as there needs to be. Two coils, two timing belt tensioners, two fuel filters, and two contact breakers all compound to frighten the life out of the average garage mechanic. In fact, with the help of the excellent handbook, all relevant service items could be handled by the enthusiastic owner/driver, and there would be great satisfaction in avoiding the high service costs shown in Service Details.

Such obvious items like the dipstick, brake fluid reservoirs, and battery are all easily accessible in either the front or rear of the car, and routine weekly checks pose no problems.

Little has been said so far in this test about the glass-fibre bodywork. The reason is simply that, if you did not know what the car was made of, you would never guess. There is no smell of glass-fibre, the doors shut with a delightful dull thud, there is no sign anywhere of star-crazing of the gel coat, and the finish of the paintwork is as good as that which can be expected on steel. There is the obvious advantage of saved weight, avoided minor parking blemishes, and absence of rusting. For these reasons as well as many others, the Ferrari Dino 308 GTB is guaranteed a place in treasured collections in the years ahead.

Conclusions

The Ferrari is so good in most respects that the areas of shortcomings stand out like sore thumbs. Maranello Concessionaires are working on an alternative facia covering to avoid the screen reflection problem, but there are still some areas that need improvement. The clutch pedal effort is unjustifiably high and out of character with the light weight of other controls. The large turning circle and length of the 308 do not allow for parking easily in confined spaces. When into a space, the absence of a check strap on the doors could allow them—and other cars—to be dented too easily while one struggles from the car. On the performance side, the loss of high speed stability in crosswinds is regrettable and hard to understand.

All round, one is lost in admiration for the superb quality of the mechanical engineering, the standard of finish of the body and interior details, and the all-round efficiency. It is the best Ferrari we have yet driven.

---

9 DINO 308GTB—Road & Track, USA

Everything about it says use me

Ferrariphiles take heart. If you're dismayed because Ferrari can't sell the Boxer in the U.S. and upset with the Dino 308's relatively sedate styling, we've got good news for you. The 308 GTB is everything you've come to expect from the Ferrari and more. True, it doesn't have the breathtaking performance of the big-engine 12-cylinder models, but if that's the only criterion you use for judging this latest Ferrari you might as well quit reading now. The trend these days is away from super powerful and super thirsty cars like the Boxer, Bora and Countach and toward smaller-engine cars stressing total refinement rather than brute power. And the 308 is a dramatic demonstration of how well Ferrari has coped with the pressing demands of emissions, safety, higher fuel prices and lower speed limits while retaining all the prestige and fun for which this marque has become famous.

The 2-seat 308 GTB supersedes the Dino 308 GT4 2 + 2 and in a sense is a successor to the Dino 246. Although it's not the first production model from Maranello with anything but a 12-cyl engine, it is the first Ferrari with other than a 12 to actually carry the Ferrari *name*. That might seem like a subtle distinction, but to image-conscious Americans that point is all important. Many are the 246 and 308 GT4 Dinos we've seen with Ferrari script embellishing the hood or rear deck.

Those who dismissed the Dino 308 GT4 with hardly a second glance have every reason to cheer the Ferrari 308 GTB. Stunning to look at, dramatic, sensuous and pleasant from every angle are just a few of the comments the Pininfarina styling elicited. The excellent finish also merits mention. The 308 GTB is the first production

Ferrari with a fibreglass body. The surface is smooth and ripple-free and the paint is as good as we've seen on the best steel-body cars. A real compliment. We've heard rumors that after the initial batch of glass-body 308 GTBs, production will be switched over to steel; if you like the weight saving and no-rust virtues of fibreglass you'd better place your order early.

Compared to the Dino 308, the 308 GTB is shorter, narrower, lower and lighter. But the only two significant differences are the 92.1 in. wheelbase—same as the Dino 246 and 8.4 in. less than the 308 GT4—and a 150 lb lighter curb weight which make for even more responsive steering and handling. Mechanically the 308 GTB has a lot in common with both its Dino predecessors. It's a transverse mid-engine design with a 5-speed transmission, independent suspension by unequal-length A-arms and coil springs all around and a vented disc brake at each corner. The major difference between the 246 and the 308s is the engine. Whereas the 246 has a 65-degree 2418 cc 4-cam V-6, the 308s have a 90-degree 2926 cc 4-cam V-8.

Entry and exit are about what you'd expect. The car is low and the sills are wide and you just don't slide into the hip-hugging bucket seats. But for an enthusiast the rewards are well worth the extra effort. However, this note of caution: Because of the unusual outside door latches, passengers tend to bend the latch over rather than pull it out from the door. Broken latches and friendships can be prevented with a word of warning.

Inside there's an instant race-car feeling. The leather-covered seats are those typical Ferrari comfortable lay-back buckets. The Dino 308 GT4 seats seem almost bolt upright in comparison. Stick out your hands and feet and you discover the padded steering wheel and the ideally positioned pedals. Move your right hand off the

wheel and it's drawn to the shift knob as if by a magnet. Major controls for lights, high beams and washer and wiper are logically arranged on steering column stalks.

Although some of the interior details are reminiscent of the Dino 246, modern design is evident in several areas. The sun visors are recessed (they don't pivot to the sides, however) into the headliner for a savings in headroom, and the dash is covered in black vinyl instead of a fuzzy dust-collecting material. Like the Lancia Scorpion the ends of the dash continue into door bolsters which conceal the inside door latches. But Ferrari carries the ideal one step further. In the 308 GTB the bolsters arch down the doors and double as armrests. They're comfortable yet they don't get in the way of the driver's arms when he's hard at work. Other thoughtful touches: a dead pedal to the left of the clutch, a metal kickplate to the right of the throttle pedal to prevent scuffing the vinyl covering on the console and the use of a glare-reducing brush finish on all chrome except around the ashtray.

Despite the lay-down driving position there's surprisingly good outward vision. You have to use caution when nosing the 308 GTB up close to another solid object and the rear quarters require above average attention, but otherwise the driver's view of the world around him is unobstructed.

Inadequate ventilation seems to be a fact of life for the exoticar buyer. The Dino 308 GT4 received better than passing grades in this critical comfort area and the Ferrari 308 is better still. The three round dash-top vents put out acceptable amounts of air once the car is at speed and, for around town driving, air flow can be boosted by a fan (one speed only). And for once some thought has gone into the design of the air-conditioning outlets. Besides the dash-top outlets there are two central below-dash vents that can be adjusted to blow cold air directly on the occupants. But a quieter fan would be appreciated.

Ferrari everywhere on this Dino 308GTB

The important gauges are grouped in a pod directly in front of the driver, but we were less enthusiastic about the positioning of the clock and oil temperature gauge. Both are tucked away under the dash on the driver's left and are hardly visible. The design of the small console box located between the seats is also illogical. The cover lacks a push-button latch so you always need a key to open it. And several drivers complained about the neck and gut grabbing restraint system.

There's a reason why the 308 GTB, with the same horsepower and less weight, is slower than its Dino counterpart. The engine is flexible and very tractable, even to the point of accepting lugging down to 2000 rpm in 5th gear without complaint, but tromp on the throttle from rest and the engine stumbles and sputters. Revving the engine and dropping the clutch was no solution; this resulted in nothing but clutch slip. The technique adopted consisted of driving away gently, bringing the revs up to 3000 rpm and then nailing the throttle. The 0–30 mph time is a second or more slower than it should be, a handicap the 308 GTB only began to overcome in the upper speed ranges.

It's amazing how Ferrari can make a V-8 sound so unique. It's not as silky smooth or melodious as a V-12 but neither does it sound like a typical throbbing high-performance Detroit V-8. The engine is mechanically noisy; but belt-driven cams and valve gear, induction hiss and some transfer-drive whine impart a tone that is music to an enthusiast's ears. The exhaust, however, is loud and harsh even for a Ferrari, and at a steady 55–60 mph cruise the droning gets to be a bit fatiguing. Above 80 mph the exhaust becomes much more pleasant!

As is typical of Ferraris, shifting can't be hurried. The gated shifter requires a deliberate and firm hand. Once the driver realizes things can't be rushed, the lever

ROAD TEST
FERRARI
308 GTB

SCALE: 10" DIVISIONS

PRICE

List price, west coast..........$29,525
List price, east coast..........$28,500
Price as tested, west coast $29,990
Price as tested includes standard
  equipment (air conditioning,
  leather upholstery, power windows), metallic paint ($315),
  dealer prep ($150)

IMPORTERS

Modern Classic Motors
Box 2026, Reno, Nevada 89505

Chinetti-Garthwaite Imports, Inc.
Paoli, Pennsylvania 19301

GENERAL

Curb weight, lb	3085
Test weight	3415
Weight distribution (with	
driver), front/rear, %	42/58
Wheelbase, in.	92.1
Track, front/rear	57.5/57.5
Length	166.5
Width	67.7
Height	44.1
Ground clearance	3.0
Overhang, front/rear	41.1/33.3
Usable trunk space, cu ft	5.3
Fuel capacity, U.S. gal.	21.1

ENGINE

Type	dohc V-8
Bore x stroke, mm	81.0 x 71.0
Equivalent in.	3.19 x 2.80
Displacement, cc/cu in.	2926/179
Compression ratio	8.8:1
Bhp @ rpm, net	240 @ 6600
Equivalent mph	138
Torque @ rpm, lb-ft	195 @ 5000
Equivalent mph	104
Carburetion	Four Weber (2V)
Fuel requirement	premium, 96-oct
Exhaust-emission control equipment:	
air injection, thermal reactor	

DRIVETRAIN

Transmission	5-sp manual
Gear ratios: 5th (0.95)	3.53:1
4th (1.24)	4.60:1
3rd (1.69)	6.27:1
2nd (2.37)	8.79:1
1st (3.58)	13.28:1
Final drive ratio	3.71:1

ACCOMMODATION

Seating capacity, persons	2
Seat width	2 x 19.0
Head room	35.5
Seat back adjustment, deg	30

CHASSIS & BODY

Layout ....mid engine/rear drive
Body/frame ...... tubular frame with
  separate fiberglass body
Brake system.......10.7-in. vented
  discs front, 10.9-in. vented discs
  rear; vacuum assisted
Swept area, sq in. 449
Wheels .... cast alloy, 14 x 7½
Tires ....Michelin XWX, 205/70VR-14
Steering type .... rack & pinion
  Turns, lock-to-lock 3.3
  Turning circle, ft 39.3
Front suspension: unequal-length A-
  arms, coil springs, tube shocks,
  anti-roll bar
Rear suspension: unequal-length A-
  arms, coil springs, tube shocks,
  anti-roll bar

INSTRUMENTATION

Instruments: 180-mph speedo,
  10,000-rpm tach, 99,999 odome-
  ter, 999.9 trip odo, oil press., oil
  temp, coolant temp, fuel level,
  clock
Warning lights: brake failure, parking brake, alternator, low fuel, fan
  on, rear-window heat, lights on,
  seatbelts, hazard, high beam, directionals

MAINTENANCE

Service intervals, mi:
Oil change	6000
Filter change	6000
Chassis lube	none
Tuneup	15,000
Warranty, mo/mi	12/10,000

CALCULATED DATA

Lb/bhp (test weight)	14.2
Mph/1000 rpm (5th gear)	20.7
Engine revs/mi (60 mph)	2900
Piston travel, ft/mi	1355
R&T steering index	1.30
Brake swept area, sq in./ton	263

RELIABILITY

From R&T Owner Surveys the average number of problem areas for all
models surveyed is 12. An average of
7 of these problem areas is considered serious enough to constitute
reliability areas that could keep the
car off the road. As owners of earlier-
model Ferraris reported 7 problem
areas and 4 reliability areas we
expect the overall reliability of the
Ferrari 308 GTB to be better than
average.

ROAD TEST RESULTS

ACCELERATION

Time to distance, sec:
0-100 ft	4.0
0-500 ft	9.6
0-1320 ft (¼ mi)	16.7

Speed at end of ¼ mi, mph .. 86.0
Time to speed, sec:
0-30 mph	3.9
0-40 mph	5.4
0-50 mph	7.4
0-60 mph	9.4
0-70 mph	12.0
0-80 mph	14.8
0-100 mph	22.6

SPEEDS IN GEARS

5th gear (6350 rpm)	132
4th (7700)	127
3rd (7700)	96
2nd (7700)	67
1st (7700)	43

FUEL ECONOMY

Normal driving, mpg	13.0
Cruising range, mi (1-gal. res)	261

HANDLING

Speed on 100-ft radius, mph	34.7
Lateral acceleration, g	0.804
Speed thru 700-ft slalom, mph	61.9

BRAKES

Minimum stopping distances, ft:
From 60 mph	163
From 80 mph	288

Control in panic stop........very good
Pedal effort for 0.5g stop, lb ... 20
Fade: percent increase in pedal
  effort to maintain 0.5g decelera-
  tion in 6 stops from 60 mph......nil
Parking: hold 30% grade? ...... no
Overall brake rating..................good

INTERIOR NOISE

All noise readings in dBA:
Idle in neutral	66
Maximum, 1st gear	85
Constant 30 mph	72
50 mph	75
70 mph	79
90 mph	82

SPEEDOMETER ERROR

30 mph indicated is actually .. 31.0
50 mph	49.0
60 mph	59.0
70 mph	69.0
80 mph	78.0
Odometer, 10.0 mi	9.7

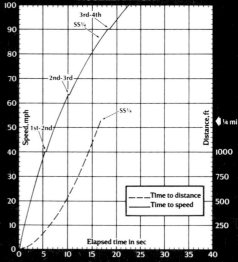

ACCELERATION

3rd-4th
SS¼
2nd-3rd
1st-2nd
SS¼
Speed, mph
Distance, ft
¼ mi

- - - Time to distance
—— Time to speed

Elapsed time in sec

falls into the proper gate with no fear of a missed shift. But when we shifted at the 7700 rpm redline, more often than not the lever slid into the proper gate but the transmission remained in neutral. An unhappy turn of events to say the least.

Balanced handling is what mid-engine cars are all about, and the 308 GTB is about the best balanced of any we have tested. The shorter wheelbase, lighter weight and the same-size Michelin XWX radials but 1 in. wider wheels make for even more precise and nimble response than the already excellent Dino 308. The new model is more than 3 mph faster through our slalom and was also marginally quicker around the skidpad. The latter performance was measured only in the normally slower clockwise direction because the oil pressure dropped to zero when the car was turning right and we terminated testing to avoid damaging the engine. The dry-sump lubrication Paul Frère wrote about (March 1976) would prevent such behavior, but unfortunately, this system isn't fitted to U.S. 308 GTBs.

The 308 corners with very little roll and the most predictable of mid-engine handling characteristics. At normal road speeds it's very neutral, at the limit there's mild understeer, and if you back off the throttle when cornering hard the 308 tightens its line slightly. This is a combination that results in a safe and predictable car for novice and experienced driver alike. The steering is marvelous, totally lacking the vague stiff action at low speeds that's normally a Ferrari characteristic. The steering is so direct, responsive and predictable the driver almost feels as if the tires are four rubber nerve endings transmitting just the right amount of road feel to the arms and brain.

The ride, as expected, is firm, well controlled and wonderfully supple. But the revised springing and damping result in a softer ride than the Dino 308 GT4.

The difference is most noticeable in the 308 GTB's dip-taking ability: It bottoms more easily than its Dino counterpart.

Installing the same size tires on wider wheels stretches the sidewalls and generally results in a stiffer ride. The 308 GTB's Michelins refute this generalization; the car has a softer ride over lane divider dots than the already impressive Dino 308.

In everyday use the 308 GTB's brakes score high grades. Pedal effort was not quite as positive or progressive as we like, but based on other Dinos we've tested we'd say this was the exception rather than the rule. More disturbing was the tendency toward front locking during panic stops. The 60–0 and 80–0 mph stopping distances were longer than we expect for a car of the Ferrari's speed potential because the driver had to modulate the pedal. This is not the best trait for a car that will be driven by people whose only credentials are good credit.

Many people will look at the Ferrari's nearly $30,000 price tag and wonder incredulously how any car could be worth that much. They don't realize that a car is more than the sum of its parts. To understand the 308 GTB you have to experience the sound of a 4-cam V-8 revving to 7000 rpm; or the elation of taking your favorite corner 10 mph faster than you ever did before and realizing, afterward, that you could have gone 10 mph faster; or the pure sensual joy of flying down the road at the speeds the car was designed to be driven at and exploring the limits of this fabulous machine.

Yes, the Ferrari 308 GTB offers a balanced blend of styling, performance, comfort, ride and handling few cars can match. But there's more to it than that. It's a blending of man and machine that makes the two feel and act as one. That's what makes the 308 GTB such a great car.

Dino racing record

This list includes all significant International and national events contested by Dino models in Formula 1, Formula 2, Tasman Formula and sports and prototype racing from 1957.... Many retired sports cars raced extensively in American events of little importance—only typical events are included owing to pressure of space.

1957

28-4-57 Naples GP, Posillipo, Italy

RESULT	DRIVER	GRID QUALIFI-CATION	MODEL	CHASSIS NUMBER
3rd	Luigi Musso	q3	156 F2	0011

14-7-57 Coupe de Vitesse, Reims-Gueux, France

1st	Maurice Trintignant	PP	156 F2	0011

22-9-57 Modena GP, Italy

2nd *Heat 1*	Luigi Musso	q3	1893 cc F1	0011
4th *Heat 1*	Peter Collins	q	1893 cc F1	0012
2nd *Heat 2*	Musso	q2		
4th *Heat 2*	Collins	q4		

Musso 2nd and Collins 4th on aggregate

27-10-57 Moroccan GP, Casablanca

Rtd	Peter Collins	q	246 F1	0012
Rtd	Mike Hawthorn	q	2195 cc F1	0011

1958

19-1-58 Argentine GP, Buenos Aires

2nd	Luigi Musso	q5	246 F1	0011
3rd	Mike Hawthorn	q2	246 F1	0001
Rtd	Peter Collins	q3	246 F1	0012

2-2-58 Buenos Aires City GP, Argentina

1st *Heat 1*	Mike Hawthorn *FL*	q4	245 F1	0001
3rd *Heat 1*	Luigi Musso	q6	246 F1	0011
Rtd *Heat 1*	Peter Collins	q5	246 F1	0012
Rtd *Heat 1*	Wolfgang von Trips	q7	246 F1	0002
3rd *Heat 2*	Musso	q3		
Rtd *Heat 2*	Hawthorn	PP		

DNS—Collins and Phil Hill, Trips having crashed the latter's car in Heat 1. Musso 2nd on aggregate

7-4-58 Sussex Trophy, Goodwood, UK

2nd	Peter Collins	–	206S sports	0740

Glover Trophy Formula 1

RESULT	DRIVER	GRID QUALIFI-CATION	MODEL	CHASSIS NUMBER
1st	Mike Hawthorn = *FL*	q3	246 F1	0003

13-4-58 Syracuse GP, Sicily

1st	Luigi Musso *FL*	PP	246 F1	0001

13-4-58 Trofeo Shell 2-litre Division races, Monza, Italy

1st *Heat 1*	Gino Munaron *FL*	PP	206S	0740
Rtd *Heat 2**	Gino Munaron			

*While leading—race won on aggregate by Colin Davis's 1500 OSCA

27-4-58 Naples GP, Posillipo, Italy

Rtd	Luigi Musso *FL*	PP	206S sports	0740

4-5-58 BRDC International Trophy, Silverstone, UK

1st	Peter Collins	q4	246 F1	0002

Sports Car Race

3rd	Mike Hawthorn	–	296S sports	0746

18-5-58 MONACO GP, Monte Carlo

2nd	Luigi Musso	q10	246 F1	0001
3rd	Peter Collins	q9	246 F1	0002
Rtd	Mike Hawthorn *FL*	q6	246 F1	0003
Rtd	Wolfgang von Trips	q12	246 F1*	0011

*Used 2-litre engine in practice, 2.4 in race

25-5-58 DUTCH GP, Zandvoort

5th	Mike Hawthorn	q6	246 F1	0003
7th	Luigi Musso	q12	246 F1	0001
Rtd	Peter Collins	q10	246 F1	0002

15-6-58 BELGIAN GP, Spa—Francorchamps

2nd	Mike Hawthorn *FL*	PP	246 F1	0003
6th	Olivier Gendebien	q6	246 F1	0011
Rtd	Peter Collins	q4	246 F1	0002
Rtd	Luigi Musso	q2	246 F1	0004

29-6-58 Two Worlds Trophy 500-Miles, Monza

Rtd*	Phil Hill	q12	'296MI'	0007

*Car failed in 63-lap Heat 1 'Prix Esso'—second heat being same-distance 'Prix Mobil'

6-7-58 FRENCH GP, Reims-Gueux

RESULT	DRIVER	GRID QUALIFI-CATION	MODEL	CHASSIS NUMBER
1st	Mike Hawthorn FL	PP	246 F1	0003
3rd	Wolfgang von Trips	q21*	246 F1	0002
5th	Peter Collins	q4	246 F1	0001
Rtd	†Luigi Musso	q2	246 F1	0004

*No practice time, †Fatal accident

19-7-58 BRITISH GP, Silverstone

1st	Peter Collins	q6	246 F1	0002
2nd	Mike Hawthorn FL	q4	246 F1	0003
Rtd	Wolfgang von Trips	q11	246 F1	0001

3-5-58 GERMAN GP, Nürburgring

4th	Wolfgang von Trips	q5	246 F1	0004
5th F2	Phil Hill	q10	156 F2	0011
Rtd	Mike Hawthorn	PP	246 F1	0003
Rtd	†Peter Collins	q4	246 F1	0002

†Fatal accident

24-8-58 PORTUGUESE GP, Oporto

2nd	Mike Hawthorn FL	q2	246 F1	0003
5th	Wolfgang von Trips	q6	246MI F1	0007

7-9-58 ITALIAN GP, Monza

2nd	Mike Hawthorn	q3	246 F1	'0005'*
3rd	Phil Hill FL	q7	246 F1	0004
Rtd	Wolfgang von Trips	q6	256 F1	0006*
Rtd	Olivier Gendebien	q5	246MI F1	0007

*See text

19-10-58 MOROCCAN GP, Casablanca

2nd	Mike Hawthorn	PP	256 F1	'0005'
3rd	Phil Hill	q5	246 F1	0004
Rtd	Olivier Gendebien	q6	246MI F1	0007

1958 World Championship Points Scores:

Hawthorn (total 49 points) 42 allowed on best six performances:
WORLD CHAMPION DRIVER
Collins (posthumous) 5th = with Harry Schell, 14 points
Musso (posthumous) 7th = with Maurice Trintignant, 12 points
Hill and von Trips 10th = with Jean Behra, 9 points

1959

18-4-59 Aintree '200', Liverpool, UK

1st	Jean Behra	q	256 F1	0004
2nd	Tony Brooks	q	246 F1	0003

25-4-59 Syracuse GP, Sicily

2nd	Jean Behra FL	q2	156 F2	0011

2-5-59 BRDC International Trophy, Silverstone, UK

4th	Phil Hill	q8	246 F1	0002
Rtd	Tony Brooks	q3	246 F1	0003

3-5-59 Coppa Sant'Ambroeus, Monza, Italy

1st	Giulio Cabianca*	–	196S sports	0740

*Scuderia Eugenio Castellotti entry

10-5-59 MONACO GP, Monte Carlo

RESULT	DRIVER	GRID QUALIFI-CATION	MODEL	CHASSIS NUMBER
2nd	Tony Brooks	q4	246 F1	0003
4th	Phil Hill	q5	246 F1	0002
Rtd	Cliff Allison	q15	156 F2	0011
Rtd	Jean Behra	q2	246 F1	0004

24-5-59 Targa Florio, Sicily

Rtd	Cabianca/Scarlatti	–	196S sports	0740

31-5-59 DUTCH GP, Zandvoort

5th	Jean Behra	q4	246 F1	0011
6th	Phil Hill	q12	246 F1	0003
9th	Cliff Allison	q15*	256 F1	0004
Rtd	Tony Brooks	q8	246 F1	0002

*No practice time

7-6-59 ADAC 1000 km, Nürburgring, Germany

Rtd	Cabianca/Scarlatti	–	196S sports	0740

20/21-6-59 Le Mans 24-Hours, Sarthe, France

Rtd	Cabianca/Scarlatti	–	196S sports	0740

3-7-59 FRENCH GP, Reims-Gueux

1st	Tony Brooks	PP	256 F1	0002
2nd	Phil Hill	q3	246 F1	0003
4th	Olivier Gendebien	q11	246 F1	0004
Rtd	Dan Gurney	q12	246 F1	0007
Rtd	Jean Behra	q5	246 F1	0011

Coupe de Vitesse Formula 2

Rtd	Cliff Allison	q2	156 F2	0012

2-8-59 GERMAN GP, AVUS, Berlin

1st Heat 1	Tony Brooks FL	PP	246 F1*	0002
2nd	Dan Gurney	q3	246 F1	0007
3rd	Phil Hill	q6	246 F1	0003
Rtd	Cliff Allison	q14**	246 F1	0004

*For reasons of driver psychology the '256' cam-covers had been replaced on the larger engines by standard '246' type. Which engines were in fact used remains unclear
**Reserve—not allowed to start Heat 2

1st Heat 2	Brooks	PP		
2nd	Hill	q3		
3rd	Gurney	q2		

Aggregate Result: 1st Brooks, 2nd Gurney, 3rd Hill

23-8-59 PORTUGUESE GP, Monsanto Park, Lisbon

3rd	Dan Gurney	q6	246 F1	0007
9th	Tony Brooks	q10	246 F1	0002
Rtd	Phil Hill	q7	246 F1	0003

23-8-59 Messina 300 km, Sicily

2nd	Giulio Cabianca	–	196S sports	0740

5-9-59 RAC Tourist Trophy, Goodwood, UK

Rtd	Scarlatti/Scarfiotti	–	196S sports	0740

13-9-59 ITALIAN GP, Monza

RESULT	DRIVER	GRID QUALIFICATION	MODEL	CHASSIS NUMBER
2nd	Phil Hill *FL*	q5	246 F1	0003
4th	Dan Gurney	q4	246 F1	0007
5th	Cliff Allison	q8	246 F1	0004
6th	Olivier Gendebien	q6	246 F1	0011
Rtd	Tony Brooks	q2	246 F1	0002

20-9-59 Pontedecimo–Giovi Hill-Climb, Italy

2nd	Giorgio Scarlatti	–	196S sports	0740

12-12-59 UNITED STATES GP, Sebring, Florida

3rd	Tony Brooks	q4	246 F1	0004
6th	Wolfgang von Trips	q6	246 F1	0002
Rtd	Phil Hill	q8	246 F1*	0006
Rtd	Cliff Allison	q7	246 F1	0003

*Experimental two-cam V6 engine in F2-type chassis with coil-spring IRS

14-12-59 All-Ferrari Event, Nassau, Bahamas

2nd	Ricardo Rodriguez	–	196S sports	0776

1959 World Championship Points Scores:

2nd	Brooks	27 points
4th	Hill	20 points
7th	Gurney	13 points
12th	Gendebien	3 points
Allison,		
and Behra	(posthumous)	2 points

Constructors' Championship:

Ferrari 2nd 32 points (Cooper, Champions with 40 points)

1960

7-2-60 ARGENTINE GP, Buenos Aires

2nd	Cliff Allison	q7	246 F1	0001
5th	Wolfgang von Trips	q5	246 F1	0005
8th	Phil Hill	q6	246 F1	0007*
10th	José Froilan Gonzalez	q11	246 F1	0004

*Possibly Sebring '0006' modified

31-1-60 Buenos Aires 1000 km, Argentina

Rtd	Scarfiotti/Gonzalez	–	246S sports	0778

19-3-60 Syracuse GP, Sicily

1st	Wolfgang von Trips	q5	156 F2	0011

23-3-60 Sebring 12-Hours, Florida

Rtd	Rodriguez/Rodriguez	–	196S sports	0776

8-5-60 Targa Florio, Sicily

2nd	von Trips/Hill	–	246S* sports	0784
4th	Mairesse/Scarfiotti/ Cabianca		246S sports	0778
7th	Rodriguez/Rodriguez	–	196S sports	0776

*Possibly larger 296 engine in this car?

14-5-60 BRDC International Trophy, Silverstone, UK

5th	Phil Hill	q4	246 F1	0003
8th	Cliff Allison	q7	246 F1	0004

22-5-60 ADAC 1000 km, Nürburgring, Germany

RESULT	DRIVER	GRID QUALIFICATION	MODEL	CHASSIS NUMBER
Rtd	Scarlatti/Cabianca	–	246S sports	0778*
Rtd	Ginther/Scarfiotti	–	246S sports	0784
Rtd	Rodriguez/Rodriguez	–	196S sports	0776

*Car thoroughly burned out in refuelling fire. Subsequently rebuilt, today in Pierre Bardinon's Mas du Clos collection, Aubusson, France

29-5-60 MONACO GP, Monte Carlo

3rd	Phil Hill	q10	246 F1	0004**
6th	Richie Ginther	q9	246'P'F1*	0008
'8th' NRF	Wolfgang von Trips	q8	246 F1	0011
DNS	Cliff Allison	PA†	246 F1	0003**

*Prototype mid-engined Formula 1 car, †PA practice accident

**Shown as listed by Ferrari but probably transposed in fact. Allison crashed a 232 cm wheelbase car, Hill raced a 222 cm. What is probably '0003's' frame surviving today is the 222 cm

6-6-60 DUTCH GP, Zandvoort

5th	Wolfgang von Trips	q15	246 F1	0004*
6th	Richie Ginther	q12	246 F1	0006
Rtd	Phil Hill	q13	246 F1	0005

*Quoted by Ferrari but almost certainly 222 cm '0003'

19-6-60 BELGIAN GP, Spa–Francorchamps

4th	Phil Hill =*FL*	q3	246 F1	0007
Rtd	Wolfgang von Trips	q10	246 F1	0004
Rtd	Willy Mairesse	q12	246 F1	0005

3-7-60 FRENCH GP, Reims-Gueux

'11th' NRF	Wolfgang von Trips	q6	246 F1	0004
'12th' NRF	Phil Hill	q2	246 F1	0007
Rtd	Willy Mairesse	q5	246 F1	0005

16-7-60 BRITISH GP, Silverstone

6th	Wolfgang von Trips	q7	246 F1	0005
7th	Phil Hill	q10	246 F1	0007

24-7-60 Solituderennen, Stuttgart, Germany

1st	Wolfgang von Trips *FL*	q2	156'P'F2*	0008
7th	Phil Hill	q12	156 F2	0011

*Mid-engined Monaco car, re-engined and modified for Formula 2

1-8-60 Silver City Trophy, Brands Hatch, England

4th	Phil Hill	q18	246 F1	0004
9th	Richie Ginther	q13	246 F1	0006

14-8-60 PORTUGUESE GP, Oporto

4th	Wolfgang von Trips	q9	246 F1	0005
Rtd	Phil Hill	q10	246 F1	0004

4-9-60 ITALIAN GP, Monza

1st	Phil Hill *FL*	PP	246 F1	0007
2nd	Richie Ginther	q2	246 F1	0003
3rd	Willy Mairesse	q3	246 F1	0006
5th (1st F2)	Wolfgang von Trips	q6	156'P' F2	0008

2-10-60 Modena GP, Italy

2nd	Richie Ginther	q6	156 F2	0011
3rd	Wolfgang von Trips	q3	156'P' F2	0008

1960 World Championship Points Scores:

5th	Hill	16 points		
6th	von Trips	10 points		
8th	Ginther	8 points		
13th	Mairesse	4 points		

Constructors' Championship:

Ferrari 3rd 24 points (Cooper, Champions with 40, Lotus 2nd with 32)

1961

25-3-61 Sebring 12-Hours, Florida

		GRID QUALIFI-		CHASSIS
RESULT	DRIVER	CATION	MODEL	NUMBER
7th	Hall/Constantine	–	246S* sports	0778
18th	Helburn/Fulp/ Hudson		196S* sports	0776
Rtd	Ginther/von Trips	–	246SP sports	0790
Rtd	Hugus/Connell	–	246S* sports	0784

*Front-engined models

25-4-61 Syracuse GP, Sicily

1st	Giancarlo Baghetti	PP	156 F1	0008

30-4-61 Targa Florio, Sicily

1st	Trips/Ginther/ Gendebien FL	–	246SP sports	0790
Rtd	Hill/Gendebien	–	246SP sports	0796

14-5-61 MONACO GP, Monte Carlo

2nd	Richie Ginther =FL	q2	156 F1	0001
3rd	Phil Hill	q5	156 F1	0003
'4th' NRF	Wolfgang von Trips	q6	156 F1	0002

14-5-61 Naples GP, Posillipo, Italy

1st	Giancarlo Baghetti FL	q3	156 F1	0008

22-5-61 DUTCH GP, Zandvoort

1st	Wolfgang von Trips	q2	156 F1	0004
2nd	Phil Hill	PP	156 F1	'0003/2'*
5th	Richie Ginther	q3	156 F1	0001

*According to Ferrari at the time, this used a new chassis frame since Monaco - presumably a wide engine bay frame for the 120° engine replacing the Monaco 65°

28-5-61 ADAC 1000 km, Nürburgring, Germany

3rd	Ginther/Gendebien/ Trips	–	246SP sports	0790
Rtd	Hill/Trips	–	246SP sports	0796

10/11-6-61 Le Mans 24-Hours, Sarthe, France

Rtd*	Trips/Ginther	–	246SP sports	0790

*After running never lower than fourth

18-6-61 BELGIAN GP, Spa-Francorchamps

1st	Phil Hill	PP	156 F1	0003
2nd	Wolfgang von Trips	q2	156 F1	0004
3rd	Richie Ginther FL	q5	156 F1	0001
4th	Olivier Gendebien	q3	156 F1	0002

2-7-61 FRENCH GP, Reims-Gueux

1st	Giancarlo Baghetti	q12	156 F1	0008
9th	Phil Hill FL	PP	156 F1	0003
'15th' NRF	Richie Ginther	q3	156 F1	0001
Rtd	Wolfgang von Trips	q2	156 F1	0004

15-7-61 BRITISH GP, Aintree, Liverpool

		GRID QUALIFI-		CHASSIS
RESULT	DRIVER	CATION	MODEL	NUMBER
1st	Wolfgang von Trips	q4	156 F1	0004
2nd	Phil Hill	PP	156 F1	0003
3rd	Richie Ginther	q2	156 F1	0001
Rtd	Giancarlo Baghetti	q19	156 F1	0008

6-8-61 GERMAN GP, Nürburgring

2nd	Wolfgang von Trips	q5	156 F1	0004
3rd	Phil Hill FL	PP	156 F1	0003
8th	Richie Ginther	q14	156 F1	0001
Rtd	Willy Mairesse	q13	156 F1	0002

15-8-61 Pescara 4-Hours, Italy

Rtd	Ginther/Baghetti FL	PP	246SP sports	0796

10-9-61 ITALIAN GP, Monza

1st	Phil Hill	q4	156 F1	0002
Rtd	†Wolfgang von Trips	PP	156 F1	0004
Rtd	Giancarlo Baghetti FL	q6	156 F1	0003
Rtd	Ricardo Rodriguez	q2	156 F1	0006
Rtd	Richie Ginther	q3	156 F1	0001

†Fatal accident

30-9-61 Canadian GP, Mosport Park, Toronto

Rtd	Ricardo Rodriguez	–	246S sports	0784
6th	Buck Fulp	–	196S sports	0778*

*Joel Finn has shipping papers for these NART entries, listing the 2-litre 196S as 0778 - the salvaged 1960 Nürburgring 1000 km pit-fire car which the team had raced at Sebring this season

10-12-61 Nassau Trophy, Oakes Field, Bahamas

Rtd*	Ricardo Rodriguez	–	246S sports	0784

*After leading

1961 World Championship Points Scores:

Hill 38 points total of which five best (34 points) counted, **WORLD CHAMPION DRIVER**

2nd	Trips (posthumous)	33 points
5th	Ginther	16 points
9th	Baghetti	9 points
13th =	Gendebien	3 points

Constructors' Championship:

FERRARI WORLD CHAMPIONS 40 POINTS (Lotus 2nd 32, Porsche 3rd 22)

1962

11-2-62 Daytona 3-Hours, Florida

2nd	Hill/Ricardo Rodriguez FL	–	246/62 sports	0796
8th	Fulp	–	246S sports	0784

24-3-62 Sebring 12-Hours, Florida

13th	Fulp/Ryan	–	248SP sports	0806
Rtd*	Rodriguez/Rodriguez	–	246SP/62 sports	0790

*Engine failed when leading after 5 hours

1-4-62 Brussels GP, Heysel, Belgium

RESULT	DRIVER	GRID QUALIFI-CATION	MODEL	CHASSIS NUMBER
3rd *Heat 1*	Willy Mairesse	q4	156 F1	0006
1st *Heat 2*	Willy Mairesse	q3		
1st *Heat 3*	Willy Mairesse FL	PP		

Winner overall on aggregate

23-4-62 Pau GP, France

2nd	Ricardo Rodriguez	q2	156 F1	0003
5th	Lorenzo Bandini	q6	156 F1	0006

28-4-62 Aintree '200', Liverpool, UK

3rd	Phil Hill	q8	156 F1*	0007
4th	Giancarlo Baghetti	q9	156 F1	0001

*Latest car, using inboard gearbox between engine and final drive

6-5-62 Targa Florio, Sicily

1st	Mairesse/Rodriguez/			
	Gendebien FL*	–	246SP/62	0796
2nd	Baghetti/Bandini	–	196SP/62	0804
DNS**	Hill/Gendebien	–	268SP/62	0802

*Mairesse FL **Effectively written off in Hill's practice accident

12-5-62 BRDC International Trophy, Silverstone, UK

4th	Innes Ireland	q6	156 F1	0001

20-5-62 DUTCH GP, Zandvoort

3rd	Phil Hill	q9	156 F1	0004
4th	Giancarlo Baghetti	q12	156 F1	0007
Rtd	Ricardo Rodriguez	q11	156 F1	0003

27-5-62 ADAC 1000 km, Nürburgring, Germany

1st	Hill/Gendebien FL*	PP	246SP/62	0790
Rtd	Rodriguez/Rodriguez	–	268SP/62	0806
Rtd**	Baghetti/Bandini	–	196SP/62	0804

*Hill FL **When running 4th

20-5-62 Naples GP, Posillipo, Italy

1st	Willy Mairesse =FL	q2	156 F1	0001
2nd	Lorenzo Bandini			
	=FL	PP	156 F1	0006

3-6-62 MONACO GP, Monte Carlo

2nd	Phil Hill	q9	156 F1	0007
3rd	Lorenzo Bandini	q10	156 F1	0001
'7th' NRF	Willy Mairesse	q4	156 F1	0004

9-6-62 Player's '200', Mosport Park, Canada

Rtd	Innes Ireland	q4	246SP/62	0790

10-6-62 Fornovo-Monte Casio Mountain Climb, Italy

1st	Ludovico* Scarfiotti			
		see App. 2	196SP/62	0804

*Many sources spell Scarfiotti's christian name 'Lodovico'—Ferrari confirm 'Ludovico' as correct. In fact he signed autographs both ways!

17-6-62 BELGIAN GP, Spa-Francorchamps

3rd	Phil Hill	q4	156 F1	0009
4th	Ricardo Rodriguez	q7	156 F1	0003
Rtd	Giancarlo Baghetti	q14	156 F1	0001
Rtd	Willy Mairesse	q6	156 F1	0004

17-6-62 Mont Ventoux Mountain Climb, Bédoin, France

1st	Ludovico Scarfiotti	–	196SP/62	0804

23/24-6-62 Le Mans 24-Hours, Sarthe, France

RESULT	DRIVER	GRID QUALIFI-CATION	MODEL	CHASSIS NUMBER
Rtd*	Rodriguez/Rodriguez	–	246SP/62	0796
Rtd**	Baghetti/Scarfiotti	–	268SP/62	0798

*Ran first before retirement at 12 hours **Ran 3rd, then 2nd, before retirement at 18 hours

8-7-62 Trento-Bondone Mountain Climb, Montevideo-Vason, Italy

1st	Ludovico Scarfiotti	–	196SP/62	0804

21-7-62 BRITISH GP, Aintree

Rtd	Phil Hill	q12	156 F1	0007

22-7-62 Freiburg-Schauinsland Mountain Climb, Baden, Germany

1st	Ludovico Scarfiotti	–	196SP/62	0804

5-8-62 GERMAN GP, Nürburgring

6th	Ricardo Rodriguez	q10	156 F1	0006
Rtd	Phil Hill	q12	156 F1	0002
Rtd	Lorenzo Bandini	q18	156/'62P' F1	0008
10th	Giancarlo Baghetti	q13	156 F1	0007

6-8-62 Guards Trophy, Brands Hatch, UK

1st	Mike Parkes FL	PP	246SP/62	0790

19-8-62 Mediterranean GP, Pergusa, Sicily

1st	Lorenzo Bandini			
	=FL	PP	156 F1	0009
2nd	Giancarlo Baghetti			
	=FL	q2	156 F1	0003

25-8-62 Ollon-Villars Mountain Climb, Lausanne, Switzerland

2nd	Ludovico Scarfiotti	–	196SP/62	0804

SCARFIOTTI 1962 EUROPEAN MOUNTAIN CHAMPION

16-9-62 ITALIAN GP, Monza

4th	Willy Mairesse	q10	156 F1	0008
5th	Giancarlo Baghetti	q11	156 F1	0003
8th	Lorenzo Bandini	q17	156 F1	0006
11th	Phil Hill	q15	156 F1	0002
'14th' NRF	Ricardo Rodriguez	q11	156 F1	0007

9-12-62 Nassau Trophy, Oakes Field, Bahamas

8th	Lorenzo Bandini	–	268SP/62	0798*
Rtd	Buck Fulp	–	196SP	0804

*Often reported as Phil Hill's Targa Florio practice crash car, 0802, but Joel Finn's shipping papers collection shows number '0798' applied to this chassis

1962 World Championship Points Scores:

6th	Hill	14 points
11th	Baghetti	5 points
12th =	Ricardo Rodriguez and Bandini	4 points
14th =	Mairesse	3 points

Constructors' Championship:

BRM 1st, Lotus 2nd, Cooper 3rd . . .

1963

24-3-63 Sebring 12-Hours, Florida

'34th'	Fulp/Heuer	–	268SP	0798

5-5-63 Targa Florio, Sicily

RESULT	DRIVER	GRID QUALIFI-CATION	MODEL	CHASSIS NUMBER
2nd	Scarfiotti/Bandini/Mairesse	–	196SP/63	0802
Rtd	Lualdi/Bini	–	196SP/63	0790

11-5-63 BRDC International Trophy, Silverstone, UK

Rtd	John Surtees	q7	156 F1	0001
Rtd	Willy Mairesse	q9	156 F1	0002

26-5-63 MONACO GP, Monte Carlo

4th	John Surtees *FL*	q3	156 F1	0001
Rtd	Willy Mairesse	q7	156 F1	0003

??-?-63 Stallavena-Boscochiesuanuova Hill-climb, Italy

1st	Edoardo Lualdi-Gabardi	–	196SP/63	0790

2-6-63 Coppa della Consuma Hill-climb, Italy

1st	Edoardo Lualdi-Garbardi	–	196SP/63	0790

9-6-63 Laguna Seca USRRC, Monterey, California

17th	Doug Thiem	–	196SP/62	0806

9-6-63 BELGIAN GP, Spa–Francorchamps

Rtd	John Surtees	q10	156 F1	0003
Rtd	Willy Mairesse	q3	156 F1	0002

23-6-63 DUTCH GP, Zandvoort

3rd	John Surtees	q5	156 F1	0003
6th	Ludovico Scarfiotti	q11	156 F1	0002

23-6-63 Mont Ventoux Mountain Climb, Bédoin, France

5th	Edoardo Lualdi-Gabardi	–	196SP/63	0790

30-6-63 FRENCH GP, Reims-Gueux

Rtd	John Surtees	q4	156 F1	0003
DNS*	Ludovico Scarfiotti	–	156 F1	0002

*Injured in practice accident

14-7-63 Trento-Bondone Mountain Climb, Montevideo-Vason, Italy

6th	Edoardo Lualdi-Gabardi	–	196SP/63	0790

20-7-63 BRITISH GP, Silverstone

2nd	John Surtees *FL*	q5	156 F1	0790

28-7-63 Cesana-Sestriere Mountain Climb, Torino, Italy

8th	Edoardo Lualdi-Gabardi	–	196SP/63	0790

26-7-63 Pensacola USRRC, Florida

3rd	Doug Thiem	–	196SP/62	0806

??-?-63 Cumberland race meeting, Maryland, USA

	Bob Grossman*		246S	0784

*Buck Fulp and William Cooper both raced Dinos in the USA, along with Tom O'Brien, later Dick Hutchins, who ran the V8 268SP '0798' . . . following its front-line NART service

4-8-63 GERMAN GP, Nürburgring

RESULT	DRIVER	GRID QUALIFI-CATION	MODEL	CHASSIS NUMBER
1st	John Surtees *FL*	q2	156 F1	0002
Rtd*	Willy Mairesse	q7	156 F1	0003

*Injured in race accident

18-8-63 Mediterranean GP, Pergusa, Sicily

1st	John Surtees *FL*	PP	156 F1	0002

25-8-63 Ollon-Villars Mountain Climb, Lausanne, Switzerland

4th	Edoardo Lualdi-Gabardi	–	196SP/63	0804

8-9-63 ITALIAN GP, Monza

Rtd	John Surtees	PP	Aero 156 F1	0004
Rtd	Lorenzo Bandini	q6	156 F1	0002

28-9-63 Canadian GP, Mosport Park, Toronto

Rtd	Lorenzo Bandini	–	268SP	0798

6-10-63 UNITED STATES GP, Watkins Glen

5th	Lorenzo Bandini	q9	156 F1	0002
Rtd	Lorenzo Bandini	q3	156 F1	0003*

*Surtees raced tube-frame car after using new Aero, initially numbered '0004' in practice. Works records show he raced '0004' in the GP. Not so

27-10-63 MEXICAN GP, Mexico City

DIS	John Surtees	q2	Aero 156	'0003'*
Rtd	Lorenzo Bandini	q7	Aero 156	'0001'*

*New monocoque chassis shown under these numbers formerly applied to the tube-frame cars in Ferrari records

14-12-63 Rand GP, Kyalami, South Africa

1st	John Surtees *FL*	PP	Aero 156	'0003'*
2nd	Lorenzo Bandini	q3	156 F1	0001

*Officially listed as above
Result repeated in both Rand GP heats: *1st* Surtees, *2nd* Bandini on aggregate

28-12-63 SOUTH AFRICAN GP, East London

5th	Lorenzo Bandini	q5	Aero 156	'0001'
Rtd	John Surtees	q4	Aero 156	'0003'

1963 World Championship Points Scores:

4th	Surtees	22 points
9th =	Bandini	6 points
15th =	Scarfiotti	1 point

Constructors' Championship:

1st Lotus 54, and BRM 36, 3rd Brabham 28

1964

12-4-64 Syracuse GP, Sicily

2nd	Lorenzo Bandini*	*FL PP*	Aero 156	0001

*Surtees won in the new 'Aero' 158 V8

2-5-64 BRDC International Trophy, Silverstone, UK

Rtd	John Surtees	q7	Aero 156	0003

10-5-64 MONACO GP, Monte Carlo

'10th' NRF	Lorenzo Bandini	q7	Aero 156	0003

NB—Surtees raced Aero 158 . . . all succeeding entries show V6-engined performances only . . .

11-7-64 BRITISH GP, Brands Hatch

RESULT	DRIVER	GRID QUALIFI-CATION	MODEL	CHASSIS NUMBER
5th	Lorenzo Bandini	q8	Aero 156	0003

19-7-64 Solituderennen, Stuttgart, Germany

Rtd	Lorenzo Bandini	q4	Aero 156	0003

26-8-64 GERMAN GP, Nürburgring

3rd	Lorenzo Bandini	q4	Aero 156	0003

6-9-64 ITALIAN GP, Monza

9th	Ludovico Scarfiotti	q7	Aero 156	0001

23-8-64 AUSTRIAN GP, Zeltweg Airfield

1st	Lorenzo Bandini	q4	Aero 156	0003

25-10-64 MEXICAN GP, Mexico City

6th	Pedro Rodriguez	q9	Aero 156	0003

1964 World Championship Points Scores:

Surtees 40 points **WORLD CHAMPION DRIVER**

Bandini 23 points 4th
Rodriguez 1 point 19th

Constructors' Championship:

FERRARI WORLD CHAMPIONS, 45 points
2nd BRM 42, 3rd Lotus 38

1965

25-4-65 Monza 1000 km, Italy

Rtd	Biscaldi/Baghetti	–	166P Coupé	0834

16-5-65 Rome GP sports car event, Vallelunga, Italy

1st (class)	Giancarlo Baghetti	–	166P Coupé	0834

23-5-65 ADAC 1000 km, Nürburgring, Germany

4th	Bandini/Vaccarella	–	166P Coupé	0834

18/19-6-65 Le Mans 24-Hours, Sarthe, France

Rtd	Baghetti/Casoni	–	166P Coupé	0834

11-7-65 Trento-Bondone Mountain Climb, Montevideo-Vason, Italy

1st	Ludovico Scarfiotti	–	206P Coupé	0834

25-7-65 Cesana-Sestriere Mountain Climb, Torino, Italy

1st	Ludovico Scarfiotti	–	206S spyder	0834*

*166P Coupé chassis re-engined, now with open spyder bodywork

8-8-65 Freiburg-Schauinsland Mountain Climb, Baden, Germany

1st	Ludovico Scarfiotti	–	206S spyder	0834

29-8-65 Ollon-Villars Mountain Climb, Lausanne, Switzerland

1st	Ludovico Scarfiotti	–	206S spyder	0834

19-9-65 Gaisberg Mountain Climb, Salzburg, Austria

5th	Ludovico Scarfiotti	–	206S spyder	0834

SCARFIOTTI 1965 EUROPEAN MOUNTAIN CHAMPION

NB – V8 and flat-12 engines used exclusively in Ferrari's Formula entries during the 1965 season

1966

26-3-66 Sebring 12-Hours, Florida

5th	Bandini/Scarfiotti	–	206S spyder	0842

25-4-66 Monza 1000 km, Italy

RESULT	DRIVER	GRID QUALIFI-CATION	MODEL	CHASSIS NUMBER
9th	Bandini/Scarfiotti	–	206S spyder	0842
Rtd	Biscaldi/Casoni	–	206S Coupé	–
DNS*	Vaccarella/Bondurant	–	206S spyder	–
13th	Attwood/Piper	–	206S spyder	010

*Badly damaged by Bondurant in practice accident

30-4-66 RAC Tourist Trophy, Oulton Park, UK

Rtd	Mike Parkes	–	206S spyder	010

8-5-66 Targa Florio, Sicily

2nd	Baghetti/Guichet	–	206S Coupé	0852
13th	Biscaldi/Casoni	–	206S spyder	0842
Rtd*	Parkes/Scarfiotti	–	206S spyder	004

*Held 3rd place before retirement

22-5-66 Spa 1000 km, Francorchamps, Belgium

6th*	Attwood/Guichet	–	206S spyder	0852

*Won its class by miles . . .

5-6-66 ADAC 1000 km, Nürburgring, Germany

2nd	Bandini/Scarfiotti	–	206S spyder	004
3rd	Rodriguez/Ginther	–	206S spyder	–
WDN*	Attwood/Piper	–	206S spyder	–

*Withdrawn due to tyres fouling bodywork during race

22-5-66 MONACO GP, Monte Carlo

2nd	Lorenzo Bandini FL	q5	246T F1	0006

1-5-66 Syracuse GP, Sicily

2nd*	Lorenzo Bandini	q2	246T F1	0006

*Behind Surtees's winning 312 V12 F1 prototype car . . .

12-6-66 Rossfeld Mountain Climb, Berchtesgaden, Germany

2nd	Ludovico Scarfiotti	–	206S	0842

13-6-66 BELGIAN GP, Spa-Francorchamps

3rd	Lorenzo Bandini	q5	246T F1	0006

18/19-6-66 Le Mans 24-Hours, Sarthe, France

Rtd	Vaccarella/Casoni	–	206S Coupé	–
Rtd	Kolb/Follmer	–	206S spyder	–
Rtd	Salmon/Hobbs	–	206S spyder	–

16-7-66 Guards Trophy, Brands Hatch British GP Meeting

6th*	Mike Parkes	–	206S spyder	–

24-7-66 Cesana-Sestriere Mountain Climb, Torino, Italy

1st	Ludovico Scarfiotti	–	206S spyder	0842

31-7-66 Freiburg-Schauinsland Mountain Climb, Baden, Germany

2nd	Ludovico Scarfiotti	–	206S spyder	0842

7-8-66 GERMAN GP, Nürburgring

Rtd	Ludovico Scarfiotti	q4	246T F1	0006

7-8-66 Coppa Citta di Enna, Pergusa, Sicily

1st	'Pam'*	–	206S spyder	–
Rtd	Nino Vaccarella	–	206S spyder	–

*Marcello Pasotti

28-8-66 Sierre-Montana Mountain Climb, Martigny, Switzerland

RESULT	DRIVER	GRID QUALIFICATION	MODEL	CHASSIS NUMBER
1st	Ludovico Scarfiotti	–	206S spyder	0842

SCARFIOTTI 2nd 1966 EUROPEAN MOUNTAIN CHAMPIONSHIP

28-8-66 USRRC Buckeye Cup, Lexington, Ohio, USA

6th*	Charlie Kolb	–	206S spyder	–

*2nd in class

29-8-66 Guards Trophy, Brands Hatch, UK

DNS*	Mike Parkes	–	206S spyder	–

*Demolished car thoroughly in practice accident

4-9-66 ITALIAN GP, Monza

UNC*	Giancarlo Baghetti	q16	246T F1	0006

*Unclassified although 10th on road at finish; covered insufficient distance after lying a strong 5th . . .

4-9-66 USRRC Road-America '500', Elkhart Lake, Wisconsin, USA

Rtd	Charlie Kolb		206S spyder	–

18-9-66 Bridgehampton USRRC, Long Island, USA

Rtd	Charlie Kolb	–	206S spyder	–
Rtd	Pedro Rodriguez	–	206S spyder	–

15-lap Qualifying Event

3rd	Kolb			

9-10-66 Prix du Tyrol, Innsbruck, Austria

4th	Edoardo Lualdi-Gabardi	–	206S spyder	010?

11-10-66 Tulln-Langenlebarn Airfield, Vienna, Austria

2nd	Edoardo Lualdi-Gabardi	–	206S spyder	010?

16-10-66 Laguna Seca, Monterey, California

14th Heat 1	Pedro Rodriguez	–	206S spyder	–
25th Heat 2	Rodriguez			

18th overall on aggregate

Consolation Race

9th	Pedro Rodriguez	–	206S spyder	–

02-?-66 SCCA Nationals, Vineland, New Jersey

5th	Bob Hutchins	–	268SP	0798

1967

4/5-2-67 Daytona 24-Hours, Florida

Rtd*	Kolb/Fulp	–	206S	
Rtd	Gregory/Gregg	–	206S	

*After leading works Porsches in 2-litre class

1-4-67 Sebring 12-Hours, Florida

Rtd	Rodriguez/Guichet	–	206S	–
Rtd	Muller/Klass	–	206S spyder	–
Rtd	Kolb/Crawford	–	206S	–
Rtd	Williams/Casoni		206S	–

25-4-67 Monza 1000 km, Italy

RESULT	DRIVER	GRID QUALIFICATION	MODEL	CHASSIS NUMBER
Rtd	Klass/Williams	–	206S spyder	004
Rtd	Casoni/'Shangri-La'	–	206S spyder	–
Rtd	Ravetto/Starrabba	–	206S spyder	–
Rtd	Biscaldi/Pianta	–	206S spyder	–
DNS*	Facetti/Nicodemi	–	206S spyder	030?
UNC	'Pam'/Lualdi	–	206S spyder	–

*Crashed by Facetti in practice

14-5-67 Targa Florio, Sicily

4th	Williams/Venturi	–	206S spyder	–
Rtd	Casoni/Klass	–	206S spyder	–
Rtd	Latteri/Capuano	–	206S spyder	018?

21-5-67 Carrera en Cuesta al Montseny Mountain Climb, Barcelona, Spain

3rd	Mario Casoni	–	206S spyder	024?

28-5-67 ADAC 1000 km, Nürburgring, Germany

DNS*	Scarfiotti/Klass	–	246P spyder	004
DNS**	Guichet/Muller	–	206S spyder	026

*The works 2.4 V6 prototype car broke a piston in practice and was withdrawn
**The Ecurie Filipinetti car was destroyed by fire early in practice; subsequently rebuilt for Pierre Bardinon

25-6-67 Reims 12-Hours, France

Rtd	Rodriguez/Guichet	–	206S spyder	–

9-7-67 Trento-Bondone Mountain Climb, Montevideo-Vason, Italy

2nd	Ludovico Scarfiotti	–	206SP spyder	0842
Penalty	Gunther Klass	–	206S spyder	004
Rtd	Edoardo Lualdi-Gabardi	–	206S spyder	–
DNS	Mario Casoni	–	206S spyder	024?

NB No further Mountain Championship entries made following Klass's death in Group 7 206SP, apparently 0842, during practice for the Mugello circuit race 23-7-67 . . .

9-7-67 Rouen-les-Essarts Formula 2, France

Rtd	Jonathan Williams	q13	166F2	0002

23-7-67 Mugello, Italy

DNS*	Scarfiotti/Vaccarella	–	206SP spyder	004
DNS*	Williams/Klass	–	206S spyder	010

*Works entries withdrawn after Klass's fatal accident in Group 7 hill-climb car being used at Mugello as training hack . . .

1968

6-1-68 New Zealand GP, Pukekohe, Auckland

1st	Chris Amon FL	q2	246T/68	0004?

13-1-68 Levin GP, New Zealand

1st	Chris Amon FL	q3	246T/68	0004

20-1-68 Lady Wigram Trophy, Christchurch, New Zealand

2nd	Chris Amon =FL	q2	246T/68	0004

3/4-2-68 Daytona 24-Hours, Florida

Rtd	Kolb/Rodriguez	–	206S Coupé	–

27-1-68 Teretonga Trophy, Invercargill, New Zealand

4th	Chris Amon	PP	246T/68	0004

11-2-68 Surfers' Paradise, Queensland, Australia

RESULT	DRIVER	GRID QUALIFI-CATION	MODEL	CHASSIS NUMBER
Rtd	Chris Amon	PP	246T/68	0004

18-2-68 Warwick Farm '100', Sydney, Australia

4th	Chris Amon	q3	246T/68	0004

25-2-68 Australian GP, Sandown Park, Melbourne

2nd	Chris Amon FL	q2	246T/68	0004

4-3-68 South Pacific Championship, Longford, Tasmania

7th	Chris Amon	q3	246T/68	0004

AMON TASMAN CHAMPIONSHIP RUNNER-UP

31-3-68 Barcelona Formula 2, Spain

3rd	Chris Amon	q7	166 F2	0008
Rtd	Jacky Ickx	q5	166 F2	0010

7-4-68 BOAC '500', Brands Hatch, UK

DIS*	Dean/Beckwith	–	206S spyder	004

*Disqualified for re-welding broken steering column bracket in paddock instead of in the pits during the race . . .

7-4-68 Deutschland Trophy, Hockenheim, Germany

6th Heat 1	Chris Amon	q6	166 F2	0006
7th Heat 2	Amon	q6		

5th overall on aggregate

12-4-68 Good Friday, Oulton Park, UK

3rd	Tony Dean	–	206S spyder	004
15th	Hans Wangstre	–	206S spyder	–

13-4-68 Post Trophy, Rufforth, UK

1st	Ben Moore FL	–	206S spyder	004

21-4-68 Eifelrennen Formula 2, Nürburgring Sudschleife, Germany

4th	Brian Redman FL	q4	166 F2	0008
Rtd	Jacky Ickx	PP	166 F2	0010

25-4-68 Monza 1000 km, Italy

18th	Terigi/Cecchini	–	Fiat Dino	–

5-5-68 Targa Florio, Sicily

22nd	Wangstre/Christofferssen	–	206S spyder	–

19-5-68 ADAC 1000 km, Nürburgring, Germany

Rtd	Wangstre/Christoffersen	–	206S spyder	–
DNS*	De Cadanet/McKay	–	206S spyder	024

*Due to inexperience of ex-Brescia Corse car unable to start it

5-5-68 Limbourg GP Formula 2, Zolder, Belgium

3rd Heat 1	Chris Amon	q2	166 F2	0006
8th Heat 1	Jacky Ickx	–	166 F2	0010
1st Heat 2	Ickx	q8		
2nd Heat 2	Amon	q2		

Amon 2nd and Ickx 4th on aggregate . . .

5-5-68 Post Trophy, Croft, UK

1st	Tony Dean	–	206S spyder	004

3-6-68 London Trophy, Crystal Palace, UK

RESULT	DRIVER	GRID QUALIFI-CATION	MODEL	CHASSIS NUMBER
5th Heat 1	Jacky Ickx	–	166 F2	0010
Rtd Heat 2	Ickx	q5		

Ickx 15th on aggregate . . .

3-6-68 RAC Tourist Trophy, Oulton Park, UK

'4th' NRF*	Tony Dean	–	206S spyder	004
12th	De Cadanet/McKay	–	206S spyder	024

*Spun out 6 laps from finish, but retained 4th overall and 1st in 2-litre class on distance covered before incident . . .

16-6-68 Rhein Cup Formula 2, Hockenheim, Germany

5th	Jacky Ickx	q3	166 F2	0006
8th	Chris Amon	q8	166 F2	0008

16-6-68 Anderstorp Inaugural, Sweden

Rtd	Wangstre/Christofferssen	–	206S spyder	–
–	De Cadanet	–	206S spyder	024

23-6-68 Lottery GP Formula 2, Monza, Italy

7th	Mario Casoni	q4	166 F2	0006
Rtd*	Derek Bell	PP	166 F2	0010
Rtd*	Tino Brambilla	q5	166 F2	0008
Rtd*	Giancarlo Baghetti	q18	166 F2	0002

*All three cars involved in multiple accident

2-7-68 Vila Real 6-Hours, Portugal

11th	Mario Araujo Cabral	–	206S spyder	024

2-7-68 Martini Trophy, Silverstone, UK

4th*	Tony Dean	–	206S spyder	004

*1st in class

3-7-68 Post Trophy, Croft, UK

1st	Tony Dean	–	206S spyder	004

14-7-68 Tulln-Langenlebarn Formula 2, Vienna, Austria

12th Heat 1	Derek Bell	q?	166 F2	0010
Rtd Heat 1	Chris Amon	q?	166 F2	0008
7th Heat 2	Bell			
8th Heat 2	Amon			

Bell 7th and Amon 12th on aggregate

14-7-68 Watkins Glen 6-Hours, New York State

7th	Rodriguez/Kolb	–	206S	–

28-7-68 Zandvoort Formula 2, Holland

1st Heat 1	Derek Bell	PP	166 F2	0010
3rd Heat 2	Tino Brambilla FL	q3	166 F2	0008
14th Final	Bell	PP		
Rtd Final	Brambilla	q3		

8-8-68 News Trophy, Rufforth, UK

1st	Tony Dean	–	206S spyder	004

Formule Libre Trophy

1st	Dean	–	206S spyder	004

15-8-68 Holts Trophy, Crystal Palace, London, UK

1st	Tony Dean = FL	–	206S spyder	004

15-8-68 Coppa Citta di Enna, Pergusa, Sicily

5th	Pietro Lo Piccolo	–	206S	–

25-8-68 Mediterranean GP, Pergusa, Sicily

RESULT	DRIVER	GRID QUALIFI-CATION	MODEL	CHASSIS NUMBER
3rd	Tino Brambilla	–	166 F2	0008
5th	Derek Bell	–	166 F2	0012
6th	Jacky Ickx	–	166 F2	0010
16th	Mario Casoni	–	166 F2	0002

28/29-9-68 Le Mans 24-Hours, Sarthe, France

'18th'*	Mesange/Martin	–	Fiat Dino	–
Rtd	Chevalier/Lagier	–	206S	–

*Too far behind to be classified as a finisher

13-10-68 Preis von Württemburg Formula 2, Hockenheim, Germany

1st	Tino Brambilla *FL*	–	166 F2	0004
3rd	Derek Bell	–	166 F2	0010

27-10-68 Rome GP Formula 2, Vallelunga, Italy

1st *Heat 1*	Tino Brambilla *FL*	PP	166 F2	0004
2nd *Heat 1*	Andrea de Adamich	q2	166 F2	0012
6th *Heat 1*	Derek Bell	q7	166 F2	0010
1st *Heat 2*	Brambilla *FL*	PP		
3rd *Heat 2*	De Adamich	q2		
6th *Heat 2*	Bell	q6		

Brambilla *1st*, De Adamich 2nd and Bell 6th on aggregate

9-11-68 Rand 9-Hours, Kyalami, Johannesburg, South Africa

2nd	Tony Dean/Basil von Rooyen	–	206S spyder	004

23-11-68 Cape 3-Hours, Killarney, Cape Town, South Africa

5th	Tony Dean/Basil von Rooyen	–	206S spyder	004

1-12-68 Temporada 1, Buenos Aires, Argentina

1st	Tino Brambilla *FL*	q3	166 F2	0004
2nd	Andrea de Adamich	q2	166 F2	0012

7-12-68 Temporada 2, Oscar Cabalen Autodrome, Cordoba, Argentina

1st	Andrea de Adamich	q2*	166 F2	0012
Rtd	Tino Brambilla	q?	166 F2	0004

*Shared fastest practice time with Jochen Rindt's Brabham

15-12-68 Temporada 3, El Zonda, San Juan, Argentina

1st	Andrea de Adamich	q2	166 F2	0012
Rtd	Tino Brambilla	q3	166 F2	0004

22-12-68 Temporada 4, Buenos Aires, Argentina

1st *Heat 1*	Andrea de Adamich	q2	166 F2	0012
Rtd *Heat 1*	Tino Brambilla	PP	166 F2	0004
6th *Heat 2*	De Adamich	PP		
DNS *Heat 2*	Brambilla			

DE ADAMICH TEMPORADA FORMULA 2 CHAMPION

1969

4-1-69 New Zealand GP, Pukekohe

1st	Chris Amon	PP	246T/69	0008
4th	Derek Bell	–	246T/69	0010

11-1-69 Levin International, New Zealand

1st	Chris Amon	q2	246T/69	0008
Rtd	Derek Bell	q3	246T/69	0010

18-1-69 Lady Wigram Trophy, Christchurch, New Zealand

RESULT	DRIVER	GRID QUALIFI-CATION	MODEL	CHASSIS NUMBER
3rd	Chris Amon =FL	q3	246T/69	0008
5th	Derek Bell	q4	246T/69	0010

25-1-69 Teretonga Trophy, Invercargill, New Zealand

3rd	Chris Amon	q3	246T/69	0008
5th	Derek Bell	q4	246T/69	0010

2-2-69 Australian GP, Lakeside, Brisbane

1st	Chris Amon *FL*	PP	246T/69	0008
2nd	Derek Bell	q3	246T/69	0010

1/2-2-69 Daytona 24-Hours, Florida

Rtd	Kolb/Biscaldi	–	206S	–

9-2-69 Warwick Farm '100', Sydney, Australia

Rtd	Chris Amon	q2	246T/69	0008
2nd	Derek Bell	q5	246T/69	0010

16-2-69 Sandown Park, Melbourne, Australia

1st	Chris Amon *FL*	q2	246T/69	0008
5th	Derek Bell	q6	246T/69	0010

AMON TASMAN CHAMPION, Bell 4th

21-2-69 Sebring 12-Hours, Florida

9th	Kolb/Rodriguez	–	206S	–
36th*	Posey/Dini	–	206GT	–

*Class winner

30-3-69 Silverstone, UK

16th	Tony Beeson		206S spyder	004*

*Now acquired by Alain de Cadanet

4-4-69 Good Friday, Snetterton, UK

11th	Alain de Cadanet	–	206S spyder	004

7-4-69 Thruxton Formula 2, UK

6th	Tino Brambilla		166 F2	0004
10th	Clay Regazzoni		166 F2	0014
Rtd	Derek Bell		166 F2	0012

13-4-69 Deutschland Trophy, Hockenheim, Germany

Rtd	Tino Brambilla		166 F2	0014
DIS*	Clay Regazzoni		166 F2	0012

*Disqualified for tow-starting on pit road

13-4-69 BOAC '500', Brands Hatch, UK

15th	De Cadanet/Beeson	–	206S spyder	004

25-4-69 Monza 1000 km, Italy

Rtd	'Matich'/'Meo'	–	206S spyder	016?
DNQ	De Cadanet/Walton	–	206S spyder	004

27-4-69 Eifelrennen, Nürburgring Nordschleife, Germany

5th	Derek Bell		166 F2	0012
Rtd	Tino Brambilla		166 F2	0004
Rtd	Clay Regazzoni		166 F2	0014

4-5-69 Targa Florio, Sicily

26th	'Cinno'/Barbuscia	–	206S spyder	–
30th	'Sancho'/'Zorba'	–	Fiat Dino	–

11-5-69 Jarama Formula 2, Spain

RESULT	DRIVER	GRID QUALIFI-CATION	MODEL	CHASSIS NUMBER
6th	Tino Brambilla		166 F2	0004
8th	Derek Bell		166 F2	0012
11th	Clay Regazzoni		166 F2	0014

11-5-69 Francorchamps 1000 km, Spa, Belgium

DNS*	De Fierlandt/'Elde'	–	206S spyder	010?

*Léon Dernier ('Elde') damaged this car severely in a practice accident which caused it to burn out. Alain de Cadanet bought the wreckage from Jacques Swaters of Ecurie Francorchamps, but it was not rebuilt successfully, merely retained as a source of spares once restored.

1-6-69 ADAC 1000 km, Nürburgring, Germany

Rtd	Christofferssen/ Wangstre	–	206S	–
Rtd	De Cadanet/Walton	–	206S spyder	004

14/16-6-69 Le Mans 24-Hours, Sarthe, France

DNS*	Pedro Rodriguez/ Mieusset	–	206S	–

*NART entry collided with team's GTB in practice, eliminating both

22-6-69 Lottery GP Formula 2, Monza, Italy

5th	Derek Bell	q5	166 F2	0012
Rtd	Tino Brambilla	q4	166 F2	0004
Rtd	Clay Regazzoni	q11	166 F2	0014

NB—Following this event the works Dino F2 cars were withdrawn—this marked the end of Ferrari works team participation in Formula 2

6-7-69 Vila Real 6-Hours, Portugal

6th	De Cadanet/Walton	–	206S spyder	004

20-7-69 Mugello, Italy

–	'Cinno'/Barbuscia	–	206S spyder	–
–	'Matich'/Lado	–	206SP spyder	016?
–	Baldi/Dolfi	–	206GT	–

15-8-69 Coppa Citta di Enna, Pergusa, Sicily

6th	Pietro Lo Piccolo	–	206S spyder	022?

17-8-69 Karlskoga Kannonloppet, Sweden

11th	Alain de Cadanet	–	206S spyder	004*

*Now glass-fibre bodied, replacing original alloy shell

31-8-69 Mantorp Park, Sweden

–	Alain de Cadanet	–	206S spyder	004

28-12-69 Bay Park International, Mount Maunganui, New Zealand

2nd	Graeme Lawrence	q2	246T/69	0008

1970

4-1-70 Levin International, New Zealand

1st	Graeme Lawrence	FLPP	246T/69	0008

10-1-70 New Zealand GP, Pukekohe

3rd	Graeme Lawrence	q5	246T/69	0008

17-1-70 Lady Wigram Trophy, Christchurch, New Zealand

Rtd	Graeme Lawrence	q7	246T/69	0008

24-1-70 Teretonga Trophy, Invercargill, New Zealand

4th	Graeme Lawrence	q3	246T/69	0008

8-2-70 Surfers' Paradise, Queensland, Australia

RESULT	DRIVER	GRID QUALIFI-CATION	MODEL	CHASSIS NUMBER
3rd	Graeme Lawrence	q6	246T/69	0008

15-2-70 Warwick Farm '100', Sydney, Australia

3rd	Graeme Lawrence	PP	246T/69	0008

22-2-70 Sandown Park, Melbourne Australia

2nd	Graeme Lawrence	q4	246T/69	0008

LAWRENCE TASMAN CHAMPION

3-5-70 Targa Florio, Sicily

11th	Lo Piccolo/ Calascibetta	–	206SP spyder	022?
–	'Cinno'/Barbuscia	–	206S spyder	

19-7-70 Mugello 500 km, Italy

14th	Pietro Lo Piccolo	–	206SP spyder	022?
Rtd	'Cinno'	–	206S spyder	–

1971

16-5-71 Targa Florio, Sicily

30th	Verna/Cosentina	–	246GT	–
Rtd	Terra/Lo Piccolo	–	206SP spyder	022?

30-5-71 ADAC 1000 km, Nürburgring, Germany

'26th'*	Komusin/Mullers	–	246GT	–

*Finished, but too far behind to be classified

1972

25-4-72 Monza 1000 km, Italy

Rtd	Lo Piccolo/Terra	–	206S spyder	–

10/11-6-72 Le Mans 24-Hours, Sarthe, France

17th	Laffeach/Doncieux	–	246GT	–

1974

15/16-6-74 Le Mans 24-Hours, Sarthe, France

Rtd	Lafosse/Gagliardi	–	308GT(C)4	–

THE 'S' AND 'SP' DINO SPORTS 1958–1963

206S '0704' — first Dino 4-cam 2-litre 1958, debut Goodwood Easter Monday driven by Collins. Rebuilt 1959 as 196S 2-cam with Fantuzzi bodywork

296S '0746' unique Dino 4-cam 2.9-litre 1958, debut Silverstone May meeting driven by Hawthorn. Re-engined with Testa Rossa 3-litre V12 for Nürburgring 1000 km, retired until 1960 when re-worked, rebodied and re-engined as TR-V12 and sold to Chinetti, USA

196S '0776' — 1959 production Fantuzzi Dino 2-cam 2-litre sold to Chinetti for Rodriguez boys with Don Pedro Rodriguez paying the running costs and repair bills, debut Nassau 1959, raced through 1960 then to Buck Fulp, Tom O'Brien, Harry Zweifel in Switzerland, Rob Walker, Johnny Lurani 1979 for Beppe Lucchini, Italy 1979

246S '0778' — 1960 2.5-litre 4-cam Dino prototype chassis type '544' engine type '169', debut Buenos Aires 1000 km and burned out at Nürburgring 1000 km 1960—rebuilt and ran as 196S 2-litre—*with Bardinon, France, 1979*

246S '0784' — 1960 2.5-litre 4-cam Dino second chassis debut at Targa Florio 1960 placed second—rebodied as high-tail car for Chinetti and Ricardo Rodriguez, Canadian GP 1961, *with Bardinon, France, 1979*

246SP '0790' — 1961 2.5-litre 4-cam mid-engined prototype, better of the two cars, debut Sebring 1961, won Targa Florio 1961 low-tail bodied form 1962, rebuilt 1963 as 196SP 2-litre 2-cam for Edoardo Lualdi-Gabardi

246SP '0796' — 1961 2.5-litre 4-cam mid-engined second car debut Targa Florio 1961 crashed—rebodied as 246SP/62 prototype raced by Hill/Rodriguez at Daytona 1962 and won Targa Florio that year—chassis lengthened to accept V12 engine as step towards 1963 250P development—used as training hack for the 1963 Targa Florio, caught fire and burned out, wreck apparently scrapped ... only one of these cars not to survive

268SP '0798' — 1962 2.6-litre V8 2-cam debut Le Mans 1962—to Chinetti USA and raced extensively by Tom O'Brien and Dick Hutchins—*with Bardinon, France, 1979*

268SP '0802' — 1962 car began life as press conference 286 V6 2-cam 2.8-litre then race debut as 268 V8 2.6-litre should have come in the Targa Florio but crashed in practice. Rebuilt as letter-box nose 196SP 2-litre 2-cam for 1963 and second in Targa Florio. Sold engineless to Chinetti and became road-going coupé with US V8 engine for female customer

196SP '0804' — 1962 2-litre 2-cam car chassis type '561' debut Targa Florio, Scarfiotti's European Mountain Champion 1962, to Chinetti USA for Buck Fulp, Peter Giddings UK 1969, via David Clarke *to current owner, John Godfrey...*

248SP '0806' — 1962 2.4-litre 2-cam V8 debut Sebring, re-engined as 268SP, 2.6-litre 2-cam V8 and reappeared Nürburgring 1000 km 1962—sold to Doug Thiem USA 1963 as 196SP 2-litre 2-cam V6—*with Bardinon, France, 1979*

Ricardo Rodriguez speeds his beautiful NART-entered Dino 246S '0784' around Nassau's rough Oakes Field airport circuit before retirement from the 1961 Nassau Trophy Race

Dino engine specifications

YEAR	MODEL	CLASS	BORE × STROKE	CAPACITY	VEE°	CAMSHAFTS	POWER	@ RPM
1957	156	F2	70 × 64.5 mm	1489.35 cc	65°	Four	c. 175 bhp @ 8500	
1957	196	F1	77 × 71 mm	1983.72 cc	65°	Four	c. 220 bhp @ 8500	
1957	226	F1	81 × 71 mm	2195.18 cc	65°	Four	c. 240 bhp @ 8500	
1957	246	F1	85 × 71 mm	2417.33 cc	65°	Four	c. 270 bhp @ 8300	
1958	246	F1	85 × 71 mm	2417.33 cc	65°	Four	c. 280 bhp @ 8500	
1958	156	F2	70 × 64.5 mm	1489.35 cc	65°	Four	c. 180 bhp @ 9000	
1958	206S	Spts	77 × 71 mm	1983.72 cc	65°	Four	c. 222 bhp @ 8500	
1958	296S	Spts	85 × 87 mm	2962.08 cc	65°	Four	c. 300 bhp @ 8000	
1958	296MI	Track	85 × 87 mm	2962.08 cc	65°	Four	c. 316 bhp @ 8250	
1958/9	156S	Exp	72 × 64.5 mm	1575.67 cc	60°	Two	c. 165 bhp @ 8000	
1959	256	F1	86 × 71 mm	2474.54 cc	65°	Four	c. 290 bhp @ 8800	
1959	156	F2	70 × 64.5 mm	1489.35 cc	65°	Four	c. 180 bhp @ 10,000	
1959	246	F1 Exp	85 × 71 mm	2417.33 cc	60°	Two	c. 250 bhp @ 8000	
1959*	196S	Spts	77 × 71 mm	1983.72 cc	60°	Two	c. 195 bhp @ 7800	
1959*	196GT	GT Exp	77 × 71 mm	1983.72 cc	60°	Two	c. 175 bhp @ 7500	
1960	246/256 F1 and 156 F2 as above							
1960	156	F2 Exp	73 × 58.8 mm	1476.60 cc	65°	Four	c. 185 bhp @ 9200	
1960	276S	Spts	90 × 71 mm	2710.09 cc	60°	Two	c. 255 bhp @ 7500	
1961	156	F1	73 × 58.8 mm	1476.60 cc	120°	Four	c. 190 bhp @ 9500	
1961	246SP	Spts	85 × 71 mm	2417.33 cc	65°	Four	c. 270 bhp @ 8000	
1961	156	F1 Exp	81 × 48.2 mm	1496.43 cc	65°	Four	c. 200 bhp @ 10,500	
1961	156	F1 Exp	67 × 70 mm	1480.73 cc	65°	Four	c. 185 bhp @ 9500	
1962?	196S	Spts	77 × 71 mm	1983.71 cc	60°	Two	c. 210 bhp @ 7500	
1962	286SP	Spts	90 × 75 mm	2862.78 cc	60°	Two	c. 260 bhp @ 6800	
1962	248SP	Spts Exp	77 × 66 mm	2458.70 cc	90°	Two	c. 250 bhp @ 7400	
1962	268SP	Spts	77 × 71 mm	2644.96 cc	90°	Two	c. 260 bhp @ 7500	
1963	156 inj	F1	73 × 58.8 mm	1476.60 cc	120°	Four	c. 205 bhp @ 10,500	
1963	186GT	Exp	77 × 64 mm	1788.14 cc	60°	Two	c. 156 bhp @ 7000	

*Both these engines first ran in late-1958

YEAR	MODEL	CLASS	BORE × STROKE	CAPACITY	VEE°	CAMSHAFTS	POWER	@ RPM
1965	166P	Spts	77 × 57 mm	1592.57 cc	65°	Four	c. 175 bhp @	9000
1965	206P	HlClm	86 × 57 mm	1986.61 cc	65°	Four	c. 205 bhp @	8800
1966	206S	Spts	86 × 57 mm	1986.61 cc	65°	Four	c. 205 bhp @	8800
1966	246T	Tasman	85 × 71 mm	2417.33 cc	65°	Four	c. 280 bhp @	8500
1966	246	F1	85 × 71 mm	2417.33 cc	65°	Four	c. 280 bhp @	8500
1967	166	F2	86 × 45.8 mm	1596.25 cc	65°	Four	c. 210 bhp @	10,500
1968	246T	Tasman	90 × 63 mm	2404.73 cc	65°	Four	c. 285 bhp @	8900
1968	166	F2	79.5 × 53.5 mm	1596.25 cc	65°	Four	c. 225 bhp @	10,600
1968	206GT	Prod	86 × 57 mm	1986.6 cc	65°	Four	c. 180 bhp @	8000
1969	246T	Tasman	90 × 63 mm	2404.73 cc	65°	Four	c. 300 bhp @	8900
1969	166	F2	79.5 × 53.5 mm	1596.25 cc	65°	Four	c. 232 bhp @	11,000
1969	246GT	Prod	92.5 × 60 mm	2419.20 cc	65°	Four	c. 195 bhp @	7500
1974	308GT	Prod	81 × 71 mm	2926.90 cc	90°	Four	c. 250 bhp @	7700
1974	208GT	Prod	66.8 × 71 mm	1990.26 cc	90°	Four	c. 180 bhp @	7700

NB

While engine specification tables as approved by the factory look very nice and clean and clinical, the truth in the metal is often—if not invariably—rather different. As proof of this truism consider the five engines (three acquired minus heads) available to Anthony Bamford's JCB Excavators team for his 1960 Formula 1 Dino 246 during the 1979 season. Their numbers, bore and stroke dimensions and approximate displacements were as follows, as opposed to the quoted 85 × 71 mm, 2417 cc:

'0003'—85 × 70 mm, 2383 cc; '0003A'*—85.4 × 71 mm, 2440 cc; '0004'—85.1 × 71 mm, 2423 cc; '0790'**—85 × 71 mm, 2417 cc (hooray); '0790/2'—85.5 × 70 mm, 2394 cc . . . they are all meant to be 2417 cc.

*Numbered thus by David Clarke's Graypaul Motors preparation team under Dick Clarson to differentiate it from the sister engine with the same number—these being the original units, the second one lacking cylinder heads, which came from Chinetti with the car. It was apparently Ferrari practice to provide each new car with one complete engine installed plus an available short-engine spare.

**'0790' and '0790/2' were of course sports car engines without the very rare double-bodied magneto of the Formula 1 246/2360.

Acknowledgements

Reproduction of the Dino road car tests features used in these pages was arranged through the good offices of Dick Bartkus and Tony Hogg of *Road & Track* magazine in the USA, and of Editors Ray Hutton, Quentin Spurring and Tony Curtis of *Autocar, Autosport* and *Motor* magazines in the UK, plus Godfrey Eaton of the British Ferrari Owners' Club magazine, allowing to reproduce what we considered to be the best and most objective published assessments of Dino models from the Fiat through the Ferrari 206GT to the 308GTB—whether one describes that as a Dino in face of the International marketing men and the customer unconscious of the Dino story, or not. To these colleagues thanks a million.

The rest of this mammoth task would not have been completed on schedule without the invaluable help of contacts at Ferrari, Modena and Maranello, who went far beyond the call of duty to allow me some insight into the factory's racing records. This is not a worshipful history, but I hope it is an objective, quite accurate and affectionate one which in some small part repays the effort they invested on my behalf.

I must especially thank Phil Hill for his long hours examining page proofs and for giving the impression he was enjoying it. His advice and clear recall were invaluable as he added so much humanity to what could have been an epic story of only nuts-and-bolts. Thanks Phil....

Pete Coltrin, American in Modena—or Mudville as he usually calls it—was a fount of all knowledge and of more fascinating photographs than we could possibly use. John Godfrey—owner of the 1962 European Mountain Championship-winning Dino '0804'—has been researching the definitive history of those 1961–63 cars for over eight years. That work will be a must when it appears; in the meantime I owe John a debt of gratitude for his patience in putting-up with my sharpened shovel, and for telling me which questions to ask—so pointing me in the direction of the truth. Joel Eric Finn in Connecticut has forgotten more about Italian sports-racing cars in general and Ferraris in particular than most enthusiasts could shake a stick at. I am indebted to him for his learned counsel on all things Ferrari and for the loan of photographs and original factory records material. Neil Corner, owner of the 1960 Italian GP-winning car, supplied a mass of information and photographs on that year's cars, while Anthony Bamford allowed me to dig deep into the background of his JCB Excavators 1960 246 with which Willie Green dominates British historic car racing as I write. Dudley Mason-Styrron, owner-restorer of the famous 1966 206S, '004' was another who spent time providing invaluable photographs and information.

Denis Jenkinson allowed me to ferret through his priceless archive of photographs, notes and publications compiled over thirty years of following the motor racing scene for *Motor Sport* magazine. Geoff Goddard turned out all manner of Dino photographs and remained patient even when I appeared on his doorstep in the darkness wanting to unearth a Targa Florio negative of some obscure Sicilian racing an even more obscure car which I thought might have been a Dino—but was not. Thanks to John Dunbar and Maurice Seldon of *Motor Sport* magazine's photographic studio; to Jerry Sloniger in Germany; to Jesse Alexander and Henry N. Manney in California, to Jean-Louis Piccard of *Automobile Year* in Switzerland; to Giancarlo Amari, the curator of the Biscaretti Museum in Turin, Italy; to Mark Konig of Maranello Concessionaires; to Dick Clarson of Graypaul Motors; to Quentin Spurring and Nigel Roebuck of *Autosport* magazine here in the UK; to Peter Brockes of the National Motor Museum library at Beaulieu; to John Surtees, to Tony Brooks, to Derek Bell, to American Dan Gurney and Andrea de Adamich. To Chuck Queener of the excellent Ferrari enthusiasts' magazine *Cavallino*; David Hodges; Cyril Posthumus; GianBeppe Panicco of Bertone; Fredi Valentini of Pininfarina; Michael Lee of JCB Excavators; Willie Green, 1979's Dino champion driver; Luca di Montezemolo and the Fiat UK press officers; to Dr Peter Rudge for advice on matters medical—and to those who prefer anonymity at Ferrari. To all those I have inevitably forgotten—thank you.

BIBLIOGRAPHY

Ferrari history in general has been examined so often by various authors that some degree of duplication is inevitable, even in a relatively untouched area such as the Dinos. For further reading on Ferraris in general the author recommends:

The Enzo Ferrari Memoirs: My Terrible Joys—Hamish Hamilton, London 1963 *et seq*

Challenge Me the Race—Mike Hawthorn, William Kimber, London, 1958 *et seq*

Champion Year—Mike Hawthorn, William Kimber, London, 1959 *et seq*

Ferrari—The Man, The Machines—Edited by Stan Grayson, Automobile Quarterly Publications, Princeton NJ, USA, 1975

Ferrari Sports and Gran Turismo Cars—Warren F. Fitzgerald, Richard F. Merritt and Jonathan Thompson, CBS Publications, USA, 1975

The Ferrari Formula 1 Cars 1948–1976—Jonathan Thompson, Aztex Corp., Tucson, Ariz. USA 1976

Ferrari Sport et Prototypes—Antoine Prunet, Editions EPA, Paris, France, 1978

Ferrari—The Early Spyders & Competition Roadsters—Dean Batchelor, Batchelor Publications, USA, 1975

Ferrari—Hans Tanner, Foulis & Co, London 1959 *et seq*, 4th Edition Haynes Publishing, Yeovil 1974, 5th edition extended and amended by Doug Nye 1980

Motor Sport Racing Car Reviews—annual publication 1948–1958, author Denis Jenkinson, published by Tee & Whiten and J. Mead Ltd, London

Contemporary car descriptions, news items and race reports from:

Motor, Autocar, Motor Sport, Motoring News, Autosport, Motor Racing, Sporting Motorist magazines in the UK; *Auto Italiana* and *Autosprint* Italy; *Sport Auto* France; *Road & Track* and *Sports Car* USA; also annual publications *Automobile Year* 1957–79 published by Edita SA, Lausanne, *Autocourse* 1959–79 UK, *Motor Racing Year* 1961–1970 UK, plus personal sources as acknowledged.

Index

The 'Dino' badges are derived from Dino Ferrari's personal signature. Here we show Dino's handwriting compared with the casting on the early coupé 166 cam cover. Beneath the 166 logo is the road car front badge with the yellow background, followed by the script from the back panel of a 246GT. The last badge has a marked change in shape and that is found on the rear panel of a Fiat Dino 2400 Spyder

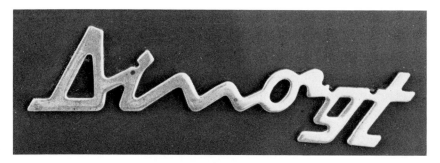